THE LIFE OF CHRIST

the Smart Guide to the Bible™ series

Robert C. Girard

Larry Richards, General Editor

THOMAS NELSON
Since 1798

NASHVILLE   DALLAS   MEXICO CITY   RIO DE JANEIRO   BEIJING

The Life of Christ
The Bible Smart Guide™ Series
Copyright © 2007 by GRQ, Inc.

Published in Nashville, Tennessee, by Thomas Nelson. Thomas Nelson is a trademark of Thomas Nelson, Inc.

Originally published by Starburst Publishers under the title *Life of Christ: God's Word for the Biblically-Inept Volumes 1 and 2*. Now revised and updated.

Thomas Nelson, Inc. titles may be purchased in bulk for educational, business, fundraising, or sales promotional use. For information, please e-mail SpecialMarkets@ThomasNelson.com.

Scripture quotations are taken from the New King James Version® (NKJV), copyright 1982 by Thomas Nelson, Inc. Used by permission. All rights reserved.

To the best of its ability, GRQ, Inc., has strived to find the source of all material. If there has been an oversight, please contact us, and we will make any correction deemed necessary in future printings. We also declare that to the best of our knowledge all material (quoted or not) contained herein is accurate, and we shall not be held liable for the same.

General Editor: Larry Richards
Managing Editor: Lila Empson
Associate Editor: W. Mark Whitlock
Scripture Editor: Deborah Wiseman
Assistant Editor: Amy Clark
Design: Diane Whisner

ISBN 13: 978-1-4185-0999-6

Printed in the United States of America
09 10 RRD 9 8 7 6 5 4 3

Introduction

Welcome to *The Life of Christ—The Smart Guide to the Bible*™. This is a new commentary designed to uncomplicate the Bible. You will have fun as you discover what's in this amazing book that has had such a huge influence on the culture in which we live. I intend to change your outlook on the Bible forever.

To Gain Your Confidence

The Life of Christ—The Smart Guide to the Bible™ is designed to make the Bible user-friendly. I've taken a sound educational approach. I've also put a lot of effort into keeping things simple while allowing you to participate in an exciting adventure of enlightenment and joy when you discover what the Bible is all about.

The best source of information needed to understand the Bible is the Bible itself—"the real thing." That's why I often use other Bible references to shed light on Bible statements I'm trying to explain. The Bible is its own best commentary.

What Is the Bible?

The Bible is a collection of sixty-six books organized in two sections: an "Old" Testament of thirty-nine books and a "New" Testament of twenty-seven books. The Old Testament was written by different authors and poets, mostly of Hebrew heritage, between 1400 and 400 BC. It deals with events before the birth of Jesus Christ that mostly center on the nation of Israel. The New Testament was written in sixty years between AD 40 and AD 100. It tells about the birth, life, teachings, death, and resurrection of a historical person named Jesus, and about the movement begun by the people who believed Jesus was the Son of God.

Why Study the Bible?

First, even though the Bible was written a long time ago by ordinary people, it is a special book. It is special because God is its source. The writers of the Bible claim more than 2,600 times that they are speaking or writing God's words. Millions of people over thousands of years have believed them.

Second, the Bible is the best-selling book in history, and for good reason. It offers answers to the questions we wonder about. How did the world begin? What is my purpose in life? What makes people act the way they do? What will happen to me when I die? To help us understand the answers to those questions, God gave us the Bible. Many, many people have found relief and comfort in its pages. Third, even people who don't believe the Bible owe it to themselves to find out what's in it. The Bible's stories and images have shaped Western society. The moral code in the Bible has been used as the source of most of our laws. Everyone who wants to be fully educated needs to have some knowledge of this influential book.

The Life of Jesus Christ

The person whose story is told in the New Testament is Jesus, also known as "Christ," "Jesus Christ," "the Lord Jesus Christ," and "Jesus of Nazareth." If the stories and teachings of Jesus recorded in the New Testament are true (and millions of Christians worldwide stake their lives on the belief that they are!), then Jesus was the most unusual person who ever lived. The study of his life and accomplishments is one of the most important pursuits in which anyone can engage.

The Early Years

Jesus was the firstborn son of a young Jewish woman named Mary from the crossroads town of Nazareth, Galilee. An unmarried virgin, she conceived Jesus through the miraculous overshadowing of the Holy Spirit. She and her fiancé, a God-fearing Jew named Joseph, were told by the angel Gabriel that Mary's boy-child was God's Son, the Messiah-Savior, Immanuel ("God with us"), sent from the heavenly world according to centuries-old promises God had made through the Old Testament prophets. Jesus was born in Bethlehem, Judea, and grew to manhood in Nazareth.

The Teaching Years

When he was thirty years old, Jesus began to preach. In the synagogues of Galilee, he announced that he was the one God sent to liberate people, give them new sight, and show them God's love and forgiveness. Jesus described a set of values and a lifestyle totally contradictory to typical human thinking and attitudes. He made repentance, humility, teachability, giving of oneself, hunger for righteousness, reconciliation, nonviolence, faithfulness, and forgiveness the measure of true success, prosperity, and happiness. He attacked religious hypocrisy and judgmentalism as enemies of true spirituality.

The Gathering Crowds

Jesus's unique personality, claims, and teachings led to national and family division. People from all walks of life were attracted to him, put their faith in him, and their lives were changed. Most who followed were from the disadvantaged, oppressed segments of Jewish society—the poor, sick, crippled, mentally ill, hungry, weak, and powerless. He healed, fed, and accepted them all. He performed many miracles to meet their needs and to demonstrate his authenticity.

The crowds coming to see and hear him became so huge, and the opposition to his message became so determined and constant, he could no longer preach in the synagogues but had to take his ministry out of doors. Out in the countryside his audiences came to number in the tens of thousands. While attracted to him, nearly all struggled with his refusal to live up to widely held, inaccurate, supernationalistic messianic expectations based on faulty interpretations of Old Testament prophecies.

The kingdom Jesus was putting together was not the political-military force the listeners had been taught to expect. And he insisted the authentic kingdom of God could not come to them until they recognized him as King of their hearts and Lord of their daily lives and actions. Jesus wanted his followers to look to him to supply not only their material but also their spiritual needs.

The members of the religious establishment (Bible scholars and clergy) saw in Jesus a threat to their positions of power and influence. Most chose to align themselves against him. He exposed and condemned their hypocrisy, legalism, and pride. Their disapproval and persistent slander quickly evolved into organized opposition and a conspiracy to assassinate him.

His Disciples

From those who were responsive, Jesus called twelve as apostles and began training them for leadership in his movement. They believed in him and remained loyal even while other disciples turned away. "Lord, to whom shall we go?" Simon Peter said. "You have the words of eternal life. Also we have come to believe and know that You are the Christ, the Son of the living God" (John 6:68–69 NKJV). Even so, they continued to struggle with the same messianic inaccuracies as the rest of the people.

Just the Facts, Ma'am

The approach taken in this commentary is to present the facts of Jesus's story as the New Testament writers recorded them and to provide a simple explanation of those facts where necessary. When facts from the culture and history of Jesus's times can help us understand more clearly the significance of some event or report or teaching, I will share those facts, too. My goal is to present a picture of Jesus accurately and simply, consistent with the way the New Testament pictures him.

Not everything Jesus did or said is recorded in the Bible. One New Testament writer insists that if everything were told, "even the world itself could not contain the books that would be written" (John 21:25 NKJV). So many thousands were touched and changed by his life, and his was a life Bible writers insist began before time (John 1:1) and will continue forever (Isaiah 9:6–7).

The Four Gospels

The four gospels—Matthew, Mark, Luke, and John—represent four pictures of the same person—Jesus Christ. The four New Testament versions of the life of Christ were written by three Jewish men and one Greek. None include a byline identifying the author. But from earliest times, the church has attributed the four to Matthew, Mark, Luke, and John.

These accounts do not pretend to be objective. These men are convinced that the Jesus about whom they write is exactly what he claimed—Son of God, Savior, Messiah, King. They are not writing to encourage speculation and further research about who Jesus is. They know who he is. And each aims to help readers know Jesus of Nazareth. The contents of their books are not inventions to spark a Christ-legend. Each is carefully composed from eyewitness testimony and well-researched fact.

The Life of Christ in the Four Gospels

Gospel	Author	Target	Date
Matthew	Matthew, also known as Levi. A tax collector who worked for the Roman government before Jesus invited him to join his team. As one of the Twelve, he spent three years with Jesus and was appointed by him as his first apostle. He was an eyewitness to most of the events of which he writes.	The Jewish people. To prove Jesus was the promised Messiah, Matthew carefully documents Jesus's fulfillment of Old Testament prophecies.	Written between AD 50 and AD 70 (no way to tell exactly). Early Christians considered Matthew's to be the first of the four authoritative accounts of Jesus's life.
Mark	John Mark, also called "John" or "Mark." Companion to Paul, Barnabas, and Peter. Markwas an eyewitness in a limited sense. He was personally acquainted with Jesus and present at key points in the story he tells (see Mark 14:51–52). Peter was Mark's major source of information.	Primarily Romans and others unfamiliar with the Old Testament or biblical theology. Pictures Jesus as a man of action and authority—the kind of man who would appeal to the pragmatic, militaristic Romans.	Probably written near the time of Peter's martyrdom in Rome, AD 68.

The Life of Christ in the Four Gospels (cont'd)

Gospel	Author	Target	Date
Luke	Luke, a well-educated Greek that Paul calls "Luke the beloved physician" (Colossians 4:14 NKJV). Authored both the third Gospel and Acts. His use of medical language indicates the writing of a physician (and his writing was readable!). He was Paul's companion, even in jail. Luke was not an eyewitness. He probably first heard the story from Paul and his missionary team. He wrote his Life of Christ after thoroughresearch, mostly done in Caesarea where Paul was imprisoned for two years.	Greeks and other Gentiles, like himself. His Life of Christ focuses on Jesus's relationships with all sorts of people—especially women, the poor, and the oppressed.	Written between AD 58, while Paul was in jail in Caesarea, and AD 63, when Paul was under house arrest in Rome.
John	John, an "insider"—one of the Twelve who was with Jesus for three years. When Jesus called him, John was a partner in a fishing business on the Sea of Galilee with his brother James and their father, Zebedee. Like the other Life of Christ authors in the New Testament, John never identifies himself by name. He calls himself "the disciple whom Jesus loved" (John 21:20 NKJV).	The whole world. The heartbeat of his writing m ay be summed up in a sentence called "the golden text of the Bible" —John 3:16: Because God loves the world of human beings, he gave his Son so that whoever puts their faith in him might escape spiritual disaster and live forever!	John was the last of the original apostles to write—between AD 75 and AD 100.

Gospel Harmony

This commentary will use all four Gospels—Matthew, Mark, Luke, and John—to tell the story. The first three are called synoptic Gospels. That is, while each author has distinctive purposes in mind, all three take the same basic approach to telling the story. John marches to a slightly different drumbeat. He focuses more on Christ as a person and the teachings and signs that prove Jesus is the Son of God. The first three report many of the same incidents. A few are reported by all four. My approach will be to collect the facts from all four and focus on the events of Jesus's life in chronological order (which is not always easy to figure out). Watch for the Gospel Harmony icon, which tells when and where an event is reported by more than one writer.

The Original Language of the Good News

Archaeological discoveries and evidence from the New Testament show the Jews were trilingual:

1. Aramaic had once been the language of the aristocracy, but by Jesus's time it had filtered down to the lower classes and was used in daily conversation.

2. Hebrew was the language of religious life at synagogues and the temple and was also used in daily conversation.

3. Greek, like English today, was the universal language spoken all over the world. Alexander the Great (who preceded the Romans in conquest of the area) had invented a language called *koine* (koy-nay) or "common" Greek. As his empire spread, Alexander instituted the use of koine Greek from Europe to Asia. Most Jews were fluent in it. It was the language for interaction with Roman authorities and trade with foreigners. Palestinian Jews also spoke and wrote Greek in their communication with each other.

There is evidence Jesus was fluent in all three languages. The New Testament was originally written in common Greek so as to be read and understood by people all over the Roman Empire. By Jesus's time scholars believe much of the Old Testament had been copied onto papyrus scrolls. It is likely the gospel writers used papyrus as well.

A Word About Words

There are several interchangeable terms: Scripture, Scriptures, Holy Scriptures, Word, Word of God, God's Word, gospel. All these mean the same thing and come under the broad heading called the Bible. I may use each of these terms at various times.

The word "Lord" in the Old Testament refers to Yahweh, the God of Israel. In the New Testament it refers to Jesus Christ, God's Son.

The Ultimate Purpose of a "Life of Christ"

The Bible was never given by God as an end in itself. And knowing what the Bible says and means is not all there is to being an authentic God-worshipper. The Bible is a means to an end. The end and goal of learning God's Word is to know God. The reason for learning about Jesus Christ is that by knowing him we can know his Father, God.

When we maintain an openness about Jesus of Nazareth, God rewards us with understanding. Many types of people can profit from reading about Jesus:

- New believers just beginning in their new way of life
- Untaught or untrained believers—new and old
- Seekers of God and truth who have not fully embraced him
- Respected unbelievers—friends, neighbors, relatives, business associates

The Life of Christ—The Smart Guide to the Bible™ speaks to such people.

Expect to be surprised and excited about the knowledge you are about to gain. No one who ever lived is as surprising and exciting as Jesus Christ.

About the Author

Bob Girard spent many years in the pastorate, during which he wrote several influential books and had a popular radio ministry, *Letters to the Church at Phoenix*. For many years Bob wrote adult Sunday school lessons for Scripture Press. He is the author of other books in The Smart Guide to the Bible™ series, including *The Book of Acts* and *The Book of Hebrews*. Bob is retired and lives in a house he built in Rimrock, Arizona.

About the General Editor

Dr. Larry Richards is a native of Michigan who now lives in Raleigh, North Carolina. He was converted while in the Navy in the 1950s. Larry has taught and written Sunday school curriculum for every age group, from nursery through adult. He has published more than two hundred books, and his books have been translated into some twenty-six languages. His wife, Sue, is also an author. They both enjoy teaching Bible studies as well as fishing and playing golf.

Understanding the Bible Is Easy with These Tools

To understand God's Word you need easy-to-use study tools right where you need them—at your fingertips. The Smart Guide to the Bible™ series puts valuable resources adjacent to the text to save you both time and effort.

Every page features handy sidebars filled with icons and helpful information: cross references for additional insights, definitions of key words and concepts, brief commentaries from experts on the topic, points to ponder, evidence of God at work, the big picture of how passages fit into the context of the entire Bible, practical tips for applying biblical truths to every area of your life, and plenty of maps, charts, and illustrations. A wrap-up of each passage, combined with study questions, concludes each chapter.

These helpful tools show you what to watch for. Look them over to become familiar with them, and then turn to chapter 1 with complete confidence: You are about to increase your knowledge of God's Word!

Study Helps

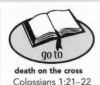

The thought-bubble icon alerts you to commentary you might find particularly thought-provoking, challenging, or encouraging. You'll want to take a moment to reflect on it and consider the implications for your life.

Don't miss this point! The exclamation-point icon draws your attention to a key point in the text and emphasizes important biblical truths and facts.

death on the cross
Colossians 1:21–22

Many see Boaz as a type of Jesus Christ. To win back what we human beings lost through sin and spiritual death, Jesus had to become human (i.e., he had to become a true kinsman), and he had to be willing to pay the penalty for our sins. With his <u>death on the cross</u>, Jesus paid the penalty and won freedom and eternal life for us.

The additional Bible verses add scriptural support for the passage you just read and help you better understand the <u>underlined text</u>. (Think of it as an instant reference resource!)

How does what you just read apply to your life? The heart icon indicates that you're about to find out! These practical tips speak to your mind, heart, body, and soul, and offer clear guidelines for living a righteous and joy-filled life, establishing priorities, maintaining healthy relationships, persevering through challenges, and more.

This icon reveals how God is truly all-knowing and all-powerful. The hourglass icon points to a specific example of the prediction of an event or the fulfillment of a prediction. See how some of what God has said would come to pass already has!

What are some of the great things God has done? The traffic-sign icon shows you how God has used miracles, special acts, promises, and covenants throughout history to draw people to him.

Does the story or event you just read about appear elsewhere in the Gospels? The cross icon points you to those instances where the same story appears in other Gospel locations—further proof of the accuracy and truth of Jesus's life, death, and resurrection.

Since God created marriage, there's no better person to turn to for advice. The double-ring icon points out biblical insights and tips for strengthening your marriage.

The Bible is filled with wisdom about raising a godly family and enjoying your spiritual family in Christ. The family icon gives you ideas for building up your home and helping your family grow close and strong.

Isle of Patmos
a small island in the
Mediterranean Sea

something significant had occurred, he wrote down the substance of what he saw. This is the practice John followed when he recorded Revelation on the **Isle of Patmos.**

What does that word really mean, especially as it relates to this passage? Important, misunderstood, or infrequently used words are set in **bold type** in your text so you can immediately glance at the margin for definitions. This valuable feature lets you better understand the meaning of the entire passage without having to stop to check other references.

the big picture

Joshua
Led by Joshua, the Israelites crossed the Jordan River and invaded Canaan (see Illustration #8). In a series of military campaigns the Israelites defeated several coalition armies raised by the inhabitants of Canaan. With organized resistance put down, Joshua divided the land among the twelve Israelite

How does what you read fit in with the greater biblical story? The highlighted big picture summarizes the passage under discussion.

what others say

David Breese
Nothing is clearer in the Word of God than the fact that God wants us to understand himself and his working in the lives of men.[5]

It can be helpful to know what others say on the topic, and the highlighted quotation introduces another voice in the discussion. This resource enables you to read other opinions and perspectives.

Maps, charts, and illustrations pictorially represent ancient artifacts and show where and how stories and events took place. They enable you to better understand important empires, learn your way around villages and temples, see where major battles occurred, and follow the journeys of God's people. You'll find these graphics let you do more than study God's Word—they let you *experience* it.

Chapters at a Glance

PART FOUR: Turn Toward the Cross

PART FIVE: Six Days to Glory

PART SIX: The Price of Redemption

PART SEVEN: Sonrise

Part One
GIFT CHILD

Chapter 1: Breaking News

Chapter Highlights:
- **The Long Wait**
- **Mission Possible**
- **The Magnificat**
- **Baby Baptist**
- **Desert Prep School**

Let's Get Started

In 5 BC two special baby boys were born in the land of Israel.

go to

cousins
Luke 1:36

They were <u>cousins</u>. One was born into the priestly clan of Aaron. The other, though born into poverty, was from the royal line of David. They were born six months apart. An angel sent from God predicted both births. Each set of parents was told that in the plan of almighty God, their son was slated to be a man of destiny.

Although each would have a very short time to minister, these two men were part of a strategy to bring the grace of God to all people. The lives of both would end violently in their early thirties. The first would be beheaded. The second would be crucified. The first would be known as the greatest prophet ever born. The second would be known as the Son of God—"the only begotten of the Father." The first would introduce the second to the world, then fade from the scene. The second would sit on the throne of a never-ending king-dom. In the Bible, the life of Christ begins with the birth stories of these two men whose lives and destinies were so intertwined.

Israel's Long Wait

> **JOHN 1:14** *And the Word became flesh and dwelt among us, and we beheld His glory, the glory as of the only begotten of the Father, full of grace and truth.* (NKJV)

When "the only begotten of the Father" was born into the human family in the person of Jesus of Nazareth, Israel was under the thumb of another in the long series of foreign armies that oppressed its citizens for seven centuries. The Romans ruled with a fist of iron. They brought with them such big-government "blessings" as heavy taxation, poverty, and martial law. Of all the Roman Empire's con-quered peoples, the Jews were the most zealous for freedom. They were programmed by the promises of God to consider only national sovereignty and personal liberty the norm. Centuries of oppression had failed to take the edge off their yearning to be free.

go to

royal family
2 Samuel 7:12–16

eternal government
Isaiah 9:6–7;
Psalm 45:5–6

Shiloh
one to whom
tribute/obedience
belongs

Judah
descended from
third son of Jacob,
father of Israel's
leading tribe

Immanuel
God with us

Anointed
chosen for kingly,
priestly, or prophetic
authority

favor
grace, lovingkind-
ness, mercy

David
figurative title for
Messiah-King

Come, O Come, Immanuel!

Israel's obsession with national sovereignty rose from the belief that God would send a deliverer from King David's <u>royal family</u> to drive the conquerors into the sea and establish an <u>eternal government</u> that would end slavery, poverty, and oppression forever and bring Israel to prominence among the nations. Ancient prophecies, messages from God about the present and future, fanned the fire of hope. God himself created the yearning for freedom and national sovereignty by promising the Messiah! In Hebrew, *Messiah* means "Anointed One." In Greek, the word is translated "Christ."

Samples of Old Testament Promises of the Coming King

Scripture Reference	Promise of the King
Genesis 49:10	The nations will obey the scepter-bearer ("**Shiloh**") a member of **Judah**'s clan.
Deuteronomy 18:18	God will give Israel a prophet like Moses who will speak God's Words.
2 Samuel 7:12–16	One of King David's offspring will reign forever.
Isaiah 7:14	A young woman will bear a son who will be called **Immanuel**.
Isaiah 9:6–7	A native son of Israel will establish an eternal kingdom of peace, justice, and righteousness.
Isaiah 61:1–4	The **Anointed** One will end oppression, mend heartbreak, free captives, proclaim God's **favor**.
Ezekiel 37:21–28	Israel will be restored to its homeland, and a king called **David** will rule forever.

Zacharias and Elizabeth

LUKE 1:5–7 *There was in the days of Herod, the king of Judea, a certain priest named Zacharias, of the division of Abijah. His wife was of the daughters of Aaron, and her name was Elizabeth. And they were both righteous before God, walking in all the commandments and ordinances of the Lord blameless. But they had no child, because Elizabeth was barren, and they were both well advanced in years.* (NKJV)

A Jewish man named Zacharias and his wife, Elizabeth, were childless and "well advanced in years." They had given up hope of conceiving. Because they and the people around them believed faithful servants of God would be blessed with children, this was hard to understand. They had been faithful. To face the "declining years" without children and grandchildren to care for them was disappointing and cause for anxiety.

Still, they were two of the "good guys" who kept the hope of the promised Messiah alive in their hearts. Luke 1:6 reports:

- They were both righteous before God.
- They observed all God's commandments and all his ordinances blamelessly.

Sweet-Smelling Serendipity

During a priestly division's period of service at the temple, specific tasks were assigned by **lot** (Luke 1:9). One of the most honored jobs was burning incense, which represented <u>prayers rising</u> to God. Zacharias won the coveted assignment. When it came time to burn incense, the old priest was left alone inside the **holy place** in the temple. All the others were outside, with the other worshippers, praying. At the signal, Zacharias burned the sweet-smelling stuff on the **altar of incense** just outside the **veil** that covered the **Holy of Holies** from view. To Zacharias, this was probably the mountaintop experience of his life. But he had no idea just how high the mountaintop was going to be!

Angel at the Altar

As the sweet-smelling smoke wafted heavenward, a being straight out of heaven suddenly stood right there beside the incense altar. A bolt of terror shot through Zacharias's old frame. Zacharias braced himself for death. But the angel's first words disarmed his fears: "Do not be afraid, Zacharias" (Luke 1:13 NKJV). The angel wasn't there to terminate the faithful priest, but to deliver some incredible news.

Silent Witness

To Zacharias's practical mind, the news that he and Elizabeth would become parents was just too good to be true! There were limits even to what a believer like him could believe—especially considering he was an old man and his wife was no spring chicken! Zacharias's faith needed proof—so the angel gave him proof:

lot
Proverbs 16:33;
18:18

prayers rising
Revelation 5:8

lot
drawing straws or throwing dice to settle an issue

holy place
second most sacred room in the temple

altar of incense
stand for burning incense

veil
thick curtain barring the way into the Holy of Holies

Holy of Holies
most sacred room, housing the ark of the covenant

Zacharias emerged from the temple speechless. Usually the incense offering was followed by a benediction for waiting worshippers. The old priest could only gesture. They concluded he'd seen a vision (Luke 1:22).

Zacharias completed his week of temple duties, then went home to his wife in the hills of Judea (Luke 1:39). Although speechless, Zacharias could write (verse 63). He probably wrote every detail of his experience for Elizabeth to read, including the child's name.

Upon discovery she was pregnant, Elizabeth went into five months of seclusion—not because there was any shame in pregnancy. Exactly the opposite. Among Jews childbearing was cause for celebration. To be childless was a tragedy. Some considered it punishment by God. Elizabeth had endured put-downs from people who failed to recognize what a godly person she was. Maybe she wanted to be sure that when she told the neighbors she was pregnant, it showed!

Mission Possible

> LUKE 1:26–28 *Now in the sixth month the angel Gabriel was sent by God to a city of Galilee named Nazareth, to a virgin betrothed to a man whose name was Joseph, of the house of David. The virgin's name was Mary. And having come in, the angel said to her, "Rejoice, highly favored one, the Lord is with you; blessed are you among women!"* (NKJV)

In the sixth month of Elizabeth's pregnancy the same angel who met Zacharias in the temple visited the town of Nazareth in Galilee. Once again, we overhear a private conversation—this time between the angel Gabriel and a young woman named Mary. Gabriel's greeting indicates Mary had a relationship with God that was alive and well.

Get the Nursery Ready!

If the angel's greeting troubled Mary (verse 29), she must have felt the wind knocked out of her when he got to the main message he'd come to deliver. It was enough to send any teenage girl into panic. But God's man Gabriel wisely paved the way with the encouraging word that she need not be afraid because God was on her side and was about to do her a "high favor." The news that changed Mary's life forever was that she was about to become pregnant and give birth to a boy to whom she was to give the name Jesus, meaning "Savior."

"How Can This Be?"

LUKE 1:34 *Then Mary said to the angel, "How can this be, since I do not know a man?" (NKJV)*

Good question (Luke 1:34). Mary knows the facts of life. It will be a while before she and Joseph complete their engagement period and consummate their marriage. She has never had sex with him or any other man. Without that, how can she conceive the promised child? Mary seems to understand that conception of her special baby will take place immediately and that no man will be involved. Unlike Zacharias, who couldn't believe without further certification of the angel's prophecy (verse 18), Mary is simply puzzled about how what is about to happen will happen. No problem. Gabriel answers her question with delicate reserve.

1. "The Holy Spirit will come upon you" (Luke 1:35 NKJV). It is a mistake to imagine some sort of "mating" between the Holy Spirit and Mary. Jesus uses these same words to describe the entrance of the Holy Spirit into the lives of his disciples on the Day of Pentecost. It is a way of saying the conception of Jesus in the womb of the Virgin was an act of God—a miracle.

2. "The power of the Highest will overshadow you" (1:35 NKJV). In Scripture, God's presence is often indicated by the appearance of an overshadowing cloud. The presence and power of God himself would perform a totally new act of creation in her womb to produce a "holy" child—free from sin of any kind.

The Mystery of the Virgin Birth

The virgin birth of Jesus Christ is the root from which everything the New Testament says about him grows. Theologians and ordinary men struggle with it. But to the mind willing to believe "nothing is impossible with God," it is not at all hard to accept. Both Luke and

go to

Pentecost
Acts 1:8

overshadowing cloud
Exodus 13:21;
14:19–20;
1 Kings 8:10–12;
Isaiah 6:4

Matthew state it up front as a fact, which they are convinced explains the unusual nature of the man, Jesus, and the amazing things he said and did.

A Visit with Elizabeth

After her unconditional surrender to the will of God (Luke 1:38), Mary needs time to process all she has been told and to prepare for the months ahead. So she hurries from the well-watered grassy hills of Galilee to the desert-dry hills of Judea for a visit with her relative Elizabeth (1:39–45). The angel Gabriel had cited Elizabeth's pregnancy as proof to Mary that "with God nothing will be impossible" (1:36–37 NKJV). Elizabeth would understand. Aside from Elizabeth's husband, Zacharias, Mary may have been the first to see the older woman since she became pregnant six months earlier and entered her self-imposed seclusion. The exchange that took place upon Mary's arrival was astonishing.

1. The baby in Elizabeth's womb jumped at the sound of Mary's greeting. Elizabeth interpreted the fetal leap as the unborn prophet's joyful recognition of the mother of the unborn Christ.

2. The Holy Spirit gave Elizabeth exactly the words Mary needed to hear, reassuring her that what was happening to her was a result of God's grace and blessing, and that her faith would be rewarded.

3. Elizabeth acknowledged the divine origin of Mary's unborn child, calling him "my Lord" (1:43 NKJV).

The Magnificat

LUKE 1:46–48 *And Mary said:*
"My soul magnifies the Lord,
And my spirit has rejoiced in God my Savior.
For He has regarded the lowly state of His maidservant;
For behold, henceforth all generations will call me blessed."
(NKJV)

eighth day
Genesis 17:12;
Leviticus 12:3

named
Luke 2:21

Upon Elizabeth's greeting, Mary broke into singing a joyful poem of worship (Luke 1:46–55). Christians call it "The Magnificat." The song magnifies the saviorhood of God and puts the arrival of the Messiah in a revolutionary perspective. The "arm" of the Lord is an Old Testament reference to the promised Messiah—the Christ child she was carrying. She says that God "has shown strength with His arm" and "has scattered the proud in the imagination of their hearts" (Luke 1:51 NKJV). She sees his arrival as continuing God's program in the present and future. The specific deeds she mentions fulfill the revolutionary longings of the Jewish people (and, for that matter, all oppressed people). Mary's boy will ignite the fires of a most unusual revolution!

Baby Baptist

LUKE 1:57–58 *Now Elizabeth's full time came for her to be delivered, and she brought forth a son. When her neighbors and relatives heard how the Lord had shown great mercy to her, they rejoiced with her. (NKJV)*

Jewish law prescribed that baby boys should be circumcised the <u>eighth day</u> after birth. Among first-century Jews the child was also <u>named</u> on that day. Without consulting the parents, presumptive relatives picked a family name (Why bother trying to talk to old Zacharias about anything? He was deaf and dumb as a post! [see Luke 1:20]). The boy should, they decided, be named Zacharias, after his father.

"His Name Is John"

"No!" shouted Elizabeth over the cacophony of noisy kinfolk. "He shall be called John" (the name the angel gave him—Luke 1:13).

thirty years
Luke 3:23

Unheard of! They went to Zacharias and, with a lot of arm waving, asked him for the final word. His handwritten answer was more emphatic than his wife's: "His name is John" (Luke 1:63 NKJV).

Obedience to the angel's instructions demonstrated the old priest's faith. The last shred of doubt (1:18) disappeared, along with his inability to speak. Once he had his faith and tongue back, Zacharias's speech returned when he named the child "John" according to the angel's instructions.

Zacharias

- praised the Lord for keeping his promises (1:68–75).
- prophesied about his son's place in God's redemptive plan (1:76–79).

Like Mary's Magnificat, Zacharias's song has been set to music. It's called the "Benedictus."

Desert Prep School

Zacharias and Elizabeth's boy grew up in the desert (1:80), where he spent <u>thirty years</u> preparing for the strategic task of introducing his cousin Jesus to Israel when it was time for Jesus to begin his messianic ministry. Jesus would one day say of John: "Among those born of women there is not a greater prophet than John the Baptist" (Luke 7:28 NKJV).

Chapter Wrap-Up

- Seven hundred years of oppression and four hundred years of prophetic silence—without a fresh message from God—left Israelites either hungry for the Messiah or settling for a hopeless existence.

- The angel Gabriel announced to a childless old priest named Zacharias that he and his wife, Elizabeth, would soon be parents of a son who would grow up to be the great prophet (John the Baptist) who would prepare Israel for the arrival of the Christ. (Luke 1:5–25)

- Six months later the same angel appeared to the Virgin Mary and revealed God's plan for her to be mother of the Messiah, the Son of God. The virgin birth was possible because conception took place through the overshadowing of the Holy Spirit. (Luke 1:26–38)
- On a visit to Elizabeth in Judea, Mary's faith was affirmed. Mary composed a song of worship that Christians call "The Magnificat." It was a song magnifying God for the spiritual and social revolution the birth of her baby would bring to Israel. (Luke 1:39–55)
- Elizabeth and Zacharias's baby was born and named "John." He grew up in the Judean desert until the time his ministry as Christ's forerunner began. (Luke 1:56–80)

Study Questions

1. What great world power was oppressing the Jews at the time of John's and Jesus's conceptions and births?

2. Identify three Old Testament promises upon which the Jewish expectations of Christ's birth were based.

3. What "miracle" kept Zacharias from expressing his doubts?

4. Identify the three "revolutions" Mary's song (Luke 1:46–55) says the "arm" of the Lord (Christ) has accomplished.

Chapter Highlights:
• Senseless Census
• No Room at the Inn
• Three Ceremonies
• "Magic" Visitors
• Herod the Great . . .
Con Man

Chapter 2: Mary's Little Lamb

Let's Get Started

MATTHEW 1:18 *Now the birth of Jesus Christ was as follows: After His mother Mary was betrothed to Joseph, before they came together, she was found with child of the Holy Spirit. (NKJV)*

Joseph took the news of Mary's pregnancy hard. He found her story unbelievable, but he did not want to make a spectacle of breaking off the relationship. He was leaning toward a quiet little divorce—a private transaction between himself and the synagogue leaders (Matthew 1:19). As he made plans to do this, "an angel of the Lord appeared to him in a dream" (Matthew 1:20 NKJV)—most likely a repeat performance by the angel <u>Gabriel</u>. The angel in the dream verified Mary's story—the child she carried was "of the Holy Spirit" (Matthew 1:20 NKJV). The dream-angel went on to reaffirm what Mary herself must have told him:

go to

Gabriel
Luke 1:19, 26

God with us
Isaiah 7:14

1. The baby is a "Son" (Matthew 1:21 NKJV).

2. His name is "Jesus"—Greek for Joshua, which means "Yahweh is salvation"—"for He will save His people from their sins" (Matthew 1:21 NKJV).

3. The conception in the womb of a virgin fulfills Old Testament prophecy (Matthew 1:22–23; Isaiah 7:14).

4. Mary's son will be "Immanuel"—no ordinary child—"which is translated, '<u>God with us</u>'" (Matthew 1:23 NKJV).

Joseph woke up convinced. Fear that Mary had been unfaithful vanished. He immediately changed his plans. He "took to him his wife" (Matthew 1:24 NKJV). Joseph and Mary did not share physical intimacy until after the miracle child was born.

Senseless Census

LUKE 2:1–3 *And it came to pass in those days that a decree went out from Caesar Augustus that all the world should be regis-*

David's hometown
1 Samuel 16:1–13

tered. This census first took place while Quirinius was governing Syria. So all went to be registered, everyone to his own city. (NKJV)

Hundreds of years earlier the prophet Micah had predicted Christ would be born in the little town of Bethlehem, Judea—King <u>David's hometown</u>—about five miles south of Jerusalem (Micah 5:2). Mary and Joseph lived in Nazareth, Galilee, about eighty or ninety miles north of Bethlehem (see appendix A). Without being aware of its participation in God's redemptive plan, the mighty Roman Imperial government made the arrangements for the fulfillment of Micah's prophecy. They decreed a census for the purpose of increasing taxes. That census brought Joseph and Mary to Bethlehem in time for Jesus to be born there.

what others say

Charles R. Swindoll

Without realizing it, mighty Augustus was only an errand boy for the fulfillment of Micah's prediction . . . a pawn in the hand of Jehovah . . . a piece of lint on the pages of prophecy. While Rome was busy making history, God arrived . . . The world didn't even notice. Reeling from the wake of Alexander the Great . . . Herod the Great . . . Augustus the Great, the world overlooked Mary's little Lamb. It still does.[1]

The authors of the New Testament Gospels (especially Luke) are careful to set the events of Jesus's life in the context of the times in which they happened (see Illustration #1). Luke, a doctor, wrote his Gospel to give an "orderly account" (Luke 1:3 NKJV) of the facts about Jesus's life, so providing an accurate historical setting for Jesus's birth was important to him.

Illustration #1
Historical Events
Surrounding Christ's
Birth

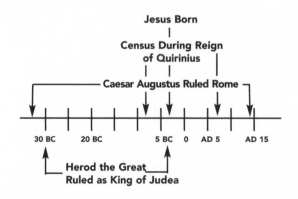

No Room at the Inn

LUKE 2:4–7 *Joseph also went up from Galilee, out of the city of Nazareth, into Judea, to the city of David, which is called Bethlehem, because he was of the house and lineage of David, to be registered with Mary, his betrothed wife, who was with child. So it was, that while they were there, the days were completed for her to be delivered. And she brought forth her firstborn Son, and wrapped Him in swaddling cloths, and laid Him in a manger, because there was no room for them in the inn.* (NKJV)

After their arrival, Mary went into labor, and the child—the focus of centuries of expressed Jewish hopes and the secret longings of a whole world languishing in sin's disastrous consequences—was born.

The Bible doesn't actually say the birth of Jesus took place in a stable. Here are the facts:

- There was no room in the inn.
- Mary wrapped the baby in cloths (clean rags) and laid him in a manger.
- The traditional conclusion based on those facts is that a stable was the birthplace. Other possibilities are as follows:
  - A very poor home where the family and animals were sheltered under the same roof
  - The courtyard of the inn where there might be a manger
  - Outdoors where Joseph and Mary camped for the night

> **what others say**
>
> **Michael Card**
>
> We know from Scripture that Jesus wept as a man. It is naïve to think he did not cry as a baby. Tears are a basic part of what it means to be human. It is one of the sad signs of our fallen world that the first sign we give to show that we're alive is a cry. It is to this fallen world that Jesus came, not an imaginary one without tears.[2]

Sheepherders Hear the Good News

The scene shifts to the hills near Bethlehem. Mary and Joseph are not the only ones spending the night without decent shelter. There

Sabbath
seventh day, Jewish
day of rest

are shepherds nearby living outdoors to protect flocks of sheep assigned to their care. They are the first to be told Christ has been born in Bethlehem. Their part in the story helps fill in some blanks. Without the report of the announcement to the shepherds, we would not know the following:

1. Jesus was born in the middle of the night (Luke 2:8).

2. What time of year it was (or wasn't).

Most of the year Bethlehem's climate is mild and lends itself to keeping flocks in the hills all night. But in winter in that mountainous area nights are cold, so most flocks are in the sheepfold, protected against winter storms. This may rule out December as the logical time of Christ's birth. (Not to worry: The Bible gives no command to celebrate Christmas on a specific day—December 25 is probably as good a day as any!)

what others say

William Barclay

It is a wonderful thing that . . . the first announcement of God came to some shepherds. Shepherds were despised by orthodox good people of the day. They were quite unable to keep the details of the ceremonial law; they could not observe the meticulous hand-washings and rules and regulations. Their flocks made far too constant demands on them; and so the orthodox looked down on them. It was to simple men of the fields that God's message first came.[3]

Three Ceremonies

LUKE 2:21 *And when eight days were completed for the circumcision of the Child, His name was called JESUS, the name given by the angel before He was conceived in the womb. (NKJV)*

Old Testament Law called for three ceremonies to get a baby boy off to a good start:

1. Circumcision (Luke 2:21; Leviticus 12:3). The eighth day after birth, the ceremonial surgery took place that set a male child apart as a son of Israel. The procedure was usually performed by the father. Even if the eighth day fell on the **Sabbath**, when work of any kind was forbidden, this act could be done. The coupling of

the day of circumcision with the naming of the child was not pre-scribed by law, but over the years it became a custom among the Jews (Luke 1:59; 2:21). Mary's baby was called Jesus the same day he was set apart as a Jew. This took place in Bethlehem.

2. Redemption of the firstborn (Luke 2:23; Numbers 18:15–16). A firstborn son was to be considered especially set apart for and belonging to the Lord. Soon after he was a month old, he was to be taken to the temple and a **redemption price** of **five shekels** was to be paid to the priest in the child's behalf.

3. Purification after childbirth (Luke 2:22, 24; Leviticus 12). For forty days after the birth of a son, a Jewish woman was required to avoid the temple and all religious ceremonies (for a daughter, eighty days). This was considered her time of "purification." On the forty-first day, she could be declared ceremonially clean if she went to the temple and made two offerings—a lamb for a **burnt offering** and a dove for a **sin offering**.

The trip from Bethlehem to the temple in Jerusalem, for these last two ceremonies, was made when Jesus was about six weeks old.

redemption price
to "buy back" the firstborn son, who, by Law, belongs to the Lord

five shekels
Jewish coins equal-ing two ounces of silver

burnt offering
sacrificial animal burned, signifying surrender to God

sin offering
sacrifice to atone for sin or ceremonial uncleanness

> what others say
>
> **Matthew Henry**
>
> [about Mary's sin offering] Christ was not conceived or born in sin, as others are, yet, because he was made under the law, he complied with it.[4]

The Messiah Watchers

LUKE 2:28–30 *[Simeon took Jesus] up in his arms and blessed God and said:*
"Lord, now You are letting Your servant depart in peace,
According to Your word;
For my eyes have seen Your salvation." (NKJV)

Simeon "came by the Spirit into the temple" (Luke 2:27 NKJV) and recognized the baby in Joseph's arms as the one for whom he had been waiting. The words Simeon spoke as he held the child became a hymn sung in early church gatherings and known as *Nunc dimittis* ("Now Let Me Depart"). In six-week-old Jesus, Simeon believed he was seeing God's salvation in personal form—the light by which

Gamaliel
Acts 5:34–40

prophetic gift
1 Corinthians 14;
Ephesians 4:11

redemption in Jerusalem
Israel's deliverance from oppression

Hillel
influential Jewish teacher

Pharisee
"separated one," teacher of Jewish law and religious tradition

the Lord would disclose himself not only to Israel but to "all peoples" (Luke 2:31 NKJV). After blessing the special little family, Simeon issued four prophetic predictions concerning the child Jesus (2:34–35):

1. He will cause many people to fall (John 3:16–17).

2. He will cause many people to rise (John 5:21; 11:25–26).

3. He will be opposed and rejected (John 1:10–11).

4. He will expose the thoughts of people's hearts (John 3:19–21).

As Simeon wrapped up his prophecy, Anna approached, thanking God. She too recognized the child as the one who would bring about **"redemption in Jerusalem"** (Luke 2:38 NKJV). She shared news about him with other "quiet ones in the land" (Psalm 35:20 NKJV), who she knew were eager to hear the news.

Outside the New Testament, Jewish writers mention a deeply spiritual man named Simeon living in Jerusalem at this time. He was the son of Rabbi **Hillel** and father of the famous **Pharisee** Gamaliel. He had a prophetic gift, the ability to speak messages from God. This may have been the man who met Joseph, Mary, and baby Jesus in the temple.

"Magic" Visitors

> MATTHEW 2:1–2 *Now after Jesus was born in Bethlehem of Judea in the days of Herod the king, behold, wise men from the East came to Jerusalem, saying, "Where is He who has been born King of the Jews? For we have seen His star in the East and have come to worship Him." (NKJV)*

The Magi may have been aware of messianic prophecies, or Old Testament predictions about the expected deliverer from God. One such prophecy said, "A Star shall come out of Jacob; a Scepter shall rise out of Israel" (Numbers 24:17 NKJV).

The Eastern custom of paying homage to the rulers of other nations on special occasions was well known. In keeping with this protocol the illustrious Magi traveled to Jerusalem—if from Babylon, it was a thousand-mile, six-month journey—to honor the newborn King. The inference is drawn from the three kinds of gifts mentioned in Matthew 2:11 that there were three travelers. Matthew nowhere states how many there were. Given the distance and wildness of the country through which they had to travel, it is likely they traveled in a caravan, including not only the distinguished visitors but their servants and bodyguards.

Herod the Great . . . Con Man

MATTHEW 2:7 *Then Herod, when he had secretly called the wise men, determined from them what time the star appeared.* (NKJV)

It's not surprising, knowing the monstrous paranoia of King Herod, that he would be "troubled" to hear that a new king of the Jews was in the wings, waiting, he suspected, to take his throne (Matthew 2:3 NKJV). Herod seemed to understand immediately his new rival was "the Christ" (Matthew 2:4 NKJV).

Wise Men Worship Christ

Contrary to the impression given in an untold number of "manger scenes," the distinguished visitors did not arrive at the manger along with the shepherds the night Jesus was born. By the time they came, Joseph had moved his family into a house (Matthew 2:11). Jesus was probably a toddler between six months (the travel time from Babylon) and "two years" (the upper age of infants Herod murdered—2:16 NKJV). When the Magi entered the house they did three things that must have astounded his parents (2:11 NKJV):

1. "They fell down"—protocol for coming into the presence of a king required them to fall to their knees, lean forward, and press their foreheads to the floor.

2. They "worshiped Him"—the Greek word for worship literally means to "kiss the hand"—a show of reverence for royalty or deity.

3. "They presented gifts to Him"—each one symbolized something significant:

- "gold"—recognition of Jesus's kingship
- "frankincense" for burning in worship—recognition of Jesus's priesthood
- "myrrh," an embalming spice—recognition of the importance of Jesus's death, his saviorhood

A Different Way Home

The Magi disobeyed King Herod's orders to report back to him. One of them had a dream that convinced them to return to their own country by an alternate route—avoiding Jerusalem and the murderous old king altogether (Matthew 2:12).

what others say

John F. MacArthur Jr.

The magi, "having been warned by God in a dream not to return to Herod . . . departed for their own country by another way." . . . There almost seems to be a double meaning in that statement. They returned to their own country by a different geographical route, to be sure. But they also were now followers of another way in the spiritual sense. That's true of everyone who turns to Christ and becomes one of his worshipers in spirit and truth.[6]

Chapter Wrap-Up

- When Joseph learned Mary, the woman to whom he was pledged to be married, was pregnant by the Holy Spirit, he found it too incredible to believe. He decided to divorce her quietly. Before he could do so, an angel in a dream convinced him to believe Mary's story and to marry her. He did. (Matthew 1:18–25)

- Though the baby Christ was born in circumstances of extreme poverty, his arrival brought great joy to Mary and Joseph, the watching angels, some shepherds who were first told the news, and Simeon and Anna, who met them in the temple. His arrival also brought predictions from Simeon of opposition from his countrymen and suffering. (Luke 2:1–38)

- After his dedication at the temple, a group of Eastern wise men followed an unusual star to Jerusalem and then on to Bethlehem where they bowed before the Christ child and gave him gifts. (Matthew 2:1–12)

Study Questions

1. Describe the dilemma Joseph faced when he learned of Mary's pregnancy. How was the problem resolved?

2. How did God move national and international governments to arrange for Christ to be born in Bethlehem? How does knowing that change your view of today's current events?

3. At what time of year were shepherds most likely to be out in the fields watching over their sheep at night? What was special about the sheep they were likely guarding?

4. Identify the three ceremonies required by Jewish law when a first baby boy was born.

5. What or who were the Magi? And how can we learn from their actions?

Chapter 3: And God Said, "Today I Am a Man!"

Let's Get Started

Jesus's mother, Mary, rejoiced in his birth. His earthly father, Joseph, did too. Two old saints at the temple saw him as their salvation. A delegation of foreign stargazers brought him rich gifts. But in the halls of political and religious power, the response ranged from cool to downright terrifying. By the time the little boy Jesus took his first steps, he found himself running for his life from people obsessed with ending it all before it had barely started!

expatriates
people who leave their native country

Midnight Escape

MATTHEW 2:13 *Now when they had departed, behold, an angel of the Lord appeared to Joseph in a dream, saying, "Arise, take the young Child and His mother, flee to Egypt, and stay there until I bring you word; for Herod will seek the young Child to destroy Him." (NKJV)*

It was the middle of the night after the Magi had left for home. The "angel of the Lord" in Joseph's dream spoke with urgency. Joseph was unaware of the threat to his family's safety looming huge and gaining terrifying intensity while he slept.

The Magi had not returned to Herod to report baby Jesus's location (Matthew 2:12), and the king was in a towering rage. Determined to do whatever it took to destroy the new rival, that very night he had ordered a regiment of his soldiers to go to Bethlehem in the morning to break into every home and to kill every male child two years old and younger!

Before dawn, Joseph and his little family were well on their way southward to Egypt. The trip from Bethlehem into Egypt would have been more than 150 miles, depending on where they stopped. Thousands of Jewish **expatriates**, perhaps some relatives of Joseph or Mary, lived in a number of Egyptian cities. A million Jews lived in Alexandria alone (about three hundred miles from Bethlehem), but Mary and Joseph would not have needed to go that far to find a place to stay.

The Boy from Nowhere

MATTHEW 2:19–21 *Now when Herod was dead, behold, an angel of the Lord appeared in a dream to Joseph in Egypt, saying, "Arise, take the young Child and His mother, and go to the land of Israel, for those who sought the young Child's life are dead." Then he arose, took the young Child and His mother, and came into the land of Israel. (NKJV)*

Joseph, Mary, and Jesus stayed in Egypt until an angel brought word of Herod's death. Matthew carefully reports how God led each movement of the family, and how each step they took fulfilled messianic prophecy. One statement Matthew attributes to the prophets—"He shall be called a Nazarene" (2:23 NKJV)—puzzles Bible students because it's not found in any of the prophets' writings. However, the statement is completely consistent with the spirit of all the messianic prophecies. For example, Isaiah 53:1–3 describes God's special Servant (Christ) as without beauty or majesty, despised, rejected, and not esteemed. Nazareth was decidedly not on Israel's list of "most desirable places to live." It was a little "nowhere town." To be called a "Nazarene" was to be called a "good-for-nothing." Nobody expected anybody who was somebody to come from Nazareth. The attitude expressed by Nathanael was typical. When Philip told him the man he believed was the Christ came from Nazareth, Nathanael retorted: "Can anything good come out of Nazareth?" (John 1:46 NKJV).

Jesus as a Teen

The only extended personal glimpse we have of the boy Jesus is just as he enters puberty, at twelve years of age when a Jewish boy became a **"son of the commandment,"** a member of the congregation, and personally accountable for the responsibilities of the Law of Moses. On that day, at his bar mitzvah, the boy stood before parents, elders, and friends and declared: "Today, I am a man!"

According to custom, his parents then took the young man to Jerusalem for Passover (Luke 2:41). When the festival was over, they headed home, along with the group of relatives and friends who had traveled from Nazareth together. The women usually started out several hours before the men, because the men traveled faster.

prophecy
Matthew 2:15, 18, 23;
Hosea 11:1;
Jeremiah 31:15

son of the commandment
English for bar mitzvah

Evidently, Joseph thought Jesus had left with Mary and the women, and Mary thought Jesus had stayed behind to walk with the men. At day's end, when the men caught up and camp was set up for the night, they discovered that Jesus was not in either group! Anxiously, Mary and Joseph returned to Jerusalem to look for him. After three days of searching, they found him at the temple with the teachers.

At feast times, the practice of the members of the Jewish **Sanhedrin** (elders) was to sit in the temple courtyard and discuss theological questions raised by anyone who cared to listen. All the time his parents hunted for him, Jesus was there. Starting out for Galilee alone would have been too dangerous for the twelve-year-old. So, knowing his parents would return and find him, he spent the days "sitting in the midst of the teachers, both listening to them and asking them questions" (Luke 2:46 NKJV). This process—asking questions and listening to the teachers—is how young rabbis were trained. It's the method Jesus would later use in training his own disciples.

Sanhedrin
seventy leaders who served as High Council and Supreme Court in Hebrew law

priest
mediator, go-between (Latin: bridge)

propitiation
sacrifice covering sins, making fellowship between God and people possible

"Today I Am a Man"

HEBREWS 2:17–18 *Therefore, in all things He had to be made like His brethren, that He might be a merciful and faithful High **Priest** in things pertaining to God, to make **propitiation** for the sins of the people. For in that He Himself has suffered, being tempted, He is able to aid those who are tempted. (NKJV)*

Even though he knew he was God's Son, Jesus returned to Nazareth with Joseph and Mary and, for another eighteen years, voluntarily submitted to their parental authority and to the protocols of the human community.

---

what others say

Robert L. Thomas and Stanley N. Gundry

Jesus grew up as the oldest of the children in a rather large family. Joseph supported the family through carpentry in which Jesus assisted. Joseph apparently died during the period before Jesus' public appearance and, by implications in the gospels and early church fathers, we can presume Jesus became the provider for his mother and younger brothers and sisters (Mark 6:3). He therefore seemingly continued to work at carpentry until the beginning of his public ministry. His frequent mention of articles of furniture, houses, plows, yokes, and the like in his teaching reflects an intimate acquaintance with items built by carpenters.[1]

go to

genealogies
Luke 3:23–38;
1 Chronicles 1–9

David's throne
Romans 1:3

**more than one
name**
John 1:42

marry the widow
Deuteronomy
25:5–10

Roots: Jesus's Family Heritage

Two New Testament writers list Jesus's human heritage. Many people, starting to read the New Testament at the beginning, find their heads swimming with an unfamiliar list of difficult-to-pronounce names with which Matthew fills his first seventeen verses. Bo-o-or-ing! However, Jewish readers, for whom Matthew is writing, would have seen the relevance of the list immediately because it establishes Jesus's credentials as the Messiah. To Jewish readers, <u>genealogies</u> were extremely important to identify who was and who was not to be counted among "God's chosen people."

Luke traces Jesus's roots back to Adam, the first human (Luke 3:38). Matthew starts with Abraham, the first Jew (Matthew 1:1–2). From Abraham to David the two lists are the same. From David to Joseph they are quite different. Bible scholars give a variety of reasons for the difference:

1. Matthew gives the royal descent of Jesus, establishing his right to <u>David's throne</u>.

2. Matthew gives Joseph's family tree, while Luke gives Mary's.

3. The differences may be explained by the fact that many Jewish men were known by <u>more than one name</u>.

4. The differences may be due to the fact that in Jewish culture it was common practice, when a man died, for his brother to <u>marry the widow</u> and raise children in his own name or in the name of the deceased.

We don't have enough data to know for sure which explanation is correct. These things we know:

- Luke's list shows the humanity of Christ and his identification with, not just the Jews, but with all mankind. Christ's roots go deeper in the human family than any single nation or race—he came from and for all people!

- Matthew's list shows that Jesus was legally Joseph's son. Under Jewish law that established his right to claim David's throne.

Why Was It Necessary for Christ to Be a Man?

PHILIPPIANS 2:8 *And being found in appearance as a man, [Christ] humbled Himself and became obedient to the point of death, even the death of the cross. (NKJV)*

The claim of all the New Testament writers is that the child in the manger was God. But the New Testament never lets us forget Jesus was as much man as he was God. The plan of God could only be accomplished through a Redeemer who was an authentic man. In his Philippians 2 declaration above, Paul reveals the major reason Christ must be human.

The Son of God had to become a son of man to make it possible for him to die. As God he was immortal and indestructible. As man he was **mortal**—he could die. To pay the penalty human sin deserved so human sinners could be forgiven, it was necessary for Christ to be authentic man.

what others say

Robert E. Coleman

In the fullness of time, God's plan to take upon himself the experience of man assumed material form in the incarnation of Christ . . . The new Being was not a man who became God; he is God who became man, coming into history from the outside.[2]

Chapter Wrap-Up

- To save the baby Jesus from Herod's murderous intentions, an angel warned Joseph to get out of Bethlehem posthaste! He took Mary and the baby to Egypt until after Herod's death. Then another angel told him when it was safe to return to Israel. (Matthew 2:13–23)

- After returning from Egypt, Jesus grew up in Nazareth, among relatives and neighbors. After his bar mitzvah, on a trip to the Passover Feast in Jerusalem, Jesus disclosed his understanding of his special relationship to his Father in heaven. (Matthew 2:39–52)

- Both Matthew and Luke give genealogies of Jesus that demonstrate his human roots. Matthew traces his legal heritage and rightful claim to David's throne through his adoptive father, Joseph. Luke shows his natural human heritage through Mary, tracing Jesus's roots back to Adam, the first man, and to God, the Creator. (Matthew 1:1–17; Luke 3:23–38)

Study Questions

1. What is significant about each of the following statements: (a) "Out of Egypt I called My Son" (Matthew 2:15 NKJV), and (b) "He shall be called a Nazarene" (Matthew 2:23 NKJV)?

2. When did religious education of a Jewish child begin?

3. What does *bar mitzvah* mean? When was it celebrated? What did it signify?

4. How can the differences between the two genealogies of Jesus (Matthew 1; Luke 3) be explained?

Part Two
THE REVOLUTION BEGINS

Chapter 4: Shout in the Desert

Let's Get Started

LUKE 3:1–2 *Now in the fifteenth year of the reign of Tiberius Caesar, Pontius Pilate being governor of Judea, Herod being tetrarch of Galilee, his brother Philip tetrarch of Iturea and the region of Trachonitis, and Lysanias tetrarch of Abilene, while Annas and Caiaphas were high priests, the word of God came to John the son of Zacharias in the wilderness.* (NKJV)

prophecies
Luke 1:14–17

Isaiah's prophecy
Isaiah 40:3–5

Luke wanted readers to know the time, and to understand that the story of John the Baptist and Jesus of Nazareth was no "once upon a time" invention. It was thoroughly factual and set solidly in the history of that time. Knowing the names of five political leaders and two religious leaders who were running things, we can calculate that John began to preach sometime in late AD 28 or early AD 29.

Desert Crier

LUKE 3:3–4 *And he went into all the region around the Jordan, preaching a baptism of repentance for the remission of sins, as it is written in the book of the words of Isaiah the prophet, saying:*
"The voice of one crying in the wilderness:
'Prepare the way of the LORD;
Make His paths straight.'" (NKJV)

John was the son of Zacharias the priest and Elizabeth, his wife, who had been unable to have children until baby John came along. Along with his surprising birth came prophecies that he would prepare Israel for Christ's arrival. Thirty years later, at the right moment on God's timetable, John emerged from seclusion and began to broadcast what was about to happen and how to prepare for it. Matthew, Mark, and Luke agree—John's ministry was the fulfillment of Isaiah's prophecy of a desert "voice" calling Israel to prepare for arrival of the Messiah-King.

gospel harmony

Matthew 3:1–6
Mark 1:2–6
Luke 3:2b–6

Old Testament Prophecies Fulfilled by John's Ministry

Where Predicted	What Is Predicted	Where Fulfilled
Malachi 3:1	God would send his messenger ahead to prepare the way for Christ.	Mark 1:2
Isaiah 40:3	Christ's arrival would be preceded by a "voice" crying in the wilderness.	Matthew 3:3; Mark 1:3; Luke 3:4
Isaiah 40:4–5	The ministry of the messenger would be spiritually comparable to a road-building project to prepare for the arrival of a king.	Luke 3:5–6

what others say

William Barclay

When a king proposed to tour a part of his dominions in the east, he sent a courier before him to tell the people to prepare the roads. So John is regarded as the courier of the King. But the preparation on which he insisted was a preparation of heart and of life. "The king is coming," he said. "Mend, not your roads, but your lives."[1]

John the Baptist called on all Israel to "repent" (Matthew 3:2 NKJV). He proclaimed a new government ("the kingdom") and yet he did not, as might be expected, make his revolutionary announcement in Jerusalem, the nation's governmental center. Instead he preached first to a handful of country folk living along the Jordan River, twenty miles to the east of the capital city. His first audiences may have been outnumbered by lizards and scorpions.

News of the desert crier spread like a prairie fire, and soon hundreds were coming out of the cities and towns of Israel just to see and hear the radical desert revivalist. He touched in them a deep, unsatisfied hunger for some word from God to make the tinder-dry desert of their spirits blossom <u>like a rose</u>.

Winner of the Elijah Look-Alike Contest

John's skin was blackened by the desert sun. His eyes blazed from a face full of disorderly beard. (At least that's how I imagine him.) Matthew and Mark give us the authorized portrait (Matthew 3:4; Mark 1:6): John the Baptist wore a homespun camel's-hair shirt, which he kept wrapped around himself with a wide leather belt.

go to

like a rose
Isaiah 35:1

John's menu was always a tasty selection of crunchy insects—locusts—made palatable by the strong, sweet taste of wild honey. The New Testament nowhere else publishes descriptions of its characters—not even Jesus. Why tell how John dressed and what he ate?

appearance of Elijah
Malachi 4:5;
Matthew 11:14;
17:10–13

heroic
1 Kings 18

It all had special meaning for people looking for the Messiah. The prophets predicted that Christ's arrival would be preceded by the <u>appearance of Elijah</u>, most <u>heroic</u> of Old Testament prophets. Near the end of his ministry, Elijah sent word to the king of Israel that because the king had consulted with an idol instead of God, he would never recover from injuries he had suffered in a fall. When the king asked for a description of the man who had the audacity to send such a message, he was told, "A hairy man wearing a leather belt around his waist." From this description, the king recognized his prophet of doom as Elijah (2 Kings 1:2–8 NKJV).

John the Baptist emerged from the same desert where Elijah spent most of his life. He preached with the same fireball fervor as Elijah. He dressed like Elijah. As the angel predicted before his birth, he came in Elijah's "spirit and power" (Luke 1:17 NKJV).

Repentance

MATTHEW 3:8 *Therefore bear fruits worthy of repentance.* *(NKJV)*

The New Testament Greek word for repentance is *metanoia*—a change in mind and attitude. As John (and later Jesus) spells out its meaning, it calls for change in basic personal values and lifestyle.

The meaning of repentance can be seen in what John told people who came to hear him.

Sadducees
powerful priestly
class who ran the
temple

tax collectors (KJV: publicans)
collectors of Roman
taxes for profit

soldiers
either temple militia
sent by the high
priest, Roman
troops, or both

1. Pharisees and **Sadducees** (religious leaders) were corrupt, hypocritical, and pompous. When they came for baptism, John compared them to snakes fleeing before a desert brushfire (Matthew 3:7; Luke 3:7). He told them their days of authority were numbered if they didn't change their stingy, self-centered ways and start sharing what they had with others (Matthew 3:8–10; Luke 3:8–11).

2. He told **tax collectors** to be honest and to collect only what the law demanded, instead of cheating the public (Luke 3:12–13).

3. **Soldiers** came, under orders to see what kind of message the people were hearing. When they asked what he thought they should do to prepare for Christ's coming, he told them to stop falsely accusing people and extorting money by threats of violence (Luke 3:14).

what others say

John Killinger

It is interesting that [John's] answer is couched in terms of simple justice. People who have more property than they need are to divide with those who have none. Those who have food are to share with those who are hungry. Tax collectors are to do their duty but forgo the often-exorbitant fees they have been accustomed to extracting for personal use. Soldiers are to live simply and honestly, not using their positions to rob or to falsely accuse people of crimes and confiscate their property . . . They imply a new orientation in life, a new spirit, so that God, not personal profit, becomes the center of the person's life.[3]

Shocking Baptism

John urged his listeners to publicly dramatize their willingness to change by joining him for a soaking in the Jordan River. Gentiles in the process of converting to Judaism were baptized in special baptismal pools to symbolize giving up idol worship, as well as cleansing from idolatry and pagan sins. But lifelong Jews did not need baptism. They were already God's special people.

John insisted that people who all their lives thought of themselves that way—as "God's people"—be baptized as if they were just emerging from darkest paganism! In confrontational conversation with the religious leaders, he argued that being born into the privileged Hebrew bloodline, the right nation, and the correct religion was insufficient preparation for receiving the Lord (Matthew 3:9; Luke 3:8).

What John Said About Jesus

LUKE 3:15–18 *Now as the people were in expectation, and all reasoned in their hearts about John, whether he was the Christ or not, John answered, saying to all, "I indeed baptize you with water; but One mightier than I is coming, whose sandal strap I am not worthy to loose. He will baptize you with the Holy Spirit and fire. His winnowing fan is in His hand, and He will thoroughly clean out His threshing floor, and gather the wheat into His barn; but the chaff He will burn with unquenchable fire." And with many other exhortations he preached to the people. (NKJV)*

Messianic expectations were in the air. As Messiah-minded Jews observed John's Elijah-like preaching and appearance, it was inevitable that some would begin to wonder if he might be the Christ. John never encouraged this idea, but faithfully pointed his listeners to the one who was approaching on his heels.

Water Fellowship

Matthew 3:11–12
Mark 1:7–8
Luke 3:15–18

MATTHEW 3:13–17 *Then Jesus came from Galilee to John at the Jordan to be baptized by him. And John tried to prevent Him, saying, "I need to be baptized by You, and are You coming to me?" But Jesus answered and said to him, "Permit it to be so now, for thus it is fitting for us to fulfill all righteousness." Then he allowed Him. When He had been baptized, Jesus came up immediately from the water; and behold, the heavens were opened to Him, and He saw the Spirit of God descending like a dove and alighting upon Him. And suddenly a voice came from heaven, saying, "This is My beloved Son, in whom I am well pleased." (NKJV)*

One fine day as kingdom seekers responded to John's preaching by coming down to the Jordan to be baptized, a young stranger moved toward the water with the other seekers. John recognized him as the one about whom he had been speaking.

no sins
2 Corinthians 5:21;
Hebrews 4:15

friend of sinners
Luke 5:29–32;
15:1–2

instinctively knew
The Holy Spirit
revealed it to him.

Matthew 3:13–17
Mark 1:9–11
Luke 3:21–22

John **instinctively knew** this man was no sinner. He protested. Jesus insisted, saying that it was appropriate for him and John to do the right thing, whatever it might be.

The Bible agrees with John's assessment: Jesus had <u>no sins</u> of his own over which to repent. Why, then, did he need to be baptized, which for all others was a sign of repentance for forgiveness of sins?

Why Did Jesus Need to Be Baptized?

Baptism launched Jesus's career with a public declaration that he was one of us—a human being. The task the Father in heaven had dispatched him to earth to do required him to be human. When people watched him go down into the Jordan River, they had no doubt they were observing the actions of a man, not some sort of special semi-man or semi-god with whom it would be impossible for them to identify. After his baptism gossips would slander him as a liar, a blasphemer, a <u>friend of sinners</u>, and a drunk. No surprise, then, for Jesus to show up at the Jordan River in a crowd of repentant sinners, to file down into the water at the preacher's invitation and declare he was forsaking sin and committing himself to righteousness—just like the others.

By presenting himself for baptism, Jesus was not confessing that he was a sinner. He was saying,

1. "I'm with John."

2. "I'm committed to live a righteous life."

3. "I want to live under God's reign."

4. "I'm one of you."

> **what others say**
>
> **Clark Peddicord**
>
> Jesus' identification with the sinful people of Israel was similar to what Moses did in the wilderness after the Israelites had sinned by making themselves a gold calf as an idol (Exodus 32:30–32). God accepted Jesus' perfect repentance for his people just as he had that of Moses. This is shown by the heavens tearing open and the Holy Spirit descending on Jesus.[4]

anointing
confer on someone authority

mediatorial
between God and sinners to fulfill his/her calling

Henry Alford

Two circumstances may be noticed respecting the manner of the descent of the Spirit: It was as a dove—the Spirit as manifested in our Lord was gentle and benign. This was not a sudden and temporary descent of the Spirit, but a permanent though special **anointing** of the Savior for his holy office . . . And from this moment his ministry and **mediatorial** work (in the active official sense) begins.[5]

Chapter Wrap-Up

- The gospel (good news) centers in Jesus of Nazareth. By carefully documenting the timing of his story, the New Testament writers make it clear that Jesus is a real person who lived a real life at a specific time in history, which they carefully document. (Luke 3:1–2)

- The importance of Jesus of Nazareth was highlighted by the commission of John the Baptist to urge the Jews to turn from their sins in preparation to receive the Messiah. (Matthew 3:1–6)

- Preparing to receive Christ is compared to building a roadway for a king. The "earthmoving" machinery is a spiritual transaction called "repentance"—willingness to change in the basic structures of one's life. (Matthew 3:7–10)

- John invited his hearers to present themselves for a special kind of baptism, which symbolized a humiliating acknowledgment that, though they were lifelong Jews, they needed to be taught how to live in the kingdom of God from the ground up. (Luke 3:7–14)

- John insisted he was not the Christ, but that a person was coming after him who surpassed John in greatness and power to bring real change into people's lives. This Christ would baptize believers with the Holy Spirit and with fire (discipline, suffering, and judgment of sin in their lives). (Matthew 3:11–12; Luke 3:16–17)

- Jesus asked John to baptize him, in order to complete his identification with human beings, to announce his agreement with John's ministry and message, and to publicly commit himself to live a righteous life under the reign of God. (Matthew 3:13–17)

- At his baptism, the Holy Spirit was seen descending on Jesus in dove-like form, anointing him with authority for his ministry. A heavenly voice announced that Jesus was the Son of God and that God was pleased with him. (John 1:32–34)

Study Questions

1. What made the people of Israel think that a special prophet would signal the coming of Christ? What sort of prophet were they looking for?

2. What one word describes the essence of John the Baptist's message? What does it mean, and how does that word relate to your life?

3. What specific changes did John call for in the following groups of people: Pharisees and Sadducees? Tax collectors? Soldiers?

4. What was there about John's baptism that was so shocking and humbling?

5. List the three ways Christ's baptism is greater than John's.

6. Jesus was given two things to get him going on his life's work—the Spirit came on him like a dove, and a heavenly voice assured him of his relationship with and approval by God. How has God affirmed you as his child in Christ?

Chapter Highlights:
- Testing, Testing
- The Invisible Peril
- Sneak Attack
- Three Proposals
- Test Passed

Chapter 5: First Blood

Let's Get Started

Following his baptism by John the Baptist, Jesus was purposely led by the Holy Spirit into the wild country surrounding the Jordan River and the Dead Sea. There God's <u>archenemy</u>, the devil, would test the young Messiah's grasp of his mission and what would be necessary to accomplish it.

Testing, Testing

MATTHEW 4:1–2 *Then Jesus was led up by the Spirit into the wilderness to be tempted by the devil. And when He had fasted forty days and forty nights, afterward He was hungry. (NKJV)*

gospel harmony

Matthew 4:1–11
Mark 1:12–13
Luke 4:1–13

Jesus's testing came in the form of (1) forty days and nights in a desert environment without food, and (2) pressure from the **devil** to sidestep the plan of God. This would be the first face-to-face skirmish in the <u>Holy War</u> Jesus had been sent to fight against the <u>evil forces</u> that mastermind the present **world order**.

Why Are Christians Tested?

The Bible mentions several reasons why Christians are tested:

- So we can know for certain our faith is genuine (1 Peter 1:7)
- So we can be changed into Christ's likeness (Romans 8:28–29)
- So the spirit world (angels and devils) can see a visible demonstration of God's wisdom worked out in believing humanity (Ephesians 3:10–13)

go to

archenemy
Luke 10:18–19;
1 Peter 5:8–9

Holy War
Ephesians 6:10–18

evil forces
Ephesians 1:21;
1 John 5:19

devil
evil being also
known as Satan

world order
human society in
opposition to God

what others say

William Barclay

What we call temptation is not meant to make us sin; it is meant to enable us to conquer sin. It is not meant to make us bad, it is meant to make us good. It is not meant to weaken

young
Luke 3:23

us, it is meant to make us emerge stronger and finer and purer from the ordeal. Temptation is not the penalty of being a man, temptation is the glory of being a man.[1]

The Invisible Peril

Jeshimmon was the Hebrew name for the wild country west of the Dead Sea into which the Holy Spirit led Jesus for the specific purpose of being tempted. The name means "Devastation." It is an untamed area of sand and crumbling limestone. The hills are heaps of dust. Rocks are bare and jagged.

The ruggedness of the land, the risks from lions, bears, and other dangerous animals who inhabited it, coupled with the rigors of going forty days and nights without food, do not suggest "the Jesus portrayed in many paintings—a fair-skinned, scrawny wimp."[2] This Jesus must have been brawny—a man who could endure the challenges involved in his temptation.

Jesus went into this rugged desert accompanied only by the Spirit of God. God's affirming voice heard at his baptism still rang in his ears: "This is My beloved Son, in whom I am well pleased" (Matthew 3:17 NKJV). The call to saviorhood burned in his young heart. He had questions, issues to be sorted out. He knew he was God's Son. And he knew he was a man. Awareness of his human limitations and the awesomeness of his task set the tone of his thoughts and prayers.

what others say

Saint John Chrysostom

You see how the Spirit led him, not into a city or public arena, but into a wilderness. In this desolate place, the Spirit extended the devil an occasion to test him, not only by hunger, but also by loneliness, for it is there most especially that the devil assails us, when he sees us left alone and by ourselves.[3]

Baudelaire

The devil's cleverest ruse is to make men believe that he does not exist.[4]

Sneak Attack

Paintings, movies, and other portrayals of Jesus's desert temptations picture the devil approaching in visible humanoid, animal, or reptilian form. But nowhere in the three New Testament accounts is the tempter said to have appeared in visible form. He may have. There is no reason why he could not have done so. But I wonder.

Matthew 4:3 (NKJV) says the tempter "came" and spoke to Jesus. It doesn't say if his coming was visible. Luke 4:3 says the devil spoke to him. It doesn't say Jesus could see him.

Hebrews 4:15 (NKJV) says Jesus "was in all points tempted as we are," which would indicate the temptations he experienced in Judea's wild lands must have come to him as they do to us—not as outward struggles with an easily recognized enemy, but as confusing battles in the mind. It is a lot more difficult to recognize the enemy when he camouflages himself in our imaginations.

Again, there is no reason to assume that Satan did not visibly appear to Jesus or that some supernatural transportation to the temple pinnacle did not take place. Nothing in the text demands that we reject the literal view. But so often we fail to consider that Jesus did experience temptation in the realm of his mind.

key point

what others say

Thomas à Kempis

At first [temptation] is a mere thought confronting the mind; then imagination paints it in stronger colors; only after that do we take pleasure in it, and the will makes a false move, and we give our assent.[5]

Three Fascinating Proposals for Missing God's Plan

For forty days, Jesus faced the barren waste, braved the wild beasts (Mark 1:13), and fielded deceptive suggestions by a tempter intent on diverting him from the work to which God had sent him. On the surface, every temptation seemed reasonable, and each represented a less costly way to do God's work than the way called for in God's plan.

water to wine
John 2:1–11

5,000
John 6:1–13

4,000
Mark 8:1–9

legions of angels
Matthew 26:53–54

spiritual gifts
Romans 12;
1 Corinthians 12

material possessions
Acts 4:32–35;
2 Corinthians 8, 9

Proposition 1: Feed Yourself

MATTHEW 4:3–4 *Now when the tempter came to Him, he said, "If You are the Son of God, command that these stones become bread." But He answered and said, "It is written, 'Man shall not live by bread alone, but by every word that proceeds from the mouth of God.'" (NKJV)*

Jesus had the power to change stones to bread. Miracles would be a daily occurrence for him. Later he would turn <u>water to wine</u>. He would feed <u>5,000</u> hungry hangers-on with a child's lunch. He would do it again for <u>4,000</u>. In the desert, toe-to-toe with the enemy, he had not eaten for nearly six weeks. Matthew's matter-of-fact understatement says, "He was hungry" (4:2 NKJV). How could it possibly upset some great eternal plan if a couple of rocks became breakfast? On the surface, the suggestion made sense and seemed harmless.

Why Turning Rocks to Bread Was a Bad Idea

It was a devilish strategy to get Jesus to divert the gifts of God from the "others-focus" that saviorhood requires. At no time did Jesus use his miraculous powers to gratify himself. Even at his arrest he could have called <u>legions of angels</u> to rescue him, but he refused. The work of God cannot be accomplished through self-indulgence. The gifts God gives—<u>spiritual gifts</u> or <u>material possessions</u>—are not for the receiver's personal benefit alone, for pride of ownership, or to gain power over others. They are given to meet the needs and hungers of others, as well as our own.

The suggestion to turn stones to bread was a bad idea because it challenged the wisdom that God's priorities take precedence over felt human needs. Jesus chose to be guided by the Word and wisdom of God, not merely his appetites and wants (Matthew 4:4).

Proposition 2: Choose Sensationalism as a Shortcut to Acceptance

MATTHEW 4:5–7 *Then the devil took Him up into the holy city, set Him on the pinnacle of the temple, and said to Him, "If You are the Son of God, throw Yourself down. For it is written:*
'He shall give His angels charge over you,'
and,

'In their hands they shall bear you up,
Lest you dash your foot against a stone.' "
Jesus said to him, "It is written again, 'You shall not tempt the
Lord your God.' " (NKJV)

Either the devil was allowed to physically transport Jesus to the **temple pinnacle** or, as I've suggested, Jesus imagined himself on that high perch looking down on the gathering worshippers below. In his mind's eye, Jesus saw himself standing on that high point. All he would need to do to attract Israel's attention would be to jump from the platform as worshippers gathered, land on his feet 450 feet below, and walk away unharmed. The Jews (who were always looking for miraculous signs) would be convinced by this phenomenal feat to instantly accept him as Messiah (at least that's how the tempter's reasoning went).

To make resisting temptation tougher, this brainstorm came with the refrain of an Old Testament hymn that seemed to say it was consistent with Scripture (Psalm 91:11–12).

Why a Quantum Leap Off the Temple Peak Was a Bad Idea

The rule of God is not established by sensational display. It grows like <u>yeast</u>, quietly taking over a batch of bread dough; or a <u>mustard seed</u>, germinating and growing into a sheltering bush without fanfare. Jesus is credited with many miracles. A few were spectacular. But he healed people and asked them not to tell. People looking for spectacles of power were disappointed. He repeatedly proved his messiahship, but never by putting on a flashy show of power. He **de-emphasized** visible proofs, expecting people to believe based on <u>his words</u>, <u>without visible proof</u>.

Jesus rejected the intriguing suggestion he take a quick leap to celebrity, because it would violate the delicate trust relationship between himself and his Father God. When Jesus cited the Scripture "You shall not tempt the Lord your God" (Matthew 4:7 NKJV; Deuteronomy 6:16), he used a different Greek word for tempt than the one used in Matthew 4:1. The new word means "to test as an attempt to coerce." The Old Testament verse Jesus quoted means, "Don't try to force God to do what you want him to do by contriv-

go to

yeast
Matthew 13:33

mustard seed
Matthew 13:31–32

de-emphasized
John 4:48

his words
John 7:16–17

without visible proof
John 20:29

temple pinnacle
platform where a trumpeter sounded the call to the morning sacrifice; a 450-foot drop to the Kedron Valley below

de-emphasized
played down

ing a test to make him prove himself."[6] The devil was suggesting Jesus back God into a corner to make him act the way he wanted God to act.

Proposition 3: Follow the Bloodless Road to the Kingdom

MATTHEW 4:8–10 *Again, the devil took Him up on an exceedingly high mountain, and showed Him all the kingdoms of the world and their glory. And he said to Him, "All these things I will give You if You will fall down and worship me." Then Jesus said to him, "Away with you, Satan! For it is written, 'You shall worship the LORD your God, and Him only you shall serve.'" (NKJV)*

Jesus found himself on the summit of a peak so high all the earth's empires were visible. Spread before him were splendid palaces, shining thrones, gleaming cities, fabulous wealth, beauty, and political power.

"All these things I will give You if You will fall down and worship me" (Matthew 4:9 NKJV).

What Sort of Suggestion Was This, Really?

The original Greek word for worship (Matthew 4:9) literally means "to kiss." To the early Greeks it meant "to do homage by kissing the hand." The word was not primarily used to describe worship of deity, but respect for a prince or king.[7] Jesus was being tempted to grant the devil respect as a legitimate ruler—perhaps an equal—as a way to find an easier, less painful way than death on the cross to bring the world's kingdoms under the reign of God.

"Away with you, Satan!" shouted Jesus. "For it is written, 'You shall worship the LORD your God, and Him only you shall serve'" (Matthew 4:10 NKJV; Deuteronomy 6:13).

what others say

William Barclay

What the tempter was saying was, "Compromise! Come to terms with me! Don't pitch your demands quite so high! Wink just a little at evil and questionable things—and then people will follow you in their hordes."[8]

Passing with Flying Colors

For six weeks the black-hearted <u>world ruler</u> had done his dirt. But now it was clear that his sulfur-yellowed teeth would have nothing to chew on but the bitter, gritty grist of failure. He had failed to deter the young Messiah from his mission. So the devil left Jesus (Matthew 4:11), planning to resume his attack at another time when his intended victim was again vulnerable (Luke 4:13). As Satan leaves we learn three important things about him:

go to

world ruler
John 12:31

1. He is not able to be everywhere at once.

2. He has limited access to people.

3. We can expect him to be relentless—to attack again.

As for Jesus, passing the test seemed to invigorate him. Matthew and Mark tell of angels ministering to him following the Temptation. This desert duel confirmed four realities for Jesus:

1. His oneness with human beings in their vulnerability to temptation

2. The genuineness of his faith and messianic vision

3. The reality of his relationship with God as Son

4. The presence and power of the Holy Spirit in his life

Chapter Wrap-Up

- Jesus was led by the Holy Spirit into the desert to be tempted. Temptation is a fact of life for every human being; it demonstrates our readiness to do God's will. (Matthew 4:1–11)

- The devil is a real person to whom the Bible gives many names describing his wicked character. He tempted Jesus when he was most vulnerable. (Mark 1:12–13)

- The devil proposed that Jesus (1) turn stones to bread to feed his hunger, (2) leap off the temple to demonstrate how God would protect him, and (3) give the devil respect as an equal in exchange for control over the nations of the world. (Luke 4:3–12)

- Using Scripture, Jesus exposed the deceptiveness of each temptation, passed the test, and ordered the devil to leave. Angels ministered to him. (Matthew 4:4, 7, 10–11)

Study Questions

1. Which of the following tactics did Jesus use in dealing with each temptation?: (a) called for angels to help him, (b) gritted his teeth and dug in his heels—willpower, (c) tried to reason with the tempter, (d) quoted Scripture to expose the deception, (e) ignored the temptation until it went away, and (f) ordered Satan to leave.

2. What were the three things the devil tempted Jesus to do? Why might each have appealed to Jesus?

3. What would have been wrong with (a) turning stones to bread, (b) jumping off the temple pinnacle, or (c) showing the devil some respect?

4. What is your greatest temptation right now? What does Jesus's experience teach you about how to deal with it?

Chapter 6: Descent from Splendor

Let's Get Started

In his introduction to the Life of Christ, the apostle-historian-author John takes us back, back, back—into the mysterious sphere we call **eternity**. There we are introduced to a person with a history like no other born on this planet. There we discover answers to questions raised by the angelic announcements to Mary, Joseph, and the shepherds, and the amazing pilgrimage of the Magi. A tantalizing string of unusual events and pronouncements mark Jesus's early life. He was not just another religious leader like Buddha or Muhammad. Jesus was and is unique.

A Hymn to Him

JOHN 1:1–2 *In the beginning was the Word, and the Word was with God, and the Word was God. He was in the beginning with God. (NKJV)*

The first sentences of John 1 are the lyrics of an <u>early Christian hymn</u> sung in first-century churches, accompanied by simple stringed instruments—lyre or harp—or without accompaniment. John adapted this hymn and made it "the overture to the **gospel** narrative of the career of the **incarnate Word**."[1]

go to

early Christian hymn
Luke 1:40–55, 68–79;
Colossians 1:15–20;
Philippians 2:6–11;
1 Timothy 3:16

eternity
reality outside and not limited to time

gospel
good news

incarnate Word
God's expression of himself in human form

what others say

Michael Card

I find it touching that before this passage was ever made the topic of theological debate, it was a simple hymn. Before it was preached, it was sung. Without reasoning and argumentation the early believers embraced these complex incarnational truths by means of a simple melody . . . And so with music those early saints sang their way to belief in the unbelievable.[2]

in the Spirit
John 14:16–21

original Twelve
Luke 6:13–16

disciples
Christian believers,
followers of Christ

pagan
non-Christian,
unbeliever

apostles
Christ's special
ambassadors sent
out to establish the
church

martyred
killed because of
their faith in Christ

Logos
spoken word;
reason, thought

The Heady Wine of Distilled Faith

Why is John's version of the Jesus story different from the versions of Matthew, Mark, and Luke? The operative word is "different," not "contradictory." His account was written around AD 80 to AD 90. A generation had passed since he and the others spent those three years with Jesus. With the passage of time, their understanding of Jesus and what they experienced with him became clearer. In the process of telling and retelling the story to the growing band of **disciples** and their **pagan** neighbors, the Christians improved their ability to communicate the truth that had captivated them. Under the Spirit's inspiration and protection, these insights and experiences distilled into an orderly understanding of the person and work of Jesus Christ.

By the time John wrote, most of the other **apostles** had been **martyred**. After fifty-plus years of walking with Jesus <u>in the Spirit</u>, John was the only one of the <u>original Twelve</u> left to write from the vantage point of a half century of experience with him.

The Cosmic Secret of Christ's Uniqueness

In a stroke of communication genius, John introduced the principal character of his Life of Christ by building on an idea with which his readers, both Jews and Gentiles, were already familiar. Thinking people of that day believed in the existence of a spiritual force in the universe called "the Word." In Greek, the universal language of the Roman Empire, this force was known as the **Logos**.

First-Century Ideas About the Logos (Word)

Group	Who/What They Believed the "Word" to Be
Greeks (Plato's disciples)	Divine wisdom that directs everything in the universe.
Greeks (Stoics)	Soul of the universe.
Romans	Universal principle by which life exists and is sustained.
Assyrians/Babylonians	Raging cosmic power from which there is no escape.
Egyptians	Creative substance from mouth of deity that maintains the universe.
Jews (Old Testament)	Action of the Almighty (Psalm 33:6). Means by which God accomplishes his purpose in history (Isaiah 55:11).
Jews (Philo of Alexandria)	Agent of creation, God's thought, expression of wisdom, medium through which he governs the world, means by which humans know God, Advocate/High Priest through which people find God and forgiveness.

go to

face of Jesus Christ
2 Corinthians 4:6;
Hebrews 1:2–3

know God
John 14:7–11

the Shema
Deuteronomy 6:4

Christ
Anointed One,
Messiah, King

> **what others say**
>
> **Lawrence O. Richards**
>
> In Hebrew thought, "the Word of God" was his active self-expression, that revelation of himself to humanity through which a person not only receives truth about God, but meets God face-to-face.[3]

The Ultimate Expression of God

JOHN 1:14, 17 *And the Word became flesh and dwelt among us, and we beheld His glory, the glory as of the only begotten of the Father, full of grace and truth . . . For the law was given through Moses, but grace and truth came through Jesus Christ.* (NKJV)

The Word is bigger than language. The Word of God has never been an impersonal force, but an extension of God himself, a living person. The Word has a name, Jesus, and has a title, **Christ** (John 1:17). The clearest, most complete communication of God's character in language human beings can understand is visible in the life, personality, words, and works of Jesus of Nazareth. Jesus is the expression of God in human form. Anyone who wants to know what kind of person God is, how God thinks, what God cares about, what God is doing, and what God expects from us, needs to look no farther than the <u>face of Jesus Christ</u>. Know Jesus, and you <u>know God</u>.

The Big Three-in-One

The four historians who wrote the New Testament's Lives of Christ were committed to the distinctive Hebrew concept of monotheism. With Jews everywhere they confessed the traditional faith:

"The LORD is one!" (<u>the *Shema*</u>). None of these men would ever deny that truth. There is and always has been only one God. His expression of himself in Jesus Christ does not change that.

The introduction of the concept of the living Word, who existed with God and is the co-Creator through whom God made the universe, opens up a mind-bending mystery! Struggling with this mystery has led Christians to the belief that the one, true God is a Trinity. The word "Trinity" is not found in the Bible. But Old

go to

together
Matthew 28:19

Trinity
one Being
expressed in three
personalities

Testament references to God in plural terms, coupled with New Testament references to God the Father, Son, and Holy Spirit <u>together</u>, lead Christians to conclude the Bible's one God is "God in three persons, Blessed **Trinity**."[4]

One God in Three Persons: Father, Son, and Holy Spirit

Old Testament Plural References to God	Genesis 1:26 Genesis 3:22 Isaiah 6:8 Psalm 33:6 with John 1:1–3; 20:22 (*Elohim*, Hebrew name for God, is "a plural noun, generally taken as a plural of majesty."[5])
Father, Son, and Holy Spirit Identified Together as God	Isaiah 42:1 with Matthew 12:15–18 Luke 3:21–22 John 3:34–35 John 14:16–26 John 15:26 John 16:13–15 Acts 2:32–33 Acts 10:36–38 Romans 1:3–4 Romans 8:9–11 2 Corinthians 1:21–22 2 Corinthians 13:14 Galatians 4:4–6 2 Thessalonians 2:13–14 Titus 3:4–6 Hebrews 9:14 1 Peter 1:2
Jesus's Claims of Oneness with God	John 8:18 John 10:30 John 14:9 John 20:28–29 Matthew 28:19

what others say

Robert E. Coleman

Any formulation of the triune nature of God proves inadequate, for the very reason that human intelligence cannot explain the divine mind. Yet only by the Trinity can the person and mind of God be understood.[6]

The Right to Become God's Children

JOHN 1:10–13 *He was in the world, and the world was made through Him, and the world did not know Him. He came to His own, and His own did not receive Him. But as many as received Him, to them He gave the right to become children of God, to those who believe in His name: who were born, not of blood, nor of the will of the flesh, nor of the will of man, but of God. (NKJV)*

born of God
John 3:3–8;
1 Peter 1:23

Spirit of God does
John 3:5–8

light
John 3:19–21

Being born a human being does not make a person a son or daughter of God in the way John is describing. He names two things people often think give them the right to be called "children of God" and declares that neither of them is enough!

1. Becoming children of God has nothing to do with "natural descent." Racial or national heritage or being born on the right side of the railroad tracks does not make a person a child of God.

2. Becoming children of God is not as simple as a mental "human decision." A person can't become God's child by gritting his or her teeth and determining to do it . . . somehow!

"The will of man" (John 1:13 NKJV) simply repeats, for emphasis, the truth that nobody simply makes up his or her mind to be a Christian. Becoming God's child is something God must do for us and in us. Coming into God's family requires another kind of birth—a person must be "born of God."

key point

There is a decision to be made, but the other kind of birth that makes us children of God is a miracle.

How Can an Ordinary Person Be Born Again?

Being born of God and gaining the right to become children of God is something the Spirit of God does in the life of a person who welcomes Christ's light. From the human perspective, spiritual birth hinges on two attitudes (John 1:11–12 NKJV):

1. *"Receive Him."* The original word for "receive" was used to describe a man taking a wife or adopting a child. It implies entering a committed, lifelong relationship with Jesus Christ.

His name
stands for everything Christ is, character, values, and person

flesh
real humanity

dwelt
became like one of us

only
Christ is unique

grace
favor, generosity, joy, mercy

truth
complete reliability, integrity, reality

2. *"Believe in His* [Jesus Christ's] *name."* The Amplified Bible gives additional meanings hidden in the original word for "believe": "believe in (adhere to, trust in and rely on) **His name**."[7]

what others say

Billy Graham

It is only when you are born again that you can experience all the riches God has in store for you. You are not just a living person, you are truly ALIVE![8]

What's God Really Like?

JOHN 1:14, 18 *And the Word became flesh and dwelt among us, and we beheld His glory, the glory as of the only begotten of the Father, full of grace and truth . . . No one has seen God at any time. The only begotten Son, who is in the bosom of the Father, He has declared Him.* (NKJV)

In the person and life of Jesus Christ, God

- exhibited himself in human form—"the Word became **flesh**,"

- exhibited himself up close and personal—"**dwelt** among us,"

- exhibited himself in one special person—"the **only** begotten of the Father," and

- exhibited himself as kind, loving, benevolent, and truthful—"full of **grace** and **truth**."

Chapter Wrap-Up

- In his approach to telling the Life of Christ, John drew on a half century of experience with Christ and sharing the good news with all sorts of people.

- The Bible's God is a God who speaks to people. His clearest expression of himself is Christ, whom early Christians identified as God's living Word. (John 1:1–2)

- When Christ came into the world, many failed to recognize him for who he was. Those who do recognize, receive, and believe in him are spiritually reborn as God's children. (John 1:10–13)

- John's viewpoint in his Life of Christ is that Jesus is God's clearest expression of himself to people, and people can know what God is really like by looking at Jesus. (John 1:14–18)

Study Questions

1. Why is John's Gospel different from the Gospels of Matthew, Mark, and Luke?

2. How does a person become a child of God?

3. What did the Word (Christ) do to show human beings what God is really like?

Chapter 7: Choices at Jordan

Let's Get Started

JOHN 1:19–20 *Now this is the testimony of John, when the Jews sent priests and Levites from Jerusalem to ask him, "Who are you?" He confessed, and did not deny, but confessed, "I am not the Christ." (NKJV)*

As John's crowds increased, it was inevitable that the authorities would take notice. Representatives of Jerusalem's religious intelligentsia were sent to the wild country near the Jordan River town of **Bethany** to question the feisty prophet about his message and work. The writer who is telling the story is not anti-Semitic—he himself is a Jew, as is Jesus. When he uses the term "the Jews," he does not refer to rank-and-file Jewish people, but to the Jewish leaders who wielded power through an official governing body known as the Sanhedrin. But the majority of Jewish leaders opposed Jesus to the death. The three groups mentioned as John's interrogators were the priests, the Levites, and the Pharisees.

PRIESTS (1:19)—descendants of Aaron, Moses's brother, in charge of religious services at the temple. John's father, Zacharias, was a priest (Luke 1:5). The priests would be especially interested in the activities of a member of a priestly family.

LEVITES (1:19)—descendants of the <u>patriarch</u> Levi (Moses and Aaron's ancestor) who were the temple police, musicians, and teachers. Their teaching role explains their concern about the content of John's teaching.

PHARISEES (1:24)—Israel's "pure religionists." They portrayed themselves as serious students of the **Law** of God, but in practice were more committed to their **traditions**. Some were genuinely godly men, but their outward legalism usually led to spiritual pride that hid real godliness behind a smoke screen of rule-bound religion.

patriarch
Genesis
29:31–30:24;
35:16–18; 49:1–28

Bethany
not Bethany near
Jerusalem, but
another town east of
the Jordan, twelve
miles from Jericho
(see appendix A)

Law
Old Testament
commandments

traditions
extrabiblical religious rules and
regulations

go to

Elijah
Malachi 3:1; 4:5–6;
1 Kings 18;
Matthew 11:14

prophet
Matthew 16:14;
Mark 6:15;
Luke 9:19

like himself
Deuteronomy
18:15–22

Day of the Lord
time when God
implements some
specific act of salva-
tion: judgment,
Christ's coming

John's Authority

JOHN 1:21 *And they asked him, "What then? Are you Elijah?"*
He said, "I am not." "Are you the Prophet?" And he answered,
"No." (NKJV)

This committee demanded to see John's credentials. Who did he
think he was? He had not gone through the proper channels, nor
was he sanctioned by anyone in authority.

John stuck to his guns. His response to those who questioned his
identity was always the same: "I am not the Christ."

People speculated on two other possible identities for the River
Prophet. John said "No" to both.

First, he insisted he was not "Elijah" (John 1:21). An Old
Testament prophecy predicted <u>Elijah</u> would come to prepare Israel
for the **Day of the Lord**. Many believed this meant the famous Old
Testament prophet would be literally resurrected. In that sense, John
was not Elijah, so he denied it. However, the angel who spoke to
John's father before his birth promised he would minister "in the
spirit and power of Elijah" (Luke 1:17 NKJV).

Second, John denied he was one known as "the Prophet." All sorts
of prophets were expected before Messiah's coming. Centuries earlier, Moses told Israel to be ready to welcome a <u>prophet</u> <u>like himself</u>.
(Early Christians believed the miracle-working, Moses-like prophet
was Christ.)

---

what others say

Lawrence O. Richards

The fact is that few of us understand the role we are playing
in God's great plan. John was more significant than he suspected, even though he recognized his commission to call
Israel back to God in preparation for the coming of the
Messiah. You and I as well may be more significant in accom-
plishing God's purposes than we suspect![1]

Upsetting Institutional Protocols

JOHN 1:24–25 *Now those who were sent were from the*
Pharisees. And they asked him, saying, "Why then do you baptize
if you are not the Christ, nor Elijah, nor the prophet?" (NKJV)

Dissatisfied with John's answers, some Pharisees pressed the cross-examination: "Where, then, did you get your authority to baptize?" Baptism was normally administered by temple priests to pagan proselytes converting to Judaism. John upset the applecart by baptizing people who were already (they thought) "God's people." Grassroots Jews readily admitted their **spiritual poverty** and came to him for baptism like brand-new converts. None of this had been approved by the established authorities, nor was it likely to be!

One Among You

JOHN 1:26 *John answered them, saying, "I baptize with water, but there stands One among you whom you do not know." (NKJV)*

John did not directly answer the Pharisees' question. He picked up on the subject of baptism to explain where his work fit on the list of spiritual priorities. But water baptism was not the gut issue; it was merely a warm-up for the main event. Top priority was the Christ issue. Christ was in the wings, ready to take center stage. You don't know him, John said. But he is **"among you,"** even as we speak!

for baptism
Matthew 3:16–17;
Luke 3:21–22

spiritual poverty
sense of something
lacking in one's spiritual life

among you
in Israel or there in
the crowd

> what others say
>
> **Leon Morris**
>
> This should not be taken as indicating that (John) did not regard his baptism as important. He did. He does not depreciate it. But his baptism is not an end in itself. Its purpose is to point men to Christ. John's interest is in the Christ and nothing less.[2]

John did not know Jesus was the promised Messiah until he saw the ultimate proof. The Lord had told him to watch for a special sign—a dove-like form descending from heaven to settle upon a certain man. The dove-form would be the Holy Spirit, and the man upon whom it fluttered down would be "the Son of God." It happened when Jesus came to John for baptism.

Connecting with God's Lamb

JOHN 1:36–37 *And looking at Jesus as He walked, he said, "Behold, the Lamb of God!" The two disciples heard him speak, and they followed Jesus. (NKJV)*

John the Baptist's effectiveness in preparing people to receive Christ is seen in what happened the next day. He was in conversation with two of his **disciples** when Jesus walked by. John's greatness was most conspicuous in the selfless way he released his closest followers to switch their allegiance to Jesus.

The two disciples to whom John had spoken hurried to catch up. Jesus turned around and asked what they were looking for. They called him **Rabbi** or "Teacher," and asked where he was staying. He motioned for them to come. One of two who spent time with Jesus that day was a man named Andrew.

Immediately after spending time with Jesus, Andrew went looking for his brother Simon Peter and said to him, "We have found the Messiah" (John 1:41 NKJV).

You Are Rocky!

> JOHN 1:42 *And [Andrew] brought [Simon] to Jesus. Now when Jesus looked at him, He said, "You are Simon the son of Jonah. You shall be called Cephas" (which is translated, A Stone). (NKJV)*

Meeting Simon for the first time, Jesus could see his potential. He gave Simon a new name in keeping with the change their encounter would bring and the destiny toward which it would lead. All three of Simon's names mean basically the same thing: "Rock."

The First Five

The next day Jesus left for Galilee. Five men—from the Galilean town of Bethsaida—joined him. Three he had met the day before: Andrew, John (the unnamed disciple), and Simon Peter. The other two would be added on the way. Either before he headed north along the Jordan River road or after they got to **Bethsaida** (see appendix A), Jesus looked up the fourth man, Philip, and said, "Follow Me" (John 1:43 NKJV). Philip, in Andrew-like fashion (compare John 1:41 and 45), went looking for his friend (or brother) Nathanael and told him what he believed about Jesus.

Philip said to Nathanael: "We have found Him of whom Moses in the law, and also the prophets, wrote—Jesus of Nazareth, the son of Joseph" (John 1:45 NKJV).

point of access
John 14:6; Acts 4:12

Six Titles for Jesus in John 1:29–50

1. Lamb of God (verses 29, 36)

2. Son of God (verses 34, 49)

3. Rabbi (verses 38, 49)

4. Messiah (Christ) (verse 41)

5. King of Israel (verse 49)

6. Son of Man (verse 51)

Ladder to God

JOHN 1:51 *And He said to him, "Most assuredly, I say to you, hereafter you shall see heaven open, and the angels of God ascending and descending upon the Son of Man." (NKJV)*

Jesus assured the honest Israelite, Nathanael, that before their relationship was over he would experience and understand magnificent spiritual truths. Jesus's statement looked ahead to his entire ministry on behalf of people. He was saying "I, personally, am the point of access and communication between heaven and earth—between God and human beings."

Chapter Wrap-Up

- The Jewish religious authorities in Jerusalem sent a team of investigators to John the Baptist to check out his claims. He denied that he was Christ, Elijah, or the prophet Moses promised. He claimed only to be a voice sent to prepare the way for the Lord. (John 1:19–28)

- John the Baptist introduced Jesus as the Lamb of God and told how he knew the truth about Christ. (John 1:29–34)

- John the Baptist introduced two of his own disciples to Jesus, and they left John to follow Jesus. This started a chain reaction in which three others were introduced to Christ and began to follow him as serious disciples. (John 1:35–49)

- Jesus claimed to be, personally, the point of access and communication between God and people. (John 1:50–51)

Study Questions

1. What three religious-political groups were represented in the investigative delegation sent to establish John's identity?

2. Who did John the Baptist claim to be? Where did he get his authority?

3. How did John know Jesus was the Son of God?

4. Of the first five disciples who joined up with Jesus, which two were introduced to Jesus by a friend or relative?

5. List the six titles for Jesus used by people in John 1:29–51 to describe him. Which one best describes the way you see Jesus today? Why?

Chapter 8: The Gush of New Wine

Chapter Highlights:
- Wedding Etiquette
- What Made Jesus So Angry?
- Superficial Faith
- Nicodemus

Let's Get Started

Coptic
the church in Egypt and North Africa

JOHN 2:1–2 *On the third day there was a wedding in Cana of Galilee, and the mother of Jesus was there. Now both Jesus and His disciples were invited to the wedding. (NKJV)*

Three days after John the Baptist introduces Jesus to his Jordan River audience as "the Lamb of God," the scene shifts to the sleepy up-country village of Cana, about nine miles from Nazareth, Galilee (see appendix A). A wedding festival was in progress. Jesus's mother was there—she was probably a relative. Jesus and his five new friends were among the invited guests.

A **Coptic** gospel says Mary was a sister of the bridegroom's mother. The Monarchian Prefaces to the New Testament say the groom was John, author of the fourth Gospel, whose mother was Mary's sister, Salome.

Wedding Etiquette

A strong element of reciprocity attached itself to wedding customs. If a guest did not bring an appropriate gift, he might, in certain situations, face legal action. If the groom did not properly entertain his guests, he could face censure.

At the Cana nuptials such a social disaster raised its ugly head out of the wine barrels and threatened to destroy the celebration. A miscalculation occurred so serious that it had the ominous potential to bring repercussions on the bridegroom's family, cloud the marriage, and disrupt the couple's standing in the community. The problem? The wine—which was supposed to be enough for a week of celebrating—ran out!

Mary, Jesus's mother, was apparently responsible for some of the festival arrangements—at least she felt responsible. She had authority over the servants—when she gave orders, they obeyed (John 2:5). Aware of the far-reaching consequences of the waning drink, she immediately swung into action to solve the problem.

go to

timetable
John 7:6, 8, 30;
12:23;
Matthew 26:18, 45;
Mark 14:41

master of the feast
master of cere-
monies, emcee, or
headwaiter

Same Son, New Relation

JOHN 2:4–5 *Jesus said to her, "Woman, what does your concern have to do with Me? My hour has not yet come." His mother said to the servants, "Whatever He says to you, do it." (NKJV)*

At first glance, Jesus's response to his mother's implied suggestion that he do something about the wine shortage seems harsh. It was an unusual way for a son to address his mother, but the Greek word for "woman" is not disrespectful or harsh. One translator interprets it "Lady, let me handle this in my own way."[1]

His response signals a new phase in the relationship between himself and Mary. He is no longer merely her obedient son, but also her Messiah.

When Jesus said, "My hour has not yet come," it was a thinly veiled hint that even he was not ultimately in charge. The shape and timing of his activities were determined by the <u>timetable</u> of God's will. He would act when the time was right. Mary, never slow to catch on, always desiring God's best, got the message. But she did not take Jesus's response as a no.

Steps to a Miracle

Every Jewish home in those days had large containers reserved for water used in the ceremonial washings involved in day-to-day Jewish life. At this home in Cana, there were six stone pots that held 120 to 180 gallons of water.

"Fill the waterpots with water," Jesus instructed the servants. They did as he said. The jars were filled "to the brim," leaving no room for additional ingredients.

"Draw some out now, and take it to the **master of the feast**" (John 2:8 NKJV).

> **what others say**
>
> **Leonard I. Sweet**
>
> Instead of showing up at the door with the gift of a bottle of wine, as moderns particularly are wont to do, he made 180 gallons of wine after he got there.[2]

Signs of Saviorhood

JOHN 2:11 *This beginning of signs Jesus did in Cana of Galilee, and manifested His glory; and His disciples believed in Him. (NKJV)*

larger number
John 21:25

The changing of ceremonial water into the best wine at the wedding was, the author John notes, the "beginning" sign, proving Jesus was the special, God-sent person John the Baptist, the New Testament writers, and he himself insisted he was. John's Life of Christ lists seven such signs. John chose these seven from a much <u>larger number</u> of Jesus's known miracles and uses them to illustrate specific aspects of Jesus's personality and ministry.

Seven Signs in John to Back up Jesus's Claims

John's Report	Sign	Response
John 2:1–11	Water changed to wine	(2:11) Disciples trusted him.
John 4:46–54	Royal official's son healed	(4:50, 53) Official and family believed.
John 5:1–18	Paralyzed man healed at Bethesda Pool	(5:9) Man's faith seen in his actions; (5:18) leaders wanted to kill Jesus.
John 6:1–14	Feeding of the 5,000	(6:14) People believed Jesus a prophet; (6:66) many disciples left him.
John 6:16–21	Walking on water	(6:21) Disciples took Jesus into the boat.
John 9:1–41	Restored blind man's sight	(9:11, 17, 33, 36) Man's faith developed; (9:16, 24, 29, 40–41) Pharisees opposed Jesus.
John 11:1–44	Raised Lazarus from the dead	(11:27) Martha confessed faith; (11:45) many Jews believed; (11:53) Sanhedrin plots to kill Jesus.

what others say

Henry H. Halley

This first miracle was done at a wedding feast, on a festive occasion, ministering to human joy, making people happy, as if Jesus wanted to announce, right at the start, that the religion which he was now introducing into the world was no religion of asceticism, but a religion of natural joy.[3]

three Passovers
John 2:13; 6:4;
11:55

the other
Matthew 21:12–13;
Mark 11:15–19;
Luke 19:45–48

After the wedding, Jesus and his five friends spent a few days in Capernaum where his mother and brothers now lived, then headed for Jerusalem. It was spring—time for the annual Feast of Passover celebrating Israel's freedom and nationhood. This would be the first of at least <u>three Passovers</u> Jesus attended during his brief ministry.

New Wine Floods the Temple Swap Meet

JOHN 2:14–16 *And He found in the temple those who sold oxen and sheep and doves, and the money changers doing business. When He had made a whip of cords, He drove them all out of the temple, with the sheep and the oxen, and poured out the changers' money and overturned the tables. And He said to those who sold doves, "Take these things away! Do not make My Father's house a house of merchandise!"* (NKJV)

New Testament historians record two times when Jesus angrily invaded the temple, driving out people conducting for-profit business in its courts. This one came just as his public ministry was starting and introduced his authority. <u>The other</u> happened during the last week of his life.

What Made Jesus So Angry?

What brought the "gentle" Jesus to a point of violent outrage was the misuse of God's house and God's law to make a fast buck! The rules of Jewish religious life required Jewish males living within walking distance to come to Jerusalem every year for the Passover. If they lived outside the homeland, they were to make it to the festival as often as possible—at least once in their lifetime. This brought huge crowds—sometimes as many as two and a quarter million—to the feast.

Three additional regulations made these throngs easy pickings for enterprising profiteers:

- *Rule 1: Temple Tax.* Every Jewish male over nineteen years of age was required to pay a half-shekel tax (two days' wages) for temple maintenance. This could only be paid in official temple coinage; foreign money had to be exchanged. Shrewd money changers made huge profits, charging the equivalent of one-fourth of a day's wage for each half-shekel. For the poor this rate constituted a real hardship.

- *Rule 2: Paschal Lambs.* Each man was required to sacrifice a lamb without blemish the afternoon before the Passover meal. Temple inspectors, appointed by the high priest, examined all animals before sacrifice. If a lamb was purchased outside the temple, it was more likely to be rejected by the inspectors than if bought from temple marketeers.

- *Rule 3: Alternate Sacrifice.* Those too poor to offer a lamb were allowed by law to offer a pair of doves. Sacrificial doves had to have a stamp of approval from the same temple inspectors as those who ruled on the lambs. Temple dove-sellers were known to charge as much as a hundred times more than their outside counterparts.

claim to messiahship
Psalm 69:9;
John 2:17

at his trial
Matthew 26:59–61

as he died
Matthew 27:39–40

According to some sources, the geniuses behind this profitable conspiracy were the high priest and his family. People appointed to lead worship padded their greedy pockets by scamming the faithful—especially the poor.

The brains behind the exploitive sanctuary swap meet demanded Jesus produce the credentials that gave him the right to close down their lucrative swindle. They did not argue that the seamy business was out of place in God's house. They seemed to understand that cleaning corruption out of the church was appropriate messianic activity. Jesus's zeal for God's house amounted to a <u>claim to messiahship</u>. What they were looking for was a "miraculous sign" to back up his claim (John 2:18).

The Ultimate Proof of Jesus's Authority

JOHN 2:19 *Jesus answered and said to them, "Destroy this temple, and in three days I will raise it up." (NKJV)*

Talk about rocking the temple! The author explains that "this temple" Jesus was talking about was "His body" (2:21 NKJV). His statement was a metaphor, meaning "Watch for the greatest proof of all—the miracle of my resurrection!" Even his disciples did not fully grasp his meaning until "He had risen from the dead" (2:22 NKJV).

He might as well have been talking to the wall. The Jewish leaders were looking for trouble, and they completely misconstrued his words. They would later use his statement to accuse him <u>at his trial</u> and mock him with it <u>as he died</u>!

The Cure for Superficial Faith

JOHN 2:23–25 *Now when He was in Jerusalem at the Passover, during the feast, many believed in His name when they saw the signs which He did. But Jesus did not commit Himself to them, because He knew all men, and had no need that anyone should testify of man, for He knew what was in man.* (NKJV)

Many people "saw the **signs**" Jesus did in Jerusalem during the Passover and "believed in His name." No specific signs or miracles are described, other than shutting down the illegal temple market. In Bible terms the phrase "his name" often refers to a person's character. The greatest sign of Jesus's authenticity went deeper than miracles. People became convinced he was the genuine article by simply observing the character and personality of the man himself.

what others say

Billy Graham

I had heard the message . . . Intellectually, I accepted Christ to the extent that I acknowledged what I knew about him to be true. That was mental assent. Emotionally, I felt that I wanted to love him in return for his loving me. But the final issue was whether I would turn myself over to his rule in my life.[4]

Nicodemus

JOHN 3:2 *This man [Nicodemus] came to Jesus by night and said to Him, "Rabbi, we know that You are a teacher come from God; for no one can do these signs that You do unless God is with him."* (NKJV)

Before the Passover ended and Jesus returned to Galilee, he was visited by an influential man named Nicodemus.

Nicodemus came to Jesus after dark, perhaps because he did not wish to be seen by his religious and political colleagues who were already lining up against Jesus. Considering his position in the community, it was amazing that he would risk coming at all. Considering the Sanhedrin's negative stance toward Jesus, Nicodemus said three startling things:

• He called Jesus "Rabbi"—respected teacher.

• He recognized Jesus was "from God."

- He acknowledged that Jesus's works showed God was "with him."

kingdom of God
place where God reigns as King

His greeting also discloses a startling revelation concerning the ruling council: "We know" indicates the Sanhedrin understood that Jesus had been sent from God. And they opposed him anyway!

What Was Really Bothering Nicodemus?

JOHN 3:3 *Jesus answered and said to him, "Most assuredly, I say to you, unless one is born again, he cannot see the kingdom of God." (NKJV)*

Jesus "knew all men" (John 2:24 NKJV). Without polite chitchat, he went directly to the point. He knew the famous Pharisee was thinking about the **"kingdom of God."** Nicodemus had seen something in Jesus that ignited a spark of messianic hope.

The truth was, as brilliant a student of the Bible as Nicodemus was, he did not really understand the nature of God's kingdom as Jesus modeled it in his actions and attitudes.

Jesus immediately hit Nicodemus twice with the hard truth that if he expected to see or live under the reign of God, he would need to be "born again." Jesus said it twice. Each time he prefaced it with, "Most assuredly, I say to you." Literally, his words were "Amen! Amen!" To the Hebrew listener, this meant the statement about to be made was absolutely certain, dependable, truthful, and binding.

The Intellectual Response

JOHN 3:4 *Nicodemus said to Him, "How can a man be born when he is old? Can he enter a second time into his mother's womb and be born?" (NKJV)*

Chalk one up for the brilliant lawyer-teacher. Nicodemus knew the biological facts of life. But, even though he was one of Israel's top thinkers, he was ignorant of the spiritual facts of life.

Jesus was not telling Nicodemus he needed a religious ceremony. He was talking about an inner spiritual transaction that can only be called "miraculous." Trace Jesus's reasoning in John 3:3–8. Jesus said five things about spiritual rebirth:

go to

washing
Ephesians 5:26–27;
Titus 3:5

power
2 Peter 1:3, 16

willpower
John 1:12–13

effects
1 Corinthians 12;
Ephesians 2:10

1. New birth is an eye-opening experience that makes a person able to "see" God's kingdom (verse 3) and enables him or her to "enter" it (verse 5).

2. New birth involves "water" (verse 5). Water is a reference to the cleansing (washing) away of past sins and the guilt for them.

3. New birth is a work of the Holy Spirit (verses 5–6), a miracle of God's life-restoring power, not the result of human effort or willpower apart from God.

4. Spiritual rebirth is a "must" and that should surprise no one (verse 7). Stacking the weaknesses that go with being human against the challenging teachings of Scripture, an honest seeker is forced to admit that living well without some sort of radical personal renewal is a "mission impossible."

5. New birth is a mysterious work of God's Spirit, the effects of which can be observed but never fully explained (verse 8). Trying to explain being "born of the Spirit" is like trying to explain the wind. You can hear the rustling of trees and grass and observe the effects of a hurricane, but to control or fully explain where the wind "comes from and where it goes" (John 3:8 NKJV) is beyond even the most brilliant meteorologist.

---

what others say

Blaise Pascal

There is a God-shaped vacuum in every man that only Christ can fill.[5]

New Birth—A Simple, Earthy Thing

JOHN 3:10, 12 *Jesus answered and said to him, "Are you the teacher of Israel, and do not know these things? . . . If I have told you earthly things and you do not believe, how will you believe if I tell you heavenly things?" (NKJV)*

Nicodemus shook his head in disbelief. He's thinking, "This is the most incredible idea I've ever heard!"

Jesus found it incredible that Nicodemus, Israel's top teacher, should be so baffled by the simple concept. Lost pagans believe in it, for heaven's sake! They perform mysterious rituals dramatizing new birth. Why should it be so difficult for a brilliant Bible scholar?

Oswald Chambers

Our part as workers for God is to open men's eyes that they may turn themselves from darkness to light; but that is not salvation, that is conversion—the effort of a roused human being. I do not think it is too sweeping to say that the majority of nominal Christians are of this order; their eyes are opened, but they have received nothing . . . When a man is born again, he knows that it is because he has received something as a gift from Almighty God and not because of his own decision.[6]

Chapter Wrap-Up

- At a wedding in Cana, Galilee, Jesus performed his first miraculous proof that he was the Messiah—turning water into wine. His disciples became convinced. His relationship with his mother entered a new phase. (John 2:1–11)

- Jesus angrily drove the sacrifice-sellers and money changers out of the temple of Jerusalem, closing down their illicit and spiritually destructive business and establishing his authority over Jewish worship. (John 2:12–22)

- Many people believed Jesus's claims after his purge of the temple and confrontation with the leaders, but he knew their faith was shallow and uninformed, so he held back from committing himself to them as their king. (John 2:23–25)

- Nicodemus, the influential Pharisee, visited Jesus to check his legitimacy as Israel's Messiah-Savior. Jesus told Nicodemus he needed to be spiritually reborn if he expected to understand and experience God's kingdom. (John 3:1–12)

Study Questions

1. Why was Jesus so angry with the profit-making businesses in the temple?

2. What three rules of Jewish religious life were the temple businesses misusing? How were they misusing each rule?

3. What did Nicodemus believe about Jesus when he came to him at night?

4. What first aroused your interest in Jesus? Why?

Chapter 9: Operation Rescue

Let's Get Started

JOHN 3:16 *For God so loved the world that He gave His only begotten Son, that whoever believes in Him should not perish but have everlasting life.* (NKJV)

John 3:16 is "the background of the canvas on which the rest of the Gospel is painted."[1]

God loved them
Deuteronomy 7:7–9;
23:5;
Isaiah 63:9;
Jeremiah 31:3

Love Shock

The idea that God loves all people came as a shock to Nicodemus. Israelites believed <u>God loved them</u>. They were, after all, "God's chosen people." Hatred of sinners and Gentiles was considered appropriate. Jesus exploded this cherished bit of first-century Hebrew theology and practice when he declared God's love, not just for the "chosen," good, religious, and God-fearing, but also for skeptics, God-haters, pagans, and synagogue dropouts—the world!

> **what others say**
>
> **Saint Augustine**
> God loves each one of us as if there was only one of us to love.[2]

Christ's Mission: Love, Not Judgment

JOHN 3:17–18 *For God did not send His Son into the world to condemn the world, but that the world through Him might be saved. He who believes in Him is not condemned; but he who does not believe is condemned already, because he has not believed in the name of the only begotten Son of God.* (NKJV)

Matthew 21:12–13
Mark 11:15–19
Luke 19:45–48

High on the list of Nicodemus's expectations for the Messiah was that he would bring judgment. The sight of Jesus, eyes blazing, chasing profiteers out of the temple (John 2:15–16), may have been

go to

walk in the light
1 John 1:5–10

what convinced some people to believe he was the one (John 2:23). Pharisees like Nicodemus, who instinctively mistrusted the priestly establishment that ran the temple, were probably among those who tentatively applauded the Nazarene's brash actions. When Nicodemus saw the merchants scrambling to escape Jesus's whip, visions of the purifier-Messiah-judge leaped to mind (Malachi 3:1–5). He was right. Jesus was all of that.

Pharisees thought Christ's judgment would be directed mainly against Gentiles. His initial purge was against Jewish religious leaders using God's house for personal profit. Now he was telling Nicodemus his mission was not to bring God's wrath to sinners, but to rescue them (John 3:17). One by one the Pharisee's cherished prejudices were being overturned.

> **what others say**
>
> **Leon Morris**
>
> Salvation . . . judgment. These are the two sides to the same coin. The very fact of salvation for all who believe implies judgment on all who do not.[3]

The "Guilty" Verdict

JOHN 3:19–21 *And this is the condemnation, that the light has come into the world, and men loved darkness rather than light, because their deeds were evil. For everyone practicing evil hates the light and does not come to the light, lest his deeds should be exposed. But he who does the truth comes to the light, that his deeds may be clearly seen, that they have been done in God. (NKJV)*

Wherever Jesus went, some people were attracted to the genuineness and purity of the life they saw in him. They came to him and believed, even though it meant exposure of personal sin. They faced up to their sins and committed themselves to walk in the light. Others hated the self-exposure that came with listening to Jesus. They rejected the truth, persisting in dishonesty and denial. They did not welcome his light. But it was too late. Light had come. Sin had been exposed. They stood condemned by their choice to turn away from the light.

Changing of the Guard

JOHN 3:22 *After these things Jesus and His disciples came into the land of Judea, and there He remained with them and baptized.* (NKJV)

Soon after his conversation with Nicodemus, Jesus left Jerusalem for Jordan River country, where he and his disciples apparently linked up for a while with John the Baptist. The inference in John 3:22–26 is that there was a brief time when Jesus and John worked side by side, preaching and baptizing. People kept coming. The spiritual awakening grew as the **cousins** and their coworkers ministered together at **Aenon** on the Jordan.

Sunrise, Sunset

JOHN 3:26 *And they came to John and said to him, "Rabbi, He who was with you beyond the Jordan, to whom you have testified—behold, He is baptizing, and all are coming to Him!"* (NKJV)

While they worked together, something happened that pointed out the necessity for the two ministries (Jesus's and John's) to separate. It also demonstrated John's integrity as a man of God. John's ministry began to fade. Fewer people came to him for baptism, while increasing numbers flocked to the nearby venue where Jesus was preaching. Some of John's disciples became alarmed. It was a human response, but showed they did not fully understand John's mission. John understood. It was he who sent many of his disciples to Jesus (see John 1:35–36). God's design was for the crowds around John to dwindle while those around Jesus increased.

The Greater Good

JOHN 3:27–30 *John answered and said, "A man can receive nothing unless it has been given to him from heaven . . . The friend of the bridegroom, who stands and hears him, rejoices greatly because of the bridegroom's voice. Therefore this joy of mine is fulfilled. He must increase, but I must decrease."* (NKJV)

go to

cousins
Luke 1:36

cousins
The mothers of John and Jesus were relatives.

Aenon
"place of springs"; seven springs pour into the Jordan in a quarter mile

go to

execution
Mark 6:17–29

gospel harmony

Matthew 4:12
Mark 1:14
Luke 3:19–20

The great forerunner explained to his nervous supporters what was going on. John the Baptist made a statement calculated to encourage his disciples to follow Christ. He compared his ministry with Christ's. There was no contest.

John's Arrest

LUKE 3:19–20 *But Herod the tetrarch, being rebuked by him concerning Herodias, his brother Philip's wife, and for all the evils which Herod had done, also added this, above all, that he shut John up in prison.* (NKJV)

After John urged his disciples to shift their allegiance to Jesus, the end of the Baptist's ministry came abruptly. On a trip to Rome, Herod Antipas, tetrarch of Galilee, had seduced his brother's beautiful young wife, Herodias, and convinced her to leave her husband for him. The sordid process involved divorcing his own wife. The Jewish people were outraged. Courageously, John publicly rebuked Antipas and Herodias. Herodias never forgave him. The prophet's arrest was the first step toward <u>execution</u>.

First-century Jewish historian Josephus reports Herod had a second reason for John's arrest: He feared the popular prophet was about to lead a revolution against him.[4]

Rendezvous

the big picture

John 4:1–9

On his way to Galilee Jesus traveled through Samaria. At noon he sat down at a well to rest. A Samaritan woman came to draw water, and Jesus asked her to give him a drink.

"He needed to go through Samaria" (John 4:4 NKJV) does not mean the only route to Galilee was through Samaria. Most travelers took the Samaritan route because it was the shortest. But the strictest Jews took the Jordan River road around Samaria in order to avoid contact with its racially and religiously mixed citizens.

Jesus did not allow ethnic prejudice to affect his choices. He headed north across the border into Samaritan territory: by divine arrangement, he had a date with destiny at **Jacob's well** near Sychar. He and his companions arrived at the well at **high noon**.

The prejudice of Jews against Samaritans was based on a history of bad feelings:

- Samaritans were a <u>mixed race</u> whose ancestors were relocated in northern Israel after the <u>Assyrian conquest</u> in 722 BC.
- Samaritans practiced a <u>corrupted</u> form of Jewish <u>worship</u> centered at Mount Gerazim rather than Jerusalem.
- Samaritans <u>hindered</u> the rebuilding of Jerusalem after the **Babylonian <u>exile</u>**.

Weary God-Man

"Jesus therefore, being wearied from His journey, sat thus by the well" (John 4:6 NKJV). John's simple report of the weariness, hunger, and thirst of Jesus reveals an important fact: Jesus, who would one day be worshipped throughout the world as God's Son, was an authentic human who experienced the physical needs common to human beings.

go to

Jacob's well
Genesis 33:18–19;
48:22;
Joshua 24:32

mixed race
2 Kings 17:24

Assyrian conquest
2 Kings 17

corrupted worship
2 Kings 17:25–41

hindered
Nehemiah 4

exile
2 Kings 24:14

Jacob's well
dug by Jacob; still used today

high noon
sixth hour of the day, which began with the first hour (sunrise)

Babylonian exile
586 BC
Nebuchadnezzar destroyed Jerusalem, deported Jews to Babylon

swine's flesh
Pork was ceremonially unclean, eating it was forbidden.[6]

> **what others say**
>
> **Ronald B. Allen**
>
> We must learn to think rightly about the One who is God and man. To learn to think rightly about his humanity is to rediscover the meaning of our own humanity created in the image of God.[5]

The Woman of Sychar

Jesus's men went into the town of Sychar, about a half mile away, to buy lunch. Jesus sat alone at the ancient well. A woman approached to draw water. Jesus said to her, "Give Me a drink" (John 4:7 NKJV). It was the beginning of a conversation that was unlikely to have taken place in polite society of those times.

- First, she was a Samaritan (John 4:7). "Let no man eat of the bread of the [Samaritans]," the rabbis taught, "for he who eats their bread is as he who eats **swine's flesh**!"

living water
John 7:37–39

patriarchs
Jacob and his sons
(Genesis 49)

messianic promises
Old Testament pre-
dictions concerning
Christ

- Second, she was a woman (verse 7). The rules of etiquette stated it was improper for a man to talk to a woman in public.
- Third, she was a social pariah. It was noon, the hottest part of the day. Respectable ladies came to draw water in the cool of morning or evening. She came to the well alone to avoid their stares.

The woman was shocked that this Jewish male should speak to her. "How is it that You, being a Jew, ask a drink from me, a Samaritan woman?" (4:9 NKJV). The statement "For Jews have no dealings with Samaritans" (4:9 NKJV) may also be translated, "Jews do not use dishes Samaritans have used." With no bucket of his own with which to draw water (verse 11), Jesus the Jew was asking this Samaritan to give him a drink out of hers.

Cool, Clear Water

JOHN 4:10–14 *Jesus answered and said to her, "If you knew the gift of God, and who it is who says to you, 'Give Me a drink,' you would have asked Him, and He would have given you living water." The woman said to Him, "Sir, You have nothing to draw with, and the well is deep. Where then do You get that living water? Are You greater than our father Jacob, who gave us the well . . . ?" Jesus answered and said to her, "Whoever drinks of this water will thirst again, but whoever drinks of the water that I shall give him will never thirst. But the water that I shall give him will become in him a fountain of water springing up into everlasting life." (NKJV)*

Jesus swept aside the woman's first response and cut to the real issue. He knew she was thirsty physically and spiritually.

She misunderstood his first statement (perhaps purposely), but it grabbed her attention nonetheless. As the story unfolds we get a clear picture of this woman. She was acquainted with failure, having five failed marriages, but she was no dummy. The man before her was making outrageous claims. In spite of social protocols and prejudices, she was willing to converse with Jesus.

The promise of <u>living water</u> sounded glorious. She probably envisioned a stream or spring from which she could draw water. No more hot, dusty trips to this well. Her comment to Jesus also showed that she was not an atheist—she believed in God, the **patriarchs**, and the **messianic promises** (John 4:12, 19–20). One day, she knew, Christ (the Messiah) would unravel the mysteries of life (4:25).

Muddying the Living Water

JOHN 4:15–17 *The woman said to Him, "Sir, give me this water, that I may not thirst, nor come here to draw." Jesus said to her, "Go, call your husband, and come here." The woman answered and said, "I have no husband." Jesus said to her, "You have well said, 'I have no husband,' . . ." (NKJV)*

The woman's response was flippant. But Jesus cut to the chase and cornered her about her life of sin. The woman told the truth but not the whole truth.

Her eyes popped wide open when he revealed that he knew about her five failed marriages and the "significant other" she was now living with outside marriage (4:17–18).

The woman at the well was convinced the man talking to her was a prophet (4:19). According to Samaritan theology, there had not been a real prophet since Moses. God promised to send another prophet <u>like Moses</u>. This Moses-like prophet would be the Messiah. The woman may have begun to wonder if the man talking with her might be that prophet—Messiah.

So she brought up a religious controversy: Samaritan worship on Mount Gerazim is just as good as Jewish worship in Jerusalem (4:20). Or she may have been expressing honest spiritual need, like saying, "Where can I find God?"

Samaritans recognized only the first five books of the Old Testament and rewrote parts of the Old Testament to make Mount Gerazim, not Jerusalem, the focal point of important events in the history of Israel. According to revisionist Samaritan history, Abraham <u>offered Isaac</u> on Mount Gerazim, he and <u>Melchizedek</u> met there, and most of the significant events in the lives of the patriarchs took place near there.

The Right Place to Meet God

JOHN 4:21–24 *Jesus said to her, "Woman, believe Me, the hour is coming when you will neither on this mountain, nor in Jerusalem, worship the Father. You worship what you do not*

like Moses
Deuteronomy 18:18

offered Isaac
Genesis 22:1–18

Melchizedek
Genesis 14:18–20

whole person
Romans 12:1

worth
Revelation 5:9–13

adoration
Luke 10:27

worship
reverence, respect,
adoration, praise
(Greek: "to kiss the
hand")

Mount Zion
hilltop site of the
temple in Jerusalem

know; we know what we worship, for salvation is of the Jews. But the hour is coming, and now is, when the true worshipers will worship the Father in spirit and truth; for the Father is seeking such to worship Him. God is Spirit, and those who worship Him must worship in spirit and truth." (NKJV)

The woman was thirsty for peace. She sincerely wanted to know the right place to offer a sacrifice to atone for her sins, where peace with God could be made.

Worship Revolution

Jesus turns typical thinking about **worship** upside down. Everything he said about it was based on the fact that "God is Spirit" (John 4:24 NKJV) and can't be limited to a geographical location— neither Mount Gerazim nor **Mount Zion**. Because he is Spirit, worshipping him is not a matter of sacred locations, shrines, or ceremonies, but of the <u>whole person</u> acknowledging the <u>worth</u> of God in sincere <u>adoration</u>. So what is the state of your worship?

> ### what others say
>
> **J. I. Packer**
>
> Christ's point is that while man, being "flesh," can only be present in one place at a time, God, being "spirit," is not so limited. God is non-material, non-corporeal, and therefore nonlocalized. Thus . . . the true condition of acceptable worship is not that your feet should be standing in either Jerusalem or Samaria, or anywhere else for that matter, but that your heart should be receptive and responsive to his revelation.[7]

Harvest of Hearts

JOHN 4:25–26 *The woman said to Him, "I know that Messiah is coming" (who is called Christ). "When He comes, He will tell us all things." Jesus said to her, "I who speak to you am He." (NKJV)*

The cat is out of the bag. Jesus is the promised Messiah. His clear claim affirmed the woman's suspicions. As Jesus's disciples approached with lunch, she left her water pot and headed for the village on her first mission of sharing her discovery. This woman of questionable character was uniquely qualified to attract the attention of the men of the village, who immediately headed out to see for themselves if what she was telling them was true.

The disciples were surprised to see Jesus talking with the woman (4:9). They were equally amazed that he had no interest in the food they brought. He said he'd already eaten (4:32). Doing the work of God had satisfied his hunger (4:34).

Motioning toward the group of Samaritans making their way toward the well, Jesus added, "Don't tell me it's still four months to harvest. Look at the fields. They are already ripe. It's time for harvest—now!" He was right. Many of the Samaritans the woman rounded up put their faith in Jesus. When they met him for themselves, they too became convinced he was "the Savior of the world" (John 4:42 NKJV).

Chapter Wrap-Up

- In conversation with Nicodemus, Jesus revealed God's motive of love in sending him to bring eternal life to people who put their faith in him. (John 3:13–21)

- Though it is painful for John's disciples, John the Baptist explained that his ministry had to fade away so the ministry of Jesus Christ could grow. (John 3:22–36)

- In order to avoid a premature confrontation with the Pharisees, Jesus headed north to Galilee. He felt compelled to stop at Jacob's well for a strategic encounter with a spiritually needy woman. (John 4:1–15)

- The woman was surprised when she discovered how much Jesus knew about her. She brought up the controversy between Samaritans and Jews over worship, and Jesus used it to teach important and revolutionary principles of true worship. (John 4:16–24)

- Jesus confirmed the woman's growing faith in him, directly claiming to be Christ. She returned to the village to tell the men about him. Many came to see him and believed. (John 4:25–42)

Study Questions

1. If Christ came into the world to save and not to judge, how did his coming result in judgment for many?

2. Did John the Baptist see himself as a success or a failure when more people began to follow Jesus than followed him? Explain.

3. What was the basis for the mutual animosity between Jews and Samaritans?

Part Three
GALILEE: BATTLE FOR
HOME TURF

Chapter 10: The Rugged Hills of Home

Chapter Highlights:
- Prophet's Honor
- Long-Distance Service
- Hometown Boy
- Choosing Apostles
- Authority and Power

Let's Get Started

Jesus and his disciples stayed in Sychar, Samaria, for two days, "harvesting." Then they moved on, heading north into the Galilean hill country—the hills of home.

Prophet's Honor

go to

three other occasions
Mark 6:4;
Matthew 13:57;
Luke 4:24

knew people
John 2:24

hometown people
Luke 4:16–30

leave him
John 6:60–66

diet of miracles
John 4:48

JOHN 4:43–45 *Now after the two days He departed from there and went to Galilee. For Jesus Himself testified that a prophet has no honor in his own country. So when He came to Galilee, the Galileans received Him, having seen all the things He did in Jerusalem at the feast; for they also had gone to the feast.* (NKJV)

Jesus made the statement about a prophet having "no honor in his own country" on <u>three other occasions</u> recorded in the New Testament. In all the others it came in the midst of conflict or rejection. Here there is no conflict. Jesus's ministry is off to a flying start.

So why this sour note? Jesus was no dummy. He <u>knew people</u>. Despite his early welcome in Galilee, his own <u>hometown people</u> would soon turn on him. Many Galileans who hung around him at first would <u>leave him</u> when he started saying things they didn't want to hear. He knew the faith of many was not soundly based because it depended on a steady <u>diet of miracles</u>. Knowing all this, he launched the Galilean phase of his ministry with power and courage.

> **what others say**
>
> **Josephus**
>
> They [Galileans] were fond of innovations and by nature disposed to changes and delighted with seditions. They were ready to follow a leader who would begin an insurrection. They were quick in temper and given to quarreling . . . They were more anxious for honor than for gain.[1]

Synagogue Agog

LUKE 4:14–15 *Then Jesus returned in the power of the Spirit to Galilee, and news of Him went out through all the surrounding region. And He taught in their synagogues, being glorified by all.* (NKJV)

The **synagogue** was the center of Galilean life, ever since the days of the Babylonian exile when the Jews had no temple in which to meet. By lifelong family custom, Jesus attended synagogue every **Sabbath** (Luke 4:16). He knew how to use it to introduce his message.

Long-Distance Service

JOHN 4:46–47 *So Jesus came again to Cana of Galilee where He had made the water wine. And there was a certain nobleman whose son was sick at Capernaum. When he heard that Jesus had come out of Judea into Galilee, he went to Him and implored Him to come down and heal his son, for he was at the point of death.* (NKJV)

News of the young miracle worker reached all levels of Galilean society. Twenty miles away in the lakeside city of Capernaum (see appendix A), one of King Herod's top officials was desperate. His son was near death. He heard Jesus was in Cana. So he mounted his horse and made the daylong trip to the one person he believed could help.

"Unless you people see **signs** and **wonders**," Jesus told him, "you will by no means believe" (John 4:48 NKJV). This was not just for the frantic father, but for the gawking Galileans craving the spectacular, withholding full acceptance until Jesus gave proof after proof of his power. In the original language, the "by no means" in his statement is an emphatic double negative, indicating the intensity of his feelings. He welcomed people who believed <u>because of the miracles</u>, but he longed for those who would believe because of his character and teachings.

what others say

William Barclay

There could be no more improbable scene in the world than an important court official hastening 20 miles to beg a favor from a village carpenter. First and foremost, this courtier swallowed his pride. He was in need, and neither convention nor custom stopped him bringing his need to Christ.[2]

Taking Jesus at His Word

JOHN 4:49–50 *The nobleman said to Him, "Sir, come down before my child dies!" Jesus said to him, "Go your way; your son lives." So the man believed the word that Jesus spoke to him, and he went his way.* (NKJV)

The anxious royal restated his request, more urgently this time. Jesus did not give the man exactly what he asked for. The request was based on the faulty belief that for healing to take place, Jesus had to be physically present with the sick person. Jesus gives the father what he wants but in an unexpected way.

The man's departure for home was evidence of his faith and recognition of Jesus's authority. No tangible sign was given, just Jesus's word. It was all the man had to hang on to. On his way, servants met him with the news of his son's recovery. Synchronizing their sundials, they discovered the fever had broken at the very moment Jesus said, "Your son lives" (John 4:52–53).

Hometown Boy

LUKE 4:16 *So He came to Nazareth, where He had been brought up. And as His custom was, He went into the synagogue on the Sabbath day, and stood up to read.* (NKJV)

The Sabbath custom in first-century synagogues was for seven men to mount the **bima** and read from the sacred scrolls (see Illustration #2) of Holy Scripture spread out on the *migdal ez*. They stood to read, sat to explain. As a young man who had grown up in the synagogue, Jesus served as one of these reader-explainers. Home again, he was asked to fulfill his old duties. Stories of his preaching and wonderworks had preceded him (Luke 4:23). The hometown folk were anxious to see if the stories were true—if their "hometown boy" had made good. The *chazzan* handed him the scroll of Isaiah. He opened it to chapter 61. According to custom, he read in **Hebrew** while an interpreter translated it into **Aramaic**.

This is what Jesus read:

LUKE 4:18–19
The Spirit of the LORD is upon Me,
*Because He has **anointed** Me*
To preach the gospel to the poor;

bima
platform

migdal ez
"wooden tower," lectern

chazzan
attendant in charge of the sacred scrolls

Hebrew
language used in religious activities

Aramaic
most commonly used language in daily conversation

anointed
granted authority and power

Matthew 13:54–58
Luke 4:16–31

He has sent Me to heal the brokenhearted,
To proclaim liberty to the captives
And recovery of sight to the blind,
To set at liberty those who are oppressed;
*To proclaim the **acceptable year of the LORD**. (NKJV)*

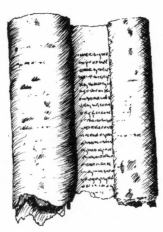

"I'm the One!"

Jesus sat down. What he said next immediately divided the congregation: "Today this Scripture is fulfilled in your hearing" (Luke
4:21 NKJV). In plain English, he claimed himself to be Isaiah's
"anointed" one. He explained that it was he who was commissioned
by the Lord God and given authority:

Year of Jubilee
Leviticus 25:8–55

**acceptable year of
the LORD**
time of grace; also
Year of Jubilee

- to give hope and dignity to the poor, downtrodden, and under-
  privileged;

- to liberate people in bondage physically, psychologically, and
  spiritually;

- to give sight to people who are blind because of physical dis-
  ability, spiritual darkness, or lack of insight into God's perspective;

- to release the oppressed, those weighed down by spiritual, political, social, psychological, or economic forces; and

- to announce that the long-awaited day of God's grace had
  arrived, that all debts were canceled and all slaves were freed, as
  in the Year of Jubilee.

A Prophet from God?

At first they were amazed at the grace flowing with such authority from their young neighbor's lips (Luke 4:22). Then, as if to deny the hope his words inspired, they began to express doubts.

"Isn't this Joseph the carpenter's son? Isn't his mother's name Mary? Aren't his brothers James, Joseph, Simon, and Judas? Aren't all his sisters with us living in Nazareth? Where then did this man get all these things he says and does?" Initial admiration changed to offense.

"No prophet is accepted in his own country," Jesus said (Luke 4:24 NKJV). Then he reminded them of stories from the lives of two esteemed Bible prophets:

Matthew 13:55–58
Mark 6:1–6
Luke 4:22–30

1. Elijah found refuge in the home of a <u>pagan widow</u> and miraculously supplied her needs, while Israel suffered under famine because of unfaithfulness to God.

2. Elisha healed the leprous pagan military commander, <u>Naaman</u>, while Israel's lepers remained unhealed because of the nation's idolatry.

Jesus forced acceptance or rejection of his claims by suggesting through these stories that God loved pagans as well as Jews, and would bypass "the chosen people" if they refused to honor him and rescue needy Gentiles. This was not what the home folks wanted to hear. Suddenly the synagogue became a mob! They drove Jesus from the platform.

With the same authority with which he had offered them grace, Jesus now turned to face the angry mob. Shaking his head over their disbelief, he walked straight through the crowd, left Nazareth, and never looked back.

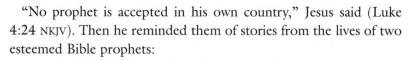

what others say

Leslie F. Brandt

Many who heard his message that day took offense and cast him out of the synagogue. They could not endure being reminded that the God of history was as concerned about the poor and foreign widows as he was about the children of Israel and that he sent his prophets to minister to them.[3]

pagan widow
1 Kings 17:7–24

Naaman
2 Kings 5:1–19

go to

followed him
John 1:35–4:54

apostleship
ambassadorship,
oversight of church
development

oracles
messages directly
from God rather
than through a mes-
senger

Choosing Apostles

MATTHEW 4:18–20 *And Jesus, walking by the Sea of Galilee, saw two brothers, Simon called Peter, and Andrew his brother, casting a net into the sea; for they were fishermen. Then He said to them, "Follow Me, and I will make you fishers of men." They immediately left their nets and followed Him.* (NKJV)

The recruitment of the twelve men Jesus trained for leadership in his movement did not happen with a single encounter. John the Baptist introduced the first five men to Jesus. They <u>followed him</u> for several weeks. Upon return to Galilee, some apparently went home to Capernaum, rejoined their families, and resumed their previous jobs, while Jesus preached his way to Nazareth. Now it was time for phase two in their progress toward **apostleship**.

Two sets of brothers, Peter and Andrew, and James and John, were working down by the lake. All fishermen by trade. Not poor, not rich. Just ordinary workingmen with families to support and mundane jobs to do. Peter and Andrew were "casting a net into the sea." The other two, James and John, were in a boat with their senior fishing partner, their father, Zebedee, "mending their nets" (dragnets) in preparation for a fishing trip (Matthew 4:21 NKJV). First Jesus called Peter and Andrew to join him. Then he called James and John. "I will make you become fishers of men," he said (Mark 1:17 NKJV).

"This Is Your Captain Speaking!"

LUKE 4:32 *And they were astonished at His teaching, for His word was with authority.* (NKJV)

The next Sabbath, Jesus and his fishing crew went to the synagogue in Capernaum. Jesus was asked to teach. As the spellbound audience listened, the meeting was interrupted by the screams of a man possessed by a "demon." The controlling spirit cried out, identifying Jesus as "the Holy One of God" (Luke 4:34 NKJV).

what others say

Albert Barnes

Jesus was open, plain, grave, useful, delivering truth as became the **oracles** of God; not spending his time in trifling disputes and debating questions of no importance, but confirming his doctrine by miracles and argument . . . He showed that he had authority to explain, to enforce, and to change the **ceremonial laws**.[4]

Neil T. Anderson

When Satan harasses you, you may be prone to languish in the shadows of your misery . . . You cry out for God to deliver you, like Jesus miraculously and instantaneously delivered the demonized people in the Gospels. But when you read through the epistles it is obvious that your deliverance has already been accomplished in Christ's work on the cross and his resurrection . . . But it is your responsibility to exercise your authority and resist the devil, renounce participation in his schemes, confess sin, and forgive those who have offended you.[5]

go to

power of God
Luke 4:14;
John 3:2

ceremonial laws
religious rules in
Exodus, Leviticus,
Numbers,
Deuteronomy

Authority and Power

LUKE **4:35–36** *But Jesus rebuked him, saying, "Be quiet, and come out of him!" And when the demon had thrown him in their midst, it came out of him and did not hurt him. Then they were all amazed and spoke among themselves, saying, "What a word this is! For with authority and power He commands the unclean spirits, and they come out." (NKJV)*

gospel harmony

Matthew 8:14–17
Mark 1:29–34
Luke 4:38–41

The people who witnessed the deliverance of the demonized man used two words to describe Jesus's command of evil spirits:

- "Authority"—the Greek word means "freedom of choice and action." Jesus acted spontaneously, of his own will, without regard to accepted protocols.
- "Power"—the Greek word sounds like "dynamite" and means "strength," "energy," "effectiveness," or "force." It's the term used for the power of God.

Chapter Wrap-Up

- Jesus's return to Galilee was met with a warm reception by the Galileans. But he knew as he launched his preaching tour of Galilean towns that warmth would soon change to a mix of acceptance and opposition. (John 4:43–45; Luke 4:14–16)

- Upon arrival in Cana, Galilee, a royal official came from Capernaum with an urgent request that Jesus go there and save the official's dying son. Jesus healed the son without going to Capernaum. The official's entire household believed on Jesus. (John 4:46–54)

- In his hometown of Nazareth, Jesus revealed he was the fulfillment of Old Testament prophecies concerning the Messiah. He told them God loved Gentiles too. His former neighbors ran him out of town. (Luke 4:16–30)

- Jesus moved his headquarters to Capernaum. He demonstrated his messianic authority by calling four men to follow him, by powerful teaching, and by acts of healing and deliverance from evil spirits. (Matthew 4:13–22; 8:14–17)

Study Questions

1. What kind of believers is Jesus looking for?

2. How did Herod's royal official demonstrate his faith?

3. Name three of the five things Jesus said the Lord had anointed him to do. Which comes closest to the thing you personally need most?

4. Why did Jesus's hometown folk fail to believe in him?

5. What does Jesus's power to command evil spirits and heal diseases tell us about his teachings?

6. How has Jesus's authority grabbed your attention recently? How is it freeing you?

Chapter 11: The Mighty Kingdom of the Weak

Let's Get Started

MARK 1:35–38 *Now in the morning, having risen a long while before daylight, He went out and departed to a solitary place; and there He prayed. And Simon and those who were with Him searched for Him. When they found Him, they said to Him, "Everyone is looking for You." But He said to them, "Let us go into the next towns, that I may preach there also, because for this purpose I have come forth." (NKJV)*

Mentor
John 7:16

The young Messiah faced crucial decisions. In the dizziness of celebrity he must talk with his <u>Mentor</u>. He had to pray. As he would often do during the next three years, he got up before sunup, hiked to a quiet place, and before the rest of the world opened its eyes, he had a conversation with his Father in heaven. He cleared his mind of distractions, asked directions, and got a fresh grip on the vision of what he had been sent to do. By the time Simon and the others found him, he knew what he must do next. His decision blew away the smoke screen of success.

> ### what others say
>
> **Elizabeth O'Conner**
> We came to know that if we were going to learn to pray, we were going to have to pray. Christ ever remains the great teacher of prayer.[1]

Unwrapping the Kingdom Dream

So far in the New Testament's telling of Jesus's story, the kingdom of God has not been defined. Jesus's teachings and the model of his life with his disciples put flesh on the bones of the kingdom concept. He challenges the Jews' ultranationalistic expectations. His followers are shown how to enter in and experience the kingdom. In the process it becomes clear that the kingdom of God is not merely something that happens in the hearts of individuals who get right

greatness
Matthew 20:25–28

with God, one by one. Jesus is clearly intent on leading the development of a new society, a new nation, a distinct counterculture that exists and thrives, and pledges allegiance to Christ as King, right smack-dab in the middle of the kingdoms, societies, nations, and cultures of this rebellious world!

Matthew 4:23–25
Mark 1:39
Luke 4:44

> what others say
>
> **Howard A. Snyder**
>
> I am convinced that a properly biblical understanding of the Kingdom of God is possible only if the church is understood—predominantly, if not exclusively—as a charismatic community and God's pilgrim people, his kingdom of priests . . . a radically biblical, caring community of believers totally sold out to Jesus Christ . . . [The church] must be seen as God's people in relation to God's kingdom or, in other words, the messianic community, the community of the king.[2]

Kingdom of the Powerless

MATTHEW 4:23 *And Jesus went about all Galilee, teaching in their synagogues, preaching the gospel of the kingdom, and healing all kinds of sickness and all kinds of disease among the people.* (NKJV)

Christ breaks all the rules that normally govern where and how a kingdom gets its power. History has shown him to be the most powerful monarch who ever reigned, but Jesus's strategies all reflect "God's descending way of becoming a servant."[3] Greatness is measured in terms of servanthood and sacrifice.

As Matthew tells the story (4:23–24), Jesus preached "the gospel of the kingdom" wherever people would listen. News quickly spread that he had power to heal. People came from everywhere around Galilee. Soon his crowds took on a distinct flavor: the diseased, pain-racked, mentally and emotionally disturbed, epileptics, quadra- and paraplegics—the broken, weak, harassed, suffering, sick, vulnerable, confused, driven, and addicted. The most needy people of that day were brought by friends or dragged themselves out of their sickbeds and places of confinement and loneliness. They found their way to Jesus because they had heard from somebody that he could help.

What a way to build a kingdom!

what others say

Joni Eareckson Tada

It is the "least of the brethren" and "the weakest members of the body" who are to be given special places of honor . . . Those who are helpless, no matter what their handicap, see themselves in the Man of Sorrows because he became one of them. Jesus' message was clear. We are all without help or hope as long as we are without him. But he was also clear that his good news was, in some way, especially for those who suffer the helplessness and hopelessness that physical infirmity can often bring.[4]

Fishing for "Sinners"

One morning Jesus again walked by the lake. The ever-present crowds surrounded him. It was the same stretch of beach where earlier he had called four fishermen to leave their work and join him. Again the boats were pulled up to shore and the men were washing their nets. Needing a better vantage point from which to talk to the crowd, Jesus climbed into the boat belonging to his friend Simon (Peter) and asked him to anchor the boat a little offshore. Jesus sat down in the boat to teach. His voice resonated off the water, which acted like a megaphone, so the crowd on shore could hear him.

Go Fish!

As his talk ended, Jesus turned to his friend and said, "Let's go catch some fish!" (Luke 5:4).

Simon, fastest tongue in the west, thought Jesus needed to be better informed about the ins and outs of Galilean fishing. He and his partners were exhausted. They'd fished these waters all night and caught nary a minnow!

"Nevertheless at Your word I will let down the net," Simon says with resignation (Luke 5:5 NKJV).

Suddenly, fish began to hit the nets, more than Peter and Andrew could handle! They called for James and John to row over and help. Both boats were soon full of fish.

As the overloaded boats struggled to make shore, Peter fell to his knees before Jesus, overcome by awareness of his unworthiness to be

go to

by law
Leviticus 13, 14

sinful man
a first-century
Jewish idiom for a
synagogue dropout

leper
person with
Hansen's disease;
incurable in Bible
times, ulcers eat
away at skin, ten-
dons, muscle, and
bone

in the presence of such authority, confessing himself a **sinful man**.
The whole fishing crew shared the same awe.

"Do not be afraid. From now on you will catch men," Jesus said
(Luke 5:10 NKJV). This was the third time he had approached these
four about being his disciples. This time, they burned their bridges
behind them and "forsook all and followed Him" (5:11 NKJV).

Raggedy Man

> LUKE 5:12 *And it happened when He was in a certain city,
> that behold, a man who was full of leprosy saw Jesus; and he fell
> on his face and implored Him, saying, "Lord, if You are will-
> ing, You can make me clean." (NKJV)*

Society's only defense against leprosy was quarantine. <u>By law</u>, the
leper was required to live alone or with other lepers outside the camp.
He or she could have no normal human contact. Untouchable, a leper
was unemployable and reduced to begging, although he or she could
expect to suffer nine years before dying. Josephus reports lepers were
treated as if they were dead men.

The psychological effects were the worst aspects of the leper's suffering. A sense of guilt and rejection by God often went with the disease, even though the leper was not personally responsible for
acquiring it. No one needed to be touched more than the outcast
leper. Jesus knew this.

As he lay before Christ, this leper felt something he may not have felt
for a very long time. A hand reached down and touched his diseased
flesh. "I am willing; be cleansed," Jesus said (Luke 5:13 NKJV). The
horrors of the awful disease were swept away in a word and a touch.

gospel harmony

Matthew 8:1–4
Mark 1:40–45
Luke 5:12–16

Joyful Disobedience

Jesus gave the cleansed leper two commands:

1. "Tell no one" (Luke 5:14 NKJV). Jesus often gave this instruction
   to healed people. Reasons?

   • To forestall a premature popular movement to crown
   Jesus king before he had a chance to demonstrate the kind
   of kingdom he was building

- To keep the cleansed leper from getting sidetracked retelling his story instead of following the procedure Moses prescribed for verification of the cure

- To keep crowds to manageable size so as not to hinder his freedom to go anywhere he needed to go in ministry (see Mark 1:45)

2. "Go and show yourself to the priest" (Luke 5:14 NKJV). This involved a sacrifice and two examinations by a priest, a week apart, to officially certify healing had taken place. Reasons?

- To obey <u>God's Law</u>
- To officially remove the stigma of leprosy
- To give "a testimony" to the priests of Jesus's messiahship

We can't be sure the man ever went to the priests. We know he disobeyed Jesus's first instruction. As a result, the numbers of people coming to see Jesus exploded. He could no longer take his message inside the city limits, but was forced to meet people in the countryside.

<u>The Paralysis of the Unforgiven</u>

MATTHEW 9:2 *Then behold, they brought to Him a paralytic lying on a bed. When Jesus saw their faith, He said to the paralytic, "Son, be of good cheer; your sins are forgiven you." (NKJV)*

On Jesus's return to Capernaum, representatives of official Judaism showed up at **his home**. He was surrounded by Pharisees and lawyers when four men came carrying a paralyzed friend on a stretcher. Unable to get through the door, they climbed to the roof, removed some tiles, and let the man down into the room in front of Jesus.

To the shock of the gathered Bible scholars, Jesus said to the paralyzed man, "Your sins are forgiven you."

The room became deafeningly silent. The religionists stared at Jesus, incredulous. No one spoke, but they were thinking volumes! **"Blasphemy**! Only God can forgive sins!"

"Which is easier, to say, 'Your sins are forgiven you,' or to say, 'Arise and walk'?" Jesus asked (Matthew 9:5 NKJV). The deafening

God's Law
Leviticus 14

his home
probably the home of his mother

blasphemy
slanderous speech directed toward God or man

silence persisted. "But that you may know that the Son of Man has power on earth to forgive sins," Jesus said, and then to the paralytic, "Arise, take up your bed, and go to your house" (9:6 NKJV).

The man got up, picked up his bed, and walked out the door shouting "Hallelujah!" (or some expression of thanks to God).

Why Are These Sinners Celebrating?

MATTHEW 9:9–12 *As Jesus passed on from there, He saw a man named Matthew sitting at the tax office. And He said to him, "Follow Me." So he arose and followed Him. Now it happened, as Jesus sat at the table in the house, that behold, many tax collectors and sinners came and sat down with Him and His disciples. And when the Pharisees saw it, they said to His disciples, "Why does Your teacher eat with tax collectors and sinners?" When Jesus heard that, He said to them, "Those who are well have no need of a physician, but those who are sick." (NKJV)*

"These are the ones I came to heal," Jesus replied. He did not defend their lifestyle. He called them to change (Luke 5:32). Jesus was concerned with the social outcasts of his day. He spent time with them. He loved them. They <u>listened</u>, and many became disciples.

In contrast, the Pharisees believed it was their religious duty to stay so far away from the ungodly that they would not even teach them the Law. Eating with these people was worse than talking to them, so the Pharisees thought, because sharing a meal meant you recognized and welcomed the sinners.

To Jesus, political and religious correctness was useless. Introducing wandering souls to God's grace was what he lived for.

New Shirts and Old Wineskins

MATTHEW 9:16–17 *No one puts a piece of unshrunk cloth on an old garment; for the patch pulls away from the garment, and the tear is made worse. Nor do they put new wine into old wineskins, or else the wineskins break, the wine is spilled, and the wineskins are ruined. But they put new wine into new wineskins, and both are preserved. (NKJV)*

Jesus's response to his critics was to compare the joyous celebration at Matthew's house with a happy seven-day Jewish wedding fes-

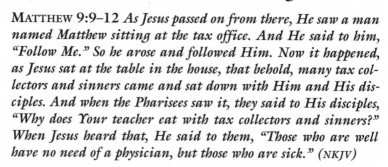

go to

listened
Luke 15:1–2;

gospel harmony

Matthew 9:1–8
Mark 2:1–12
Luke 5:17–26

Matthew 9:9–13
Mark 2:13–17
Luke 5:27–32

gospel harmony

Matthew 9:14–17
Mark 2:18–22
Luke 5:33–39

tival (Matthew 9:15). The bride and groom and their guests dressed in their finest and feasted for seven days.

Jesus used three illustrations to describe religious people who could not force such an idea into the narrow package of their preconceptions:

1. They were old shirts on which new patches had been sewn (Matthew 9:16). When washed, the new patch would shrink and tear the old shirt apart!

2. They were old wineskins unsuitable to handle the fermenting process of new wine (Matthew 9:17). As grape juice ferments it gives off gases, causing pressure. Old, inflexible wineskins explode. The skin is ruined. The wine is lost.

3. They were addicted to "old wine" (Luke 5:39 NKJV).

What Is the "New Wine"?

The "new wine" is new life experienced and lived in response to Christ as King. For individual followers of Christ and for their religious structures and institutions, the person responsive to Christ must be flexible—willing to change and grow. Old wineskins represent the rigidity of religion by rules, regulations, and ritual. New wineskins represent the flexibility of personal relationship with the King.

key point

Chapter Wrap-Up

- The greatest concern in Jesus's preaching and ministry was and is the establishment of the kingdom of God. As crowds gathered, it became apparent his kingdom was not built on the exercise of power, but on weakness, servanthood, and sacrifice. (Matthew 4:17–25)

- Jesus demonstrated his authority over nature and men. He issued the final call for four fishermen to join him in catching people. They left everything and followed. (Matthew 4:18–22; Luke 5:1–11)

- Jesus broke social rules by touching and healing a leper. The leper told everyone, making it impossible for Jesus to take his ministry into some cities. (Mark 1:40–45)

- Jesus healed a man whose paralysis was linked with guilt for unforgiven sin, and confronted hypocritical reasoning about forgiveness. (Luke 5:17–26)

- Jesus called Matthew to leave his crooked tax-collecting job to follow him as a disciple. Matthew invited his friends to dinner to meet Jesus. The Pharisees became unglued. Jesus reminded them that it was the sick who need a doctor. (Matthew 9:9–13)

- Jesus warned the Pharisees that their rigid attitudes kept them from enjoying the new spiritual relationship he was offering, as surely as a new patch destroyed an old shirt and new wine busted an old wineskin. (Luke 5:33–39)

Study Questions

1. What did Jesus do when success at Capernaum threatened to deter him from his main mission?

2. What did Jews hearing Jesus preach the nearness of the kingdom already believe about the kingdom of God? What did they fail to understand, which caused them confusion?

3. When Simon saw the power of Christ, what did he confess?

4. What did Jesus do to prove he had the authority to forgive sins?

Chapter 12: Religion Gone Rigid

Let's Get Started

JOHN 5:2–4 *Now there is in Jerusalem by the Sheep Gate a pool, which is called in Hebrew, Bethesda, having five proches. In these lay a great multitude of sick people, blind, lame, paralyzed, waiting for the moving of the water. For an angel went down at a certain time into the pool and stirred up the water; then whoever stepped in first, after the stirring of the water, was made well of whatever disease he had.* (NKJV)

Feast of Tabernacles
festival commemorating Israel's forty years of desert wandering

The Pool of Bethesda was not far from the temple area in Jerusalem (see Illustration #3). Its five porches were always filled with sick people. Some feel that the information given in John 5:4 portrays a highly questionable notion in that the idea of God working in "lottery-like" fashion seems grossly inconsistent with what the Bible reveals about God.

Jesus visited the place during a feast (likely the **Feast of Tabernacles**). His attention was drawn to a man by the pool who had been unable to walk for thirty-eight years.

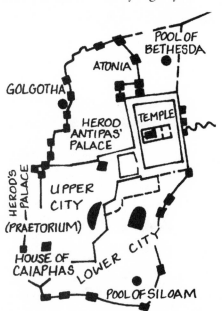

Illustration #3
Map of Jerusalem—
This map of Jerusalem shows the location of the Pool of Bethesda where the paralyzed man had gone for thirty-eight years.

go to

Ten Commandments
Exodus 20:3–17

Sabbath
the seventh day,
meant for rest

The $64,000 Question

JOHN 5:6–7 *[Jesus] said to him, "Do you want to be made well?" The sick man answered Him, "Sir, I have no man to put me into the pool when the water is stirred up; but while I am coming, another steps down before me."* (NKJV)

"Do you want to be made well?" Some might wonder why Jesus asked this question. This man had been incapacitated for thirty-eight years.

Actually, it's a pretty good question. Nearly four decades of helplessness can leave a man hopeless, depressed, and passive. Suddenly being able to do things for yourself, after thirty-eight years of depending on other people, means having to take responsibilities you're not used to and may not want!

The Unexpected Cure

JOHN 5:8–9 *Jesus said to him, "Rise, take up your bed and walk." And immediately the man was made well, took up his bed, and walked. And that day was the Sabbath.* (NKJV)

The cure was instantaneous. The man must have been shocked out of his wits! He got up, folded his mat, threw it over his shoulder, and walked away. It wasn't an act of faith, but obedience. The man didn't even know who the healer was (5:13)!

The simplicity in the way the healing is reported masks the bomb blast detonated in the last phrase of verse 9: "And that day was the Sabbath."

You had to be seriously Jewish to understand the fuss that simple fact set off. When religious leaders saw the man carrying his bed through the streets on the **Sabbath** they made a citizen's arrest—"It is against the law to carry a bed on the Sabbath day." If you know the <u>Ten Commandments</u>, that sounds reasonable.

Sabbath Keeping: A Matter of Life and Death

The official Jewish rulebook read: "If anyone carries anything from a public place to a private house on the Sabbath intentionally he is punishable by death by stoning."[1] The healed man's only defense was, "He who made me well said to me, 'Take up your bed and walk'" (John 5:11 NKJV). The authorities were not impressed. They could only see him disobeying a rule they considered on the same level as the Law of God!

Jews
not the Jewish people, but the religious leaders

blasphemous
slander against God

Jesus the Sabbath Breaker

> JOHN 5:16 *For this reason the Jews persecuted Jesus, and sought to kill Him, because He had done these things on the Sabbath.* (NKJV)

This story pinpoints the issue over which the opposition against Jesus began to crystallize. He had two strikes against him. (Strike one: He told the man to carry his bed on the Sabbath. Strike two: He healed on the Sabbath. One more strike and he's out!)

Jesus's Bizarre Defense: "Even God Breaks the Sabbath!"

> JOHN 5:17–18 *But Jesus answered them, "My Father has been working until now, and I have been working." Therefore the **Jews** sought all the more to kill Him, because He not only broke the Sabbath, but also said that God was His Father, making Himself equal with God.* (NKJV)

The religious authorities thought Jesus was claiming to be bigger than the Sabbath traditions. They were right! They understood him to be dispensing with their authority to tell people what they could or couldn't do on the Sabbath. They were right! When he identified his works with God's works, and called God "Father," they understood him to be claiming equality with God. Again, they were right! Red lights were flashing in their rule-bound brains: This was **blasphemous** insanity! (It would turn out to be strike three for Jesus.)

what others say

C. S. Lewis

A man who said the sort of things Jesus said wouldn't be a great moral teacher. He would either be a lunatic on the level of a man who says he's a poached egg, or else he would be the devil of hell; you must take your choice. Either this was and is the Son of God, or else a mad man or something

pictured
Hebrews 10:1

predicted
Hebrews 1:1;
Matthew 1:22; 2:6;
4:15–16

foreshadowed
Psalm 22

> worse. You can shut him up for a demon; or you can fall at his feet and call him Lord and God. But don't come up with any patronizing nonsense about his being a great moral teacher. He hasn't left that alternative open to us.[2]

Corroborating Witnesses

In first-century courts, according to Jewish, Roman, and Greek law, no witness could testify in his own behalf. Other witnesses must be called to testify for him. Jesus didn't need human testimony to prove his equality with God. But if Jewish leaders needed witnesses, he provided them, hoping to convince them to believe (John 5:34). In verses 33–40 Jesus called four "witnesses" to substantiate his claims. Here they are with the gist of their testimony:

Witness 1: John the Baptist: "This is the Son of God" (John 1:34 NKJV).

Witness 2: The saving mission on which God sent Jesus: "It is finished!" (John 19:30 NKJV).

Witness 3: The Father's voice (1) heard at Jesus's baptism: "You are My beloved Son; in You I am well pleased" (Luke 3:21–22 NKJV); and (2) heard by people, like Peter: "You are the Christ, the Son of the living God" (Matthew 16:16 NKJV).

Witness 4: The Old Testament Scriptures (Luke 24:44–47; John 1:45):

1. The Law of Moses <u>pictured</u> Christ's work in its rituals and sacrifices.

2. The prophets <u>predicted</u> details of his person and work.

3. The Psalms <u>foreshadowed</u> his death and resurrection.

---

what others say

John Charles Ryle

If a man is not thoroughly honest in his professed desire to find out the truth in religion—if he secretly cherishes any idol which he is resolved not to give up, if he privately cares for anything more than God's praise—he will go on to the end of his days doubting, perplexed, dissatisfied, and restless, and will never find the way to peace.[3]

"Picking" a Fight

LUKE 6:1–2 Now it happened on the second Sabbath after the first that He went through the grainfields. And His disciples plucked the heads of grain and ate them, rubbing them in their hands. And some of the Pharisees said to them, "Why are you doing what is not lawful to do on the Sabbath?" (NKJV)

Back in Galilee, Jesus and his disciples again ran head-on into the Sabbath issue. One Sabbath day as they walked through ripened grainfields, they plucked a few heads of grain, rubbed them in their hands, and snacked on the kernels.

The "Sabbath police" (otherwise known as Pharisees) were out in force, and immediately questioned the "offenders'" actions.

According to Moses's law, the poor were <u>permitted to pluck</u> standing grain in order to sustain life and limb. But according to the Sabbath traditions, hunger was no excuse for breaking the law.

Jesus disagreed with the Pharisees and stated six reasons:

1. **David** <u>violated a law</u> actually found in the **Pentateuch** and was never punished for it (Matthew 12:3–4). On the run from King Saul, David and his hungry men went into the **tabernacle** and ate **<u>consecrated bread</u>**, which could legally be eaten only by priests. He was excused because of his hunger and his greatness.

2. <u>Priests working</u> at the temple technically "break the Sabbath" every week, and the Law declares them exempt (Matthew 12:6) on the basis that service at the temple is more important than strict adherence to the Sabbath regulations.

3. "In this place there is One <u>greater than</u> the temple" (Matthew 12:6 NKJV). Christ is the One. Those who serve him (his disciples) are exempt from some Sabbath rules simply because of the greatness of the One they serve.

4. The Sabbath was set aside for the spiritual and physical refreshment of people; people were not created to be drudging slaves of <u>burdensome</u> Sabbath restrictions (Mark 2:27).

5. God's purpose in the no-work-on-the-Sabbath commandment was never to stifle <u>concern for people</u>. The leaders' condemnation

gospel harmony

Matthew 12:1–8
Mark 2:23–28
Luke 6:1–5

go to

permitted to pluck
Deuteronomy 23:25

violated a law
1 Samuel 21:1–6

consecrated bread
Leviticus 24:5–9

priests working
Numbers 28:9–10

greater than
Matthew 12:41–42

burdensome
Acts 15:10

concern for people
Hosea 6:6

David
Israel's most illustrious king

Pentateuch
first five books of the Old Testament

tabernacle
Jewish tent of worship during desert wanderings

consecrated bread
twelve loaves kept on a table, symbol of communion with God

of the disciples for eating was evidence they misunderstood the true spirit of the Sabbath (Matthew 12:7).

6. Christ is ultimately Lord and has the last word on the Sabbath, its meaning, and its purposes (Matthew 12:8; Mark 2:28; Luke 6:5).

The Reach for Renewal

Given Jesus's compassion for the physically challenged, what happened next was to be expected. He was teaching in a synagogue in Galilee. In the congregation were the ever-present religious establishment spies—"the scribes and the Pharisees" (Luke 6:7 NKJV). Also in attendance was a man with a withered right hand. It was a situation for which the scribes and Pharisees had waited. They "watched Him closely, whether He would heal on the Sabbath" (6:7 NKJV).

In "an atmosphere of glorious defiance,"[4] Jesus called the man forward so no one would miss what was about to take place. The rabbis taught that it was okay to rescue a farm animal who had fallen into a pit on the Sabbath, even if the animal was in no danger of dying (Matthew 12:11). But, unless the disease or injury was life-threatening, a person could not be given medical treatment until another day.

Matthew 12:9–13
Mark 3:1–5
Luke 6:6–10

Jesus disdained such compassionless reasoning: "Of how much more value then is a man than a sheep!" he demanded. Then he swept aside the whole catalog of nit-picking Sabbath regulations with one straightforward declaration: "Therefore it is lawful to do good on the Sabbath" (Matthew 12:12 NKJV). Turning to the man he said, "Stretch out your hand" (12:13 NKJV). The man did, and his hand was restored.

An Assassination Conspiracy Is Born

Matthew 12:14
Mark 3:6
Luke 6:11

The Pharisees had found what they were looking for—a reason to condemn Jesus. The Sabbath issue became his enemies' immediate charge against him. Mark reports they were so determined to destroy Jesus they were even willing to conspire with their worst political enemies, the Herodians (Mark 3:6). From then on they would be in every crowd that gathered to hear him, listening, building their case for his execution.

Chapter Wrap-Up

- Jesus healed a lame man at the Pool of Bethesda on the Sabbath; religious leaders questioned the man for carrying his bed; Jesus deliberately ignored unreasonable and unmerciful Sabbath regulations. (John 5:1–15)

- Jesus defended his actions by claiming equality with God in work, authority to raise the dead, and as giver of eternal life; he cited four witnesses to his claims. (John 5:16–47)

- The Sabbath issue was pressed when Jesus's disciples picked grain on the Sabbath; he healed a man on the Sabbath, declaring the Sabbath was for doing good and showing mercy, and that he was Lord of the Sabbath. His enemies conspired to kill him. (Luke 6:1–11)

Study Questions

1. What was the healed man's defense when questioned about carrying his bed? What was Jesus's defense when they accused him of breaking the Sabbath?

2. Who and what are the four witnesses Jesus calls to verify his claims?

3. How had the scribes and Pharisees neglected the meaning of "I desire mercy and not sacrifice" (Matthew 12:7 NKJV)?

4. By healing a man's withered hand on the Sabbath in the synagogue, what did Jesus demonstrate?

5. When have you fallen into the trap of "offering sacrifice" while "neglecting mercy"? What can you do today (or this week) to change that?

Chapter 13: The Inner Circle

Chapter Highlights:
- **The Power Team**
- **Jesus and the Old Testament**
- **First Things First**
- **Beware of False Prophets**

Let's Get Started

Jesus would have only three years to prepare the kingdom-of-God movement to carry on without his visible leadership. Powerful political and religious forces were already looking for the right moment to terminate him. He met the challenge with a simple but brilliant strategy. He would leave behind a cadre of spiritually powerful people. They would be equipped with careful instruction, the living model of his life, one another's support, and the gifts and power of the Holy Spirit.

sinners
Luke 5:8, 30; 15:1–2

disciples
pupils, followers

The Power Team

MARK 3:13–15 *And [Jesus] went up on the mountain and called to Him those He Himself wanted. And they came to Him. Then He appointed twelve, that they might be with Him and that He might send them out to preach, and to have power to heal sickness and to cast out demons. (NKJV)*

Matthew 10:1–4
Mark 3:13–19
Luke 6:12–16

To this point, the New Testament historians have named seven men who spent time with Jesus in the early days of his public ministry: Andrew, Simon Peter, James, John, Philip, Nathanael, and Levi (Matthew). They are identified as **"disciples."** Unnamed others also were identified that way. Luke describes "a crowd" as "disciples" of Jesus (Luke 6:17 NKJV). According to Jesus's strategy, the time came to select from the growing number of his followers those who would form the leadership team to lead the assault on the world.

By worldly standards, the people Jesus chose were poorly qualified for leadership. They were ordinary working stiffs, mostly poor but not impoverished. All were skilled at some trade or craft (like Levi's genius for cheating taxpayers!). They could read and write but were not well educated. They were untrained in theology—not a clergyman among them. Polite society denounced some of them as "<u>sinners</u>" —meaning they didn't obey the religious rules. By association with John the Baptist, several showed eagerness for Messiah's arrival.

They were part of the responsive group who'd already indicated a desire to be with Jesus (Luke 6:13).

PETER: Also called Simon and Cephas ("Rock"). Fisherman. Impulsive, brash. Introduced to Jesus by his brother Andrew. One of the first five to follow Jesus. First to confess Jesus as the Son of God (Matthew 16:15–16). One of the three closest to Jesus.

ANDREW: Peter's brother. Fisherman. Son of John (Jonah). Introduced to Jesus by John the Baptist. Brought his brother Peter to Jesus. Left fishing trade to follow Jesus.

JAMES: Brother of John. Son of Zebedee and Salome. Fisherman. Left father and fishing business to follow Jesus. Volatile personality. The brothers were nicknamed "sons of thunder" (Mark 3:17; Luke 9:51–55). One of the three closest to Jesus.

JOHN: Brother of James. Son of Zebedee and Salome. Fisherman. Ambitious (see Matthew 20:20–28). "Son of thunder." May be the "disciple Jesus loved" in the Gospel of John (see John 13:23; 19:26; 20:2; 21:7, 20–24). One of the three closest to Jesus.

PHILIP: Name means "lover of horses," which may describe either him or his father. One of the first to meet Jesus. Brought his friend (or brother) Nathanael to Jesus. Slow to catch on to who Jesus really was (John 14:7–11).

BARTHOLOMEW: Name means "son of tolmai." *Tolmai* is Hebrew for "plowman"—may have been a farmer. May be the same as

Nathanael, Philip's friend from Cana (John 21:2). Bartholomew/ Nathanael was skeptical of Jesus at first because he came from Nazareth.

MATTHEW: Name means "gift of God." Son of Alphaeus (Mark 2:14). Possibly James the Younger's elder brother. Also called Levi. Customs officer. Probably hated by fellow Jews for collecting foreign taxes.

JAMES: Son of Alphaeus and Mary, also called "James the Less" (Mark 15:40) to distinguish him from John's brother (who may have been older). Probably Matthew's brother (compare Matthew 10:3 and Mark 2:14).

THOMAS: Nicknamed Didymus, "the twin." Cautious. Yet willing to follow Jesus into danger (John 11:16). Genuine believer who struggled with uncertainty. "Doubting Thomas."

SIMON: Also called "the Zealot" or "the **Cananite**" (Mark 3:18). The "Zealot" ID indicates he was zealous for the Jewish Law and/or he was a member of the movement committed to violent overthrow of Roman rule and assassination of Jewish collaborators.

THADDAEUS: Also called "Judas the son of James" and "Jude." "Judas" is the Greek, "Jude" the Latin, for "Judah," a common Jewish name (Matthew 13:55; Acts 5:37; 9:11; 15:22). May have been son of the apostle James and grandson of fisherman Zebedee.

JUDAS ISCARIOT: Iscariot, may mean "man of Kerioth." Kerioth was a Judean town. This may indicate Judas was the only non-Galilean apostle. Father's name: Simon. Treasurer (John 12:5–6) of the apostolic group.

Christ's School of Kingdom Life

Jesus's teachings are the constitution and bylaws of "the kingdom of heaven." The most basic "kingdom teachings" are concentrated in two major "sermons": The Sermon on the Mount (Matthew 5–7) and the Sermon on the Plain (Luke 6:17–49). These may be two **versions** of the same message, or they may be two sermons delivered on separate occasions. Jesus preached these ideas all over Galilee and Judea.

Cananite
an Aramaic word meaning "Zealot"

versions
Matthew's eyewitness account; Luke's from interviews with witnesses

The Sermon on the Mount

go to

born again
John 1:12–13; 3:3–8

Beatitudes
from Latin word
for "blessed" or
"fortunate"

born-again
God's children
through believing
and receiving Jesus

the big picture

Matthew 5–7

Jesus's dream is not merely of believing individuals living heroic Christian lives alone against the world. His dream is of his followers facing the challenges of faith together, in a close-knit community guided by principles like the ones he taught in the Sermon on the Mount.

Jesus begins his description of the Christian life with nine statements known as the **"Beatitudes."** A play on words calls them "be-attitudes" because they describe attitudes that produce the kind of behavior that makes possible the unique lifestyle of the kingdom of heaven community. The Beatitudes introduce a catalog of teachings designed to pull the kingdom of God idea down from the ivory towers of heady theology and put it right in the middle of down-and-dirty situations of the everyday lives and relationships of earthlings.

Who's This Sermon For?

From celebrity seekers and enemy spies to serious truth seekers, they flocked to hear him preach. But the primary target of these teachings was the believing minority scattered among the crowds—his disciples (Matthew 5:1–2; Luke 6:20). He was drawing true believers—the **born-again**—into a special community through which his gospel could be carried to the world.

what others say

F. R. Maltby

Jesus promised his disciples three things—that they would be completely fearless, absurdly happy, and in constant trouble.[2]

Jesus's Formula for Success: The Beatitudes

MATTHEW 5:3–10

Blessed (happy, spiritually prosperous, successful) are . . .

- *The poor in spirit*—The vulnerable, confess their poverty (material/spiritual), forced to depend on God. "Theirs is the kingdom of heaven" (5:3 NKJV).

- *Those who mourn*—The broken, who weep over their sins, allow their hearts to break over what breaks God's heart. "They shall be comforted" (5:4 NKJV).

- *The meek*—The gentle, who demand nothing, give themselves to God and others, teachable, flexible. "They shall inherit the earth" (5:5 NKJV).

- *Those who hunger and thirst for righteousness*—The intense, who are dissatisfied with the depth of their own spirituality, obsessed with desire for justice, fairness. "They shall be filled" (5:6 NKJV).

- *The merciful*—The compassionate, whose lives are marked by the "inefficiency" of concern for cripples, misfits, the hurting. "They shall obtain mercy" (5:7 NKJV).

- *The pure in heart*—The single-minded, who are surrendered to Jesus, and are undefiled by their own evil and their own virtues.[3] "They shall see God" (5:8 NKJV).

- *The peacemakers*—The reconcilers, who are actively involved in healing troubles and conflicts between people. "They shall be called sons of God" (5:9 NKJV).

- *Those who are persecuted for righteousness' sake*—The despised, whose living, radical contradiction to cultural values and ways brings them rejection and trouble. "Theirs is the kingdom of heaven" (5:10 NKJV).

Strange Reasons to Celebrate

LUKE 6:22–23
> *Blessed are you when men hate you,*
> *And when they exclude you,*
> *And revile you, and cast out your name as evil,*
> *For the Son of Man's sake.*
> *Rejoice in that day and leap for joy!*
> *For indeed your reward is great in heaven,*
> *For in like manner their fathers did to the prophets. (NKJV)*

For people looking for real success, it is good to know that when you're poor, hungry, shedding tears, rejected, and hated for telling the truth, you are in excellent company—it's how God's witnesses have always been handled by a world rejecting him!

Salty Saints, Shining Cities, and Flaming Lamps

MATTHEW 5:13–16 *You are the salt of the earth; but if the salt loses its flavor, how shall it be seasoned? It is then good for nothing but to be thrown out and trampled underfoot by men. You are the light of the world. A city that is set on a hill cannot be hidden. Nor do they light a lamp and put ut under a basket, but on a lampstand, and it gives light to all who are in the house. Let your light so shine before men, that they may see your good works and glorify your Father in heaven. (NKJV)*

The old thinking about religion being "a private thing" is out the window. Jesus's followers make a visible difference. Jesus uses three down-to-earth illustrations to get this point across.

1. *Salt.* Emphasis is on the distinctive flavor life lived by the values of the kingdom brings to the world. There's a difference. You can taste it.

2. *City on a hill.* Nazareth, Jesus's hometown, was on a hill. At night its lights were visible from Cana, nine miles away. The emphasis is on the high visibility of a community of people living together by Jesus's happy values.

3. *Lamp.* Christ's followers are "the light of the world." The lamp Jesus was thinking of was a pottery bowl full of olive oil with a wick set ablaze. It fulfilled its purpose only when the wick was lit and the lamp was put where it illuminated the house.

what others say

Harry Emerson Fosdick

They were a fallible group and he knew it, but he called them "the light of the world" and the "salt of the earth." The modern reader of the Gospels often wonders at Jesus' faith in God the Father, despite his life's tragedy, but that is easier to understand than his faith in those disciples. He demanded of them a quality of life far above the average.[4]

Jesus and the Old Testament

Law or the Prophets
Old Testament

righteousness
moral harmony with
God's character

MATTHEW 5:17, 20 *Do not think that I came to destory the* **Law or the Prophet***s. I did not come to destroy but to fulfill . . . For I say to you, that unless your righteousness exceeds the righteousness of the scribes and Pharisees, you will by no means enter the kingdom of heaven.* (NKJV)

Jesus declared in no uncertain terms that nothing he taught contradicted the Old Testament Law or Prophets. His mission was to "fulfill" the Law (Matthew 5:17 NKJV). "Fulfilling the law" was the way rabbis described what they were doing when they sought to give their students a true and full understanding of God's Word. Jesus says that's what he's doing. The **righteousness** of kingdom citizens "exceeds the righteousness of the scribes and Pharisees" because in the ideal of the kingdom community, people face up to and deal with their heart motives as well as their actions.

what others say

R. T. France

The Old Testament . . . remains a permanent and crucial revelation of the will of God, but its application can no longer be by the simple observance of all its precepts as literal regulations for Christian conduct. The key to its interpretation is in Jesus and in his teaching, with its sovereign declaration of the will of God at a far deeper level than mere rule-keeping.[5]

The Lord's Prayer

MATTHEW 6:9–13 *In this manner, therefore, pray:*
Our Father in heaven,
Hallowed be Your name.
Your kingdom come.
Your will be done
On earth as it is in heaven.
Give us this day our daily bread.
And forgive us our debts,
As we forgive our debtors.
And do not lead us into temptation,
But deliver us from the evil one.
For Yours is the kingdom and the power and the glory forever.
*   Amen.* (NKJV)

The Lord's Prayer is set in the middle of Jesus's warning against spiritual dishonesty. Was that prayer intended to become what it has for many Christians—a rote recitation for formal worship—or was it intended as a practical guide for expressing the attitudes toward God necessary for living together in his kingdom?

First Things First

MATTHEW 6:19–21 *Do not lay up for yourselves treasures on earth, where moth and rust destroy . . . but lay up for yourselves treasures in heaven . . . For where your treasure is, there your heart will be also.* (NKJV)

apply it

Jesus now moves to deal with another area of human life in which the priorities of the world and the priorities of the kingdom collide. To the consternation of all who are trying to balance a quest for material success with life in the kingdom society, Jesus states flat out that it is not possible to focus on both God and money. We cannot seek what can be gained in this world and single-mindedly serve God and tend kingdom business at the same time.

Job One: The Kingdom

MATTHEW 6:25–27 *Therefore I say to you, do not worry about your life, what you will eat or what you will drink; nor about your body, what you will put on. Is not life more than food and the body more than clothing? Look at the birds of the air, for they neither sow nor reap nor gather into barns; yet your heavenly Father feeds them. Are you not of more value than they? Which of you by worrying can add one cubit to his stature?* (NKJV)

go to

our Father
Romans 8:15–17

committed to care
Matthew 7:7–11;
Philippians 4:19

Jesus goes on to point out that temptation to focus one's energy on worldly things is not just a problem for the rich. Anxiety about the lack of worldly things like food, drink, clothing, health, and longevity, is the flip side of the same broken record! Worry about such things is unnecessary since our Creator, who knows we have such needs, is also <u>our Father</u>, who is <u>committed to care</u> for us as certainly as he cares for birds and wildflowers. Birds and flowers never worry about such stuff!

Seek His Righteousness

MATTHEW 6:28–30, 33 *So why do you worry about clothing? Consider the **lilies** of the field, how they grow: they neither toil nor spin; and yet I say to you that even **Solomon** in all his glory was not arrayed like one of these. Now if God so clothes the grass of the field, which today is, and tomorrow is thrown into the oven, will He not much more clothe you, O you of little faith? . . . But seek first the kingdom of God and His righteousness, and all these things shall be added to you.* (NKJV)

The key to understanding this teaching and reaping its restful benefits is in the phrase "seek first the kingdom of God and His righteousness."

- God's kingdom is his rule. Seeking his righteousness revolves around committing to please God ahead of everything else.

- God's kingdom is the community of believers. Seeking his kingdom revolves around serving the needs of your fellow Christians and contributing to the peace and spiritual prosperity of the community of faith.

lilies
scarlet poppies and anemones, which bloom for a day then die

Solomon
Israel's richest king

thornbushes
buckthorn bush whose black berries resemble tiny grapes

thistles
desert thistle whose flower resembles a fig blossom

what others say

Leonard I. Sweet

There is no excuse for a sadsack, wallflower spirituality. God's pantry is never bare. God's party is never dull.[6]

Oswald Chambers

Never water down the word of God, preach it in its undiluted sternness; there must be unflinching loyalty to the word of God; but when you come to personal dealing with your fellow men, remember who you are—not a special being made up in heaven, but a sinner saved by grace.[7]

Beware of False Prophets

MATTHEW 7:15–17 *Beware of false prophets, who come to you in sheep's clothing, but inwardly they are ravenous wolves. You will know them by their fruits. Do men gather grapes from **thornbushes** or figs from **thistles**? Even so, every good tree bears good fruit, but a bad tree bears bad fruit.* (NKJV)

How can you tell a pseudo prophet from a true prophet? Two clues:

1. *Inspect his or her "fruit."* A good spiritual leader will be of good character. Galatians 5:19–23 says, "Now the works of the flesh are evident, which are: adultery, fornication, uncleanness, lewdness, idolatry, sorcery, hatred, contentions, jealousies, outbursts of wrath, selfish ambitions, dissensions, heresies, envy, murders, drunkenness, revelries, and the like . . . But the fruit of the Spirit is love, joy, peace, longsuffering, kindness, goodness, faithfulness, gentleness, self-control" (NKJV).

2. *Check out his or her obedience to do the will of God.* Speaking "**Christianese**," preaching powerful sermons, or doing miracles are not the signs of a sound spiritual guide. Jesus states the issue clearly: "Not everyone who says to Me, 'Lord, Lord,' shall enter the kingdom of heaven, but he who does the will of My Father in heaven" (Matthew 7:21 NKJV).

A Tale of Two Builders

MATTHEW 7:24 *Therefore whoever hears these sayings of Mine, and does them, I will liken him to a wise man who built his house on the rock.* (NKJV)

There are, Jesus insists, only two ways to build a life—one leads to success; the other, to disaster. Consider two housebuilders:

1. *The "wise builder"* gives prime attention to the foundation, being careful to build his house on bedrock. What's this bedrock? Listening to and putting into practice the teachings of Jesus.

2. *The "foolish builder"* builds his dream house in a dry wash, without a foundation. What is the nature of this sandy footing? Letting Jesus's teachings go in one ear and out the other, without making a difference.

Push comes to shove when both houses are struck by a violent storm. Life throws its worst at both, as life will do. The life built on Jesus and his wisdom weathers the storm; the life built without him collapses! The "gut issue" is the choice to submit all of life to the authority of Christ. To tell good leaders from bad ones, check their fruit and their obedience.

Chapter Wrap-Up

- Jesus chose twelve men to be with him and to become his apostles to lead his movement after his death and resurrection. (Luke 6:12–16)

- Jesus taught his disciples the basic principles of the kingdom of God, the community of believers in which they would live their lives. (Matthew 5–7; Luke 6:17–49)

- Jesus turned the world's view of success and happiness upside down with nine statements called the "Beatitudes." (Matthew 5:3–12)

- Jesus said he did not come to abolish the Old Testament but to fill up what was lacking in it by dealing with the motives behind the Ten Commandments, and showing how life among his followers was radically different from life in the world. (Matthew 5:17–48)

- He attacked religious hypocrisy and called his followers to attitudes and actions based on honesty, humility, and dependence on the Father in heaven. (Matthew 6:1–18)

- He taught the importance of having our hearts set on heavenly rather than earthly treasures. If we seek the kingdom of God first, all our needs will be supplied. (Matthew 6:19–34)

Study Questions

1. How many of his disciples did Jesus choose to be apostles? How many of the apostles can you name? Which one was a tax collector? Which ones had been fishermen? Which were brothers? Which one was a political radical?

2. Who does Jesus expect to be able to live by the teachings in the Sermon on the Mount?

3. How does Jesus "fulfill" the Old Testament Law?

4. What are three ways Jesus teaches us to express love for our enemies? (See Luke 6:27–28.)

5. Considering this past week in the light of the Sermon on the Mount (Matthew 5–7), is your "bank" on earth or in heaven? What needs to be done to change accounts?

Chapter 14: Revolution of Love

Let's Get Started

Jesus, the young prophet from Nazareth, preached the ancient truths in a strange and powerful new way, pressing each issue deeper to deal in startling new ways with his hearers' values, attitudes, and allegiances. And he had the audacity to claim listening to his teachings and putting them into practice was the only way to avert disaster!

All his speechless enemies could do was look for some violent way to silence him.

teaching
Matthew 5–7;
Luke 6:17–49

A Walk on the Wild Side

> MATTHEW 7:28–8:1 *And so it was, when Jesus had ended these sayings, that the people were astonished at His teaching, for He taught them as one having authority, and not as the scribes. When He had come down from the mountain, great multitudes followed Him. (NKJV)*

Even those who believed Jesus was the Messiah were far from comprehending what messiahship actually involved. Hebrew nationalism dominated their messianic dreams. The idea of a crucified Messiah was unthinkable. The amazing things the New Testament reports Jesus did from then on would demonstrate three things: (1) God had sent him, (2) he was who he claimed to be, and (3) he was a completely unique commander in chief leading a completely unique army of revolutionaries in the most unique revolution ever to disturb the status quo.

A Revolutionary Model of Faith

> LUKE 7:1–6 *Now when [Jesus] concluded all His sayings in the hearing of the people, He entered Capernaum. And a certain centurion's servant, who was dear to him, was sick and ready to die. So when he heard about Jesus, he sent elders of the Jews to Him, pleading with Him to come and heal his servant. And*

go to

God-fearers
Acts 10:2

grace
Ephesians 2:8–9

centurion
commander of one
hundred men;
"backbone of the
Roman army"

converted
circumcised, living
by Jewish religious
rules

amazed
the original word
indicates high
admiration

grace
God's kindness to
the undeserving

when they came to Jesus, they begged Him earnestly, saying that the one for whom He should do this was deserving, "for he loves our nation, and has built us a synagogue." Then Jesus went with them. (NKJV)

The Roman army maintained a military presence at Capernaum. A **centurion** stationed there had a dearly loved slave who was disabled with painful paralysis and near death. Slaves in Roman culture were treated as property to be used, so this owner displayed an unusual attitude toward his worker. The officer was not a Jew; he was a Roman. Most Romans would do anything to avoid duty in Israel, but this soldier loved the Jews. While he had not formally **converted** to Judaism, he was one of the non-Jewish believers called "God-fearers," who, in many cities, attended the synagogue, believed in God, studied the Scriptures, and lived by many of the Jewish rules.

At first, the centurion sent Jewish friends with the request for Jesus to come (Luke 7:3). Jesus was on his way to the centurion's house when the Roman dispatched a second group to tell Jesus he didn't deserve to have him come into his home (7:6), nor did he feel worthy to approach him personally (7:7). At some point, according to Matthew's account, the centurion himself came and expressed his urgency (Matthew 8:5–6). Jesus was **amazed** at the soldier's attitude (Luke 7:9). He shocked Jewish onlookers by asserting that nowhere in Israel had he found faith as great as this Gentile's faith! The servant was healed (7:10).

Two things were admirable and different about the centurion's faith:

something to ponder

1. He acknowledged the principle of **grace**. While the Jews who recommended that Jesus help him thought his good works made him "deserving" (Luke 7:4 NKJV), the centurion appealed for help, fully understanding he did not deserve it (7:6–7).

2. He recognized the uniqueness of Jesus's authority—that (a) his authority is similar but superior to earthly authority; (b) Jesus has authority over people and created things (e.g., disease); and (c) his authority transcends space and distance. In other words, the Roman soldier recognized Jesus as more than "just another teacher."

A Revolutionary Picture of God

Jesus and his men took a hike to the village of Nain (see appendix A). As they approached the town gate a funeral procession was headed for the **cemetery**. The bier carried the body of a woman's only son. Having already lost her husband at some point in the past, this grieving mother was in bad shape, emotionally as well as financially. A woman seldom owned property; if her husband died and she had no children to care for her, she was often left destitute.

This God Has Feelings

LUKE 7:13 *When the Lord saw her, He had compassion on her and said to her, "Do not weep." (NKJV)*

The original language says, "He was moved in his inner body parts." He cared deeply. When Jesus cared it was never just empty emotion. Whenever the New Testament records Jesus <u>feeling compassion</u> or sympathy toward someone, it also records him doing something about the situation.

This God Has Come to Help

LUKE 7:14–16 *Then He came and touched the open coffin, and those who carried him stood still. And He said, "Young man, I say to you, arise." So he who was dead sat up and began to speak. And He presented him to his mother. Then fear came upon all, and they glorified God, saying, "A great prophet has risen up among us"; and, "God has visited His people." (NKJV)*

Among first-century Jews, a God who let himself be bothered by a widow's grief was a theological scandal! Theologians thought if God could be moved emotionally—with sadness, happiness, compassion, and anger—he would be changeable and not in control.

Jesus corrects that grotesque idea. As <u>God's **expression**</u>, he shows us a God who not only cares about people and their pain, but actually feels their pain with them! As he and his entourage left town, a widow's tearstained face wore a smile.

feeling compassion
Matthew 9:36;
15:32;
Mark 8:2

God's expression
John 1:1–18

cemetery
A ten-minute walk from Nain there is a burial ground, still used today.

expression
"the Word"

go to

**courageously
confronted**
Luke 3:19–20

dove
Luke 3:21–22

introduce
John 1:35–36

dared to confront
Matthew 3:7–10

prophecies
Isaiah 61:1–2

Machaerus Castle
Herod's fortress in
the desert east of
the Dead Sea

Medal of Honor for a Revolutionary Hero

MATTHEW 11:2–4 *And when John had heard in prison about
the works of Christ, he sent two of his disciples and said to Him,
"Are You the Coming One, or do we look for another?" Jesus
answered and said to them, "Go and tell John the things which
you hear and see." (NKJV)*

John the Baptist had stood toe-to-toe with powerful people and
<u>courageously confronted</u> them with their need for spiritual change.
He was there when the Holy Spirit came down like a <u>dove</u> and identified Jesus as God's "beloved Son." He was the first to <u>introduce</u>
Jesus as "the Lamb of God." Because he <u>dared to confront</u> a wicked
king about the illegitimacy of his marriage, John was arrested and
thrown into the dungeon at **Machaerus Castle**, "one of the loneli-
est and grimmest and most unassailable fortresses in the world."[1]

Just Checking

Why, then, did such a man of faith and power send disciples to ask
Jesus if he was really the Messiah? Was it his own need for comfort
as his execution approached? Did he have doubts even after all he
had seen and said about Jesus? Or was it to redirect the allegiance of
his disciples from himself to Jesus? Whatever the reason, Jesus knew
John would recognize the fulfillment of Old Testament <u>prophecies</u>
of things Messiah would do.

So while John's messengers watched, Jesus healed the sick, freed
the demon-harassed, restored sight to the blind, cured lepers, made
the deaf hear, raised the dead, and cared for the poor.

First Prize Goes to . . . (Drum Roll, Please)

MATTHEW 11:11 *Assuredly, I say to you, among those born of
women there has not risen one greater than John the Baptist; but
he who is least in the kingdom of heaven is greater than he.
(NKJV)*

When the messengers left, Jesus paid John a high tribute. In giving this compliment, Jesus was spotlighting three things:

1. *His character:* In the raging wind of opposition to truth and justice, John was an immovable tree! No overindulged yes-man lolling about a king's palace, he was a tough-minded, rugged, uncompromising man of God (Luke 7:24–25; Matthew 11:7–8).

2. *His work:* John was a special kind of prophet. First, he prepared Israel for Messiah's arrival (Luke 7:26–27; Matthew 11:9–10). Second, in Spirit, power, and the strategic nature of his work, he was an "Elijah" (Matthew 11:14; Malachi 4:5–6; Luke 1:17).

3. *His place in history:* John was the living bridge between Old Testament prophecy and Law and the kingdom led by Jesus Christ (Matthew 11:12–13). John was the first hero of the revolution of love.

"No Matter the Game, We Won't Play!"

> LUKE 7:33–34 *For John the Baptist came neither eating bread nor drinking wine, and you say, "He has a demon." The Son of Man has come eating and drinking, and you say, "Look, a glutton and a winebibber, a friend of tax collectors and sinners!"* (NKJV)

As Jesus paid his tribute to the greatness of John the Baptist, the audience divided itself as it had from the baptizer's first desert cry for repentance. It was a divide that carried over into Jesus's ministry and would finally culminate in his death on the cross.

what others say

Leonard I. Sweet

John the Baptist's . . . funeral ethic with its fasting and flailing, its eating nothing but wild honey and locusts, its wearing nothing but a hair shirt, didn't appeal to you, Jesus is saying. But neither did my wedding ethic with its eating and drinking. What more do you want? God gave you a choice . . . a funereal faith or a dance spirituality. You rejected both.[2]

The "Impossible" Fellowship

> LUKE 8:1–3 *The twelve were with Him, and certain women who had been healed of evil spirits and infirmities—Mary called Magdalene, out of whom had come seven demons, and Joanna the wife of Chuza, Herod's steward, and Susanna, and many others who provided for Him from their substance.* (NKJV)

go to

his brothers
Mark 6:3

Jesus traveled from town to town proclaiming the kingdom of God. He did not travel alone. The twelve apostles-in-training were with him along with "many other" disciples, including a group of women whose involvement with him had led to their personal transformation and healing, and who traveled with them and paid the bills. Two things are impressive about this group of fellow travelers:

1. The invitation to enter the kingdom of God was given in a context of sharing, fellowship, and mutual care. Seeing Jesus and his disciples living together provided an instant illustration of the community life into which he was calling them.

2. The mix of people who made up this early Christian fellowship was revolutionary: a woman with a dark past, a royal lady of the king's court, a carpenter, a couple of "super-patriots," a tax collector, some pugnacious fishermen, healed psychotics, poor and rich, male and female, and at least one potential traitor. It was a group too varied to get along. They were a microcosm of the diverse peoples who make up the church—the advance contingent of the kingdom of God—today. The thing that holds such a lumpy mix of souls together and makes it an indivisible family is Jesus Christ at the center.

Family Matters

The strain of Jesus's notoriety took its toll on his family. Seeing the crowds flocking to hear him, aware of the risk of making the revolutionary claims he made, watching the opposition intensify, Jesus's relatives began to think he'd gone too far. "He is out of His mind," they concluded, and made plans to take him home and protect him from himself (Mark 3:20–21 NKJV).

When they arrived to take him away, they were unable to get into the house where he was speaking, because of the crowd that had come to hear him. They sent word to Jesus that his mother and <u>his brothers</u> were standing outside and that they wanted to talk to him. There is no record they made contact. Their plans to take him into protective custody were frustrated.

LUKE 8:21 *But He answered and said to them, "My mother and My brothers are these who hear the word of God and do it."* (NKJV)

Jesus used the occasion to announce that his true family (brothers, sisters, and mother) includes "whoever does the will of God" (Mark 3:35 NKJV). Christ's revolution of love creates more than an audience or aggregation of unrelated adherents—our Elder Brother and Lord has made true believers members of his family!

go to

brothers, sisters, and mother
Mark 10:28–30

Chapter Wrap-Up

- For his disciples, following Jesus was a march into unfamiliar territory. Examples of faith came from unexpected sources (a Roman centurion). The picture of God as personal and caring that emerged was different from the picture they had grown up with. (Luke 7:1–17)

- John the Baptist sent messengers from his prison cell to Jesus to ask if he was, for sure, the Messiah. Jesus demonstrated his authenticity by the works he did. Then he gave John high praise and explained why the Pharisees refused to listen to him. (Matthew 11:2–19)

- Jesus's family members decided he had gone too far and needed to be protected from himself. When Jesus was told his mother and his brothers were looking for him, he said that his true family consisted of those who heard the word of God and followed his will. (Mark 3:21, 31–35)

Study Questions

1. What did the centurion recognize as unique about Jesus's authority?

2. What does Jesus's response to the sorrow of the widow at Nain teach us about God?

3. Considering your life right now, would others see you as Jesus's "brother or sister" or as a distant relative? Why?

Chapter 15: The Storyteller

Chapter Highlights:
- A Seedy Saga
- Why Parables?
- Reality Teaching
- Decoding a Parable
- Jesus's Parables

Let's Get Started

The yarns Jesus spun captured the imagination of people who talked with him one-on-one, the Twelve who hung out with him, and the crowds who came to hear him preach. The Greek word *paraballein* means "to throw one thing down alongside another." Jesus's parables are sayings, stories, or metaphors he used to communicate truth by comparison.

the trail
by Lake Galilee and other places

A Seedy Saga About Listening

MATTHEW 13:3 *Then He spoke many things to them in parables, saying: "Behold, a sower went out to sow."* (NKJV)

The trail took them past a farmer seeding his field. "Look!" Jesus said. "A sower planting his crop!" Like a play-by-play announcer, Jesus described the scene as he and his companions watched. It was a familiar sight. A man with a sack of grain walked up and down the field, "broadcasting" (see Illustration #4). Again and again his hand reached into the bag of seed, and he then scattered each handful in a circular motion. A wind gust caught some seed, depositing it on the beaten footpaths between the fields. Other seed fell where the Palestinian limestone was scarcely covered with a thin layer of dirt. Still others fell into the weedy soil at the corners of the field. Most fell where the sower intended—in good soil, rich and deep enough to produce a harvest.

"That's us and the people who listen to us!" Jesus may have said. Then, without explaining the meaning of the story, he added, "He who has ears to hear, let him hear!" (Matthew 13:9 NKJV; Mark 4:9; Luke 8:8) which freely translated means, "Wake up and smell the coffee!"

fruit
John 15:2;
Galatians 5:22

enemy
Satan

the world
everything in the
present order of
things that appeals
to the soul as an
object of desire
apart from and in
rivalry with God

What Mysteries Lie Buried in the Seeding Story?

LUKE 8:9 *Then His disciples asked Him, saying, "What does this parable mean?" (NKJV)*

Jesus's disciples, seeing the puzzled looks on the faces of the crowd and struggling themselves to wrap their minds around the story's meaning, were frustrated and said, "Why do You speak to them in parables?" (Matthew 13:10 NKJV).

The key to understanding this parable is to focus on four types of listeners:

- *The seed* is the word of God—the good news of the kingdom taught by Jesus (Matthew 13:19; Mark 4:14; Luke 8:11).

- *The hard-packed path* represents people who listen to Jesus's words with closed minds. They have built around their hearts a comfort zone of religious habits, preconceived ideas, and prejudice. The Word never sinks in, and the **enemy** whisks away the new info like a buzzard snatching a scrap of roadkill! (Matthew 13:19; Mark 4:15; Luke 8:12).

- *The stony places* are people who look like they are listening, but beneath the facade of initial openness lie concretized prejudice, stubbornness, and fear. The Word of God sends down roots but runs with a dull thud into hidden resistance to anything that might disturb the comfy spiritual status quo of their shallow faith. Growth stops. Pressure comes and faith disappears (Matthew 13:20–21; Mark 4:16–17; Luke 8:13).

- *The thorny ground* pictures the listener who is genuinely receptive. Christ's words take root, sprout, and start to grow. But the listener's head is turned by distractions—anxiety, the seduction of wealth, and the nearly irresistible siren call to wallow in the world's vanities. The gagging sound you hear is the life being strangled out of some split-hearted fool trying to sing the songs of the kingdom in harmony with the discordant serenade of **the world**[1] (Matthew 13:22; Mark 4:18–19; Luke 8:14).

- *The good soil* is the responsive, teachable mind that lets Christ's teachings sink down deep, take root, wrap themselves around the hearer's welcoming heart, grow, and produce practical, profitable <u>fruit</u>. No secondary concerns are allowed to choke out the

Word. Resistance to change is displaced by teachability and responsiveness. Kingdom-of-God values (values that promote the development of the kingdom community) become apparent in the lifestyle, priorities, and personal relationships of this person.

Illustration #4
The Sower—Farmers in the ancient world walked through the fields, throwing handfuls of seed in a circular motion so that it scattered evenly on the ground. Then they used a plow to scratch the soil and lightly cover the seed.

Why Did Jesus Speak in Parables?

MATTHEW 13:34–35 *All these things Jesus spoke to the multitude in parables; and without a parable He did not speak to them, that it might be fulfilled which was spoken by the prophet, saying:*

"I will open My mouth in parables;
I will utter things kept secret from the foundation of the world." (NKJV)

Matthew, in quoting Psalm 78:2, reminds us that the Old Testament promised that Messiah would be a storyteller. Jesus was a

go to

Samuel
1 Samuel 3:1–14

brilliant teacher who never stopped teaching. Parables were a familiar teaching technique in Israel. He would have first heard God's truth in parable form from his earthly father, Joseph. It was one of the ways Hebrew parents passed their faith on to their children.

Reality Teaching

> LUKE 6:40 *A disciple is not above his teacher, but everyone who is perfectly trained will be like his teacher.* (NKJV)

Jesus's parables were part of a style of teaching in which the teacher does not depend on books or lectures alone to communicate truth. Jesus was not satisfied to cram his disciples' heads full of "amazing facts to impress their friends"! He was building lives—men and women who, under his tutelage, would become like him. He wanted them to be "perfectly trained."

To keep his disciples' learning experiences close to the realities of their day-to-day lives, Jesus capitalized on what was happening around him as he went from town to town or taught down at the beach.

Decoding a Parable

Here are some things to remember that can help us discover the meaning of Jesus's parables:

1. *Note the context in which the story is told.* Jesus used parables to answer someone's question or to shed light on some issue. When trying to figure out the meaning, look at the verses leading up to

the parable and following it. What triggered the story? What was the event, question, issue, or need the parable was told to explain, answer, or address?

lost coin
Luke 15:8–9

metaphors
figurative language

2. *Focus on the main point.* A parable is not the same as an allegory. In an allegory, every part of the story has meaning. In a parable, some details are simply part of the story. Usually a parable makes one point, and only the parts that focus on the main point are significant.

3. *Consider the culture and customs of the time.* It is valuable to know something of the culture and customs of Jesus's time. For example, to identify with the panic of the woman in Jesus's parable of the <u>lost coin</u>, we need to know that the ten coins were probably her dowry, which many Jewish women strung and wore like a necklace. The missing coin was probably a family heirloom more prized for its sentimental than actual value.

> what others say
>
> **Merril F. Unger**
>
> The mind takes a natural delight in this manner of teaching, appealing as it does not to the understanding only, but to the feelings, to the imagination, in short to the whole man . . . and all things thus learned with delight are those longest remembered.[5]

Jesus's Parables in the Four Gospels

Depending on how each defines them, various scholars say Jesus told twenty-seven to fifty parables.[6] The difference is that some include Jesus's **metaphors** among the parables, while others define a parable more strictly as a short story. Using the story definition, the number is about thirty.

The parables of Jesus fall into at least six categories:

1. Parables of the kingdom, present

2. Parables of the kingdom, future

3. Parables about resources, priorities, and material possessions

4. Parables about grace and forgiveness

5. Parables about prayer

6. Parables about various spiritual issues

Chapter Wrap-Up

- An important part of Jesus's teaching was the telling of special stories based on things familiar to his hearers, to set priorities, correct misconceptions, develop attitudes, and teach concepts necessary for life in the kingdom community. (Matthew 13:3)

- Through the parable of the sower, the seeds, and seed growth, Jesus taught about various ways of listening and responding to truth. (Matthew 13:3–9, 18–23; Luke 8:1–8, 11–15)

- Jesus's parables, like all of his teaching, were designed to help disciples keep their understanding of truth solidly related to life's realities and to pass on the teacher's likeness. His stories were crafted to hide spiritual truth from unbelievers while revealing it to believers. (Matthew 13:10–17, 34–35)

- Jesus's parables dealt with a variety of subjects. The predominant theme was life in the kingdom of God. (Matthew 13)

Study Questions

1. Define a parable.

2. In the parable of the sower and seeds, what is the seed? What do the rocky places represent?

3. What was Jesus's goal in his teaching, according to Luke 6:40?

4. What are three helpful things to remember when interpreting Jesus's parables?

5. When it comes to how you listen to God right now, are you (a) locked in on the signal, (b) moving with the music, (c) getting a lot of static, (d) channel surfing, or (e) barely picking up the signal? Why? What needs to happen to get tuned into his voice?

Chapter 16: Storms Over Galilee

Chapter Highlights:
- Calming Mental Tornadoes
- Hog Stampede
- Stilling Windstorms of Worry and Grief

Let's Get Started

MARK 4:35–38a *On the same day, when evening had come, He said to them, "Let us cross over to the other side." Now when they had left the multitude, they took Him along in the boat as He was. And other little boats were also with Him. And a great windstorm arose, and the waves beat into the boat, so that it was already filling. But He was in the stern, asleep on a pillow.* (NKJV)

Matthew 8:23–27
Mark 4:35–51
Luke 8:22–25

Jesus was bone tired from a full day of speaking and teaching. In need of rest, he told his men to head across the lake. Several were experienced boatmen who'd grown up on these waters, so he left the sailing to them, grabbed a cushion, lay down in the back of the boat, and fell asleep.

Terror on the Seas

MARK 4:38b–39 *And they awoke Him and said to Him, "Teacher, do You not care that we are perishing?" Then He arose and rebuked the wind, and said to the sea, "Peace, be still!" And the wind ceased and there was a great calm.* (NKJV)

Lightning flashed. Thunder crashed. Rain splashed. Wind whipped. Waves washed the wee watercraft. Jesus slept.

"Don't you care if we drown?" The men with Jesus were not far from wrong. Drowning was a distinct possibility. They were afraid they would be drowned. And they were afraid he would be drowned along with everything his teachings had caused them to dream of. They might as well be saying, "Don't you care if the kingdom of God sinks?"

Jesus woke, yawned, rubbed his eyes, "rebuked" the wind, and told the roaring waves to "be still!" Two things happened: The wind stopped, and the <u>sea stilled</u>.

sea stilled
Psalm 89:9

over the sea
Psalms 89:8–9;
104:5–9; 106:8–9;
107:23–32

The light dawned. As their jaws dropped open, their knees became spaghetti—this time out of sheer awe. The man whose concern they had the audacity to question when the storm hit (Mark 4:38) held power (including authority <u>over the sea</u> and the weather). They knew this power and authority belonged only to God! "Who can this be?" they said (Mark 4:41 NKJV).

They knew. And now they understood better why listening to his words was the only thing that made sense.

> ### what others say
>
> ### Robert L. Thomas and Stanley N. Gundry
>
> Here is a double miracle, the cessation of the wind and the immediate calming of the water. Ordinarily the waters would remain rough for a time after the wind stopped, but not this time.[1]

Calming Mental Tornadoes

LUKE 8:28 *When [the demon-possessed man] saw Jesus, he cried out, fell down before Him, and with a loud voice said, "What have I to do with You, Jesus, Son of the Most High God? I beg You, do not torment me!"* (NKJV)

The boat landed at a craggy limestone area overlooking the lake near Gadara (see appendix A). The cliffside was honeycombed with caves used to entomb the dead. On the grassy plateau above the tombs, a herd of some two thousand pigs was rooting, watched over by local swineherds.

As Jesus and his men pulled the boat up on shore, a notorious madman emerged from the tombs, screaming and gesturing for the intruders to leave him alone. He and his equally tormented companion (Matthew 8:28 says there were two of them) ran down the rocky cliffside toward the boat. Both were naked and covered with filth. Their bodies were scarred from slashing themselves with sharp stones in acts of self-punishment. The big one's ankles, legs, and arms bore the marks of chains and irons used to control his violence. This tortured soul, with demon-enhanced strength, had repeatedly broken the chains and escaped to haunt the tombs, where together the two madmen of Gadara filled the night with deranged wails and by day poured threats and obscenities on passersby and those who came to bury their dead.

abyss
Revelation 9:1–11;
11:7; 17:8; 20:1–3

pigs
Leviticus 11:7–8;
Isaiah 65:3–5

Legion
an army of six
thousand men

abyss
Greek for "bottom-
less" pit; realm of
the dead

> ## what others say
>
> ### Henry H. Halley
>
> The rather plain implication of Scripture is that "demoniacs" were not mere lunatics, but cases of "invaded personality"; and that demons, whatever their origin or nature, were evil spirits that did actually enter and afflict, one way or another, certain persons. It is thought to have been a special exhibition of the devil against Jesus, permitted by God during Jesus' stay on earth, to demonstrate that Jesus' power extended even into the unseen realm.[2]

An Army of Warrior Devils

Jesus knew what he was up against, and as the harassed souls stumbled and screamed their way toward him, he commanded the evil spirits to free their captives.

"What is your name?" Jesus demanded, addressing the trembling hulk before him. "My name is **Legion**; for we are many" snarled the man (Mark 5:9 NKJV). It was the cry of a man who felt like all the demon soldiers of hell had fastened themselves to him and were waging war against him from the inside.

Hog Stampede

> LUKE 8:31–32 *And they begged Him that He would not command them to go out into the **abyss**. Now a herd of many swine was feeding there on the mountain. So they begged Him that He would permit them to enter them. And He permitted them.* (*NKJV*)

Suddenly there was a commotion among the swine on the hill. They squealed and shook. Then they moved with increasing agitation toward the precipice. The swineherds ran here and there yelling, but nothing could stop the stampede. Down the rocky slope tumbled a thundering herd of two thousand crazed pigs, headlong straight into the Sea of Galilee, squealing and gurgling their last as they drowned in the blue waters of what the rabbis loved to call "the sea of God's delight."

Why did Jesus do as the evil spirits requested by letting them go into the pigs? Under the Law of Moses, pigs were ceremonially unclean. This rule tested Israel's obedience and protected them from

go to

more than a match
1 John 4:4

trichinosis
disease caused by
trichinae, carried by
pigs

exposure to **trichinosis**. In rebellion, Israel sometimes ignored this ban. By sending the demons into the pigs, Jesus "killed two birds with one stone," getting rid of the demons and disciplining the illegal swine trade in one fell swoop!

The madmen of Gadara were healed, cleaned up, put their clothes back on, stopped harassing the neighborhood, and found peace. And the whole town turned out to ask Jesus to leave (Mark 5:17)!

But the cured crazies went home to their families and reported all the good things Jesus had done for them (Mark 5:19–20). Although the cured men asked to go with Jesus when he left (Mark 5:18), Jesus said, "No." He gave them the more difficult task of being witnesses for him in that Gentile region. The healed men's obedience gave that area the gift of a believable testimony of Christ's power and an opportunity to respond.

> **what others say**
>
> **Lawrence O. Richards**
>
> Are we in danger today from these evil beings? . . . It would be wrong to suggest that possession or oppression cannot happen today . . . What the Scriptures emphasize, and what the Gospels prove, is that Jesus is <u>more than a match</u> for the evil powers of our universe.[3]

Stilling Windstorms of Worry and Grief

MARK 5:21–24 *Now when Jesus had crossed over again by boat to the other side, a great multitude gathered to Him; and He was by the sea. And behold, one of the rulers of the synagogue came, Jairus by name. And when he saw Him, he fell at His feet and begged Him earnestly, saying, "My little daughter lies at the point of death. Come and lay Your hands on her, that she may be healed, and she will live." So Jesus went with him, and a great multitude followed Him and thronged Him. (NKJV)*

Galilean synagogues had been wide open for Jesus early in his ministry, but as official opposition mounted they were rapidly closing to him. Jairus may have been initially opposed, but there is a big difference between taking an arrogant attitude toward Christ when the sun is shining and hanging on to that attitude when you're in trouble and need Christ's help! Pride isn't worth much when your child is dying! So when Jesus's boat docked at Capernaum, Jairus was waiting on the beach.

As president of the synagogue, Jairus organized and directed Sabbath services. By rabbinical rule he was expected to be a man of <u>high moral character</u>, modest, God-fearing, truthful, not greedy, hospitable, and not a gambler. In some synagogues the president was the sole authority.[4] But he risked it all for his child.

Right there in front of God and everybody, the proud president pleaded with the controversial Nazarene to come to his house and save his twelve-year-old from death.

Stopping a Blood Flood

LUKE **8:42–44** *But as He went, the multitudes thronged Him. Now a woman, having a flow of blood for twelve years, who had spent all her livelihood on physicians and could not be healed by any, came from behind and touched the border of His garment. And immediately her flow of blood stopped. (NKJV)*

On the way to Jairus's house, the crowd pushed and shoved, demanding attention. Someone was constantly pressing against him, touching him. Suddenly Jesus spun around to face the swarming mass. "Who touched Me?" he asked (Luke 8:45 NKJV).

The disciples thought it was a ridiculous question. "Who touched you?" they echoed incredulously. "Who didn't touch you?"

Their sarcasm notwithstanding, Jesus knew he'd felt something unusual in the press of the crowd. Someone had touched him in faith. As he searched the faces, a frightened woman stepped out of the mass and blurted out her painful and embarrassing story: For twelve years she hadn't stopped **bleeding**!

Old Testament Law declared a woman with a chronic menstrual flow and anyone she touched ceremonially "unclean." She could not participate in worship or community life until the bleeding stopped. The Jewish **Talmud** prescribed eleven different "cures" for her problem—several amounted to superstitious mumbo jumbo. She'd no doubt tried them all.

In a final act of desperation, the sick and lonely woman risked public condemnation, pushed through the crowd, and got close enough to reach out and touch the <u>edge</u> of Jesus's robe. Devout Jews wore a four-cornered outer robe with a tassel at each corner; the woman reached for the tassels.

go to

high moral character
1 Timothy 3:1–7;
Titus 1:5–9

bleeding
Leviticus 15:25–30

edge
Numbers 15:38–40

bleeding
chronic menstrual flow

Talmud
ancient commentaries; collections of insights of rabbis

wailing women
professional mourn-
ers hired to wail

As soon as she made contact, her bleeding stopped. She could feel it (Mark 5:29). "Daughter, your faith has made you well," Jesus said. "Go in peace" (5:34 NKJV).

Bad News: The Girl Is Dead!

MARK 5:35 *While He was still speaking, some came from the ruler of the synagogue's house who said, "Your daughter is dead. Why trouble the Teacher any further?" (NKJV)*

As soon as Jesus heard the men's words, he said, "Do not be afraid; only believe" (5:36 NKJV).

Taking Peter, James, and John with him as witnesses, Jesus followed Jairus the rest of the way to his house. Sure enough, the funeral had already started! **Wailing women** filled the place with ear-splitting, high-pitched moans and melodramatic pleas for the dead girl to speak. Others played mournful dirges on flutes. The house was a pandemonium of tragedy and grief.

Good News: The Funeral Is Canceled!

Jesus marched in and demanded the commotion to stop! "The child is not dead, but sleeping," he said (Mark 5:39 NKJV). The orderly mourning disintegrated into disorderly fits of cynical laughter.

"Out! All of you!" he demanded. Then, with only his three disciples and the girl's parents, Jesus went into the room where the child's body lay. He took her hand and told her to get up. She got up and walked through the house, greeting gape-mouthed guests who had come to join the wailing! Those who were in the room were under strictest orders that "no one should know it" (Mark 5:43 NKJV). What did he mean? Since it would be hard to keep her resuscitation from the gathered mourners, Jesus must mean the process involved—the fact that he touched her dead body and raised her up by the hand.

Chapter Wrap-Up

- In a boat sailing across the northeast corner of Lake Galilee, Jesus and his disciples were caught in a ferocious gale that threatened to scuttle the tiny boat. Jesus woke up from his nap, rebuked the wind and the waves, and the storm stopped! (Mark 4:35–41)

- On the shore of Gadara, two madmen emerged from the tombs, one having been possessed by a legion of evil spirits. Jesus sent the spirits into a herd of pigs grazing nearby, whereupon the swine plunged to their deaths in the sea. (Mark 5:1–20)

- On the beach as they returned, a synagogue president named Jairus met Jesus with the urgent request that he come and heal his young daughter, who was near death. (Luke 8:40–42)

- On the way to Jairus's house, a suffering woman reached through the crowd and touched the tassel of Jesus's robe. She was instantly healed. (Luke 8:43–48)

- Word came from Jairus's house that his daughter was dead. Jesus ignored the bad news and encouraged her father to believe. The daughter was raised from the dead at Christ's word. (Luke 8:49–56)

Study Questions

1. Where was Jesus when the storm threatened to sink the boat? When has Jesus seemed asleep in your life when you desperately needed to know he was awake?

2. How did the disciples react when the wind and waves obeyed Jesus? What does it tell us about who Jesus is?

3. How did the people of Gadara try to deal with the demon-possessed man? How is the way we treat mentally ill people today similar? Different?

4. How did the evil spirits react to the presence of Jesus? What does this say about Jesus's authority over evil spirits?

5. When they saw the former madman sitting, dressed, and in his right mind, how did the townspeople react? What does this say about their values?

Chapter Highlights:
• Help Wanted
• Offense! Offense!
• Two by Two
• Urgent Harvest
• Assault Strategy

Chapter 17: Crusade for Galilee

Let's Get Started

In the training timetable for the future leaders of the kingdom movement, it was time for the rubber to meet the road. The Twelve must be sent out in specific ministry to preach Jesus's message and to duplicate his working style. It would be a temporary sending this time. They would be "on their own" for a short while, then return for debriefing and several more months with him. But it would be a real get-their-feet-wet event. And they'd never be the same after the experience.

go to

he was moved with compassion
Matthew 14:14;
15:32; 20:34;
Mark 1:41

third preaching tour
Compare
Matthew 9:35;
Luke 4:14; 8:1.

Help Wanted

MATTHEW 9:35–36 *Then Jesus went about all the cities and villages, teaching in their synagogues, preaching the gospel of the kingdom, and healing every sickness and every disease among the people. But when He saw the multitudes, He was moved with compassion for them, because they were weary and scattered, like sheep having no shepherd.* (NKJV)

The endless crowds of needy people "got to" Jesus. By the principles of good management, an efficient leader who's really in control keeps his head, maintains a cool distance, and doesn't let himself get too emotionally entangled in people's problems. Jesus could never do that. He was too vulnerable, intentionally. When the Bible says "he was moved with **compassion**," it means he put himself in people's shoes, let himself feel their pain, and hurt with them.

The pain he shared with them moved him to help them. On his third preaching tour of Galilee, his identification with hurting people was multiplied by the hundreds of anxious faces surrounding him in each place.

gospel harmony

Matthew 9:35;
10:1–11, 14
Mark 6:6–13
Luke 9:1–6

compassion
feeling moved by
another's situation,
leading to action

ripened crop
John 4:35;
Matthew 13:23

volunteers
Isaiah 6:1–8

Urgent Harvest

MATTHEW 9:37–38 *Then He said to His disciples, "The harvest truly is plentiful, but the laborers are few. Therefore pray the Lord of the harvest to send out laborers into His harvest." (NKJV)*

As a "plentiful" harvest, the people represented a huge, critical task. The chief priests saw the crowd as "accursed" because they did "not know the law" (John 7:49 NKJV); the Pharisees considered them chaff to be burned up and destroyed.[1] Jesus saw them, not as objects of judgment and condemnation, moral refuse to be thrown away and burned, but as a <u>ripened crop</u> to be carefully, joyfully gathered and saved for God's good purposes.

Jesus ached deep inside to gather them to himself and to be their shepherd. However, there was one urgent need if this was to be accomplished: enough workers (Matthew 9:37). While physically among us, his was a single voice that could not possibly reach all the people who were ready to respond.

> ### what others say
>
> **Robert E. Coleman**
>
> Like a mother eagle teaching her young to fly by pushing them out of the nest, Jesus pushed his disciples out into the world to try their own wings.[2]

As they prayed, their hearts would share his concern. They would begin to see the task from his perspective. By the time he sent them out, they would not be draftees, but <u>volunteers</u>.

Offense! Offense!

MATTHEW 10:1, 7–8 *And when He had called His twelve disciples to Him, He gave them power over unclean spirits, to cast them out, and to heal all kinds of sickness and all kinds of disease . . . [Jesus commanded them, saying,] "As you go, preach, saying, 'The kingdom of heaven is at hand.' Heal the sick, cleanse the lepers, raise the dead, cast out demons. Freely you have received, freely give." (NKJV)*

Jesus gathered his twelve recruits for a strategy briefing. His instructions pulled together the things he'd been showing them by example all the time they'd been together. He specifically deputized them to do his work, assuring them they possessed the **authority** and **power** needed to do it.

Assault Strategy

> MATTHEW 10:11–14 *Now whatever city or town you enter, inquire who in it is **worthy**, and stay there till you go out. And when you go into a household, **greet it**. If the household is worthy, let your peace come upon it. But if it is not worthy, **let your peace return** to you. And whoever will not receive you nor hear your words, when you depart from that house or city, shake off the dust from your feet. (NKJV)*

Jesus's assault strategy was to concentrate the most energy on receptive individuals and families. This requires discernment and sensitivity. Generally, if the <u>door is open</u> to the witness, it is not closed to Christ. The Christian worker's primary concentration is to be on people most likely to respond positively, to positively influence their neighbors, and to continue the work after the evangelists leave.

No Pain, No Gain

> MATTHEW 10:16–17 *Behold, I send you out as sheep in the midst of wolves. Therefore be wise as serpents and harmless as doves. But beware of men, for they will deliver you up to councils and scourge you in their synagogues. (NKJV)*

Jesus did not sugarcoat the hardships his witnesses would face. Every prediction he made ultimately came true, if not on this trip, then later in the course of their Christian service. This short-term missionary jaunt in Galilee was the start of the toughest job these men had ever undertaken. But he wasn't a glutton for punishment. He wanted them to be "wise" and avoid trouble if they could. He urged them to be "harmless" and not give their persecutors a legitimate reason to attack.

> **what others say**
>
> **J. I. Packer**
>
> For a final example and proof of the truth that following God's guidance brings trouble, look at the life of the Lord Jesus himself. No human life has ever been so completely guided by God, and no human being has ever qualified so comprehensively for the description "a <u>man of sorrows</u>."[3]

go to

door is open
Matthew 10:40–42;
Luke 10:5–7, 16

man of sorrows
Isaiah 53:3

authority
jurisdiction, freedom to act; Jesus's delegated authority

power
spiritual energy to meet each challenge

worthy
receptive, welcoming, willing to listen

greet it
Shalom: peace, health, prosperity, God's blessing

let your peace return
withhold God's blessing

loses his life
Luke 14:26–27

will find it
Matthew 5:10–12;
Luke 6:22–23

Judas of Galilee
Acts 5:37

Swords in the Family Room

> MATTHEW 10:34–37 *Do not think that I came to bring peace on earth. I did not come to bring peace but a sword. For I have come to "set a man against his father, a daughter against her mother, and a daughter-in-law against her mother-in-law"; and "a man's enemies will be those of his own household." He who loves father or mother more than Me is not worthy of Me. And he who loves son or daughter more than Me is not worthy of Me.* (NKJV)

The cost of throwing in with Jesus Christ is revealed in startling reality when Jesus reminds his men that the message they are being sent to preach can be painfully divisive and will demand total commitment.

They can expect splits in the family tree. Since Christ's invitation is to repentance (the forsaking of sin), and since the kingdom lifestyle is so revolutionary and demands such sweeping changes in values, priorities, and personal relationships, it is inevitable that family feathers will be ruffled. Anyone digging in against change is going to be deeply disturbed when someone close to them embraces Jesus, begins to try to live by Jesus's ideas, and tells others about it. To emphasize his point, Jesus quotes Micah 7:6.

The High Cost of Winning

> MATTHEW 10:38–39 *And he who does not take his cross and follow after Me is not worthy of Me. He who finds his life will lose it, and he who <u>loses his life</u> for My sake <u>will find it</u>.* (NKJV)

"Total commitment" is a phrase tossed around glibly in athletic and military circles. No one ever called for a commitment more total than Jesus did. From the men about to take his kingdom dream to the cities of Galilee, he demanded the ultimate.

Galileans listening to Jesus say these words had vivid images of the cross in their minds. A few years before, the Romans had crushed a rebellion led by <u>Judas of Galilee</u>. In reprisal, the Roman general Varus crucified two thousand Galileans and lined the roads of Galilee with their crosses. Now Jesus's friends were being told that following him was going to be no less costly. For every man or woman who joined his uprising, there awaited . . . a cross!

Two by Two

MARK 6:7 *And He called the twelve to Himself, and began to send them out two by two, and gave them power over unclean spirits. (NKJV)*

The success of the Jesus-teams was phenomenal. As Jesus's twelve fledgling ambassadors, in teams of two, fanned out over the hills and villages of Galilee, the impact of their ministry and of Jesus himself became, more than ever, the talk of the province. The disciples were powerfully preaching the gospel of the kingdom and calling people to turn from their sins (Mark 6:12). Demons were releasing their hold on their victims. The sick were healed (6:13). The impact of Jesus was being multiplied through his men.

Flashback: The Courage and Arrest of Big John the Baptist

MARK 6:14–16 *Now King Herod heard of Him, for His name had become well known. And he said, "John the Baptist is risen from the dead, and therefore these powers are at work in him." Others said, "It is Elijah." And others said, "It is the Prophet, or like one of the prophets." But when Herod heard, he said, "This is John, whom I beheaded; he has been raised from the dead!" (NKJV)*

At this point in the story, Matthew and Mark pause for a flashback. The last time we heard from John the Baptist he was cooling his heels in the dungeon at Herod's Machaerus Castle. Herod had arrested him for publicly pointing the finger at the "king" and his new wife, Herodias, whom he had seduced and stolen from his brother Philip. In the process, Herod had divorced his legitimate wife to clear the way for the new romance. John had dared to declare the whole sordid affair illegal!

Herodias never forgave him. She would not be happy until John was dead. Herod too wanted John dead (Matthew 14:5), but he feared the prophet's political influence and, superstitiously, his spiritual power. So he kept John alive, albeit in prison. He was there for a year and a half.

When Salome Danced

MATTHEW 14:6–7 *But when Herod's birthday was celebrated, the daughter of Herodias danced before them and pleased Herod. Therefore he promised with an oath to give her whatever she might ask. (NKJV)*

At Herod's birthday party, Herodias's beautiful and voluptuous young daughter, Salome, danced for the king and his invited guests. In an expansive statement of inebriated and sexually aroused appreciation (and to impress the high mucky-mucks at the party), the tetrarch issued the above oath, offering the girl "up to half my kingdom" (Mark 6:23 NKJV).

After conferring with her mother, Herodias, Salome immediately returned to the banquet hall with her request: "I want you to give me at once the head of John the Baptist on a platter" (Mark 6:25 NKJV). Herod kept his promise. The illustrious career of Christ's forerunner came to a sudden end on the chopping block, but his influence lives today.

Chapter Wrap-Up

- Filled with compassion for the lost, harassed, and helpless crowds, Jesus asked his disciples to pray for workers to send into the fields to "harvest" those willing to be saved. (Matthew 9:35–38)

- Jesus gathered his disciples and gave them instructions on how to go throughout Galilee preaching the message of the kingdom and carrying on his work, what to expect in the way of opposition, and their need for total commitment. (Matthew 10:1–42)

- He sent them out on their mission in teams of two. (Mark 6:7)

- Many people, including King Herod, misread the effective evangelism and miracles done by Jesus and his men as evidence that the martyred John the Baptist had returned from the dead. (Mark 6:14–16)

Study Questions

1. What convinced Jesus the crowds needed a shepherd (Matthew 9:36)? Describe his feelings toward people. What was the first thing he asked his disciples to do about the need?

2. What did Jesus mean when he told his disciples he was sending them out "like sheep in the midst of wolves"? (Matthew 10:16–17)

3. How has Christ's teaching united your family? How has it divided your family? (Matthew 10:34–37)

4. Who did King Herod think Jesus was when his disciples fanned out across Galilee, casting out demons and preaching the kingdom of God? What had he done that was probably bothering his conscience?

Chapter 18: Good Bread

Chapter Highlights:
- Power Lunch
- The Royalist Movement
- Sea Walker
- Shock Diet for Malnourished Spirits

Let's Get Started

The Jewish people despised the Roman conquerors more than most conquered countries. There was always an insurrection brewing somewhere in Israel. Nowhere was anti-Roman sentiment more explosive than in Galilee. The atmosphere of political unrest had a negative effect on trade. Goods did not flow to Israel as freely as to other parts of the empire. High taxation and reluctant trade assured that food would always be in short supply. Prices were high. The rich, as usual, had all they needed. The poor, always the first to suffer under such conditions, existed on the brink of starvation.

other side
where Jordan flows into northern end of Lake Galilee

Power Lunch

> **MARK 6:34–36** *And Jesus, when He came out, saw a great multitude and was moved with compassion for them, because they were like sheep not having a shepherd. So He began to teach them many things. When the day was now far spent, His disciples came to Him and said, "This is a deserted place, and already the hour is late. Send them away, that they may go into the surrounding country and villages and buy themselves bread; for they have nothing to eat." (NKJV)*

gospel harmony

Matthew 14:13–21
Mark 6:30–44
Luke 9:10–17
John 6:1–14

Because of the clamoring crowds, Jesus and his apostolic teams, who had just returned from their preaching sweep of Galilee, couldn't find time to be alone to share what they'd experienced. Jesus suggested a getaway to the desolate hill country north of the Sea of Galilee (see Illustration #5).

As they boarded a fishing boat to escape across the lake, someone saw them. Word of their departure and direction spread like wildfire and, by the time they got to the **other side**, a crowd was waiting onshore. Even though his plan for time alone with his disciples was disrupted, Jesus's compassion for the crowds moved him to temporarily lay aside retreat plans for his two primary people-helping ministries—teaching and healing.

Philip
John 1:44; 6:5

their own faith
1 Peter 1:6–7

The Miracle Picnic

Each Gospel storyteller—Matthew, Mark, Luke, and John—gives details not noticed by the others. All four number the crowd at five thousand men. Many may have been armed,[1] thinking Jesus was a "new Moses" who would lead in a war of liberation from Roman oppression. Matthew adds that this number did not include women and children. The actual size of the crowd has been estimated at between ten thousand and fifteen thousand, depending on how many women and children were there. As the day wore on and the crowd stayed, his disciples suggested Jesus send them into neighboring villages to buy food. He turned to <u>Philip</u>, who was from the area, and asked where food might be purchased to feed the crowd.

Jesus knew what he was going to do. His question was designed to reveal to Philip and the others the strength of <u>their own faith</u>.

Illustration #5
Sea of Galilee—Map of the Sea of Galilee shows the locations of many of Jesus's miracles, including the feeding of the five thousand and his walk on water, as well as his bread-of-life conversations.

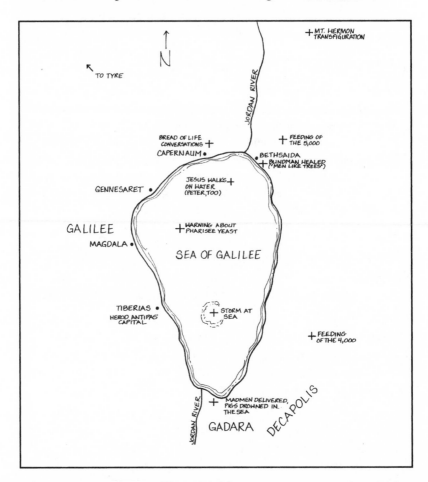

Two Responses Are Noted:

1. The response of hopelessness based on mathematical calculation. Philip says, "Two hundred denarii worth of bread is not sufficient for them, that every one of them may have a little" (John 6:7 NKJV; Mark 6:37).

2. The response of hopelessness based on a survey of available resources. Andrew says, "There is a lad here who has five **barley loaves** and two **small fish**, but what are they among so many?" (John 6:8–9 NKJV). The boy may have come from nearby Bethsaida on his way to take supper to his father or brothers herding sheep in the hills.

Jesus took the loaves in his hands and offered thanks as if presiding over a family dinner. Then he broke the bread and fish (Luke 9:16) and handed the pieces to the Twelve to distribute to the people who were seated in the soft grass. Everyone in the crowd, from all economic levels, was **"filled"** (Matthew 14:20; Mark 6:42; Luke 9:17; John 6:12).

To avoid waste of God's gifts and to emphasize the preciousness of food, after everyone had eaten his fill, the disciples collected twelve baskets of leftovers!

go to

the Prophet
Deuteronomy
18:15–19

barley loaves
rough bread of the poor; three loaves made an adult's meal

small fish
dried or pickled, to help the barley bread go down

filled
original word means not a token meal but an abundant feast

the Prophet
catchphrase for Moses-like leader expected in the last days

---

what others say

Saint Augustine

Certainly the government of the whole world is a greater miracle than the satisfying of 5,000 men with 5 loaves; and yet no man wonders at the former; but the latter men wonder at, not because it is greater, but because it is rare. For who even now feeds the whole world, but he who creates the cornfield from a few grains?[2]

The Royalist Movement

JOHN 6:14 *Then those men, when they had seen the sign that Jesus did, said, "This is truly **the Prophet** who is to come into the world." (NKJV)*

Powerful forces at work in first-century Jewish society shaped the people's response to the supernatural supper. Many battled the per-

go to

old temptation
Matthew 4:1–7;
Luke 4:5–8

at his feet
Mark 12:12;
Luke 20:19;
John 12:12–13, 19

departed
mild word for "fled"

sistent problem of poverty and hunger. The Jews hated the Roman occupation of Israel. Jewish teachers reminded the people of the messianic prophecies.

Add to these a general confusion about the miracle in which they had just participated. The feeding of the five thousand demonstrated Jesus's phenomenal ability to supply human needs—and perhaps, they reasoned, this also meant he could lift them out of near-starvation and grinding poverty. Jesus intended the miracle of the loaves and fishes to do four things:

1. To feed more than five thousand hungry people

2. To be a sign to people expecting Messiah's arrival that he was the One

3. To open the way to introduce himself as the Bread of Life

4. To show that the kingdom of God had arrived

The Case of the Reluctant Royal

JOHN 6:15 *Therefore when Jesus perceived that they were about to come and take Him by force to make Him king, He **departed** again to the mountain by Himself alone.* (NKJV)

To the young Messiah, this royalist movement was neither a compliment nor an asset. It was a "summer rerun" of an old temptation—the enticing prospect of becoming ruler of the world in some way other than the Father's plan, which involved the Cross. Whenever such temptations came, Jesus knew what to do. He climbed a mountain . . . "to pray" (Mark 6:46 NKJV).

what others say

Robert E. Coleman

If Jesus had only accommodated himself to their natural appetites, the multitudes would have been at his feet and the cross could have been avoided . . . He could have set himself upon the throne of the world. Was not this his temptation in the wilderness? That he viewed the suggestion as a satanic deception poses a bewildering problem for those activists who see his mission only in terms of social and political reformation.[3]

Sea Walker

fourth watch
3:00 to 6:00 a.m.

Moving quickly to keep them from getting trapped in royalist politics, Jesus directed them to get into the boat and to proceed to the other side of the lake. It was getting dark when they took oars in hand and headed out across the water. Jesus didn't go with them—he needed time on the mountain.

The disciples had rowed about three miles when an unpredictable weather pattern struck from the west, and they found themselves rowing hard against the wind (John 6:18). Sometime during "the **fourth watch** of the night" (Mark 6:48 NKJV), the struggling oarsmen saw a terrifying sight: In a flash of lightning or moonlight, they caught sight of a lone ghostly figure walking on top of the water, catching up to them! The disciples cried out in fear. "But immediately He talked with them and said to them, 'Be of good cheer! It is I; do not be afraid'" (Mark 6:50 NKJV).

Dancing, Dancing, Over the Bounding Main

> MATTHEW 14:28–29 *And Peter answered Him and said, "Lord, if it is You, command me to come to You on the water." So He said, "Come." And when Peter had come down out of the boat, he walked on the water to go to Jesus. (NKJV)*

Peter climbed over the side and found himself walking on top of the water, just like Jesus! What faith! But wait. What's this? Peter, God's "man of faith and power" looked around as he walked with Jesus on the surface of the water. The wind whipped the waves. Suddenly fear took the faith right out of his heart! He began to sink.

"Lord, save me!" he screamed in desperation (Matthew 14:30 NKJV). Jesus reached out his hand and pulled Peter to safety, giving him a mild reprimand for his doubt.

With Eyes (and Mouths) Wide Open

> MATTHEW 14:33 *Then those who were in the boat came and worshiped Him, saying, "Truly You are the Son of God." (NKJV)*

What did the Twelve do after seeing Jesus and Peter walk on the water? What would you do? They got on their knees right then and there and worshiped Jesus!

go to

drinking blood
Leviticus 17:10–14

what others say

Oswald Chambers

There is no delusion in Christian experience, it begins outside me by creating in me an enormous craving, akin to thirst or to hunger. This craving is created by the reality of the Redemption, not by my penetrating insight, but by what John calls "the drawing of the Father" (John 6:44).[4]

Shock Diet for Malnourished Spirits

JOHN 6:51–57 *"I am the living bread which came down from heaven. If anyone eats of this bread, he will live forever; and the bread that I shall give is My flesh, which I shall give for the life of the world." The Jews therefore quarreled among themselves, saying, "How can this Man give us His flesh to eat?" Then Jesus said to them, "Most assuredly, I say to you, unless you eat the flesh of the Son of Man and drink His blood, you have no life in you. Whoever eats My flesh and drinks My blood has eternal life, and I will raise him up at the last day. For My flesh is food indeed, and My blood is drink indeed. He who eats My flesh and drinks My blood abides in Me, and I in him. As the living Father sent Me, and I live because of the Father, so he who feeds on Me will live because of Me." (NKJV)*

What did Jesus mean? These are explosive pictures of Christian faith, and they are shocking enough to emphasize the radical nature of what it means to live by faith in Jesus. "Eating his flesh" and "drinking his blood" are metaphors for the real spiritual processes involved in being a Christian.

The response among the Galileans listening to Jesus was shock and revulsion. The Old Testament taught clearly that <u>drinking blood</u> was absolutely forbidden. Obviously, Jesus's statements were never meant to be taken literally, but figuratively. But to the Jews, even the thought of drinking blood was repulsive. Even non-Jews often find these words offensive, always puzzling.

key point

what others say

Lawrence O. Richards

The relationship with Christ symbolized by eating his flesh is initiated and sustained by faith's participation in all that Jesus is and all he has done for us . . . By faith we do participate in Jesus' death and resurrection. We have partaken of his body and blood, and received his gift of eternal life.[5]

No Place I'd Rather Be

JOHN 6:67–69 *Then Jesus said to the twelve, "Do you also want to go away?" But Simon Peter answered Him, "Lord, to whom shall we go? You have the words of eternal life. Also we have come to believe and know that You are the Christ, the Son of the living God." (NKJV)*

Peter's answer does not mean all his questions were answered. But it expresses a genuine conviction that gripped him and the others. And it glows as the brightest spot in this story.

Chapter Wrap-Up

- Jesus fed a crowd of more than five thousand people a satisfying meal using only a little boy's lunch—five barley loaves and two small fish. (Mark 6:30–44)

- Many in the crowd wanted to crown Jesus king, seeing in him the solution to their economic problems and a military-political deliverer from Roman rule. Politics was not on Jesus's kingdom agenda. He escaped to a mountain to pray. (John 6:14–15)

- Jesus's disciples got into a boat to return to Capernaum and got caught in a storm. As they struggled against the wind, Jesus came to them, walking on top of the water. (Matthew 14:22–34)

- When Jesus used the metaphor of eating his flesh and drinking his blood to press the people's need to take him into their lives and depend on him for daily spiritual sustenance, many deserted him. The Twelve reaffirmed their commitment to be with him. (John 6:52–69)

Study Questions

1. What food was available for Jesus to use in feeding the five thousand? With whom do you most identify in this story? (a) The crowd: waiting for a miracle, (b) Philip: crunching the numbers and overwhelmed, (c) Andrew: coming up short, or (d) the boy with the lunch: if Jesus wants it he can have it.

2. Can you imagine being in Peter's place and walking on the water with Jesus? What would your thoughts be at that moment?

3. What did Jesus mean when he told his followers they must eat his flesh and drink his blood?

Chapter 19: Religion Versus Reality

Let's Get Started

In the discussions growing out of the feeding of the five thousand (John 6), Jesus carried his radical ideas to still more disconcerting depths. He declared that he was the living bread, which provided spiritual sustenance for a life-giving relationship with God, and that to find eternal life, people needed to take him into their lives and feed on him. This bold claim added fuel to his enemies' fire. The chasm between Jesus and the authorities became a gaping canyon. Many rank-and-file Jews joined their leaders in opposing the brash young rabble-rouser. Even the enthusiasm of many of Jesus's friends cooled (John 6:66).

hypocrites
Greek meaning: "actors in a play"; pretenders

Tradition Versus Reality

> **MARK 7:5** *Then the Pharisees and scribes asked Him, "Why do Your disciples not walk according to the tradition of the elders, but eat bread with unwashed hands?" (NKJV)*

Matthew 15:1–20
Mark 7:1–23

Pharisees and lawyers came from Jerusalem intent on exposing Jesus and his followers as lawbreakers. Everywhere he went these religious scalp hunters were there, watching. In a classic "Aha!" moment, they saw the disciples eating without the elaborate hand-washing ceremony observed by strict Jews. They confronted Jesus about this unthinkable breach of etiquette and religious correctness. It was not an issue of hygiene or of true spirituality, but of over-scrupulous, legalistic, meaningless religious minutiae.

Nothing angered Jesus like religious nit-picking, which served no true spiritual purpose. You can almost see him shaking his head in disgust.

The Love Ban

> **MARK 7:6–9** *He answered and said to them, "Well did Isaiah prophesy of you **hypocrites**, as it is written:*

'This people honors Me with their lips,
But their heart is far from Me.
And in vain they worship Me,
Teaching as doctrines the commandments of men.'
"For laying aside the commandment of God, you hold the tra-
dition of men—the washing of pitchers and cups, and many
other such things you do." He said to them, "All too well you
reject the commandment of God, that you may keep your tradi-
tion." (NKJV)

In a tone tinged with sarcasm, Jesus turned the spotlight of truth on a glaring hypocrisy practiced by these self-appointed religious "policemen." He quoted one of the Ten Commandments: "Honor your father and your mother" (Mark 7:10 NKJV; Exodus 20:12). God considered the breaking of that particular mandate so serious, Jesus reminded them, that he prescribed the death penalty for anyone "who **curses** father or mother" (Mark 7:10 NKJV; Exodus 21:17).

Jesus blew them out of the water with his exposé of a common practice that broke the commandment to honor one's parents all to smithereens. In spite of what the Law of God said, the traditions provided a completely legal way to avoid the expense of caring for one's father and mother. All you had to do was announce to your parents that what you had been saving to help them was "**corban**." This meant it now belonged to God and was no longer available for nonreligious purposes!

The Rule of Corban was great for the temple treasury, but it allowed or forced some people to break one of God's most precious commandments! Jesus called it by its real name—hypocrisy—and used it as an example of how religious people honor man-concocted traditions above God's Law!

what others say

Dan McCartney and Charles Clayton

Tradition was quite binding, even blinding, in the Judaism of Jesus' day . . . Tradition can, if not continually challenged, lull people into a comfortable, dogmatic slumber from which they may never awake.[1]

A Clean Heart

> **MARK 7:15** *There is nothing that enters a man from outside which can defile him; but the things which come out of him, those are the things that defile a man.* (NKJV)

the heart of men
Jeremiah 17:9;
Romans 3:9–18;
Galatians 5:19–21

the five thousand
Matthew 14:15–21;
Mark 6:35–44;
Luke 9:12–17;
John 6:4–13

madman
Mark 5:18–20;
Luke 8:38–39

Later, alone with his disciples, Jesus said: "Do you not perceive that whatever enters a man from outside cannot defile him, because it does not enter his heart but his stomach, and is eliminated, thus purifying all foods?" (Mark 7:18–19 NKJV).

What Jesus was really concerned about was a person's heart, so he explained it more: "What comes out of a man, that defiles a man. For from within, out of <u>the heart of men</u>, proceed evil thoughts, adulteries, fornications, murders, thefts, covetousness, wickedness, deceit, lewdness, an evil eye, blasphemy, pride, foolishness. All these evil things come from within and defile a man" (Mark 7:20–23 NKJV).

Déjà Vu

> **MATTHEW 15:35–37** *So He commanded the multitude to sit down on the ground. And He took the seven loaves and the fish and gave thanks, broke them and gave them to His disciples; and the disciples gave to the multitude. So they all ate and were filled, and they took up seven large baskets full of the fragments that were left.* (NKJV)

Two New Testament historians report a second incident in which Jesus fed a large crowd with a tiny amount of food. The differences between this miracle meal multiplication and the feeding of <u>the five thousand</u> include the following:

- This time the crowd was four thousand men, plus women and children (Matthew 15:38).

- The scene was a desolate area in Decapolis, east of Galilee (Mark 7:31), a province with a mixed Jewish-Gentile population. Some think the liberated <u>madman</u> whom Jesus healed helped bring this crowd together.

- This time the people had gone three days without food (Mark 8:2).

- The number of loaves to work with this time was "seven, and a few little fish" (Matthew 15:34 NKJV).

go to

escape
Acts 9:23–25

Magdalene
Luke 8:1–3

Magdala
Magadan (Matthew
15:39) or
Dalmanutha (Mark
8:10)

Mary Magdalene
woman from whom
Jesus cast seven
devils

- The leftovers filled seven baskets (Matthew 15:37). The word for basket is different this time. The baskets used to gather leftovers after the five thousand were fed were long, narrow-necked baskets in which Jews carried food when they traveled. This time, the basket is the same as the one used to help Paul <u>escape</u> over the Damascus wall—large, open at the top, and used mainly by Gentiles.

- The motivation for both miracles was Christ's compassion for the hungry (Matthew 14:14; 15:32; Mark 6:34; 8:2).

- It is possible this picnic in the desert included Gentiles and Jews together—a symbol that the time was coming when non-Jews would be included in the gospel.

what others say

Lawrence O. Richards

The need for food is one of the most basic of human needs. Jesus was not only concerned about people's spiritual condition, he was moved by compassion for physical hunger as well. We cannot represent Jesus adequately if we are moved only by the need to win lost souls. To represent Jesus we must be as concerned for the hungry, the homeless, and the oppressed as our Lord was for the hungry multitudes.[2]

After the four thousand were well fed and sent home, Jesus and his men once again sailed across the lake, this time at its widest part, and landed near the lakeshore town of **Magdala**, home of **Mary Magdalene**.

The Odd Couple

Jesus's perennial detractors, the Pharisees, were waiting for him. This time, they were joined by the Sadducees, evidence that a rather strange political alliance had been formed to oppose him. Often the Pharisees appeared with their legalistic mentors, the lawyers (scribes). But to team up with the Sadducees would have required both a theological and a practical stretch.

And Herodians Make Three

The fact that the Pharisees and Sadducees, two widely divergent groups, could join forces shows how determined they were to get rid of Jesus. In fact, this theological odd couple was joined by the Herodians—a political party with little concern for theology.

Back in the boat headed across Galilee, this time for Bethsaida on the north shore, Jesus reflected on the most recent confrontation with the developing conspiracy against him. He warned his disciples about the three groups aligned against him.

Herodians
Matthew 22:16–17;
Mark 3:6; 8:15;
12:13

encourage
Mark 5:28;
Acts 5:15; 19:12

Seeing People as Walking Trees

> **MARK 8:22–24** *Then He came to Bethsaida; and they brought a blind man to Him, and begged Him to touch him. So He took the blind man by the hand and led him out of the town. And when He had spit on his eyes and put His hands on him, He asked him if he saw anything. And he looked up and said, "I see men like trees, walking." (NKJV)*

When the boat arrived at Bethsaida, someone brought a blind man with the request that Jesus "touch him." Jesus took him outside the town and "spit on his eyes." The New Testament historians report Jesus using spit in a healing process three times:

1. In taking away a speech impediment (Mark 7:33)

2. In restoring sight to a man born blind (John 9:6)

3. In restoring sight to this blind man (Mark 8:23)

People in the past thought human saliva had healing properties. We know that spit alone can't make a blind man see, but Jesus used it as a way to encourage the man's faith for healing.

This is the only miracle Jesus performed that happened in two stages. In the first stage (after Jesus's first touch), the man said, "I see men like trees, walking" (Mark 8:24 NKJV). In the second stage (after Jesus's second touch), the Bible reports, "He was restored and saw everyone clearly" (8:25 NKJV).

Chapter Wrap-Up

- Jesus's enemies accused Jesus of letting his disciples eat without the ceremonial hand-washings prescribed by tradition. He turned their accusations against them, showing how their man-made traditions were forcing people to break the laws of God. (Mark 7:1–13)

- Food, Jesus declared, has nothing to do with a person's spiritual purity. What matters is what is in the person's heart. A heart full of sin can only express itself in outward sin. Food is not a spiritual issue. All foods are ceremonially clean. (Mark 7:14–23)

- On returning to Galilee from Phoenicia, Jesus did many healing miracles and, in a repeat performance of the feeding of the five thousand, satisfied the hunger of a crowd of four thousand using a tiny amount of food. (Mark 7:31–8:10)

- The religious and political forces lining up against Jesus began to solidify, bringing together divergent groups whose only bond was refusal to accept him as Messiah. He warned his disciples to beware of letting their thinking become corrupted by these groups. (Mark 8:10–21)

Study Questions

1. What was Jesus's chief objection to the traditions of the Pharisees and lawyers? What did he call them?

2. How does Jesus's idea of being "unclean" differ from that of the Pharisees?

3. Who were the three groups forming an alliance against Jesus?

4. List three times Jesus used spit in the performance of a healing miracle.

Part Four
TURN TOWARD THE CROSS

Chapter Highlights:
- "Who Am I?"
- The Destiny of Saviorhood
- The Splendor of the Son
- King of the Mountain

Chapter 20: Road to Messiahship and Discipleship

Let's Get Started

Five of the twelve disciples had been with the controversial Jesus most of the time since the day John the Baptist introduced him as "the Lamb of God" (John 1:36 NKJV). That was the first time any of them had met Jesus. But that very first day they confessed to believing some amazing things about him:

- "We have found the Messiah," Andrew told Peter (John 1:41 NKJV).

- Philip told Nathanael he believed Jesus was "Him of whom Moses in the law, and also the prophets, wrote" (John 1:45 NKJV).

- When Nathanael met Jesus he said, "You are the Son of God! You are the King of Israel!" (John 1:49 NKJV).

Did they, at that early date, really know what they were saying? Or were they just parroting things their mentor, John the Baptist, <u>had said</u>? The full significance of the words did not really soak in until they'd spent more than three years and had some amazing experiences with Jesus. But along the way, there were signs their faith was getting a tighter grip on their hearts.

go to

had said
Matthew 3:11–12;
John 1:15, 26–27,
29–34

"Who Am I?"

MATTHEW 16:13–16 *When Jesus came into the region of Caesarea Philippi, He asked His disciples, saying, "Who do men say that I, the Son of Man, am?" So they said, "Some say John the Baptist, some Elijah, and others Jeremiah or one of the prophets." He said to them, "But who do you say that I am?" Simon Peter answered and said, "You are the Christ, the Son of the living God." (NKJV)*

gospel harmony

Matthew 16:13–23
Mark 8:27–33
Luke 9:18–22
John 6:68–69;
20:21–23

Peter spoke first. Peter always spoke first. It was apparently a combination of a quick tongue and the ability to sense the consensus of the group, because nobody argued with him when he answered for

My Father
John 6:44–45, 63, 65

rock
Acts 4:8–12;
1 Corinthians 3:11;
Ephesians 2:19–22

anointed
"smeared with olive oil," symbol of authority to reign, minister, or prophesy

revealed
revelation; God's actions of self-disclosure

church
Greek: *ekklesia*, "called-out ones"

Hades
Greek: place of the dead; some translations say "hell"

keys
authority

them all: "You are the Christ, the Son of the living God" (Matthew 16:16 NKJV).

"Christ" and "Messiah" are the same word in Greek and Hebrew. Both mean "**Anointed** One." Jesus is royalty—God's chosen Savior-King.

"Son of the living God"—Jesus claimed to be sent by God and that God was his Father. His followers came to recognize his special relationship with God as God's "one and only," God's Son and expression in a way no one else is God's Son and expression.

The Miracle of Faith

> MATTHEW 16:17 *Jesus answered and said to him, "Blessed are you, Simon Bar-Jonah, for flesh and blood has not **revealed** this to you, but* <u>*My Father*</u> *who is in heaven." (NKJV)*

Peter and others had said words before that sounded like these. What's the difference this time? This time Peter's statement of faith expressed a conviction planted deep in his heart, mind, and spirit by God himself. Such faith is a gift—even, we can say, a miracle—the miracle upon which the movement of Christ is founded.

Network on the Rocks

> MATTHEW 16:18–19 *And I also say to you that you are Peter, and on this rock I will build My **church**, and the gates of **Hades** shall not prevail against it. And I will give you the **keys** of the kingdom of heaven, and whatever you bind on earth will be bound in heaven, and whatever you loose on earth will be loosed in heaven. (NKJV)*

This is Jesus's first recorded mention of the church. He was not referring to the development of an organization or institution, but to the new fellowship of people who believed in him—the new shape the Jesus movement would take—a new network of relationships with his committed followers at its core.

key point

Some have thought Jesus was saying that Peter was the rock on which Jesus would build his church. In fact, the solid <u>rock</u> on which the church is built is none other than Jesus Christ himself. Peter and the other apostles are among the first stones laid on the foundation, but the foundation is Christ.

Keep This Under Your Hat!

MATTHEW 16:20 *Then He commanded His disciples that they should tell no one that He was Jesus the Christ.* (NKJV)

spiritual conquest
2 Corinthians 10:3–5

saviorhood
Isaiah 53;
Matthew 1:21

spiritual conquest
not physical warfare
but spiritual warfare

They were convinced he was the Messiah. But as real as their conviction was, their understanding was deeply flawed. Their kingdom dreams did not factor in the Cross. Jesus couldn't have them stirring up ill-timed hopes of a conqueror who would drive the Romans into the sea when God's timetable called first for **spiritual conquest** that required the Messiah's death! Unless they understood, their witness would only result in disillusioned converts.

The Destiny of Saviorhood

MATTHEW 16:21 *From that time Jesus began to show to His disciples that He must go to Jerusalem, and suffer many things from the elders and chief priests and scribes, and be killed, and be raised the third day.* (NKJV)

Before they could tell the world of his messiahship, they had to own the necessity of his <u>saviorhood</u>. Jesus's turn toward the cross was calculated, deliberate. Matthew, Mark, and Luke each include the word "must" in their description of what he told them about his coming death. The original word for "must" is *dei*, meaning legally or morally binding. It's used one hundred times in the New Testament to indicate necessity imposed by the will of God. Jesus believed rejection, death, and resurrection were his destiny.

> ### what others say
>
> **Robert E. Coleman**
>
> His [Jesus's] life was ordered by his objective. Everything he did and said contributed to the ultimate purpose of his life. Not for one moment did Jesus lose sight of his goal. Nothing was haphazard about his life—no wasted energy, no idle words. He was on business for God. He lived, he died, and he rose again according to schedule. Like a general plotting his course of battle, the Son of God calculated to win . . . Weighing every alternative and variable factor in human experience, he conceived a plan that would not fail.[1]

go to

out of my way
Matthew 4:10

daily
Luke 9:23;
1 Corinthians
15:30–32

self-denial
disown, renounce
one's own plans and
priorities to commit
to the will of God

crucifixion
identification with
Jesus

six days
between above
teaching and this
event

Say It Isn't So!

In Matthew's record, Peter, who'd just made the stunning confession of faith in Jesus's messiahship, took Jesus aside and started to scold him for talking about rejection and death. How negative! Such an idea was incompatible with Peter's concept of messiahship.

"Far be it from You, Lord; this shall not happen to You!" (Matthew 16:22 NKJV).

Jesus whirled around and stared at his disciples. He spoke sharply to Peter. "Get <u>out of my way</u>, Satan! You aren't looking at things from God's perspective, but from man's!" (Matthew 16:23, paraphrased).

The Road of Discipleship

MATTHEW 16:24–26 *Then Jesus said to His disciples, "If anyone desires to come after Me, let him deny himself, and take up his cross, and follow Me. For whoever desires to save his life will lose it, but whoever loses his life for My sake will find it. For what profit is it to a man if he gains the whole world, and loses his own soul? Or what will a man give in exchange for his soul?" (NKJV)*

These words were for everyone—disciples and people thinking about becoming disciples. The call to discipleship has no fine print requiring a magnifying glass to read. Followers of Jesus must know what they are getting into. Suffering and death in the course of doing God's will were his destiny as Messiah. It was also the destiny of anyone who joined him. The "must" of the cross applies as surely to followers as to their Leader. Follow Jesus and you find yourself picking up your cross <u>daily</u> and marching beside him up the road of **self-denial** and **crucifixion**, willing to face rejection, suffering, and death.

The Splendor of the Son

MATTHEW 17:1–3 *Now after **six days** Jesus took Peter, James, and John his brother, led them up on a high mountain by themselves; and He was transfigured before them. His face shone like the sun, and His clothes became as white as the light. And behold, Moses and Elijah appeared to them, talking with Him. (NKJV)*

Jesus took Peter, James, and John up this mountain to pray (Luke 9:28). They must have spent the night on the mountain. It would have taken all day to reach the top, and Luke says the disciples were overcome with sleep.

While Jesus prayed, his face and clothing began to <u>glow</u>. This is described as being **transfigured**.

Two men they intuitively recognized as Moses and Elijah appeared and talked with Jesus. Moses had led the Israelites out of slavery in Egypt to Mount Sinai where God gave the Ten Commandments to his people. Elijah was a prophet sent by God to confront a wicked king and idol worshippers in a contest to call fire from heaven.

Luke, in his account, tells what the two historical faith heroes talked about: "[They spoke] of His **decease** which He was about to accomplish at Jerusalem" (Luke 9:31 NKJV).

glow
Exodus 34:29–35

decease
John 16:7

cloud
Exodus 40:34–38;
2 Chronicles
5:13–6:2

transfigured
changed in form

decease
coming events—
confrontation with
authorities, death on
the cross, resurrec-
tion, ascension

tabernacles
temporary huts used
at the Feast of
Tabernacles

Supremacy of the Son

The bright-as-sun light roused the sleeping disciples (Luke 9:32). Their eyes popped open to the dazzling sight of Jesus like they'd never seen him before, with Moses and Elijah basking in his radiance. Surrounded by sunlight-power radiance, a 40-watt bulb went on over Peter's inventive head! He had an idea whose brilliance he was sure matched the brilliance of the vision he was seeing.

"Master, it is good for us to be here; and let us make three **tabernacles**: one for You, one for Moses, and one for Elijah" (Luke 9:33 NKJV). Three "shrines" for the three greats! What a brainstorm! "Not knowing what he said," Luke perceptively adds of Peter.

Listen Up and Calm Down

LUKE 9:34–35 *While [Peter] was saying this, a cloud came and overshadowed them; and they were fearful as they entered the cloud. And a voice came out of the <u>cloud</u>, saying, "This is My beloved Son. Hear Him!" (NKJV)*

Matthew tells that at the sound of the voice, Peter, James, and John, terrified, fell to the ground, facedown. As they lay there, scared to look, Jesus touched them and told them to get up and not

spiritual pride
Mark 9:33–42;
Matthew 20:20–21

authority
Matthew 10:1, 8;
Luke 9:1

histrionics
deliberate acting

spirit
evil spirit, demon

to be afraid (Matthew 17:6–7). When they got courage enough for a peek, "Jesus was found alone" (Luke 9:36 NKJV).

No Bragging Allowed

Again, Jesus told the three not to tell anyone what they had seen, until after his resurrection (Matthew 17:9). It would be a hard secret to keep. The difficulty of keeping this mountaintop experience to themselves may have contributed to some of the incidents that took place after they came down from the mountain—incidents that might have been triggered by spiritual pride.

You Can't Win 'Em All!

> MATTHEW 17:14–16 *And when they had come to the multitude, a man came to Him, kneeling down to Him and saying, "Lord, have mercy on my son, for he is an epileptic and suffers severely; for he often falls into the fire and often into the water. So I brought him to Your disciples, but they could not cure him."* (NKJV)

The scene was chaotic (Mark 9:14–18). Even though Jesus had given them authority to deal with evil spirits and they had some success in doing so, the nine apostles waiting in the valley were unable to deal with this one. The young Messiah took control and, in spite of the atmosphere of embarrassment, doubt, and panic, he "rebuked the demon" (Matthew 17:18 NKJV). With some last-gasp violent **histrionics**, the **spirit** left the boy at peace (Mark 9:26).

Later, in private, Jesus told the disciples that people can be set free from some kinds of evil spirits only through a process involving prayer and fasting on the part of spiritual helpers (Mark 9:28–29).

Temple Tax

> MATTHEW 17:24 *When they had come to Capernaum, those who received the temple tax came to Peter and said, "Does Your Teacher not pay the temple tax?"* (NKJV)

Jesus and his men returned to Capernaum just in time to become embroiled in the down-and-dirty world of taxes. The temple tax collectors were in town. They collared Peter and asked about "the **temple tax**." There's a pretty good chance the questioners, part of the anti-Jesus religious establishment, were hoping the answer would be "no." This would give them something else for which to accuse Jesus.

Peter took the matter to Jesus, who turned it into a teaching opportunity, giving Peter two things: (1) freedom from the obligation of the outdated religious system being replaced with personal relationship with God through Christ, on the basis of faith, and (2) God's supply of something to give.

At Jesus's instruction, Peter went to the sea and threw in a hook and line. A fish grabbed the bait, and Peter reeled it in. In the fish's mouth were four drachmas—enough to pay both Jesus's and Peter's temple tax.

Calling them sons of the kingdom, Jesus indicated his followers were free from obligation to pay the temple tax. The **temple** was part of the outdated religious system. In the new system the temple would be obsolete. On the other hand, sons of the kingdom were also free to pay the temple tax if they chose to, out of love for Jewish contemporaries who might otherwise be offended.

King of the Mountain

> **MARK 9:33–35** *Then He came to Capernaum. And when He was in the house He asked them, "What was it you disputed among yourselves on the road?" But they kept silent, for on the road they had disputed among themselves who would be the greatest. And He sat down, called the twelve, and said to them, "If anyone desires to be first, he shall be last of all and servant of all." (NKJV)*

A really childish game of "king of the mountain" erupted among the Twelve on the road to Capernaum. Wounded egos reacted to spiritual arrogance with jealousy and defensiveness. What resulted was that manly mix of bragging, put-downs, and spiritual "Can you top this?" that religious people engage in when their egos are threatened or they're struggling to gain position in the "pecking order."

temple tax
shekel annually (two days' wages), required of Jewish males over age nineteen

temple
the Jewish center of worship located in Jerusalem

Zealots
right-wing political
party committed to
the overthrow of
Roman occupation
forces

How to Be Great in the Kingdom

MATTHEW 18:2–4 *Then Jesus called a little child to Him, set him in the midst of them, and said, "Assuredly, I say to you, unless you are converted and become as little children, you will by no means enter the kingdom of heaven. Therefore whoever humbles himself as this little child is the greatest in the kingdom of heaven." (NKJV)*

It's no surprise to read that he brought a little child and put him in the middle of that puffing circle of burly fishermen, tax collectors, and **Zealots**. (Tradition says the child was Peter's son, who grew to be Ignatius of Antioch, influential Christian writer and martyr in the early AD second century.)

Their set jaws visibly relaxed at the presence of the wee one. Jesus used the child as an object lesson to teach future leaders of the church important principles of authentic spiritual excellence.

> what others say
>
> **Peter Marshall**
>
> We ask thee to give to each of us that childlike faith, that simplicity of mind which is willing to lay aside all egotism and conceit, which recognizes vanity for what it is—an empty show, which knows that we are incapable of thinking the thoughts of God, which is willing to be humble again.[2]

The New Math of Forgiveness

MATTHEW 18:21–22 *Then Peter came to Him and said, "Lord, how often shall my brother sin against me, and I forgive him? Up to seven times?" Jesus said to him, "I do not say to you, up to seven times, but up to seventy times seven." (NKJV)*

Rabbis taught one should not forgive more than three times. Peter was ready to go way beyond that. Seven times was plenty in Peter's mind.

Jesus's answer showed that there is no end to the amount of forgiveness one should extend to another. The parable of the unforgiving servant (Matthew 18:23–35), with which Jesus followed this mind-boggling statement, teaches at least two major things about forgiveness:

- We must <u>forgive</u> in order to be forgiven.

- The person who refuses to forgive will suffer because of his unforgiveness.

forgive
Matthew 5:7;
6:14–15;
James 2:13

> **what others say**
>
> **Gayle Erwin**
> Maybe Jesus was telling us that our heart for forgiving should exceed someone's ability to sin against us.[3]

Chapter Wrap-Up

- Jesus asked his twelve disciples who they thought he was. Peter, answering for the rest, said he was the Christ, the Son of God. Jesus told Peter this insight had come to him from God and that his church would be built on the reality he had just confessed. (Matthew 16:13–20)

- Then Jesus revealed to his men that his personal destiny, toward which he was soon to head, involved rejection and execution by the authorities, after which he would rise from the dead. (Matthew 16:21–23)

- For his disciples, the road ahead also held self-denial, a personal cross each would carry every day, and following the same basic trail (destiny) he was on. (Matthew 16:24–26)

- Jesus took three of his disciples with him to the top of a high mountain where he was visibly changed before them, becoming as radiant as the sun. Appearing with him were Elijah and Moses, talking with him about the ordeal ahead for him. (Matthew 17:1–8)

- Coming down the mountain, Jesus and the three were met by a desperate father with a demon-possessed son, whom Jesus's disciples had been unable to help. After chiding them all for their lack of faith, he cast the demon out and taught them that self-denial and prayer were often the only way to set people free from such evil spirits. (Mark 9:14–29)

- A childish argument developed among the Twelve as to which was most important in the kingdom. Using a little child as an example, Jesus taught them the nature of true greatness, climaxing with an important message about forgiveness. (Matthew 18:1–35)

Study Questions

1. Where did Peter get the insight expressed in his confession (Matthew 16:16)? What did Jesus say would not be able to stand against the church founded on this truth?

2. What did Jesus call Peter when Peter tried to get him to stop talking about his death (Matthew 16:23)? What did he say was wrong with Peter's perspective?

3. What two Old Testament characters appeared with Jesus on the Mount of Transfiguration (Matthew 17:1–3)? Name two possible reasons for this experience for the disciples. For Jesus.

4. How many times did Jesus tell Peter he ought to forgive someone who wronged him (Matthew 18:22)? What did he mean?

Chapter 21: Feast of Spirit and Light

Chapter Highlights:
• Back Road to Jerusalem
• Assassins in the Crowd
• River of the Spirit

Let's Get Started

After six months of skirting the limelight, Jesus made several strategic forays into Judea and Jerusalem. He would go in for a while, then back off to a distance, preparing for the final moment when the prophecies of his sacrifice and triumph would be fulfilled.

gospel harmony

Matthew 8:8–22
Luke 9:57–62

Back Road to Jerusalem

> JOHN 7:2–3, 5–6 *Now the Jews' Feast of Tabernacles was at hand. His brothers therefore said to Him, "Depart from here and go into Judea, that Your disciples also may see the works that You are doing." . . . For even His brothers did not believe in Him. Then Jesus said to them, "My time has not yet come, but your time is always ready."* (NKJV)

Jesus did not go to the feast until later. At the midpoint of the festivities, he joined the crowds in the temple area and began to teach. John doesn't tell us what he said, only that whatever it was, the leaders and people found it astonishing: "The Jews marveled, saying, 'How does this Man know letters, having never studied?'" (John 7:15 NKJV). In speaking he combined a complete grasp of Scripture with fresh <u>authority</u>.

Who Was Jesus's "Rabbi"?

> JOHN 7:16–18 *Jesus answered them and said, "My doctrine is not Mine, but His who sent me. If anyone wills to do His will, he shall know concerning the doctrine, whether it is from God or whether I speak on My own authority. He who speaks from himself seeks his own glory; but he who seeks the glory of the One who sent Him is true, and no unrighteousness is in him."* (NKJV)

He did not claim to be self-taught—that would be grounds for discreditation. He never claimed to be the originator of the ideas he

go to

authority
Matthew 7:28–29;
Mark 1:22;
Luke 4:32

shared. His answer to their question was that God was his <u>teacher</u>. His words came from his Father in heaven.

Assassins in the Crowd

teacher
John 12:49; 14:10

believe and welcome
John 5:45–47

branches
Leviticus 23:40

Hallel
Psalms 113–118

> JOHN 7:19–20 *"Did not Moses give you the law, yet none of you keeps the law? Why do you seek to kill Me?" The people answered and said, "You have a demon. Who is seeking to kill You?"* (NKJV)

Addressing the Jewish leaders, Jesus pressed the point: If they were practicing God's will even as it was revealed in the Law of Moses, they wouldn't be conspiring at that very moment to kill him. Instead they would <u>believe and welcome</u> him.

Most people listening were unaware of the leaders' plot. They wrote off Jesus's suggestion as the absurd ravings of a deranged person. But in fact the Pharisees and the chief priests had decided it was time to shut Jesus up. They dispatched a squad of temple police to arrest him (John 7:32).

River of the Spirit

> JOHN 7:37–39 *On the last day, that great day of the feast, Jesus stood and cried out, saying, "If anyone thirsts, let him come to Me and drink. He who believes in Me, as the Scripture has said, out of his heart will flow rivers of living water." But this He spoke concerning the Spirit, whom those believing in Him would receive; for the Holy Spirit was not yet given, because Jesus was not yet glorified.* (NKJV)

One of the high points each day at the Feast of Tabernacles was a procession through the streets of Jerusalem to the Pool of Siloam. At the pool a priest filled a golden pitcher with water. When the procession returned to the temple, the water was poured into a silver funnel leading to the base of the altar of burnt offering while the congregation chanted the **Hallel** and shook <u>branches</u> of palm and other trees toward the altar. When the singing ended there was a moment of silence as the priests prepared the sacrifices.[1]

It was probably during that moment of silence the voice of Jesus was heard inviting thirsty people to come to him and drink, promising everyone who believed in him streams of <u>living water</u> flowing within them.[2]

go to

living water
John 4:14

> ### what others say
>
> **Billy Graham**
>
> God does not want us to come to Christ by faith, and then lead a life of defeat, discouragement, and dissension. Rather, he wants to "fulfill every desire for goodness and the work of faith with power; in order that the name of our Lord Jesus Christ may be glorified in you" (2 Thessalonians 1:11–12, New American Standard Bible). To the great gift of forgiveness God adds also the great gift of the Holy Spirit. He is the source of power who meets our need to escape from the miserable weakness that grips us. He gives us the power to be truly good . . .
>
> If you believe in Jesus Christ, a power is available to you that can change your life, even in such intimate areas as your marriage, your family relationships, and every other relationship. Also, God offers power that can change a tired church into a vital, growing body, power that can revitalize Christendom.[3]

Greek manuscripts
copies of New Testament books, handwritten in Greek by copyists, used to make our English translations (the originals have been lost)

The Tragedy of the Unconvinced

JOHN 7:45 *Then the officers came to the chief priests and Pharisees, who said to them, "Why have you not brought Him?"* (*NKJV*)

The officers sent to arrest Jesus returned to their superiors empty-handed.

"No man ever spoke like this Man!" (John 7:46 NKJV). These were not exactly the words the chief priests and Pharisees wanted to hear. Jesus had slipped through their fingers again.

The Case of the Controversial Fragment

The oldest and best **Greek manuscripts** of John's Gospel do not contain the first eleven verses of John 8. It probably was not part of the book in its original form.

The early Christian theologian Augustine thought the story ought to be removed on grounds that Jesus's readiness to forgive the adulterous woman might encourage Christian wives to sin. Not a good argument, Saint Augustine!

go to

grace
Luke 5:20; 7:48;
John 3:17

friend of sinners
Matthew 11:19;
Luke 5:31–32;
15:1–2

grace
God's loving-
kindness toward
sinners

Even if it was written by someone other than John and inserted later, it is consistent with everything we know about Jesus. There's no reason to doubt it really happened. It illustrates beautifully the incredible grace of God we see in Jesus. And it may very well have happened in precisely the context in which it appears.

Kicking and Screaming into the Light

JOHN 8:2–6 *Now early in the morning He came again into the temple, and all the people came to Him; and He sat down and taught them. Then the scribes and Pharisees brought to Him a woman caught in adultery. And when they had set her in the midst, they said to Him, "Teacher, this woman was caught in adultery, in the very act. Now Moses, in the law, commanded us that such should be stoned. But what do You say?" This they said, testing Him, that they might have something of which to accuse Him. But Jesus stooped down and wrote on the ground with His finger, as though He did not hear.* (NKJV)

In their commitment to destroy Jesus, the religious leaders hatched scheme after scheme to embarrass or entrap him in front of the people. Most backfired. But they kept trying. In this incident they thought they'd snare him in a catch-22 and get him in trouble with both Jewish and Roman law:

- If he agreed she should be stoned, he would compromise his own way of life and his teaching of **grace** and forgiveness, and sacrifice his reputation as a <u>friend of sinners</u>.

- If he said she should not be stoned, they could accuse him of ignoring the demands of Moses's Law.

what others say

William Barclay

It is extremely unlikely that the scribes and the Pharisees even knew this woman's name. To them she was nothing but a case of shameless adultery that could now be used as an instrument to suit their purposes.[4]

Sinners in the Spotlight

JOHN 8:7 *So when they continued asking Him, He raised Himself up and said to them, "He who is without sin among you, let him throw a stone at her first."* (NKJV)

Jesus was seated in the temple court teaching when the woman was dragged before him. Sitting there he bent down and wrote on the dusty pavement with his finger. The arrogant religionists repeated their question. He looked up at them and hit them with an exploding word grenade.

He then stooped down and again wrote on the ground. Nobody knows what he wrote. There are plenty of theories:

- He was doodling to cool his anger or to buy time to think.
- He wrote a passage from the Old Testament.
- He listed the sins of the woman's accusers.
- He wrote the names of the leaders who had themselves committed adultery.
- He wrote what he said in verse 7 about the person who hadn't sinned throwing the first stone.

The men who had arranged this disgusting spectacle found themselves exposed and, one by one, they left, confronted by their own guilt.

Soon everyone was gone but Jesus and the woman standing before him. There is no record that she confessed her sin or promised to stop. Even so, Jesus told her that he did not condemn her—meaning he forgave her.

When Jesus said to the woman, "Neither do I condemn you" (John 8:11 NKJV), that did not make her innocent. It did make her forgiven. The next step was up to her. Forgiven—her record cleansed of her sin—she was now ready for a new start: "Go and sin no more," he urged (8:11 NKJV).

The Light of the World

JOHN 8:12 *Then Jesus spoke to them again, saying, "I am the light of the world. He who follows Me shall not walk in darkness, but have the light of life." (NKJV)*

This was Jesus's second "I am" declaration reported by John. It was an outright claim of Godhood. In the context of the festival, he was claiming to Israel and the world to be everything symbolized by the blazing candelabra.

Unbelieving Believers

JOHN 8:28 *Then Jesus said to them, "When you lift up the Son of Man, then you will know that I am He, and that I do nothing of Myself; but as My Father taught Me, I speak these things."* (NKJV)

"Who are you?" the people asked. Jesus's answer amounted to, "I am who I claim to be." Besides being the light of the world, Jesus was the Son of God (John 8:16, 18, 23), the bearer of God's message (8:26, 28), the one who pleases God in everything (8:29), and the one who has God with him (8:29).

At first glance, the next statement is cause for celebration: "As He spoke these words, many believed in Him" (John 8:30 NKJV).

But something was missing. Three sentences later, John reports that some of these "believers" debated with Jesus about his suggestion that they needed to be set free (John 8:32–33). Their resistance against what he was saying became so intense that Jesus called them children of the devil (8:44). And before the conversation ended, some of them picked up stones from the temple pavement to throw at him (8:59)!

---

what others say

Oswald Chambers

Obedience to Jesus Christ is essential . . . In the early stages we have the notion that the Christian life is one of freedom, and so it is, but freedom for one thing only—freedom to obey our Master.[5]

Chapter Wrap-Up

- As the Feast of Tabernacles approached, Jesus's skeptical brothers advised him to go to Jerusalem and "go public." He followed God's timing, not theirs. He left at a different time. (Luke 9:52–56; John 7:1–10)

- Halfway through the feast, Jesus arrived and began to preach. The crowd was split—some for him, some against, some confused. Temple police were dispatched to arrest him. (John 7:11–36)

- On the last day of the feast, Jesus announced that anyone who believed on him would have a river of living water flowing inside—he spoke of the Holy Spirit. Temple police returned to the high priests empty-handed. They hadn't arrested Jesus. They'd gotten caught up in his teachings. (John 7:37–53)

- A woman caught in the act of adultery was brought to Jesus for judgment. He forgave her and forced her accusers to face up to their own sins. (John 8:1–11)

- At the same festival, Jesus introduced himself as "the light of the world." People were forced to make a decision about who he was. Many believed he was telling the truth—he was everything he claimed to be. Still they rejected him; some even tried to stone him. (John 8:12–59)

Study Questions

1. Why did Jesus wait to attend the feast after it was under way?

2. According to John 7:16, who gave Jesus the things he taught and gave him the right to teach? How did Jesus suggest a person might know for sure his teachings came from God?

3. On the last day of the feast, what did Jesus promise to the people who put their faith in him?

4. Jesus accepts us "as is" and refuses to condemn us. Does knowing that free you to change, or reinforce your bad behavior? How?

Chapter 22: Bright Sonlight, Dark Shadows

Chapter Highlights:
- Witness of the Lambs
- Private Lessons
- The Good Samaritan
- Slanderous Talk
- Spiritual Astigmatism

Let's Get Started

The clock was ticking. Jesus <u>knew</u> his days were numbered. Only about six months remained before the final conflict with his enemies, which would climax in his crucifixion.

Timing was important. The ultimate crisis must not come too soon. All Israel must hear the message of the kingdom's nearness before Jesus presented himself in Jerusalem as the **Passover Lamb** on April 15, AD 29.[1]

go to

knew
Matthew 16:21;
Luke 9:44

crusade
Matthew 10;
Luke 9:1–9

Witness of the Lambs

> LUKE 10:1–3 *After these things the Lord appointed seventy others also, and sent them two by two before His face into every city and place where He Himself was about to go. Then He said to them, "The harvest truly is great, but the laborers are few; therefore pray the Lord of the harvest to send out laborers into His harvest. Go your way; behold, I send you out as lambs among wolves." (NKJV)*

With only a few months to go, Jesus commissioned a second wave of advance witnesses—seventy—to prepare the way for his arrival in cities and towns of Judea and Perea (see appendix A). Some translations say there were seventy-two, not seventy, who were sent. The difference is due to a copyist's error. Whatever amount, the number corresponds to elders assisting Moses (Numbers 11:16–27) or the number of men in the **Sanhedrin**.

The instructions given this second, larger team are essentially the same as those given the Twelve for their <u>crusade</u> in Galilee, including the warning that they are being sent "as lambs among wolves" (Luke 10:3 NKJV). The Judean response could be expected to be even more "wolflike" than what had faced Galilee campaigners.

Passover Lamb
lamb sacrificed at
the Passover Feast
to free people from
sin's slavery

Sanhedrin
the ruling council
and supreme court
of Israel

Debriefing

LUKE 10:17–20 *Then the seventy returned with joy, saying, "Lord, even the demons are subject to us in Your name." And He said to them, "I saw Satan fall like lightning from heaven. Behold, I give you the authority to trample on serpents and scorpions, and over all the power of the enemy, and nothing shall by any means hurt you. Nevertheless do not rejoice in this, that the spirits are subject to you, but rather rejoice because your names are written in heaven." (NKJV)*

Thirty-five teams of excited campaigners returned from their mission, high on success and adventure. Their message had not been rejected. Troubled people had been liberated. Demons cowered when team members confronted them using Jesus's delegated authority!

Jesus's response, "I saw Satan fall like lightning from heaven" (Luke 10:18 NKJV), was like saying, "When you guys were out there preaching the kingdom message, confronting demons, and healing sick people, I saw the devil falling in defeat before you!"

Joyful Praise

LUKE 10:21 *In that hour Jesus rejoiced in the Spirit and said, "I thank You, Father, Lord of heaven and earth, that You have hidden these things from the wise and prudent and revealed them to babes. Even so, Father, for so it seemed good in Your sight." (NKJV)*

Jesus broke into prayer, joyfully praising his Father for the fresh spiritual understanding his disciples were experiencing as they returned from their mission.

Compared to the world's sophisticated scholars, this group of simple Galileans and other relatively uneducated people were "babes."

Yet they were making spiritual discoveries the educated and clever missed seeing through the smoke screen of their pride.

love the LORD your God
Deuteronomy 6:5

your neighbor
Leviticus 19:18

> ### what others say
>
> **John Wesley**
>
> Give me one hundred preachers who fear nothing but sin, and desire nothing but God, and I care not a straw whether they be clergymen or laymen, such alone will shake the gates of hell and set up the kingdom of heaven on earth.[3]

Private Lessons

LUKE 10:25 *And behold, a certain lawyer stood up and tested Him, saying, "Teacher, what shall I do to inherit eternal life?" (NKJV)*

An expert in Jewish law pretended to be searching for the answer to life's great question: "What shall I do to inherit eternal life?" But the lawyer's question was a dead giveaway, revealing that he believed he could be saved by his deeds.

Jesus saw through the ruse and did not give the man a direct answer. Instead, he asked the lawyer three questions to make him face the issue for himself. First, Jesus asked, "What is written in the law? What is your reading of it?" (Luke 10:26 NKJV).

Every serious Jew could be expected to know by heart the answer to this legal question: "'You shall <u>love the LORD your God</u> with all your heart, with all your soul, with all your strength, and with all your mind,' and '<u>your neighbor</u> as yourself'" (Luke 10:27 NKJV).

"You have answered rightly; do this and you will live," Jesus responded (Luke 10:28 NKJV).

"And who is my neighbor?" the lawyer asked (Luke 10:29 NKJV), squirming to wriggle out of the limelight. Jesus's answer was the well-known parable of the good Samaritan.

go to

neighbor
1 John 4:20

The Good Samaritan

the big picture

Luke 10:30-35

Then Jesus told this story: A traveler on his way to Jericho was beaten, robbed, and left for dead. A priest walked by and ignored him. Then a Levite passed by and also ignored him. But when a Samaritan saw the victim, he helped him, took him to an inn, and paid the staff to look after him until he was well.

In Jesus's story, the despised outlander was the hero. After the religious people refused to get involved, the Samaritan rescued the beat-up robbery victim, transported him to safety, cared for him, and paid the bills!

Jesus then asked his second question: Which of the three in the story—priest, Levite, or Samaritan—proved to be the robbery victim's neighbor (Luke 10:36)?

"He who showed mercy on him," the lawyer answered. Jesus said, "Go and do likewise" (Luke 10:37 NKJV). The lawyer was left to ask himself, "To whom am I a neighbor?"

The Israelites of Jesus's day typically thought the ancient Love-thy-neighbor command applied only to fellow Jews. It never entered their heads that loving your neighbor might include all human beings, regardless of racial or religious background.

what others say

Leon Morris

The lawyer wanted a rule or a set of rules that he could keep and so merit eternal life. Jesus is telling him that eternal life is not a matter of keeping rules at all. To live in love is to live the life of the kingdom of God . . . Our attitude toward God determines the rest. If we really love him we love our <u>neighbor</u> too.[4]

The Flip Side of Good Samaritanism

LUKE 10:39–40 *[Martha] had a sister called Mary, who also sat at Jesus' feet and heard His word. But Martha was distracted with much serving, and she approached [Jesus] and said, "Lord, do You not care that my sister has left me to serve alone? Therefore tell her to help me." (NKJV)*

In the little village of Bethany, just five miles from Jerusalem, lived a family that was very dear to Jesus—and he to them—Mary, Martha, and Lazarus (two sisters and their brother).

The personalities of the sisters were quite different. And they expressed their deep love for Jesus in completely different ways. When he came to their house, Mary would sit on the floor near him and hang on every word he spoke. Martha was no less glad to see him, but her style was to fuss and clean and prepare meals.

There is a place for both expressions of love.

In all her busyness, however, Martha revealed mixed motives that threatened to make her "loving" labors less than loving. She complained to Jesus that Mary was not helping with the housework. Actually, she went further than that: She blamed Jesus for not caring that she had to do all the work while her sister lollygagged with him!

Jesus gently adjusted Martha's priorities. "Mary has chosen that good part, which will not be taken away from her" (Luke 10:42 NKJV).

go to

Sermon on the Mount
Matthew 5:1–48;
6:1–34; 7:1–29;
Luke 6:20–49; 11:1

Lord's Prayer
Matthew 6:9–13

what others say

Roy Irving

We can become so involved in the work of the Lord that we neglect the Lord of the work.[5]

Practical Principles of Powerful Praying

LUKE 11:1 *Now it came to pass, as [Jesus] was praying in a certain place, when He ceased, that one of His disciples said to Him, "Lord, teach us to pray, as John also taught his disciples."* (NKJV)

Jewish rabbis customarily taught their students a prayer to pray. John the Baptist had taught such a prayer to his people.

In the Sermon on the Mount Jesus gave his earlier disciples a pattern for prayer, which Christians recite as the Lord's Prayer.

Since then additional disciples had joined his ranks. One of them observed Jesus praying and asked to be taught how to pray. Jesus's response was to repeat the model prayer.

The point, as with the Matthew 6 version of it, is not to provide a little religious ritual that can be rattled off at the drop of a hymnbook. The point is to capsulize in digestible form the principles of effective prayer.

Beelzebub
Lord of Flies or
Prince of Dung,
the devil

Slanderous Talk

LUKE 11:14–15 *And [Jesus] was casting out a demon, and it was mute. So it was, when the demon had gone out, that the mute spoke; and the multitudes marveled. But some of them said, "He casts out demons by Beelzebub, the ruler of the demons." (NKJV)*

The coalition of Jesus's enemies spread the groundless slander that he performed his miracles by the power of "**Beelzebub**, the ruler of the demons." He soon discovered the coalition's lie was being believed and spread by some ordinary people in the crowds.

Spiritual Astigmatism

LUKE 11:29 *And while the crowds were thickly gathered together, [Jesus] began to say, "This is an evil generation. It seeks a sign, and no sign will be given to it except the sign of Jonah the prophet." (NKJV)*

Many in the Judean crowds were withholding acceptance of Jesus, waiting for some extraordinary demonstration of power as proof of his messiahship.

What were they waiting for? The hard, cold fact is that even if he parted the sea or stopped the sun (again!), some people still would refuse to believe. When they could not deny a miracle, they dismissed it as the work of the devil (Luke 11:15)! They'd find a way to ignore anything he did to prove he was Messiah.

"Doing Lunch" with the Enemy

LUKE 11:37–38 *And as [Jesus] spoke, a certain Pharisee asked Him to dine with him. So He went in and sat down to eat. When the Pharisee saw it, he marveled that He had not first washed before dinner. (NKJV)*

A Pharisee invited Jesus to "do lunch." Jesus knew the rules. But in order to take the conversation quickly where he wanted it to go, he deliberately broke the first rule for eating with a Pharisee: He went in and sat at the table without first doing the handwashing ritual.

This procedure had nothing to do with cleanliness. It was a ceremony to remove "defilement" from contact with sinful people, an arrogant statement of self-righteousness and spiritual superiority.

His host was surprised at Jesus's neglect. Jesus knew what he and the others were thinking. He attacked their spiritual duplicity. He accused them of being "full of greed and wickedness" (Luke 11:39 NKJV).

In effect he said: "If you Pharisees were as concerned about the persons you are on the inside as you are about this **foolish** external practice, you'd actually be clean!" (Luke 11:39–42).

Then, having set the tone for the table conversation, Jesus pronounced six **"woes"** on them for their hypocrisy (Luke 11:42–52).

foolish
Greek means froth, foam; silliness

woes
cries of grief, "Alas!"; Jesus grieves for the disaster of hypocrisy

Chapter Wrap-Up

- About six months before the climactic events at Jerusalem leading to his crucifixion and resurrection, Jesus sent a second wave of seventy disciples to the towns of Judea and Perea to prepare them for his personal arrival to preach the kingdom message there. (Luke 10:1–24)

- Jesus told the story of the good Samaritan to show his followers their love should include people who were different from them. He taught the importance of shameless praying. (Luke 10:25–11:13)

- After the resurfacing of the slander that his miracles were the work of the devil, Jesus attacked hypocrisy, climaxing with a luncheon at the home of a Pharisee where he named six calamities of hypocrisy in the lives of the Pharisees and legal experts. (Luke 11:14–53)

Study Questions

1. When the seventy returned from their preaching mission what were they most excited about? What did Jesus say they should be most excited about? What was he most excited about?

2. What two "loves" fulfill the two greatest Old Testament commandments? In the story, what did the good Samaritan do that showed he loved his neighbor?

3. Around what two factors does successful praying revolve, according to Luke 11:5–13?

Chapter 23: Seeing with New Eyes

Chapter Highlights:
- Treasure Hunt
- Matters of Life and Death
- Eye-Opening Experience
- Out with It

Let's Get Started

When the third New Testament historian, Luke, describes the crowds that came to see Jesus in Judea during his final six months of ministry he uses the Greek word *myrias* (Luke 12:1). The word means audiences numbered in the "tens of thousands."

The spiritually starved, sick, and curious thronged him in the capital province in even greater numbers than in Galilee.

greed
Exodus 20:17;
Colossians 3:5–6

covetousness
excessive desire for wealth and possessions

Treasure Hunt

> LUKE 12:13–15 *Then one from the crowd said to Him, "Teacher, tell my brother to divide the inheritance with me." But He said to him, "Man, who made Me a judge or an arbitrator over you?" And He said to them, "Take heed and beware of covetousness, for one's life does not consist in the abundance of the things he possesses."* (NKJV)

Jesus refused to get involved in the dispute. There were magistrates for that. He spoke to the deeper issue behind the man's request, the problem of **covetousness** or greed.

Matthew 6:16–21,
25–34
Luke 12:22–34

Fool's Gold

> LUKE 12:16–17 *Then He spoke a parable to them, saying: "The ground of a certain rich man yielded plentifully. And he thought within himself, saying, 'What shall I do, since I have no room to store my crops?'"* (NKJV)

Jesus told a story. What this successful farmer decided to do was tear down his too-small barns and build bigger ones, store his wealth, and live it up for the rest of his life . . . which, as it turned out, ended that very night (Luke 12:20)!

"So is he who lays up treasure for himself, and is not rich toward God," Jesus concluded (Luke 12:21 NKJV).

go to

gift
Deuteronomy 8:18;
1 Corinthians 3:7;
James 1:17

don't worry
Matthew 6:24–34

ravens
Leviticus 11:15

seek God's kingdom
Matthew 5–7;
Luke 6

literally
Acts 2:44–45;
4:32–37

ravens
unclean birds,
according to Old
Testament Law—
God cares for them

lilies
crocus, gladiolus,
anemone, iris, wild-
flowers that grow in
Palestine

Wealth was not the farmer's problem. Good crops are a gift from God. The point swirls around the farmer's question, "What shall I do?" The choices he made and the priorities those choices revealed caused God to call the farmer a "fool" (Luke 12:20 NKJV).

A man, or woman, is "rich toward God" if he can thank God for his success and wealth but hold both loosely, and if he can care about others, focus on eternity, and trust his future to God.

Radical Investment Strategy

Turning to his disciples, Jesus went deeper into the issue of money and possessions.

1. Don't worry (Luke 12:22–28). "Life is more than food, and the body is more than clothing" (Luke 12:23 NKJV). Jesus reminded them of **ravens** (12:24) and **lilies** (12:27). It's silly to think of birds stockpiling food or plants worrying about having nothing to wear. It's just as silly for people who trust God to worry about food, clothing, physical stature, or the length of life.

2. Seek God's kingdom (Luke 12:29–34). Unlike the "nations of the world," the people of God set their hearts on the "kingdom of God" (Luke 12:30–31 NKJV). To seek the kingdom is to pour one's energy into doing God's will and watching out for the well-being of fellow kingdom citizens, leaving the supply of personal necessities to a generous God (12:31–32).

3. Radical investment (Luke 12:33). The no-anxiety lifestyle makes possible a liberal, giving spirit that moves the kingdom toward its goals. Jesus told his followers to sell what they had and give to needy people. The original disciples took him literally.

Matters of Life and Death

LUKE 12:35–37 *Let your waist be girded and your lamps burning; and you yourselves be like men who wait for their master, when he will return from the wedding, that when he comes and knocks they may open to him immediately. Blessed are those servants whom the master, when he comes, will find watching. (NKJV)*

At this point Jesus added a new dimension to his teaching. During the weeks leading to the end of his earthly life, he would talk a lot about something Christians call "the second coming of Christ."

The story Jesus told urged his followers to have three bases covered at all times:

lamps burning
Matthew 5:14–16;
25:1–13

filled
John 7:38–39;
Romans 8:5–9;
Ephesians 5:15–20

1. Be dressed and ready for service (Luke 12:35). Literally, "Let your loins be girded." His listeners understood this to mean, "Be ready and working." A man doing a strenuous job would gather his robe close to his body and tuck it up under his belt, and he would say his loins were girded.

2. Keep your <u>lamps burning</u> (Luke 12:35). A lamp was a cotton wick floating in a dish of oil. To keep the light shining, the wick had to be trimmed and the oil replenished. This pictures the need to be continually faithful and **<u>filled</u> with the Spirit**.

filled with the Spirit
controlled by and responsive to Christ

3. Be watching and ready (Luke 12:37–38, 40). Be awake, alert, attentive, vigilant . . . all the time. Christ will return when it's least expected (12:40).

Ignorance Is No Excuse

> LUKE 12:47–48 *And that servant who knew his master's will, and did not prepare himself or do according to his will, shall be beaten with many stripes. But he who did not know, yet committed things deserving of stripes, shall be beaten with few. For everyone to whom much is given, from him much will be required; and to whom much has been committed, of him they will ask the more. (NKJV)*

When Christ returns, rewards and discipline will be dished out in direct proportion to what each of us has done with what we've known. Ignorance is no excuse. Judgment will be less harsh for those who know less, but all are accountable for what they know.

The Parable of the Fruitless Fig

> LUKE 13:6–9 *[Jesus] also spoke this parable: "A certain man had a fig tree planted in his vineyard, and he came seeking fruit on it and found none. Then he said to the keeper of his*

who sinned
Luke 13:1–5

who sinned
rabbis discussed
whether an unborn
child could sin in the
womb

vineyard, 'Look, for three years I have come seeking fruit on this fig tree and find none. Cut it down; why does it use up the ground?' But he answered and said to him, 'Sir, let it alone this year also, until I dig around it and fertilize it. And if it bears fruit, well. But if not, after that you can cut it down.'" (NKJV)

The parable makes several points related to God's judgment and the need for repentance:

- True repentance is demonstrated by visible fruit—change, action (Luke 3:8, 10–14).

- Spiritual fruitlessness invites disaster (Luke 13:7).

- Delayed calamity does not mean God approves of the way we are living (Romans 2:4). God, in patient love, often delays judgment to give time to repent (2 Peter 3:9).

- God's patience has limits—we can wait too long to change (Luke 13:9).

Eye-Opening Experience

JOHN 9:1–5 *Now as Jesus passed by, He saw a man who was blind from birth. And His disciples asked Him, saying, "Rabbi, who sinned, this man or his parents, that he was born blind?" Jesus answered, "Neither this man nor his parents sinned, but that the works of God should be revealed in him. I must work the works of Him who sent me while it is day; the night is coming when no one can work. As long as I am in the world, I am the light of the world." (NKJV)*

The sight of this blind man who had never seen the light of day brought up a puzzling theological question from Jesus's friends: Whose fault is it? "**Who sinned**, this man or his parents, that he was born blind?" (John 9:2 NKJV).

Jesus's response to the question was that this man's trouble had nothing to do with who sinned. A more important dynamic was at work. The blind man's struggle provided opportunity for the work of God to be displayed in his life (John 9:3). The work of God was why Jesus was in the world (9:4–5). What was this the work of God? To be "the light of the world" (9:5).

"Here's Mud in Your Eye!"

JOHN 9:6–7 *When [Jesus] had said these things, He spat on the ground and made clay with the saliva; and He anointed the eyes of the blind man with the clay. And He said to him, "Go, wash in the pool of Siloam" (which is translated, Sent). So he went and washed, and came back seeing. (NKJV)*

A delightful confusion broke out among the neighbors when the blind beggar showed up on the street where he lived, seeing. Attention was quickly turned from the no-longer-blind man to the one who gave him his sight: "a man called Jesus" (John 9:11 NKJV).

Sabbath Squad to the Rescue!

JOHN 9:14–16 *Now it was a Sabbath when Jesus made the clay and opened his eyes. Then the Pharisees also asked him again how he had received his sight. He said to them, "He put clay on my eyes, and I washed, and I see." Therefore some of the Pharisees said, "This Man is not from God, because He does not keep the Sabbath." Others said, "How can a man who is a sinner do such signs?" And there was a division among them. (NKJV)*

The unsuspecting neighbors immediately took the man to the Pharisees. There's no indication they were trying to get him in trouble. They assumed religious leaders, steeped in theology, could put this event into perspective.

The Pharisees' immediate response was to declare that the miracle worker could not be a man of God because he broke the Sabbath! None seemed to care that the beggar's ordeal was over. The great sin of religious legalists was (and is) that they care more for their institutions and traditions than for people! When they asked the man his opinion of Jesus, he answered, "He is a prophet" (John 9:17 NKJV).

Give God the glory!"
Joshua 7:19

official edict
first official attack
against Christian
believers

**put out of the
synagogue**
excommunicated

The Third Degree—Round Two

> JOHN 9:18–21 *But the Jews did not believe concerning him,
> that he had been blind and received his sight, until they called
> the parents of him who had received his sight. And they asked
> them, saying, "Is this your son, who you say was born blind?
> How then does he now see?" His parents answered them and
> said, "We know that this is our son, and that he was born blind;
> but by what means he now sees we do not know, or who opened his
> eyes we do not know. He is of age; ask him. He will speak for
> himself." (NKJV)*

The parents of the no-longer-blind man were brought in. They
confirmed the healed man was their son and that he had been blind
from birth. Asked if they knew how it was possible he could now see,
though, they "pleaded the Fifth," refusing to answer on grounds of
possible self-incrimination.

They feared an **official edict** by the religious leaders: "If anyone
confessed that [Jesus] was Christ, he would be **put out of the synagogue**" (John 9:22 NKJV). Religious leaders could have either (1)
permanently excluded them and given public notice that they were
accursed, cut off from friends, relatives, and God; or (2) temporarily excluded them.

The Third Degree—Round Three

> JOHN 9:24–25 *So they again called the man who was blind,
> and said to him, "Give God the glory! We know that this Man is
> a sinner." He answered and said, "Whether He is a sinner or
> not I do not know. One thing I know: that though I was blind,
> now I see." (NKJV)*

The inquisition again focused on this man, who was now seeing
for the first time.

"Give God the glory!" the inquisitors said. But they really had no
interest in God's glory. What they meant was: "Confess your sin and
agree that we are right—Jesus is a sinner!" (Condemned criminals
were challenged with those words to confess and prepare to die.)

The leaders pressed the man to repeat his story, hoping he'd con-
tradict himself (John 9:26).

The irony hit its peak when the witness assumed the role of inquisitor: "Why do you want to hear it again? Do you also want to become His disciples?" (John 9:27 NKJV). (The seeing man now sees himself as disciple of the healer.)

He'd touched their hot button! All pretext of politeness and orderly investigation were suddenly out the window, and bitterness boiled over (John 9:28–29).

Out with It

JOHN 9:31–33 *Now we know that God does not hear sinners; but if anyone is a worshiper of God and does His will, He hears him. Since the world began it has been **unheard of** that anyone opened the eyes of one who was born blind. If this Man were not from God, He could do nothing. (NKJV)*

Under attack for a stranger he barely knew, the man became more courageous and insightful. He expressed shock at their unbelief. To him it was not amazing someone should believe in Jesus—what was amazing was that anyone should fail to believe in the face of the evidence (John 9:30–33)! The man's perception of Jesus sharpened: He is definitely "from God."

The Pharisees tore the lid off their theological prejudice and threw the man's blindness into his face: The fact he'd been blind proved he was a sinner. "And they cast him out" (John 9:34 NKJV).

When You See the Son, Believe or Go Blind!

When Jesus heard the newly seeing man had been thrown out of the temple, he went looking for him. After Jesus had identified himself (after all, the man had never seen him before!), the healed man did three things (John 9:38):

- Acknowledged Jesus as Lord
- Put his faith in Jesus into words
- **Worshipped** Jesus

unheard of
The Old Testament records no incident of a blind person receiving sight.

worshipped
Greek word indicates the man prostrated himself and kissed Jesus's feet

Chapter Wrap-Up

- Jesus warned the people to guard against greed, then turned the world's concept of wealth, security, and investment priorities upside down. (Luke 12:13–34)

- Like a jeweler stringing pearls, he warned them to be ready for his return and to pay attention to the signs of the times. (Luke 12:35–48)

- He sought to correct people's thinking about the causes of calamity, and warned them to repent in preparation for the certainty of death. (Luke 13:1–9)

- In Jerusalem Jesus healed a man who had been born blind. The man witnessed to his neighbors, was interrogated by the Pharisees, and was excommunicated from the temple. Jesus met him, and he confessed faith in Jesus as Messiah. (John 9)

Study Questions

1. Place a mark on the line below to show where you see yourself between the extremes.

   Frugal to a fault ————————— Spendthrift generosity

   Now place a mark to show where you see Jesus (according to Luke 12:13–34).

2. Identify three things that are part of the investment strategy Jesus taught.

3. Identify three things to do to be ready for the second coming of Christ.

4. What did the Pharisees care most about—their traditions or making people well?

Chapter 24: Shepherd Lord

Let's Get Started

Jesus understood from the start that he had been sent by God to lead Israel into God's kingdom. The terms "King," "Master," "Rabbi," "Teacher," and "Lord" were all applied to him by his followers. But one of his own favorite ways of describing his leadership was to call himself "Shepherd." In fact, shepherds and sheep are mentioned more than six hundred times in the Bible.

After John the Baptist <u>introduced</u> Jesus and he began to preach in Galilee, people came from everywhere with their diseases, sicknesses, mental and spiritual maladies and handicaps, suffering under poverty and oppression of all kinds—harassed and helpless. And "He was moved with **compassion** for them, because they were weary and scattered, like sheep having no shepherd" (Matthew 9:36 NKJV).

go to

introduced
John 1:29–35

conversation
John 9:39–41

compassion
feeling others' pain and acting to ease it

The Good Shepherd

JOHN 10:1–3 *Most assuredly, I say to you, he who does not enter the sheepfold by the door, but climbs up some other way, the same is a thief and a robber. But he who enters by the door is the shepherd of the sheep. To him the doorkeeper opens, and the sheep hear his voice; and he calls his own sheep by name and leads them out. (NKJV)*

Jesus had just come from a tense <u>conversation</u> with the Pharisees (self-proclaimed spiritual shepherds). They had spent much negative energy denying a miracle (Jesus giving sight to a man born blind). They threatened with expulsion and censure any who dared to say they believed in Jesus, and threw the former blind man out of the temple simply for telling the truth.

What Do the Sheep-and-Shepherd Symbols Mean?

In Jesus's shepherd-and-flock allegory, the identity of the symbols is easily recognized.

shepherd
Psalm 23

devil
1 Peter 5:8

door
John 14:6;
Ephesians 2:18;
Hebrews 10:20

wolf
Matthew 10:16;
Luke 10:3;
Acts 20:29

Solomon's Porch
Acts 5:12

thief
original word
emphasizes trickery
and deceit

robber
original word indi-
cates violence in
commission of the
crime

door
the shepherd

hireling
anyone doing his
work for pay

Solomon's Porch
covered porch, east
side of temple, built
by Solomon

- The sheepfold is the kingdom of God.

- The sheep are God's people.

- The <u>shepherd</u> is Jesus (also spiritual leaders).

- The **thief** and **robber** (John 10:1) are leaders who exploit the flock for selfish purposes, victimizing rather than protecting and nurturing. The thief's goals—"to steal, and to kill, and to destroy" (John 10:10 NKJV)—fit well the goals of the <u>devil</u>.

- The stranger (John 10:5) is any false leader.

- The **<u>door</u>** or gate (John 10:7–9) is Jesus. He is the sole access to the safety of God's kingdom and has come "that they may have life, and that they may have it more abundantly" (10:10 NKJV).

- The **hireling** (John 10:12–13) is one who doesn't really care about the sheep.

- The <u>wolf</u> (John 10:12) is any enemy seeking to harm God's people.

- The other sheep (John 10:16) are Gentiles soon to be included in God's flock.

The Shepherd's Choice

JOHN 10:14–15 *I am the good shepherd; and I know My sheep, and am known by My own. As the Father knows Me, even so I know the Father; and I lay down My life for the sheep.* (NKJV)

By calling himself the good shepherd, Jesus inferred that he was the promised Messiah. However, he took the claim beyond what most Jews, including his disciples, expected of the Messiah—he said he would lay down his life for his sheep (John 10:11, 15).

what others say

Octavius Winslow

Who delivered up Jesus to die? Not Judas, for money; not Pilate, for fear; not the Jews, for envy—but the Father, for love![1]

The Hanukkah Challenge

One day at the feast Jesus was walking in the covered area called **<u>Solomon's Porch</u>**, probably because it was raining, as it often did during this winter festival. The religious leaders **surrounded** him, demanding he state openly whether or not he claimed to be Messiah.

> JOHN 10:25 *Jesus answered them, "I told you, and you do not believe. The works that I do in My Father's name, they bear witness of Me." (NKJV)*

Jesus had made amazing claims. Why did he not state flatly, publicly, that he was the Messiah?

Most Jewish people had mistaken ideas of what Messiah would be and do. When they asked, "Are you the Messiah?" they were asking if he had come to set up a political-military kingdom to liberate Israel from Roman rule. If he said openly that he was the Messiah, it could have set off a chain of political events that could only end in disaster.

But Jesus never denied his messiahship, and whenever the title was applied to him by believing followers ready to accept the truth, he <u>affirmed</u> it.

key point

<u>The Unvarnished Truth</u>

> JOHN 10:26–28 *But you do not believe, because you are not of My sheep, as I said to you. My sheep hear My voice, and I know them, and they follow Me. And I give them eternal life, and they shall never perish; neither shall anyone snatch them out of My hand. (NKJV)*

what others say

Phillip Keller

Over a period of time sheep come to associate the sound of the shepherd's voice with special benefits . . . His voice is used to announce his presence; he is there. It is to allay their fears and timidity. Or it is to call them to himself so they can be examined and counted carefully. He wants to make sure they are all well, fit and flourishing. Sometimes the voice is used to announce that fresh feed is being supplied, or salt, or minerals, or water. He might call them up to lead them into fresh pastures or into some shelter from an approaching storm. But always the master's call conveys to the sheep a positive assurance that he cares for them and is acting in their best interests.[2]

go to

affirmed
John 1:41, 49

surrounded
original word indicates a hostile crowd

go to

saved
Proverbs 28:18;
Isaiah 45:22;
John 3:16–17;
Acts 4:12

lost
Ezekiel 34:15–16;
Matthew 10:6;
Luke 19:9–10;
John 10:28

saved
rescued from
sin's eternal
consequences

lost
perishing, separated
from God because
of unforgiven sin

Until this confrontation Jesus had veiled his claims when talking to his enemies. Now, suddenly, he tore the lid off—but still did it in words carefully chosen to give his opponents little that would stand up in court.

Then he said those words that drove them crazy: "I and My Father are one" (John 10:30 NKJV).

what others say

Tim Stafford

In Jesus' life we may see God. Yet the choice to see remains with us. On any given day we may choose not to see God in Jesus. We may, without even sensing our deep and calamitous rebellion, ignore him, act as though he is merely a picture on the wall. I do so often for the simple reason that I have not yet been totally changed by the power of his glory. His Holy Spirit, however, is changing me, teaching me to recognize God in Jesus.[3]

Heartbreak Hotel

LUKE 13:23–27 *Then one said to Him, "Lord, are there few who are saved?" And He said to them, "Strive to enter through the narrow gate, for many, I say to you, will seek to enter and will not be able. When once the Master of the house has risen up and shut the door, and you begin to stand outside and knock at the door, saying, 'Lord, Lord, open for us,' and He will answer and say to you, 'I do not know you, where you are from,' then you will begin to say, 'We ate and drank in Your presence, and You taught in our streets.' But He will say, 'I tell you I do not know you, where you are from. Depart from Me, all you workers of iniquity.'" (NKJV)*

A favorite pastime for the rabbis and other religious types with time on their hands was to argue about how many or few would be **saved**. Prevailing belief was that, except for a few really gross sinners, all Jews would be saved and all non-Jews **lost**.

Jesus's response upset some cherished applecarts. (Surprise! Surprise!) Not everyone who thinks they know the password will receive access to heaven.

Herod
Luke 9:7–9; 23:6–11

Herod
Herod Antipas,
Tetrarch of Galilee

what others say

William Barclay

Jesus taught that the only aristocracy in the kingdom of God is the aristocracy of faith. Jesus Christ is not the possession of any one race of men; Jesus Christ is the possession of every man in every race in whose heart there is faith.[4]

Cracks in the Pharisee Wall

LUKE 13:31–35 *On that very day some Pharisees came, saying to Him, "Get out and depart from here, for Herod wants to kill You." And He said to them, "Go, tell that fox, 'Behold, I cast out demons and perform cures today and tomorrow, and the third day I shall be perfected.' Nevertheless I must journey today, tomorrow, and the day following; for it cannot be that a prophet should perish outside of Jerusalem.*

"O Jerusalem, Jerusalem, the one who kills the prophets and stones those who are sent to her! How often I wanted to gather your children together, as a hen gathers her brood under her wings, but you were not willing! See! Your house is left to you desolate; and assuredly, I say to you, you shall not see Me until the time comes when you say, 'Blessed is He who comes in the name of the LORD!'" (NKJV)

At that point a rather strange and touching thing happened. Some Pharisees (of all people!) warned Jesus of death threats against him by **Herod** and suggested he leave the area.

They may have been trying to scare him to keep him away from Jerusalem at Passover time, when support for him could build among the festival crowds. The fact that Jesus did not expose any hypocrisy on their parts indicates, though, that they may actually have been concerned for his safety. If they were honestly trying to protect him, they did so at the risk of censure by fellow Pharisees. If so, it comes as a surprise to discover that not all Pharisees were hostile to Jesus.

The Notoriety of God

LUKE 15:1–2 *Then all the tax collectors and the sinners drew near to Him to hear Him. And the Pharisees and scribes complained, saying, "This Man receives sinners and eats with them." (NKJV)*

mud
Luke 5:31; 7:34

shepherd theme
John 10

just
doctrinally correct,
separated, holier-
than-thou

The things Jesus was saying to the religious leaders (Luke 13:13, 21) told Israel's "lost souls" that Jesus was their friend. He associated with such people. In fact, he was often seen eating with them! Eating together implied acceptance. His reputation for going to dinner with such people became part of the <u>mud</u> with which his enemies smeared his name.

The way Jesus represented the heavenly Father in the stories he told in response to the religionists' criticism was enough, in the Pharisees' opinion, to smear God's reputation with the same mud.

Lost and Found: The 100th Sheep

LUKE 15:3–7 *So He spoke this parable to them, saying: "What man of you, having a hundred sheep, if he loses one of them, does not leave the ninety-nine in the wilderness, and go after the one which is lost until he finds it? And when he has found it, he lays it on his shoulders, rejoicing. And when he comes home, he calls together his friends and neighbors, saying to them, 'Rejoice with me, for I have found my sheep which was lost!' I say to you that likewise there will be more joy in heaven over one sinner who repents than over ninety-nine **just** persons who need no repentance." (NKJV)*

This is the first of three stories Jesus told about losing and finding prized things, and it goes back to the <u>shepherd theme</u>. Shepherds were second-class citizens, but sheep were vital to the economy and religion—the source of wool and leather, thousands of temple sacrifices, and the main course at banquets.

Symbolic parallels between a shepherd and Jesus include these:

- The shepherd represents God.
- The lost sheep represents the helplessness of people separated from God by sin.
- Leaving the flock in the open field to search for the lost one (a good shepherd would never do this except in extreme emergency) represents God's urgency.
- Jewish teachers taught that God would receive repentant sinners. But the idea that God actively pursues sinners was revolutionary to the first-century Jewish mind.

Lost and Found: The Tenth Coin

go to

dowry
Exodus 22:17;
Genesis 29:18

will
Hebrews 9:16–17

pigs
Leviticus 11:7

LUKE 15:8–10 *Or what woman, having ten silver coins, if she loses one coin, does not light a lamp, sweep the house, and search carefully until she finds it? And when she has found it, she calls her friends and neighbors together, saying, "Rejoice with me, for I have found the piece which I lost!" Likewise, I say to you, there is joy in the presence of the angels of God over one sinner who repents. (NKJV)*

The missing coin was probably part of the woman's **dowry**. A dowry coin would have been prized because it symbolized her worth as a person, her individuality, and her rights as a woman.

dowry
groom's gift to
bride's father;
father's gift to the
bride

below the dignity
"Cursed is he who
feeds swine!"
(ancient Jewish
axiom)

What this tells us about God is that the lost are precious to God for reasons relating to who he is and his character as the Creator who wants to live with his creatures in a continuing personal relationship.

Lost and Found: The Second Son

LUKE 15:11–12 *Then He said: "A certain man had two sons. And the younger of them said to his father, 'Father, give me the portion of goods that falls to me.' So he divided to them his livelihood." (NKJV)*

A father could pass his property to his heirs in one of two ways: (1) after his death by means of a last <u>will</u> and testament, or (2) while he was still alive by gifts given to his heirs. (Usually these gifts were in the form of property.)

Exceptions could be made. In this case, the younger son asked for cash. Liquid assets in hand, the younger son left for "a far country" (Luke 15:13 NKJV).

There, he blew it all! Wealth, opportunity, self-respect, youth, his future—down the tubes! When he hit bottom, he hit it hard. The only employment he could find was a low-down, poverty-level job well **below the dignity** of a son of Israel—feeding <u>pigs</u>!

The View from the Bottom

LUKE 15:17–19 *But when he came to himself, he said, "How many of my father's hired servants have bread enough and to spare, and I perish with hunger! I will arise and go to my father, and will say to him, 'Father, I have sinned against heaven and before you, and I am no longer worthy to be called your son. Make me like one of your hired servants.'" (NKJV)*

From that vantage point—he'd hit bottom—with failure staring him in the face, his arrogance buried in pigpen muck, the young man "came to himself." At this "critical threshold," far from home and keeping company with swine, this young Jew evaluated his life.

With nowhere to go but up, it was not hard to make "up" the direction of choice. The foolish young man did three smart things to turn his life around:

1. He faced up to the spiritual issues in his life (Luke 15:17).

2. He decided to go back and face the music (15:18–19).

3. He acted on his decision (15:20–21).

Parable of the Forgiving Father

> LUKE 15:20 *And he arose and came to his father. But when he was still a great way off, his father saw him and had compassion, and ran and fell on his neck and kissed him. (NKJV)*

This story is known as the parable of the prodigal son, but the father's response is the main focus. It probably ought to be renamed the parable of the forgiving father.

This father demonstrates how God responds to sinners who turn to him:

key point

1. God longs for sinners to return to him (Luke 15:20).

2. God has compassion on sinners who are on their way to him (15:20).

3. God is ready to forgive (15:20).

4. God accepts as sons and daughters, not servants, sinners who come to him (15:20, 22–24). Jesus's description of the father's enthusiastic, loving acceptance was a rebuke to self-righteous hypocrites who objected to Jesus's eating with and accepting sinners.

5. The list of the father's expressions of love and welcome is impressive:

- kisses—demonstrate unbroken affection (15:20)
- best robe—symbol of position and honor (15:22)
- ring—symbol of authority (15:22)
- sandals—symbol of a son not a slave (slaves wore no shoes) (15:22)
- fatted calf—sign the father saw the homecoming as a most special occasion (15:23)
- celebration—sign of the father's joy (15:7, 10, 23–24)
- announcement: "My son was dead and is alive again"—restored relationship (15:24 NKJV)

Chapter Wrap-Up

- In a society where sheep were extremely important to the economy and religious life, Jesus introduced himself as the Good Shepherd and promised to lay down his life for his sheep, then to take his life back by rising from the dead. (John 10:1–18)

- At Hanukkah in Jerusalem, Jesus's enemies demanded that he declare himself openly—was he the Messiah? He reminded them of how he had already made messianic claims and proven their validity by doing miracles. (John 10:22–25)

- Jesus's enemies did not believe his claims, he said, because they were not his true sheep. If they were they would recognize his voice and enjoy assurance of their salvation. (John 10:25–39)

- A question about the number of people who will be saved led to Jesus's teaching about the narrowness of the way of salvation. A parable about excuse-making invited guests underscores the truth that the kingdom of God will include a lot of people the Jews of his day did not expect to be included—namely Gentiles. (Luke 13:22–14:24)

- Criticized for welcoming and celebrating with known sinners and irreligious people, Jesus told three stories (the lost sheep, lost coin, and prodigal son) to show how God rejoices when sinners return to him and how freely he offers them his grace. (Luke 15)

Study Questions

1. Explain the meaning of the following symbols in Jesus's shepherd-and-flock allegory: (a) sheepfold, (b) sheep, (c) shepherd, (d) thief, (e) door, and (f) wolf.

2. As the ultimate Shepherd of his sheep, Jesus said he would choose when to lay down his life. What else did he say he had the authority to do?

3. What do the stories of the lost sheep, lost coin, and prodigal son teach us about God's attitude toward wayward people who turn to him? How did the elder brother react to the prodigal's return?

4. With whom do you personally identify in this story and why? The prodigal, the father, or the elder brother?

Chapter Highlights:
• The Real Rich Man
• Life-Giving Friend
• The Resurrection and
  the Life
• Assassins' Plot

Chapter 25: Your Money or Your Life

Let's Get Started

Jesus taught that welcoming repentant sinners makes God deliriously happy. But he also carefully showed his followers a clear road map to real change in their lives.

fidelity
marital faithfulness

The Real Rich Man

Jesus challenged his rookie disciples to change their attitudes toward wealth and poverty, marriage and **fidelity**, heaven and hell, life and death, and faith.

> LUKE 16:1–4 *[Jesus] also said to His disciples: "There was a certain rich man who had a steward, and an accusation was brought to him that this man was wasting his goods. So he called him and said to him, 'What is this I hear about you? Give an account of your stewardship, for you can no longer be steward.' Then the steward said within himself, 'What shall I do? For my master is taking the stewardship away from me. I cannot dig; I am ashamed to beg. I have resolved what to do, that when I am put out of the stewardship, they may receive me into their houses.'"* (NKJV)

A middle manager mishandled his boss's financial affairs to his own dishonest advantage. The boss caught him with his hand in the till and terminated his employment.

Digging ditches was no option—he was too out of shape. Begging was embarrassing. So he hatched a brilliant scheme to assure that when the boss showed him the gate he wouldn't wind up on the street.

He knew who owed his boss money. He went to the debtors one by one and offered to accept a drastically reduced amount in exchange for "paid-in-full" receipts. The olive grower got out of his debt for 50 cents on the dollar. The sharecropper got a paid-in-full receipt worth 1,000 bushels of wheat for the price of 800. With a grand conspiracy between manager and debtors, a few altered entries in the records, and the shredding of a couple of strategic memos, the manager bought a couple of cronies who would do him a big favor he'd need once he was canned.

The boss, who prided himself in being a shrewd businessman, was so impressed with the manager's cleverness, he applauded, even though it cost him 500 gallons of olive oil and 200 bushels of wheat! What impressed him was not the cost of the swindle, but its creativity.

Jesus used this parable to say to his newly converted tax men: "Now that you've gone straight, you must put your infamous creativity to work devising ways to build up the kingdom of God!" (Luke 16:8, paraphrased).

what others say

John Killinger

If we love God, we will use our money for spiritual purposes. But if we love money, we cannot use God to further our business situations. He will not be a party to our selfish designs.[1]

Mother Teresa

I think people are so preoccupied with material difficulties. In the industrial world where people are supposed to have so much, I find that many people, while dressed up, are really, really poor. By having nothing we will be able to give everything—through the freedom of poverty.[2]

The Topsy-Turvy Tale of a Poor Rich Man and a Rich Poor Man

LUKE 16:19–21 *There was a certain rich man who was clothed in purple and fine linen and fared sumptuously every day. But there was a certain beggar named Lazarus, full of sores, who was laid at his gate, desiring to be fed with the crumbs which fell from the rich man's table. Moreover the dogs came and licked his sores. (NKJV)*

Chances are this is a story that really happened. In no other parable did Jesus reveal his characters' names. The poor man in this tale was named **Lazarus**. Jesus did not name the rich man, but tradition calls him **Dives**.

This saga, like the rest of Jesus's teachings in Luke 16, relates to the handling of material possessions, but it doesn't suggest there is any connection between a person's financial status and his eternal destiny. No one goes to hell simply because he is rich. And no one goes to heaven simply because he is poor. Being rich or poor has nothing to do with a person's eternal destiny.

A Tale of Two Destinies

> LUKE 16:22 *So it was that the beggar died, and was carried by the angels to Abraham's bosom. The rich man also died and was buried. (NKJV)*

In this life, all the good things came to the rich man, while poor Lazarus got stiffed, ate garbage, and suffered the torment that goes with being too broke to buy decent food or get medical help.

But death is the great leveler—after they died, there was a great switcheroo: Lazarus left the street for a wonderful place called **"Abraham's bosom"** and got the good things; Dives went straight from his sumptuous earthly life to **hell** (Luke 16:22–24).

Mary, Martha
Luke 10:38–42

fragrant oil
John 12:1–8;
Mark 14:9

Abraham's bosom
"paradise," a hold-ing area for the righteous dead awaiting resurrection

hell
Greek: *Hades*

Lazarus
not the previous beggar, but a wealthy man

love
Greek: phileo, "good friend"

for the glory of God
John 9:2–3

glorified
John 7:39; 12:16, 23, 27–28, 31–32; 13:31; 17:1

what others say

Charles Swindoll

When Lazarus, the believer, died, his body was probably tossed in the local dump, the refuse pile. Chances are good he didn't even receive a decent burial. But his soul and spirit were taken immediately into the presence of the Lord, called here "Abraham's side." When we read, "The rich man died and was buried," we can be sure his burial was one of great pomp and elaborate ceremony. So much for his body. It is his eternal soul that interests us. We find him "in hell."[3]

glorified
Jesus used this term to refer to the end of his life—crucifix-ion, death, burial, resurrection, and ascension

Life-Giving Friend

> JOHN 11:1–4 *Now a certain man was sick, **Lazarus** of Bethany, the town of Mary and her sister Martha. It was that Mary who anointed the Lord with fragrant oil and wiped His feet with her hair, whose brother Lazarus was sick. Therefore the sisters sent to Him, saying, "Lord, behold, he whom You **love** is sick." When Jesus heard that, He said, "This sickness is not unto death, but for the glory of God, that the Son of God may be glorified through it." (NKJV)*

go to

Perea
John 10:40–42

purpose
Psalm 37:7–8;
Isaiah 40:31;
Acts 1:4–5;
Romans 8:18–25

effect
Romans 5:1–5;
1 Peter 1:6–8

When the message came about Lazarus's illness, Jesus was preaching in <u>Perea</u>, across the Jordan River, about twenty miles east of the village of Bethany (see appendix A). When his twelve friends heard him say Lazarus's illness would not end in death, they interpreted it to mean the illness was temporary—Lazarus would recover.

Jesus, however, was looking beyond his friend's sickness and death to the greatest miracle of his career (except for his own resurrection), and he saw glory for God and himself.

The Mystery of Waiting

The historian John reminds his readers that "Jesus loved Martha and her sister and Lazarus" (John 11:5 NKJV). The word for "love" here is *agape*, Greek for the most perfect kind of love. The writer's point seems to be: Don't misinterpret Jesus's next actions as a lack of love.

"So, when He heard that he was sick, He stayed two more days in the place where He was" (John 11:6 NKJV). He didn't delay his departure to Bethany because he didn't care, but precisely because he cared so much!

Upon arrival, how long did they tell him Lazarus had been dead and in the grave? Four days (John 11:17). In the first century, Jews buried the dead the same day they died. Rabbis taught that the grave should be visited for three days following burial to be sure the person was really dead. (One rabbi taught that the soul hung around for three days, hoping to return to the body; in three days it could tell by the color of the corpse's face it was really dead, then it would leave.)

Jesus, however, had a different <u>purpose</u> in his procrastination. He wanted there to be no doubt Lazarus was dead, so when he raised him from the dead there would be no doubt it was a miracle. The <u>effect</u> on the faith of his friends hinged on the official certification that Lazarus was dead.

The Ultimate Nap

JOHN 11:11–14 *"Our friend Lazarus **sleeps**, but I go that I may wake him up." Then His disciples said, "Lord, if he sleeps he will get well." However, Jesus spoke of his death, but they thought that He was speaking about taking rest in sleep. Then Jesus said to them plainly, "Lazarus is dead." (NKJV)*

go to

sleeps
Luke 8:52;
Acts 7:60;
1 Corinthians 11:30;
15:17–18

immediately awake
Luke 16:22–23;
23:43;
2 Corinthians 5:8;
Philippians 1:21–23

doubting Thomas
John 20:25

His disciples thought he meant, "He's sleeping"—a sign he was on the mend. Not so. Jesus restated it clearly: "Lazarus is dead." For the believer in Christ, death is merely a pause, a moment of sleep, from which we <u>immediately awake</u> in the presence of the Lord.

sleeps
The Bible often speaks of believers' deaths as "falling asleep."

stayed
literally, "she sat"

> ### what others say
>
> **Leon Morris**
>
> In the New Testament death for the believer is characteristically spoken of as "sleep." . . . Few things illustrate more graphically the difference the coming of Christ made than this. Throughout the ancient world the fear of death was universal. Death was a grim adversary that all men feared and no man could defeat. But Christ's resurrection altered all that for his followers. For them death no longer was a hateful foe. Its sting was drawn (1 Corinthians 15:55) . . . Death is no more now than sleep.[4]

The Resurrection and the Life

JOHN 11:16 *Then Thomas, who is called the Twin, said to his fellow disciples, "Let us also go, that we may die with Him." (NKJV)*

Thomas (sometimes called "<u>doubting Thomas</u>") was the first to confess his "faith" that they were all headed for death! But, bless his pessimistic little heart, he was the first in line to volunteer.

As they approached Bethany, word of Jesus's arrival reached Mary and Martha. It was the fourth day after Lazarus's death, the day professional mourners, flute players, and hired wailing women really hit the crescendo in their funereal racket. Martha went out to meet Jesus.

Mary was too overcome with grief. She **stayed** in the house where the mournful chaos harmonized with her heart-wrenching pain.

go to

scolding
Luke 10:40

end-time resurrection
1 Corinthians 15;
1 Thessalonians
4:13–18;
Revelation 20:4–6

source
John 1:3–4; 5:26;
14:6

alive
John 5:24; 10:10;
Romans 5:9–10;
1 Corinthians 15:22

resurrection
power and promise
to bring the dead to
life

life
source and sustainer
of all life, including
life from the dead

The Evolution of Resurrection Faith

JOHN 11:21–22 *Now Martha said to Jesus, "Lord, if You had been here, my brother would not have died. But even now I know that whatever You ask of God, God will give You." (NKJV)*

Martha was aware that Lazarus had died before the message of his illness could reach Jesus. Her "if," sometimes interpreted as <u>scolding</u>, was more likely an expression of grief and regret, mingled with enough faith to think that, if Jesus had been present, he could have kept her brother alive.

"Your brother will rise again," Jesus assured her (John 11:23 NKJV).

Martha believed in the future, <u>end-time resurrection</u>. Serious Jews did. "I know that he will rise again in the resurrection at the last day" (John 11:24 NKJV).

The Bedrock of Believing

JOHN 11:25–27 *Jesus said to her, "I am the resurrection and the life. He who believes in Me, though he may die, he shall live. And whoever lives and believes in Me shall never die. Do you believe this?" She said to Him, "Yes, Lord, I believe that You are the Christ, the Son of God, who is to come into the world." (NKJV)*

This is one of the most startling statements Jesus ever made. He was taking Martha from where her faith was to the bedrock foundation on which her faith was built.

The "**resurrection** and the **life**" was standing in front of Martha, talking with her, at that very moment! Her friend Jesus.

Jesus claimed not only to have the power to give life and raise the dead; he claimed to be the <u>source</u> of life. He meant that the existence of all forms of life was and is dependent on him and that he, personally, was and is the substance of life.

Jesus further insisted that anyone who puts his or her personal faith in him is <u>alive</u>. It is impossible to kill such a person! Death is for dead people, not those who have eternal life. Consequently, eternal death is an impossibility for the person who trusts his or her life and destiny to Jesus.

key point

Grave Sorrow

> JOHN 11:32 *Then, when Mary came where Jesus was, and saw Him, she fell down at His feet, saying to Him, "Lord, if You had been here, my brother would not have died." (NKJV)*

Mary was brought from her place of mourning to where Jesus and Martha had been talking. When she saw Jesus, the more emotional sister fell down at his feet and repeated the same "if" lament her sister had verbalized earlier.

Grave Rage

> JOHN 11:33–37 *Therefore, when Jesus saw her weeping, and the Jews who came with her weeping, He **groaned in the spirit** and was **troubled**. And He said, "Where have you laid him?" They said to Him, "Lord, come and see." Jesus **wept**. Then the Jews said, "See how He loved him!" And some of them said, "Could not this Man, who <u>opened the eyes</u> of the blind, also have kept this man from dying?" (NKJV)*

The meanings of the original words John, the author, uses in telling this story (see sidebar) reveal that, as he approached the cave where the body of Lazarus was buried, Jesus felt a very intense mix of sorrow and anger.

Anger? At the grave of his friend? We know he wasn't weeping for Lazarus (see John 11:4, 15). Why was he so angry he snorted like a horse?

Perhaps it was the unbelief represented in the hopeless wails of the professional mourners or the thought of death's destructive and unnecessary grip on humans or the tragedy of the human situation caused by humanity's sin, combined with the personal heartbreak suffered by his dear friends Mary and Martha.

Most likely, though, his rage was against the archenemy of God—the devil, the "thief" Jesus says comes against God's flock with no other purpose than "to steal, and to kill, and to destroy" (John 10:10 NKJV).

go to

opened the eyes
John 9

groaned in the spirit
literally, "snorted like a horse"; was indignant, angry, intensely displeased

troubled
Greek: inwardly distressed, troubled, disgusted

wept
literally, "shed tears"

The Death Destroyer

JOHN 11:39–40 *Jesus said, "Take away the stone." Martha, the
sister of him who was dead, said to Him, "Lord, by this time
there is a stench, for he has been dead four days." Jesus said to
her, "Did I not say to you that if you would believe you would see
the glory of God?"* (NKJV)

At the tomb, Jesus again expressed his rage with a groan (John
11:38). "Take away the stone," he said. According to custom, a
huge, flat stone had been rolled over the entrance to the **burial
cave**.

At first, Martha recoiled from the prospect of death's unpleasant
odor. But Jesus assured her that if she trusted him she should not
expect something horrible, but something wonderful (John 11:40).

At Martha's nod, several men moved to the entrance of the tomb
and rolled away the heavy stone.

Jesus prayed a simple prayer: (1) to assure that all the glory would
go to his Father in heaven for the wonder that was about to take
place, and (2) to assure that the people would see this miracle as a
sign of Jesus's messiahship.

Come!

JOHN 11:41–43 *"Father, I thank You that You have heard Me.
And I know that You always hear Me, but because of the people
who are standing by I said this, that they may believe that You
sent Me." Now when He had said these things, He cried with a
loud voice, "Lazarus, come forth!"* (NKJV)

In the words John originally wrote to describe this happening, the order Jesus shouted to the corpse in the tomb literally was: "Lazarus! Here! Outside!"

The mourners fell silent. Every eye was fixed on the dark opening of the grave cave. Nobody breathed. Something moved inside the tomb. A few shuffling sounds. Then suddenly in the entrance of the cavern appeared a startled, struggling figure wrapped from head to foot in strips of white linen!

"Take off the grave clothes and let him go!" Jesus said. Lazarus, certified dead man, was living again! Jesus's prayer for the faith of his friends' friends was answered: "Then many of the Jews who had come to Mary, and had seen the things Jesus did, believed in Him" (John 11:45 NKJV).

Assassins' Plot

JOHN 11:46 *But some of them went away to the Pharisees and told them the things Jesus did. (NKJV)*

Some who were there in Bethany comforting the sisters were Pharisee informers. They went directly from Lazarus's resurrection party to the Pharisees in Jerusalem, just two miles away, and reported what Jesus had done and the effect it was having on the people. An emergency meeting of the Sanhedrin was called.

But God was at work even among these rebellious, self-motivated men. Though it was the last thing he intended, Caiaphas, the high priest, one of Jesus's most committed enemies, spoke prophetic words the early Christians recognized as coming from God:

"You know nothing at all, nor do you consider that it is expedient for us that one man should die for the people, and not that the whole nation should perish." The New Testament historian adds this comment: "Now this he did not say on his own authority; but being high priest that year he prophesied that Jesus would die for the nation, and not for that nation only, but also that He would gather together in one the children of God who were scattered abroad" (John 11:49–52 NKJV).

Under Caiaphas's "inspired" leadership, the Sanhedrin officially agreed Jesus must die. Thus the specific plot which culminated in his crucifixion was born the day Lazarus lived again.

Chapter Wrap-Up

- With two parables Jesus taught the difference between the world's way of handling money and his followers' way. He called for creativity in investing in others, and for awareness that how we invest our possessions has eternal consequences. (John 16:1–31)

- Jesus's friend Lazarus died. He and his disciples returned to Bethany (two miles from Jerusalem), where Jesus raised Lazarus from the dead and announced, "I am the resurrection and the life" (John 11:25 NKJV).

- Some Jewish leaders put their faith in Jesus when they saw Lazarus rise from the dead. Others reported it to the Pharisees. At an emergency meeting of the Sanhedrin the high priest unwittingly prophesied Jesus would be sacrificed for the people. Plans were made to arrest and kill Jesus. (John 11:45–53)

Study Questions

1. How long had Jesus's friend Lazarus been dead when Jesus raised him from the dead?

2. In conversation with Lazarus's sister Martha, what did Jesus say could never happen? What did he mean?

3. Identify four things Martha believed about Jesus (John 11:22, 27). What did Jesus promise she would see if she believed?

Chapter 26: Final Journey to Jeruslaem

Let's Get Started

As soon as the miracle of Lazarus of Bethany was reported to the leaders at Jerusalem, they met to lay specific plans to end the young Nazarene's career (John 11:53). What else could they do? The choice was clear: Either embrace and endorse Jesus, or . . . assassinate him!

Always aware of his Father's timetable, Jesus quietly slipped out of Bethany and took his men to the Judean mountain village of Ephraim, about fifteen miles north (see appendix A). This was the final retreat before the final march to the final Passover in the Holy City.

law
Leviticus 13–14

leprosy
contagious skin disorders; Hansen's disease

Walking Dead Men

> LUKE 17:12–16 *Then as [Jesus] entered a certain village, there met Him ten men who were lepers, who stood afar off. And they lifted up their voices and said, "Jesus, Master, have mercy on us!" So when He saw them, He said to them, "Go, show yourselves to the priests." And so it was that as they went, they were cleansed. And one of them, when he saw that he was healed, returned, and with a loud voice glorified God, and fell down on his face at His feet, giving Him thanks. And he was a Samaritan. (NKJV)*

As Jesus and his men were about to enter a village in the disputed territory along the border between Galilee and Samaria, a pitiful group of ten men with **leprosy** met them. In compliance with the <u>law</u> concerning lepers, they remained outside of town, loudly calling attention to their condition. Usually the leper's cry was to protect other people from entering their quarantine zone. In this case, it was a call for help: "Jesus, Master, have mercy on us!"

Jesus immediately challenged them to act on their faith. According to Old Testament Law, healed lepers must show themselves to a priest who could certify their cure (Leviticus 14).

good light
Matthew 15:21–28;
Luke 7:2–9;
10:29–37;
John 4:4–42

With the symptoms still visible, it took faith to go to the priest as Jesus ordered. "And so it was that as they went, they were cleansed" (Luke 17:14 NKJV)—the diseased flesh became healthy, the symptoms disappeared.

One-Man Praise Band

One of the ten, when he discovered his body was free of disease, broke ranks with the others and returned, shouting praise to God at the top of his healed lungs! He threw himself down at Jesus's feet and thanked him. Luke notes, "He was a Samaritan" (Luke 17:16 NKJV).

"Were there not ten cleansed?" Jesus asked. "But where are the nine? Were there not any found who returned to give glory to God except this foreigner?" Then to the man he said, "Arise, go your way. Your faith has made you well" (Luke 17:17–19 NKJV).

Hidden in Jesus's statements are a couple of ideas worth noting:

1. Jesus used different words to describe what happened to the nine who did not thank him and what happened to the one who did.

- The original word for the healing of nine ("cleansed") simply means they were cleansed of leprosy, physically healed.

- The original for the healing of the thankful one ("made . . . well") means he was completely healed, fully restored—it's a biblical word for salvation.

2. Jews held a deep and abiding prejudice against Samaritans. Jesus delighted in showing Samaritans and foreigners in a <u>good light</u>.

what others say

Tim Stafford

Praise of God is fundamental to my relationship with him. It opens a channel of loving regard. When I bring my requests to God, I stand by him looking toward mutual concerns, but when I praise him my eyes are lifted in intimacy and warmth toward him. I look to his face.[1]

What Is This Kingdom of God?

LUKE 17:20–21 Now when He was asked by the Pharisees when the kingdom of God would come, He answered them and said, "The kingdom of God does not come with observation; nor will they say, 'See here!' or 'See there!' For indeed, the kingdom of God is within you." (NKJV)

go to

announcing
Matthew 4:17;
Mark 1:14–15;
Luke 4:43

secret
Matthew 13:33;
Luke 13:20–21

Jesus had begun his public ministry three years earlier <u>announcing</u> arrival of the kingdom of God. People looking for him to establish a visible, earthly government were still looking.

Jesus's answer said two things about the kingdom of God: (1) You can't find it by spying ("observation") to find something to use against Christ (Luke 17:20), and (2) the kingdom is a <u>secret</u> within-you operation; don't expect it to appear in some familiar form in an identifiable geographical location with a flashing neon sign saying, "Welcome to God's kingdom!"

The kingdom of God is a spiritual reality happening within and among God's people, built not on Christ's visible presence but on the presence of his Spirit.

Since the kingdom of God is "within you" and is built around the spiritual rather than visible presence of Jesus, the chief system for communication between kingdom citizens and their King is the hotline of prayer. On the road toward Jerusalem, Jesus told two stories to illustrate prayers that fulfill kingdom goals.

Prayer as a Fight for Justice

LUKE 18:1–5 Then [Jesus] spoke a parable to them, that men always ought to pray and not lose heart, saying: "There was in a certain city a judge who did not fear God nor regard man. Now there was a widow in that city; and she came to him, saying, 'Get justice for me from my adversary.' And he would not for a while; but afterward he said within himself, 'Though I do not fear God nor regard man, yet because this widow troubles me I will avenge her, lest by her continual coming she weary me.'" (NKJV)

waiting
2 Peter 3:8–9

compared
Romans 3:23

fast
skipping meals

tithe
10 percent of
income was given to
the temple

If a crooked, godless judge will grant justice when confronted with courage and persistence, God, who cares about people and loves righteousness and justice, eagerly waits for people to come to him for help! If the justice we pray for is delayed, we can be sure it is because he is <u>waiting</u> for people to repent and turn to him in faith (Luke 18:8).

Prayer as a Cry for Justification

LUKE 18:10–14 *Two men went up to the temple to pray, one a Pharisee and the other a tax collector. The Pharisee stood and prayed thus with himself, "God, I thank You that I am not like other men—extortioners, unjust, adulterers, or even as this tax collector. I fast twice a week; I give tithes of all that I possess." And the tax collector, standing afar off, would not so much as raise his eyes to heaven, but beat his breast, saying, "God, be merciful to me a sinner!" I tell you, this man went down to his house justified rather than the other; for everyone who exalts himself will be humbled, and he who humbles himself will be exalted. (NKJV)*

The next story Jesus told was especially for "some who trusted in themselves that they were righteous, and despised others" (Luke 18:9 NKJV). Self-righteousness is a hard sin to deal with, because nobody ever feels guilty for being "righteous."

This Pharisee went way beyond the requirements of the Law:

- *Fasting.* The Law required one **fast** a year, on Yom Kippur. He fasted twice a week.

- *Tithing.* The Law required a **tithe** of grain, new wine, flocks, and herds. He paid tithes on everything (Luke 11:42), even garden herbs.

Why was this admitted "bad guy" accepted by God, while the Pharisee wasn't?

The Pharisee expected God to accept him based on how he compared with other people; the tax collector <u>compared</u> himself with God and knew he didn't have a chance without God's mercy.

On Marriage and Children

go to

at the beginning
Genesis 2:24

MATTHEW 19:3 *The Pharisees also came to Him, testing Him, and saying to Him, "Is it lawful for a man to divorce his wife for just any reason?"* (NKJV)

A hot topic in that day as in ours was divorce. No culture had ever held marriage in such high esteem as the Jews did. They took God's earliest commandment to "be fruitful and multiply" (Genesis 1:28 NKJV) very seriously. According to ancient teachings, to fail to be married and produce children was to "lessen the image of God on the earth."[2]

But the rabbis, official interpreters of the Old Testament Law, were all over the map on the subject of divorce.

The Pharisees tried to get Jesus to take sides in the debate. They may have figured that, no matter which rabbi he sided with, he'd make somebody mad! Jesus refused to take the bait.

Instead he raised the marriage and divorce issue to a new level. The Pharisees had asked what was "lawful." Jesus took them back behind the Law to the story of creation in the book of Genesis.

monogamous
one man married to
one woman

polygamy
marriage to more
than one partner

Jesus on Marriage

MATTHEW 19:4–6 *And He answered and said to them, "Have you not read that He who made them <u>at the beginning</u> 'made them male and female,' and said, 'For this reason a man shall leave his father and mother and be joined to his wife, and the two shall become one flesh'? So then, they are no longer two but one flesh. Therefore what God has joined together, let not man separate."* (NKJV)

From the creation story Jesus drew these insights on marriage:

- *Man and woman.* God created marriage by making human beings "male and female," giving them to each other and commissioning them to bear children (Matthew 19:4; Genesis 1:27–28; 2:22–23).

- *Monogamy.* God's original design called for **monogamous** marriage, like Adam and Eve's—one man with one woman (Matthew 19:5; Genesis 2:24). **Polygamy** was permitted and existed among Jews even in the first century, but was never the Creator's ideal.

go to

one flesh
Ephesians 5:21–33

Moses
Deuteronomy
24:1–4

spiritual infidelity
Ezekiel 16;
Hosea 2

desertion
1 Corinthians 7:15

one flesh
man and woman
joined together in
body, mind, and
emotions

spiritual infidelity
unfaithfulness to the
covenant (relation-
ship) with God

- *Oneness.* Marriage is a man and a woman who leave all others to become "**one flesh**" (Matthew 19:5–6; Genesis 2:24). The two become "joined in such a way that they share everything in their journey of life together";[3] spiritually, emotionally, and physically; sexual union is "the ribbon that ties the marriage bundle together."

- *Permanence.* Marriage is intended to be permanent (Matthew 19:6; Malachi 2:13–16).

Jesus on Divorce

MATTHEW 19:8–9 *He said to them, "Moses, because of the hardness of your hearts, permitted you to divorce your wives, but from the beginning it was not so. And I say to you, whoever divorces his wife, except for sexual immorality, and marries another, commits adultery; and whoever marries her who is divorced commits adultery." (NKJV)*

The Pharisees were less than thrilled with his first answer, so they hit him up again: "Why then did <u>Moses</u> command to give a certificate of divorce, and to put her away?" they argued (Matthew 19:7 NKJV). (A certificate of divorce was not an important court document; it was just a written notice by a husband saying, "She is not my wife, and I am not her husband.") Jesus's response this time was clear:

- Divorce was never commanded, as the Pharisees erroneously said (Matthew 19:7). Divorce was "permitted" (Matthew 19:8; Deuteronomy 24:1).

- The reason God, through Moses, allowed divorce was because people's "hearts were hard." The Greek word for hard-hearted means obstinate, stubborn in opposing what is right or reasonable, wrongheaded.

- Jesus took a stand against divorces of convenience. However, he made an exception for divorce in cases of "sexual immorality" (Matthew 19:9 NKJV). The Greek word is usually used for sexual promiscuity, but it can also be a metaphor for **spiritual infidelity**.

- Sex with a person who is not one's marriage partner shatters the marriage covenant, often beyond repair. Marital unfaithfulness can take other forms as well (such as <u>desertion</u>).

All forms of disloyalty to one's marriage vows come from hard-heartedness, not love.

give
Deuteronomy
15:7–8, 11

Kids in the Kingdom

MATTHEW 19:13–14 *Then little children were brought to Him that He might put His hands on them and pray, but the disciples rebuked them. But Jesus said, "Let the little children come to Me, and do not forbid them; for of such is the kingdom of heaven." (NKJV)*

It is no accident that the story of parents bringing their children to Jesus follows hot on the heels of that heavy discussion of marriage and divorce.

The humility, honesty, dependence, and teachability of little children stands in refreshing contrast to the pride, infidelity, independence, and rigidity that destroy marriages. Jesus makes childlikeness the ideal for all his followers.

The Love of Money

MARK 10:17–21 *Now as He was going out on the road, one came running, knelt before Him, and asked Him, "Good Teacher, what shall I do that I may inherit eternal life?" So Jesus said to him, "Why do you call Me good? No one is good but One, that is, God. You know the commandments: 'Do not commit adultery,' 'Do not murder,' 'Do not steal,' 'Do not bear false witness,' 'Do not defraud,' 'Honor your father and your mother.'" And he answered and said to Him, "Teacher, all these things I have kept from my youth." Then Jesus, looking at him, loved him, and said to him, "One thing you lack: Go your way, sell whatever you have and <u>give</u> to the poor, and you will have treasure in heaven; and come, take up the cross, and follow Me." (NKJV)*

go to

Ten Commandments
Exodus 20

basis of faith
Ephesians 2:8–9

Yahweh
Exodus 3:14

mammon
Luke 16:13

called
Matthew 10:38;
16:24;
John 10:4, 27; 12:26

direct command
Matthew 4:19; 8:22;
9:9;
Mark 2:14;
John 1:43

young ruler
civil rather than
religious official;
too young to be
an elder

As Jesus started out on the next leg of his journey to Jerusalem, a **young ruler** ran to meet him. This young man was eager to know how to receive eternal life.

Jesus reminded him that no Jewish teacher called another "good." The rabbis said, "There is nothing that is good, but the Law."

Then Jesus listed five of the <u>Ten Commandments</u>, focusing on human relationships (not attitudes toward God). The young man said he'd kept these all his life.

Jesus looked at him and loved him. Then he struck the nerve issue standing between this man and God—his wealth (Mark 10:21).

What Jesus asked him to do would have been difficult even for a poor man! We can't help wondering why he made the way so tough for this man when he doesn't require the same level of abandonment from everyone.

Here may be some reasons:

1. Eternal life can only be obtained on the <u>basis of faith</u>—keeping commandments and being a good or successful citizen is not enough. To do what Jesus asked would require complete trust in Jesus.

2. To show the young man his failure to keep the first, most important commandment: "You shall have no other gods before Me" (Exodus 20:3 NKJV). The god this man served was not <u>Yahweh</u> but <u>mammon.</u> (The young ruler's response showed he was unwilling to serve God if it meant giving up his money. See Mark 10:22.)

3. Another reason may be hidden in the command "Follow Me" (Mark 10:21 NKJV). All believers are <u>called</u> to follow Christ, but in the four Gospels the <u>direct command</u>, "Follow Me," is nearly always associated with a call to apostleship. Did Jesus want this man to become his apostle?

Impossible for Man—Possible for God

MARK 10:23–25 *Then Jesus looked around and said to His disciples, "How hard it is for those who have riches to enter the kingdom of God! . . . It is easier for a camel to go through the eye of a needle than for a rich man to enter the kingdom of God." (NKJV)*

The disciples were amazed at this statement. Nothing was more inconceivable to them than that wealth should be a hindrance to getting into the kingdom. Common Jewish belief was that wealth was a sign of God's <u>approval</u>, and that the man who was blessed with it must be a good man.

Some say there was a gate in the wall of Jerusalem designed for human passage. This gate was so small, a camel could only pass through on its knees, and then only if it carried nothing on its back (a picture of the rich man who must give up his trust in wealth in order to enter the kingdom).

One Gospel writer, however, uses the Greek word for a literal tailor's needle here. Most think Jesus is drawing a hilarious mental cartoon—a camel trying to get through the eye of a tailor's needle—a ridiculous impossibility!

"Who then can be saved?" the disciples moaned (Mark 10:26 NKJV). "With God all things are possible," Jesus answered (10:27 NKJV).

approval
Job 1:10; 42:10;
Psalm 37:25

what others say

Ronald J. Sider

Wealth and possessions are the most common idols of us rich Westerners . . . We have become ensnared by unprecedented material luxury . . . The standard of living is the god of twentieth-century America, and the ad man is its prophet.[5]

The Sinner-King of Jericho

LUKE 19:2–6 *Now behold, there was a man named Zacchaeus who was a chief tax collector, and he was rich. And he sought to see who Jesus was, but could not because of the crowd, for he was of short stature. So he ran ahead and climbed up into a sycamore tree to see Him, for He was going to pass that way. And when Jesus came to the place, He looked up and saw him, and said to him, "Zacchaeus, make haste and come down, for today I must stay at your house." So he made haste and came down, and received Him joyfully. (NKJV)*

Of all the characters that crossed Jesus's path, few are more intriguing than Zacchaeus. He was a CEO of sinners. Hired sinners under him did his sinning for him!

Desperately needy and hungry for a new life, the love-starved little man hoped for a glimpse of Jesus as he passed by. Too proud to scream for help like blind Bartimaeus, he'd just watch while the parade of hope passed by under his lonely tree-branch perch.

It was his great good fortune, however, that the route Jesus took brought the Life-Giver directly beneath the tree in whose branches Zacchaeus sat. Jesus looked up and ordered the surprised **sycamore**-sitter to slide down and make up the bed in the guest room—Jesus would be staying the night!

Salvation of the lost, Jesus declared (Luke 19:10), was not incidental to his mission; it was his mission. The tiny taxman climbed down from his roost, welcomed Jesus into his home and life, and emerged from the encounter a changed man. "Zacchaeus stood and said to the Lord, 'Look, Lord, I give half of my goods to the poor; and if I have taken anything from anyone by false accusation, I restore fourfold'" (Luke 19:8 NKJV).

Chapter Wrap-Up

- On the border between Galilee and Samaria, ten lepers cried for help. Jesus sent them to the priest to verify their healing. Only one—a Samaritan—returned to thank him. (Luke 17:11–19)

- When asked the location of the kingdom of God, Jesus answered that it is within people (and among them) and is not built around his physical presence but is built, rather, around his spiritual presence. (Luke 17:20–25)

- Using two parables, Jesus taught that prayer is a cry for justice or justification, and that it requires persistence, humility, and frank admission of desperate personal need. (Luke 18:1–14)

- A question from some Pharisees about divorce triggered an important teaching concerning marriage and divorce. He emphasized marriage rather than divorce. Hard-heartedness was the root cause of divorce, he said. (Matthew 19:1–12)

- A rich young ruler came asking how to obtain eternal life. Jesus told him to give away everything he owned and follow him. The man went away sadly. Jesus taught his disciples that it was difficult but not impossible for the rich to enter the kingdom. (Mark 10:17–31)

- At Jericho, Jesus encountered the spiritually blind tax collector, Zacchaeus. He saved the taxman. (Luke 18:35–19:10)

Study Questions

1. What type of prayer did Jesus encourage by his parable of the widow and the judge? By the one about the Pharisee and the tax collector? Which of the two comes closest to your own heart's desire right now?

2. Identify the four major insights Jesus gave on marriage.

3. What did Jesus ask the rich young ruler to do to obtain eternal life? Why did he ask so much from him?

4. What does the Zacchaeus story tell us about Jesus? How did Zacchaeus demonstrate his readiness to receive the salvation Jesus offered? Where were you when you were first introduced to Jesus? (a) up a tree?, (b) out on a limb?, or (c) hiding, hoping he'd find you? Where are you now?

Part Five
SIX DAYS TO GLORY

Chapter 27: Parade

Chapter Highlights:
- All the King's Men
- The Hit List
- Priceless Worship
- The Victory Pageant
- Up with the Son!

Let's Get Started

God's clock was ticking. Time was running out. But still his followers failed to grasp the true nature of his kingdom and the road he must follow to claim the throne. At least seven times, Jesus had told his friends about the events that would occur in Jerusalem—his rejection, suffering, death, and resurrection. But they were <u>unable to fit</u> the idea of the King's death into their understanding of his reign.

All the King's Men

> **LUKE 19:11** *Now as they heard these things, He spoke another parable, because He was near Jerusalem and because they thought the kingdom of God would appear immediately.* (NKJV)

gospel harmony

Matthew 25:14–30
Luke 19:11–27

Jesus's disciples saw the crowds increasing. They heard the people talking.

Thousands would gather for the Passover. Many speculated that this celebration of Israel's liberation would be the ideal time to unveil the kingdom. These people clung to the notion that "the kingdom of God would appear immediately." Jesus told a story designed to chip away at their erroneous expectations.

A nobleman had been appointed king. While the man was away for his coronation, he turned his financial affairs over to ten trusted servants, giving each a **mina** to invest for him. Jesus added that the man's servants "hated him, and sent a delegation" to try to prevent his appointment (Luke 19:14 NKJV).

go to

unable to fit
Luke 18:31–34;
Mark 8:31–33

mina
about one hundred
days' wages

When the newly appointed king returned, he called his ten brokers to account for how they'd handled his money. One had earned 1,000 percent return (Luke 19:16). Another had gained 500 percent (19:18). Both were given promotions in keeping with their success.

Then came the overscrupulous man who had kept the king's money "in a handkerchief" (Luke 19:20 NKJV) because he thought the king was an **austere** man.

austere
Greek: sour, harsh,
rigid, ungenerous,
severe, disagreeable

go to
John 15:5–7;
Acts 1:10–11

resources
Acts 1:8;
1 Corinthians 12;
Romans 12

raised Lazarus
John 11

sign
proof he was the
Messiah

six days before
Sabbath—sundown
Friday to sundown
Saturday

Not only was this broker not rewarded for protecting the king's money, it was taken away from him. He ended up with nothing to show for his trouble but a reprimand! As for those subjects who tried to keep him from reigning, the king issued the order "Bring here those enemies of mine, who did not want me to reign over them, and slay them before me" (Luke 19:27 NKJV).

The interpretation revolves around four characters or groups:

- The nobleman pictures Christ.
- The imperial authority to whom he owed his appointment represents God the Father.
- The ten servants trusted to care for his business represent Christ's disciples.
- The rebellious subjects determined to keep him off the throne represent Jesus's enemies.

This story teaches that between the time Christ left the world to go to his Father and his second coming, there would be a lengthy interval. While waiting for his return, his servants would be entrusted with resources for the work he wanted them to do (Luke 19:13).

> **what others say**
>
> **Leon Morris**
>
> In the Christian life we do not stand still. We use our gifts and make progress or we lose what we have.[1]

Arrest Warrant

JOHN 11:57 *Now both the chief priests and the Pharisees had given a command, that if anyone knew where He was, he should report it, that they might seize Him. (NKJV)*

The last time Jesus was near Jerusalem, at Bethany, he had raised Lazarus from the dead. As a direct result of that **sign**/miracle, Jesus's enemies in the Sanhedrin pushed through an official edict to arrest him.

The "outlaw" arrived at Bethany, two miles from Jerusalem, at the home of Lazarus, Martha, and Mary, **six days before** the Passover (John 12:1). Bethany would be his headquarters for the next few days. Each day until Passover, he and his disciples would walk to the temple (two miles west) and return at night.

The Hit List

JOHN 12:9–11 *Now a great many of the Jews knew that He was there; and they came, not for Jesus' sake only, but that they might also see Lazarus, whom He had raised from the dead. But the chief priests plotted to put Lazarus to death also, because on account of him many of the Jews went away and believed in Jesus.* (NKJV)

The streets of Bethany were filled with curiosity seekers, hoping for a glimpse of one or both "celebrities"—Jesus or Lazarus, the man alive from the dead, as Lazarus was living proof Jesus was the Messiah.

The number of people siding with the man religious leaders viewed as "public enemy number one" increased, while the number loyal to the leaders shrank. In desperation, the clergy added Lazarus to their list of people to be assassinated! For the man who had already died once, friendship with Christ suddenly became very costly.

Priceless Worship

JOHN 12:3 *Then Mary took a pound of very costly **oil of spikenard**, anointed the feet of Jesus, and wiped His feet with her hair. And the house was filled with the fragrance of the oil.* (NKJV)

As Passover week began, a dinner in Jesus's honor was held in Bethany at the home of Simon the leper (Matthew and Mark supply the host's name).

Lazarus was there, alive and kicking, at the table with Jesus. His sister Martha, in her <u>usual role</u>, served the meal.

At some point in the party, Mary did an unusual thing: She emptied a "pound of very costly oil of spikenard" on Jesus's head and feet as he reclined at the table.

It was an extravagant act. Some witnesses found such extravagance disturbing. Mary was concentrating on Jesus—dramatizing her love, gratitude, faith, and reverence.

As the **costly** oil ran over his feet, this highborn woman let down the tresses of her long hair (something Jewish women did not do in

go to

usual role
Luke 10:38–42

oil of spikenard
precious imported oil from the Indian nard plant

costly
a year's wages, three hundred denarii

gospel harmony

Matthew 26:6–13
Mark 14:3–9
Luke 7:36–50
John 12:1–11

public), got on her knees behind him, and proceeded to wipe the excess **spikenard** from his feet <u>with her hair</u>.

The Priority of Worship

JOHN 12:4–6 But one of His disciples, Judas Iscariot, Simon's son, who would betray Him, said, "Why was this fragrant oil not sold for three hundred denarii and given to the poor?" This he said, not that he cared for the poor, but because he was a thief, and had the money box; and he used to take what was put in it. (NKJV)

Hiding behind a smoke screen of concern for the poor, Judas Iscariot protested the extravagance. The truth was, he was a petty embezzler, pilfering the kingdom community's common purse of gifts given to support Jesus's ministry. Christ's response was to tell the self-motivated critic to stop harassing the worshipper.

Jesus insisted Mary was preparing him for "**burial**," which he knew would come within the week (verse 7). In John 19:40, the same word is used for the Jewish custom of wrapping the body with spices and linen. Nard was often one of the spices used.

<u>Nobody cared more</u> about the poor than Jesus, but Judas and the other critics within his own ranks (Mark 14:4) needed to understand two realities. First, he would be with them for only six more days—whatever they were going to do to express their love had to be done soon. Second, there would always be poor people to help; after he was gone, <u>care of the needy</u> would become a high-priority expression of love to him (John 12:8).

go to

with her hair
Luke 7:36–38

burial
John 19:39–40

nobody cared more
Luke 4:18–19;
Matthew 4:23–24;
John 6:5–13

care of the needy
Matthew 25:34–45

spikenard
perfume from roots of perennial nard plant

burial
"laying out the corpse" for burial

> **what others say**
>
> **Venerable Bede**
>
> We anoint the Lord's head when we cherish the glory of his divinity, along with that of his humanity, with the worthy sweetness of faith, hope and charity, [and] when we spread the praise of his name by living uprightly. We anoint the Lord's feet when we renew his poor by a word of consolation, so that they may not lose hope when they are under duress. We wipe [the feet of] these same ones with our hair when we share some of what is superfluous to us [to alleviate] the wants of the needy.[2]

The Victory Pageant

> LUKE 19:35–38 *Then they brought [the colt] to Jesus. And they threw their own clothes on the colt, and they set Jesus on him. And as He went, many spread their clothes on the road. Then, as He was now drawing near the descent of the Mount of Olives, the whole multitude of the disciples began to rejoice and praise God with a loud voice for all the mighty works they had seen, saying:*
> *"'Blessed is the King who comes in the name of the LORD!'*
> *Peace in heaven and glory in the highest!" (NKJV)*

The next day, **Sunday**, Jesus led the way from Bethany to the Mount of Olives, about a half mile from Jerusalem. There he paused to put into operation plans for entrance into the city that would fulfill <u>messianic prophecy</u>.

Two disciples were sent into Bethphage, a tiny village in the shadow of the city wall. They would find and borrow a never-before-ridden donkey colt. If, as they untied the colt the owners asked why, they were to answer with what may have been a prearranged password, "Because the Lord has need of it" (Luke 19:31 NKJV), and the owners would let them take it.

By the time the colt arrived, pilgrims were jamming the road. Exuberant disciples made a saddle of their outer cloaks and lifted Jesus onto the back of the animal.

Matthew mentions two animals, a donkey and a colt; both had been brought (21:2, 7). Jesus rode the colt, and the mother was led along so the colt would be at ease with its first rider.

Spontaneously, people <u>laid their clothes</u> on the ground along with palm branches cut from nearby trees to form a multicolored royal carpet upon which Jesus rode in kingly triumph the last half mile into the city (John 12:13). Thousands waved <u>palm branches</u> and cheered loudly, a common practice for honoring a conqueror.

At last Jesus was doing what the <u>Galileans</u> had wanted him to do after the feeding of the five thousand. This time he accepted their acclamation of his royalty. He was the King of Israel!

Fidgety Pharisees

> LUKE 19:39–40 *And some of the Pharisees called to Him from the crowd, "Teacher, rebuke Your disciples." But He answered*

Matthew 21:1–17
Mark 11:1–11
Luke 19:28–46
John 12:9–50

messianic prophecy
Isaiah 62:11;
Zechariah 9:9;
Matthew 21:5

laid their clothes
2 Kings 9:13

palm branches
Revelation 7:9

Galileans
John 6:14–15

Sunday
now called "Palm Sunday"

wept
Greek: "wailed,"
broke into sobs

and said to them, "I tell you that if these should keep silent, the stones would immediately cry out." (NKJV)

Not everyone was thrilled. Many who watched the parade pour into the streets of Jerusalem were still asking, "Who is this?" (Matthew 21:10 NKJV). The Pharisees demanded Jesus stop his supporters from shouting those unnerving Bible slogans!

But his kingship had to be proclaimed, or the huge stones in the temple walls would find voices. This was the day for the cosmos to acknowledge, "Jesus is King!"

The Warrior

LUKE 19:41–44 *Now as He drew near, He saw the city and wept over it, saying, "If you had known, even you, especially in this your day, the things that make for your peace! But now they are hidden from your eyes. For days will come upon you when your enemies will build an embankment around you, surround you and close you in on every side, and level you, and your children within you, to the ground; and they will not leave in you one stone upon another, because you did not know the time of your visitation." (NKJV)*

As the borrowed donkey carried him through the city gate, Jesus **wept** and prophesied the city's destruction. Forty years later, every tragic detail of his prophecy (Luke 19:43–44) was fulfilled. In AD 70 Jerusalem was sacked, the temple was reduced to rubble and burned by the armies of Emperor Titus, and 1,100,000 Jews were killed.[3]

what others say

Michael Card

How can we call it the "Triumphal Entry" when Jesus was still wiping tears from his eyes? . . . The disciples were singing. Jesus was weeping . . . Jesus' first coming was characterized by misunderstanding. But there will be a Second. The misunderstood Messiah, who that day was a Lamb, will return as a Lion.

. . . Jesus will not be wiping tears of sorrow from his eyes but most likely tears of joy and relief. And he will be wiping away our tears as well.[4]

The Curse of Empty Promises

MARK 11:12–14 *Now the next day, when they had come out from Bethany, [Jesus] was hungry. And seeing from afar a fig tree having leaves, He went to see if perhaps He would find something on it. When He came to it, He found nothing but leaves, for it was not the season for figs. In response Jesus said to it, "Let no one eat fruit from you ever again." And His disciples heard it.* (NKJV)

The next morning on the way back into Jerusalem, Jesus was hungry. He stopped at a lonely, leafy fig tree beside the road to see if there were any figs left from the year before. Finding "nothing but leaves," Jesus spoke to the fruitless tree: "Let no one eat fruit from you ever again!" The tree shriveled up and died (Matthew 21:19).

Mark comments that this was not the season for figs (11:13), a fact Jesus well knew. But, the <u>fig tree</u> was a traditional symbol for the nation of Israel. The search for fruit Jesus knew wasn't there was an attention-grabber for a **symbolic** teaching he wanted to share.

go to

fig tree
Jeremiah 8:13;
29:17;
Hosea 9:10, 16;
Joel 1:7;
Luke 13:6–9

same
John 2:14–17

symbolic
called "an enacted parable"

The Redeemer's Wrath

MARK 11:15–16 *So they came to Jerusalem. Then Jesus went into the temple and began to drive out those who bought and sold in the temple, and overturned the tables of the money changers and the seats of those who sold doves. And He would not allow anyone to carry wares through the temple.* (NKJV)

For a man with a price on his head, Jesus took a big risk to reenter the city the next morning. Right under the noses of the authorities who had ordered his arrest, he stormed into the temple and single-handedly shut down the temple market, bodily ejecting entrepreneurs who were exploiting out-of-town worshippers.

He had begun his ministry with the <u>same</u> brash act.

Predictably temple officials became more committed to kill Jesus. The only reason they didn't do it then and there was fear of political repercussions. "The chief priests, the scribes, and the leaders of the people sought to destroy Him, and were unable to do anything; for all the people were very attentive to hear Him" (Luke 19:47–48 NKJV).

gospel harmony

Matthew 21:12–13
Mark 11:15–19
Luke 19:45–48

go to

time
John 2:4; 7:30; 8:20

glorified
extolled, magnified,
invested with
majesty

Up with the Son!

JOHN 12:20–21 *Now there were certain Greeks among those who came up to worship at the feast. Then they came to Philip, who was from Bethsaida of Galilee, and asked him, saying, "Sir, we wish to see Jesus." (NKJV)*

Jesus didn't respond directly to the Greeks (or perhaps he did but John did not report it). But he took the request as a signal that the time had come for his ministry to reach its climax: "The hour has come that the Son of Man should be glorified" (John 12:23 NKJV). It was his time to be **glorified** and for his message to be taken to the world.

One Life to Give

JOHN 12:27–28a *Now My soul is troubled, and what shall I say? "Father, save Me from this hour"? But for this purpose I came to this hour. Father, glorify Your name. (NKJV)*

Jesus referred to his death by explaining how a kernel of wheat has to fall into the ground and die in order to multiply (John 12:24–26).

Knowing that this was the time for which he was born, he said, "Father, glorify Your name" (John 12:28 NKJV).

> **what others say**
>
> **Leon Morris**
>
> The way to fruitfulness lies through death. Unless the wheat falls into the ground and "dies" it will not bear. It is only through "death" that its potentiality for fruitfulness becomes actual. This is a general truth. But it refers particularly to our Lord himself.[5]

The Good Sonship Seal of Approval

JOHN 12:28b *Then a voice came from heaven, saying, "I have both glorified it and will glorify it again." (NKJV)*

No sooner had Jesus's emotional prayer escaped his lips than the temple area shook with what sounded to the crowd like a clap of thunder. God affirmed that everything Jesus was and did revealed his splendor, and promised that the wonders of God would continue to be revealed in Jesus.

No Time to Ride the Fence

Sanhedrin
John 11:47–53

expelled
John 9:34

light
spiritual insight,
information

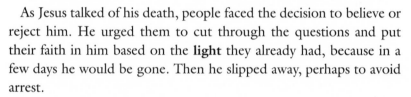

the big picture

John 12:34–50

Even after Jesus had done all those miraculous signs in their presence, the Jews still would not believe in him. Their unbelief fulfilled prophecies of Isaiah. Some people, even among the leaders, believed in him, but because of the Pharisees they would not confess their faith for fear they would be put out of the synagogue. These secret believers loved praise from men more than praise from God.

Jesus said those who believe in him believe in the one who sent him. He said he did not come to judge, but that there is a judge for those who reject him. Jesus stated that he speaks what God wants him to say.

As Jesus talked of his death, people faced the decision to believe or reject him. He urged them to cut through the questions and put their faith in him based on the **light** they already had, because in a few days he would be gone. Then he slipped away, perhaps to avoid arrest.

Decisions were made that day: Some still refused to believe (John 12:37). Others believed, even some <u>Sanhedrin</u> members. But they kept their faith to themselves for fear of being <u>expelled</u> from the synagogue (12:42–43).

Chapter Wrap-Up

- Jesus told a parable to teach his followers that there would be an interval of time between his death and his second coming, and that they would be accountable for their handling of resources he left with them to carry on his work. (Luke 19:11–27)

- By the time Jesus reached Bethany, the Sanhedrin had issued orders for his arrest. People wondered if he would show up for the feast. Lazarus, whom he'd raised from the dead, was added to the list of those to be killed so the leaders could stay in power. (John 11:55–57; 12:9–11)

- A dinner in Jesus's honor was held in Bethany with Lazarus and his sisters in charge. Mary demonstrated her love and reverence by anointing Jesus with an expensive perfume. Judas protested the "waste." Jesus accepted Mary's actions as preparation for his burial. (John 12:1–8)

- The next day Jesus rode on a young donkey in triumphal procession into Jerusalem while thousands of his disciples welcomed him as Israel's King. The Pharisees protested. He replied that the people had to cheer him, or else the stones of the temple would cry out. (Luke 19:28–40)

- When some Greeks asked to see him, Jesus took it as a signal that the climax of his ministry was near. He would be "lifted up" on a cross before the week ended. He pressed people to decide for or against him, and insisted that to accept or reject him was to accept or reject God. (John 12:20–50)

Study Questions

1. What misconception does Jesus seek to correct with the parable about the king and the men to whom he gave his money to invest? Who do the following characters represent: The king? The distant empire? The enemies? The servants? What resources do you think Jesus has given you to invest for him?

2. How did Jesus interpret Mary's anointing him with expensive oil?

3. For his triumphal entry into Jerusalem, why did Jesus choose to ride a donkey instead of a horse?

4. Why did the leaders who believed keep it a secret? In your life, how does love for "praise from men" get in the way of openly confessing your faith in Christ?

Chapter Highlights:
- **Proof of Authority**
- **The Rejected Rock**
- **The God-and-Politics Maneuver**
- **Exposé**
- **Twopenny Serenade**

Chapter 28: Ambush

Let's Get Started

Tuesday morning of Passover week found Jesus and the Twelve once again on the road from Bethany to Jerusalem and into the temple area, just inside the eastern wall.

John taught
John 1:26–35

chief priests and the elders
Sanhedrin, city fathers, "teachers of the law"

Proof of Authority

MATTHEW 21:23 *Now when [Jesus] came into the temple, the **chief priests and the elders** of the people confronted Him as He was teaching, and said, "By what authority are You doing these things? And who gave You this authority?"* (NKJV)

The coalition of enemies came demanding that Jesus reveal his credentials. If he claimed someone (other than they) authorized his actions, they could accuse him of illegally usurping the nation's and city's duly recognized authorities, and might even be able to get him in trouble with the Roman occupation government.

If he claimed the right to act as he did because of who he was (Son of God), they could charge him with blasphemy (a capital offense) because he was usurping God's authority.

Jesus caught them in their own snare. He silenced them instantly by asking a question he knew they would refuse to answer for fear of self-incrimination: "I also will ask you one thing, which if you tell Me, I likewise will tell you by what authority I do these things: The baptism of John—where was it from? From heaven or from men?" (Matthew 21:24–25 NKJV).

The power brokers of Israel were caught between a rock and a hard place. If they said John was sent by God, they would have to admit Jesus was the Messiah, because that's what John taught. If they said John's ministry and message were not from God, they would lose the people's support, because the people believed John was God's prophet.

cried
Luke 13:34;
19:41–44;
Matthew 23:37–39

The most brilliant thing they could think of to say was, "We do not know" (Matthew 11:27 NKJV). "Neither will I tell you by what authority I do these things," Jesus said (11:27 NKJV).

> **what others say**
>
> **William Barclay**
>
> If a man consults expediency rather than principle, his first question will be not, "What is the truth?" but, "What is it safe to say?" And again and again his worship of expediency will drive him to cowardly silence . . . If a man knows the truth, he is under obligation to tell the truth, though the heavens should fall.[1]

Reinventing Authority

As the foiled coalition squirmed, Jesus told four stories that exploded like a warhead, blasting the right of Israel's official leadership to lead the nation.

This was not vindictiveness. He <u>cried</u> for these men. But he could not walk softly at this point, because such men as these stole the faith of Israel!

My Two Sons

> MATTHEW 21:28–30 *But what do you think? A man had two sons, and he came to the first and said, "Son, go, work today in my vineyard." He answered and said, "I will not," but afterward he regretted it and went. Then he came to the second and said likewise. And he answered and said, "I go, sir," but he did not go.* (NKJV)

With his first story, Jesus exposed their political waffling: A farmer with two sons asked his sons to work in his vineyard. Both were rebellious. The first refused, then changed his mind and obeyed. The second thought he'd get his dad off his back by agreeing to go to work, but then didn't keep his word.

"Which of the two did the will of his father?" Jesus asked (Matthew 21:31 NKJV). "The first," they answered.

Jesus revealed the identity of the sons. The first son, who said "No" but then changed his mind, represented people the religious leaders despised most—tax collectors and prostitutes. Such "sinners" believed God's message and **repented**.

The second son, who promised his father everything and gave him nothing, represented the leaders—who considered themselves spiritually superior to tax collectors and prostitutes.

"Assuredly, I say to you that tax collectors and harlots enter the kingdom of God before you" (Matthew 21:31 NKJV).

The Wretched Renters

MATTHEW 21:33–34 *There was a certain landowner who planted a vineyard and set a **hedge** around it, dug a winepress in it and built a tower. And he leased it to vinedressers and went into a far country. Now when vintage-time drew near, he sent his servants to the vinedressers, that they might receive its fruit. (NKJV)*

At harvesttime the property owner sent servants to collect his rent. The tenants brutalized them. So the landowner sent his son. Surely they would respect him. But the terrible tenants reasoned in their twisted minds that if they killed the son, they'd own the vineyard.

Jesus's listeners easily identified the characters: (1) The **vineyard** is Israel; (2) the owner of the vineyard is God; (3) the renters are the religious leaders entrusted with the vineyard's care; (4) the landlord's servants are the **prophets** Israel rejected and killed; and (5) the son is Jesus, who would soon die at the hands of the leaders.

There's no happy ending. The wretched renters ended wretchedly. Jesus said, "Therefore what will the owner of the vineyard do to them? He will come and destroy those vinedressers and give the vineyard to others" (Luke 20:15–16a NKJV).

The Rejected Rock

LUKE 20:16b–17 *And when they heard it they said, "Certainly not!" Then He looked at them and said, "What then is this that is written:*
   'The stone which the builders rejected
   Has become the chief cornerstone'?" (NKJV)

vineyard
Isaiah 5:7

repented
turned from their
sins; changed

hedge
"wall" of thorn-
bushes to keep out
wild boars and
thieves

vineyard
OT symbol for
nation of Israel

prophets
OT preachers and
writers, John the
Baptist

Jesus reminded the people of <u>a line</u> from the **Hallel**, about "the stone which the builders rejected" becoming "the <u>cornerstone</u>." The original word indicates either (1) the "cornerstone," the first, most important stone in a building's foundation; or (2) the "capstone," the last stone placed at the top of the corner tying the building together and setting its shape (see Illustration #6).

Even though Israel rejected him, Jesus Christ is nonetheless the <u>beginning and end</u> of everything God is doing in the world!

Illustration #6
Capstone—The capstone of an arched doorway—also called the keystone—held the structure together. It was the most important piece of the arch, and without it everything would crumble.

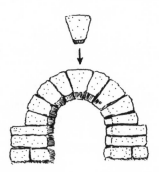

<u>The King Threw a Party and Nobody Came</u>

MATTHEW 22:1–3 *And Jesus answered and spoke to them again by parables and said: "The kingdom of heaven is like a certain king who arranged a marriage for his son, and sent out his servants to call those who were invited to the wedding; and they were not willing to come.* (NKJV)

go to

a line
Psalm 118:22

cornerstone
Acts 4:11;
1 Peter 2:7;
Ephesians 2:20

beginning and end
Revelation 1:8;
22:13

Hallel
Psalms 113–118,
sung at the Feast of
Tabernacles

Jesus's listeners were familiar with the etiquette involved in a banquet like the one in this parable. Guests were invited well in advance. A second invitation was delivered the day before the feast. Such banquets often began in the morning and lasted

Some aspects of this tale of impoliteness, impatience, and indifference are exaggerated to stress the life-and-death issues Jesus had in mind. If the king seems to us to be overreacting and overly cruel, we only need remember that the "kings" Israel knew best were the late Herod the Great (murderer of the Bethlehem babies) and his son Archelaus (butcher of three thousand Jews at a Passover Feast).

The parable makes two major points:

1. Israel was invited to celebrate the arrival of God's Son and inauguration of the kingdom, but the general populace reacted with indifference (Matthew 22:5) or open <u>hostility</u> (22:6). Both are rebellion. There would be serious <u>consequences</u> (22:7). (It is estimated that two-thirds of first-century Jews rejected Christ, and only one-third believed.)

2. Since Israel and its leaders rejected the Messiah, the invitation would be offered to <u>anyone</u> (Matthew 22:9)—good or bad (22:10). All that is required is that they put on the "wedding garments" (22:11–13)—that is, by putting their faith in Jesus, they become clothed (Romans 1:17; 3:22–24; 13:13–14) with his righteousness.

go to

hostility
Luke 4:28–29;
John 7:30, 43–44;
8:59; 10:31, 39

consequences
Luke 13:34–35;
19:41–44

anyone
John 3:16;
Acts 2:21;
Romans 10:13

taxes
poll tax, one denarius a year from ages 14 to 65

Caesar
Augustus; emperor of Rome; symbol for civil authority

Herodians
supporters of Roman occupation government

> ### what others say
>
> **Sallie McFague**
>
> Jesus, in his friendship with outcasts and sinners, is a model of friendship with God . . . The God of Jesus is the One who invites us to table to eat together as friends.[2]

The God-and-Politics Maneuver

MATTHEW 22:15–17 *Then the Pharisees went and plotted how they might entangle Him in His talk. And they sent to Him their disciples with the Herodians, saying, "Teacher, we know that You are true, and teach the way of God in truth; nor do You care about anyone, for You do not regard the person of men. Tell us, therefore, what do You think? Is it lawful to pay* **taxes** *to* **Caesar***, or not?" (NKJV)*

With the chief priests and city fathers reeling from Jesus's four-barreled attack on their authority, the Pharisees decided it was their turn to outfox him. Desperation shows in their decision to get their worst political enemies, the **Herodians**, involved in the hit-and-run assaults.

Popular enthusiasm for Jesus was running high, so they decided future attacks would be more subtle. In a sneak attack, they sent a team of rabbinical students and astute political liars to butter Jesus up, hoping flattery would get him to drop his guard (Matthew 22:16). But Jesus saw through the flattery, as the truly humble usually do.

go to

government's right
Romans 13:1–7

Sadducees
aristocrats, high
priests, ruling party;
deny supernatural,
angels

The question was carefully crafted "to entangle Him in His talk" (22:15 NKJV). If he said "Yes," the people could turn against him—some would rather die than pay Roman taxes. If he said "No," his enemies could report him to Pilate as a seditionist, and he would be arrested and executed by the Romans.

The Principle of the Citizen-Christian

MATTHEW 22:18–21 *But Jesus perceived their wickedness, and said, "Why do you test Me, you hypocrites? Show Me the tax money." So they brought Him a denarius. And He said to them, "Whose image and inscription is this?" They said to Him, "Caesar's." And He said to them, "Render therefore to Caesar the things that are Caesar's, and to God the things that are God's." (NKJV)*

Jesus turned the trap into a chance to teach an important principle of Christian citizenship: If you accept the government's currency and use it, you are bound to accept the <u>government's right</u> to impose taxes. If you benefit from the state, you are obliged to pay your dues to the state. Taxation is a universal right that goes with rulership.

On the other hand, government's authority is limited. People bear God's image, which means they have duties to God that are more inescapable than their duties to the government.

what others say

Richard J. Mouw

The authority and mandate to govern, even in totalitarian societies, are given to human beings by God, so that no one may lightly dismiss the obligation to respect and obey political powers. But in modern democracies the power of national leaders is derived from the populace . . . Democratic government grants Christians the right publicly to criticize, review, debate, and challenge current procedures and policies. Under these conditions, [Scripture] imposes on them the duty to make use of that right.[3]

Resurrection Ridicule

MATTHEW 22:23–28 *The same day the **Sadducees**, who say there is no resurrection, came to Him and asked Him, saying:*

"Teacher, <u>Moses</u> said that if a man dies, having no children, his brother shall marry his wife and raise up offspring for his brother. Now there were with us seven brothers. The first died after he had married, and having no offspring, left his wife to his brother. Likewise the second also, and the third, even to the seventh. Last of all the woman died also. Therefore, in the <u>resurrection</u>, whose wife of the seven will she be? For they all had her." (NKJV)

The intent of this fabricated yarn was to make the resurrection look ridiculous. The resurrection will happen at the end of time when righteous and unrighteous dead will rise and face judgment, but the Sadducees didn't believe there would be a resurrection.

In the first place, Jesus told them, their ignorance of the Scriptures and the **power of God** was showing (Matthew 22:29). Life after resurrection will be totally different from anything experienced in this earthly life.

In Luke's report we learn that Jesus concentrated on the future life of the <u>righteous</u>, not the lost (Luke 20:35). Putting Matthew's and Luke's reports together, we find that Jesus told them four things about the resurrection world:

1. Marriage won't be necessary—it will be replaced by a new eternal relationship (Matthew 22:30).

2. Resurrected people will be **like the angels**—they will not be angels but will be immortal with spiritual bodies and other angel-like characteristics (Matthew 22:30).

3. It will be <u>impossible</u> for them to die (Luke 20:36).

4. They will be <u>known</u> as children of God because he is the God <u>of the living</u>, not the dead (Luke 20:36).

<u>A Voice of Reason in the Madness</u>

MARK 12:28 *Then one of the scribes came, and having heard them reasoning together, perceiving that He had answered them well, asked Him, "Which is the first commandment of all?" (NKJV)*

Moses
Deuteronomy 25:5

resurrection
Job 9:25–27;
John 5:24–29;
1 Corinthians 15:12–18;
Revelation 20:4–5

righteous
Romans 3:28; 4:3

impossible
Revelation 21:4

known
John 1:12–13;
Romans 8:18–19

of the living
1 John 5:11–12

power of God
specifically, ability to raise the dead

like the angels
Greek means "equal to angels"

Matthew's report makes this sound like another question concocted by the Pharisees to trap Jesus. Mark, however, gives the distinct impression that this lawyer was at least mildly approving of the way Jesus had handled the Sadducees on the subject of the resurrection (in which, by the way, Pharisees strongly believed).

Jesus's answer to the lawyer's question sums up the fundamentals of true Judaism and Christianity in three sentences:

key point

- Monotheism: "The LORD is one" (Mark 12:29 NKJV; Deuteronomy 6:4).

- Personal relationship with God: "Love the LORD your God with all your heart, with all your soul, with all your mind, and with all your strength" (Mark 12:30 NKJV; Deuteronomy 6:5).

- Love for people: "Love your neighbor as yourself" (Mark 12:31 NKJV; Leviticus 19:18).

The lawyer added that to do these things "is more than all the whole burnt offerings and sacrifices" (the formalities of religion) (Mark 12:33 NKJV). To which Jesus responded, "You are not far from the kingdom of God" (12:34 NKJV).

what others say

Pierre Teilhard De Chardin

Some day, after we have mastered the winds, the waves, the tides and gravity, we will harness for God the energies of love and then for the second time in the history of the world man will have discovered fire.[4]

Exposé

MARK 12:34b *But after that no one dared question Him. (NKJV)*

His detractors had temporarily run out of gas. So in this rare moment when they had nothing to say, Jesus asked them the most crucial question anyone can answer: "What do you think about the Christ? Whose Son is He?" (Matthew 22:42 NKJV).

"The son of David," they replied (22:42 NKJV).

Jesus then asked, "How then does David in the Spirit call Him 'Lord'?" (22:43 NKJV). In Jewish culture it would be appropriate for a son to call his father "Lord," but not the other way around. How can Christ be David's son and David's Lord at the same time?

The only answer is what Christians call the "Incarnation"—the miracle by which God <u>became flesh</u> in the person of Jesus Christ, whose human mother was a <u>descendant</u> of King David.

became flesh
John 1:14, 18;
Philippians 2:5–8

descendant
Luke 1:29–37; 2:4

hypocrisy
Matthew 6;
Mark 7

phylacteries
Exodus 13:9, 16;
Deuteronomy 6:4–9;
11:13–21

tassels
Numbers 15:37–41;
Deuteronomy 22:12

> what others say
>
> **William Barclay**
>
> There would be few that day who caught anything like all that Jesus meant . . . They had the awed and the uncomfortable feeling that they had heard the voice of God, and for a moment, in this man Jesus, they glimpsed the very face of God.[5]

A Requiem for Hypocrisy

MATTHEW 23:2–7 *The scribes and the Pharisees sit in Moses' seat. Therefore whatever they tell you to observe, that observe and do, but do not do according to their works; for they say, and do not do. For they bind heavy burdens, hard to bear, and lay them on men's shoulders; but they themselves will not move them with one of their fingers. But all their works they do to be seen by men. They make their phylacteries broad and enlarge the borders of their garments. They love the best places at feasts, the best seats in the synagogues, greetings in the marketplaces, and to be called by men, "Rabbi, Rabbi." (NKJV)*

Jesus saves some of his biggest guns for attacks on <u>hypocrisy</u>. Again and again he opens fire on this sin.

From the amount of space given to the subject in the New Testament, it is hard to conclude anything but that Jesus classes spiritual arrogance and religious pretense among the most destructive and deadly of human transgressions—at least as far as the development of his kingdom fellowship is concerned.

In Matthew 23, he zeroes in on the problem of hypocrisy in spiritual leaders. The Pharisees gave every appearance of being spiritual. They believed they were superior in part because of their **phylacteries** (see Illustration #7) and their **tassels**. People who teach, guide, or direct the spiritual life of others are not to be seen or to see themselves in any sense "above" or superior to either those they lead or their fellow leaders.

Rabbi
teacher

phylacteries
small boxes containing Bible verses, strapped to left wrist or forehead during prayers

tassels
fringe or cord attached to cloaks remind Jews of relationship with God

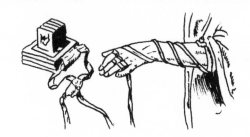

Twopenny Serenade

LUKE 21:1–4 *And He looked up and saw the rich putting their gifts into the treasury, and He saw also a certain poor widow putting in two mites. So He said, "Truly I say to you that this poor widow has put in more than all; for all these out of their abundance have put in offerings for God, but she out of her poverty put in all the livelihood that she had." (NKJV)*

One of Jesus's stinging accusations of the hypocritical teachers of Israel was that, while they carry on their pious show, they "devour widows' houses" (Luke 20:47 NKJV).

The Law required these men to support themselves so their teaching could be offered without charge. But some teachers taught that supporting a rabbi was an act that could win you a place in heaven. Some misled disciples signed over their homes!

As he spoke, Jesus looked up and saw rich and poor people putting gifts into the temple treasury box. A nearly destitute widow dropped in **two mites**.

Her gift was a flyspeck on a football field compared to the gifts of the wealthy. But Jesus declared her gift to be greater than all the others. Rather than a percentage of wealth, this poor woman gave everything she had to live on!

two mites
quadrons or lepta,
each worth about
1/64 of a denarius
(day's wage)

what others say

Saint John Chrysostom

[Jesus] paid no attention to the amount of the money. What he did heed was the wealth of her soul. If you calculate by the value of her money, her poverty is great. If you bring her intention into the light, you will see that her store of generosity defies description.[6]

Chapter Wrap-Up

- Jesus used the fig tree he had shriveled to teach his disciples about the power of faith and forgiveness. (Matthew 21:19–22; Mark 11:19–20; Luke 17:3–6)

- During the last week of his earthly ministry, even though there was a price on his head, Jesus taught in the temple. The religious and political leaders tried to trap him with questions. But, one by one, he turned the answers back on the questioners. (Luke 20:1–44)

- At the end of the debate, Jesus warned the people against following the example of the religious leaders, accusing them of failing to practice what they preach and turning Jewish religious life into an unbearable burden so they could maintain their positions of control. He gave a long lament over their hypocrisy, and wept for them and Jerusalem's rejection of him. (Matthew 23)

- Jesus said the Pharisees "devour widows' houses." He used a widow's two-mite offering to teach that the value of giving is not the amount, but the heart of the giver and the level of sacrifice. (Luke 20:45–21:4)

Study Questions

1. In the story of the two brothers (Matthew 21:28–32), who do the two brothers represent? With which brother do you most identify?

2. Which group of Jesus's enemies joined the Pharisees for the trick question about paying taxes to Caesar? What item did Jesus use in answering this question? What principle did Jesus teach in his answer?

3. What four things did Jesus tell the Sadducees about the resurrection when they tried to make it look ridiculous?

Chapter 29: Final-Hour Prophecies

Chapter Highlights:
- **The Fleeting Splendor of the Temple**
- **Beginning of the End**
- **Jerusalem's Falling**
- **Signs of Christ's Return**

Let's Get Started

During the last week of his earthly life, Jesus talked more about the future than he ever had before. Some of what he said related to his disciples' near future, some to the distant future—to "end-time events," signals of the second coming of Christ.

The Fleeting Splendor of the Temple

LUKE 21:5–7 *Then, as some spoke of the temple, how it was adorned with beautiful stones and donations, He said, "These things which you see—the days will come in which not one stone shall be left upon another that shall not be thrown down."*

So they asked Him, saying, "Teacher, but when will these things be? And what sign will there be when these things are about to take place?" (NKJV)

It was late Tuesday of Jesus's final week. As he was leaving the temple area after a fast-paced day of controversy and confrontation with angry men determined to bring him down, his disciples commented on how beautiful and impressive the sacred buildings were with all the lavish **gifts** that decorated them. But Jesus zapped his followers with a prophetic lightning bolt: This dazzling temple would be destroyed so completely not one stone would be left on another (Matthew 24:2; Mark 13:2; Luke 21:6)! He'd said it <u>before</u>.

In stunned silence the disciples followed Jesus to the Mount of Olives, outside the city. There they broke the silence with three questions (Matthew 24:3):

- "When will the temple be destroyed?"

- "What will be the sign of your coming?"

- "What will be the sign of the end of the age?"

As they sat among the ancient olive trees, Jesus gave them a telescopic glimpse into the future with a lengthy, detailed prophetic teaching.

before
Luke 19:43–44

gifts
from the rich and famous

Matthew 24:1–3
Mark 13:1–4
Luke 21:5–7

counterfeit christs
Theudas and Judas
of Galilee (Acts
5:36–37); Dositheus
and Menander

what others say

Josephus

The outward face of the temple in its front wanted nothing that was likely to surprise either men's minds or their eyes, for it was covered over with plates of gold of great weight, and, at the first rising of the sun, reflected back a very fiery splendor, and made those who forced themselves to look upon it to turn their eyes away, just as they would have done at the sun's rays. But the temple appeared to strangers, when they were at a distance, like a mountain covered with snow, for, as to those parts of it that were not gilt, they were exceeding white.[1]

The Beginning of the End

They asked for signs. Jesus told them to watch for these:

1. *A procession of deceivers* (Matthew 24:5; Mark 13:6; Luke 21:8). During the lifetimes of the apostles, **counterfeit christs** crossed the Israelite landscape like illusive desert dust devils, claiming to be the promised Messiah. Today the list of pretenders and false teachers is long and growing.

2. *Wars and rumors of wars* (Matthew 24:6–7; Mark 13:7–8; Luke 21:9–11). The period of history following Christ's resurrection was a time of great international unrest. Roman historian Tacitus said, "It was a time rich in disasters, horrible with battles, torn with seditions, savage even in peace."

   Today, television and the Internet bring live coverage of major disasters around the world while they are happening—including hunger, disease, earthquakes, civil wars, tornadoes, hurricanes, and tsunamis.

what others say

Oswald Chambers

"Do not panic." That is either the statement of a madman or of a Being who has power to put something into a man and keep him free from panic, even in the midst of the awful ter-

go to

hates Christ
John 15:18–16:4

target
Matthew 5:10–12;
Luke 6:22–23;
Acts 5:17–18;
Colossians 1:24

grow cold
2 Timothy 3:1–5;
Revelation 2:4

megatrends
major movements,
directions in society

> ror of war. The basis of panic is always cowardice. Our Lord teaches us to look things full in the face. He says—"When you hear of wars, don't be scared." It is the most natural thing in the world to be scared, and the clearest evidence that God's grace is at work in our hearts is when we do not get into panics.[2]

3. *Persecution of Christ's followers* (Matthew 24:9–10; Mark 13:9–13; Luke 21:12–19). Jesus predicted that believers would face persecution. The nameless "they" (Luke 21:12) who harass followers of Christ and demand they answer for their identification with him include religious and secular authorities ("synagogues . . . kings and governors"). The unbelieving world <u>hates Christ</u>, and his followers often become the <u>target</u> of that hatred (21:17).

4. *Intensification of trouble and opportunity* (Matthew 24:9–26; Mark 13:14–23). As the present age moves toward its end (Matthew 24:14), several observable **megatrends** will develop that spell trouble for society and the church:

- Persecution will intensify (24:9).
- Many will "fall away" from the Christian faith (24:10).
- False prophets will emerge and increasing numbers of people will be misled by them (24:11).
- Lawlessness and crime will be on the rise (24:12).
- Love—for the Lord and other people—will <u>grow cold</u>; hate will flourish (24:12).

At the same time these disturbing trends are taking place, another very important movement will make its impact: "This gospel of the kingdom will be preached in all the world as a witness to all the nations" (Matthew 24:14 NKJV; Mark 13:10).

what others say

C. Peter Wagner

> In all of history, there has never been a more exciting time than this to be a Christian. A wave of world Christians is carrying the gospel to places it has never before reached. We are indeed in the springtime of missions.[3]

go to

rubble
Matthew 23:38;
24:2;
Luke 13:35; 19:44;
21:6

again uprooted
Genesis 46–47;
2 Kings 17;
24:10–25:12;
2 Chronicles 36:20

AD 70
less than forty years
after Jesus's
prophecy

siege works
barricades

rage
"wrath," not God's
but the Romans'

Jerusalem's Falling

LUKE 21:20–24 *But when you see Jerusalem surrounded by armies, then know that its desolation is near. Then let those who are in Judea flee to the mountains, let those who are in the midst of her depart, and let not those who are in the country enter her. For these are the days of vengeance, that all things which are written may be fulfilled. But woe to those who are pregnant and to those who are nursing babies in those days! For there will be great distress in the land and wrath upon this people. And they will fall by the edge of the sword, and be led away captive into all nations. And Jerusalem will be trampled by Gentiles until the times of the Gentiles are fulfilled.* (NKJV)

This section of Luke 21 speaks directly to the disciples' question regarding the destruction of the temple: "When will these things be?" (21:7 NKJV).

Third-century Christian historian Eusebius tells of the tragic fall of the Holy City in **AD 70**.

The Roman army under Emperor Titus surrounded Jerusalem with **siege works**, completely cutting off access in or out of the city. A million Jews who had crowded into the city for protection died of starvation or the slaughter that followed; 97,000 were taken prisoner.[4] The city was leveled.

Titus had given orders for his soldiers to spare the temple, but their **rage** at the Jews was too intense. The looting and destruction got out of hand, and the once-glorious temple was reduced to burning rubble.

The large community of Christians living in Jerusalem were reminded by their prophets of Jesus's warning (Luke 21:21), and escaped to the mountains before the siege began. (Christians escaped to the Gentile town of Pella, east of the Jordan, where Herod Agrippa 2 gave them asylum.)

Following the destruction of Jerusalem, the Jews were again uprooted from their homeland and scattered among the nations, just as Jesus predicted (21:24).

Signs of Christ's Return

MATTHEW 24:3 *Now as He sat on the Mount of Olives, the disciples came to Him privately, saying, "Tell us, when will these things be? And what will be the sign of Your coming, and of the end of the age?" (NKJV)*

Jesus had told his friends several times—directly or in story—that in the future, after his death and resurrection, he would <u>return</u> to judge the world and the church.

Jesus described four events that would be developing at the time of his coming:

1. *Completion of the "times of the Gentiles"* (Luke 21:24). After its destruction, the Jewish nation would be gone, but Jerusalem and the Holy Land would be inhabited, dominated by Gentiles until their "time" was up. The end of Gentile control would be an important milestone on the prophetic calendar. After nineteen hundred years, in 1948 by edict of the United Nations, the Jews were reestablished in their homeland. In June 1967, in the Six Day War, they recaptured Old Jerusalem. Though the political dispute over Jerusalem continues, the Gentiles' time to "trample" the city appears over.

2. *The sight of the "<u>abomination</u> of desolation"* in the temple (Matthew 24:15–26; Mark 13:14–23). This was predicted by the prophet Daniel. The "abomination" is an act of sacrilege by a future ruler who makes a treaty with Israel and tries to assume the place of God. The "desolation" is the beginning of the great time of trouble (see number 3, below). Daniel 11:36 describes this ruler as a "king" who "shall do according to his own will" (NKJV). The New Testament calls him the "<u>Antichrist</u>," among other things. Two things must have taken place before this: (1) The Jews must be back in the Promised Land (they are); and (2) the temple must be rebuilt (plans are ready; you can visit the architectural model in Israel).

3. *A time of great trouble* (Matthew 24:21–26; Mark 13:19–23; Luke 21:25–26). "There will be <u>great</u> **tribulation** such as has not been since the beginning of the world until this time, no, nor ever shall be. And unless those days were shortened, no flesh would be saved; but for the **elect**'s sake those days will be shortened" (Matthew 24:21–22 NKJV). This is what students of prophecy call the Tribulation.

go to

return
Matthew 16:27;
Mark 8:38;
Luke 9:26; 12:37–40;
17:22–30

abomination
Daniel 8:13; 9:27;
11:31; 12:11

Antichrist
2 Thessalonians
2:3–11;
1 John 2:18–23; 4:3;
Revelation 13:11–18

great tribulation
Daniel 12:1;
Revelation 6–18;
Ezekiel 38, 39

elect
Romans 11:5–6;
Titus 1:1–3;
1 Peter 1:1–2

tribulation
Greek: distress,
trouble, emotional
and spiritual distress

elect
chosen people,
those who put their
faith in Jesus Christ

go to

upheavals
Isaiah 13:4–5

mental distress
Isaiah 13:6–8

Rapture
1 Thessalonians
4:15–17

Son of Man
Jesus

those days
the time of great
distress

Rapture
Latin: *rapio*, mean-
ing "to be caught
up"

4. *Signs on the earth and in the sky* (Matthew 24:29; Mark 13:24–25; Luke 21:25–26). The descriptions given may prophesy celestial phenomena (meteors, comets, unusual weather patterns, etc.), or sudden and violent national and international <u>upheavals</u>, or both. In the Bible the "sea" is often a figure of speech for masses of people. "The sea and the waves roaring" (Luke 21:25 NKJV) could be literal tidal waves, tsunamis, hurricanes, or violent demonstrations and disturbing social changes. The darkening of the sun and moon (Matthew 24:29) could result from the fires of war.

The mood of the times is described in Luke 21—<u>mental distress</u>, perplexity, pressure (21:25), fear, terror, astonishment, apprehension (21:26) over what's coming on the world.

Pow! Crash! A Blinding Flash! He Comes!

MATTHEW 24:27–31 *For as the lightning comes from the east and flashes to the west, so also will the coming of the **Son of Man** be. For wherever the carcass is, there the eagles will be gathered together.*

*Immediately after the tribulation of **those days** the sun will be darkened, and the moon will not give its light; the stars will fall from heaven, and the powers of the heavens will be shaken. Then the sign of the Son of Man will appear in heaven, and then all the tribes of the earth will mourn, and they will see the Son of Man coming on the clouds of heaven with power and great glory. And He will send His angels with a great sound of a trumpet, and they will gather together His elect from the four winds, from one end of heaven to the other. (NKJV)*

In his first coming, Jesus came silently, in the womb of Mary, the girl from Nazareth. When he comes again it will be with all sorts of heavenly fireworks (Matthew 24:27–31).

When Jesus comes, angels will be dispatched to gather the followers of Christ, living and dead, from every part of the universe (Matthew 24:31). Christians call this the "**Rapture**" of the church.

Synchronize Your Watches! . . . or Not

MATTHEW 24:36, 42 *But of that day and hour no one knows, not even the angels of heaven, but My Father only . . . Watch therefore, for you do not know what hour your Lord is coming.* (NKJV)

Jesus did not tell his disciples <u>precisely</u> when he would return. He gave them trends to watch so they'd know history was unfolding according to God's plan. He gave a few clues. He knew people would play amateur detective and try to outguess God about the timing of the Second Coming, the great Tribulation, and the Rapture.

A Six-Pack of Preparedness Parables

Jesus told a batch of parables to show his hearers how important it was to be prepared.

night burglar
Luke 12:39;
1 Thessalonians 5:2, 4;
1 Peter 3:10;
Revelation 3:3;
16:15

joyful celebrations
Jeremiah 7:34

1. *The Boss's Long Trip* (Mark 13:33–37). Christians waiting for Christ's return are like employees left in charge of the business while their boss is away. They don't know when he will return. The best way to be ready is simply to live and work so that it doesn't matter when he returns. He can come whenever he comes— they're ready 'cause they're doing what they should be doing . . . every day.

2. *The <u>Night Burglar</u>* (Matthew 24:42–44). No self-respecting sec-ond-story man calls on his cell phone to let you know when he's going to burglarize your house. If he did, his crime spree would end with one break-in, because you'd have the police waiting when he came. Jesus will return at a time least expected. We'd best be ready all the time.

3. *The Two Servants* (Matthew 24:45–51). Servant #1 faithfully car-ries out responsibilities the boss left with him. When the boss comes back, #1 is ready, even though he didn't know when to expect him. He's rewarded for a job well done. Servant #2 decides there's no hurry ("My master is delaying his coming" [24:48 NKJV]).

He puts off doing what he should be doing, mistreats his fel-low servants, and wastes his time drinking with his cronies at the local pub. He plans to get around to fixing things later, before the boss returns. He's wrong. Unexpectedly the boss comes back, drags the procrastinator out of the pub, and cuts him to pieces! The man is appointed "his portion with the hyp-ocrites" (24:51 NKJV). Because that's what an unfaithful ser-vant is.

4. *The Ten Bridesmaids* (Matthew 25:1–13). Jewish weddings were <u>joyful celebrations</u>. The bride and friends waited at her home for the groom to come and take her to his home. As they waited, messengers repeatedly announced the bridegroom was coming. Everyone rushed out to meet him, only to discover it was a false alarm. So all went back inside. Finally about midnight, the groom and his friends arrived. Together, the two groups of friends and most of the townspeople noisily proceeded to escort the couple, lamps blazing, to the groom's home, taking the longest route so the most people could express their good wishes.

The bridesmaids—ten friends of the bride—are the focus of Jesus's story. Each had a lamp. Five brought extra oil to last through the long wait. Five brought lamps but no oil, thinking perhaps they could obtain it after they arrived. It was a tragic miscalculation. When the call came at midnight that the bridegroom was coming, the bridesmaids trimmed their lamps to go meet him. In the long wait, however, the five without extra oil had fallen asleep and their lamps were going out. When they woke up they asked their five counterparts to share oil with them, but the wise young ladies only had enough to supply their own lamps. (Oil may represent the Holy Spirit and lamps the state of each one's relationship with God—either full of [under control of] the Spirit or living on yesterday's experience with God.)

While the shortsighted girls hurried to find an oil merchant in the middle of the night, the bridegroom arrived . . . for real. The procession went off to his house. The five wise bridesmaids went in and enjoyed the festivities. By the time the other five returned, the door was shut. They were left out in the cold. They missed everything!

go to

familiar ring
Luke 19:11–27

talents
58 to 80 pounds of silver per talent—value: $1,000 or more

what others say

Oswald Chambers

The parable of the ten virgins reveals that it is fatal from our Lord's standpoint to live this life without preparation for the life to come.[7]

5. *The Investment Challenge* (Matthew 25:14–30). The situation has a familiar ring. The boss departs on a long trip. (What else is new?) Jesus wanted his disciples to accept the reality of a long interval before he would set up an earthly kingdom—so he repeats it.

The master leaves three men in charge of his investments, according to their abilities. One is given five **talents** of silver ($5,000); the second, two ($2,000); the third, one ($1,000). They are to use their gifts to make money for their employer.

When he returned, an accounting took place. The first two were commended because both had doubled their money. The third had dug a hole in the ground and buried the money.

long time
2 Peter 3:8–9, 15

judge
Revelation 20:11–15

separate
Matthew 13:24–30,
36–43, 47–50;
24:40–41

righteous
Luke 18:13–14;
Romans 3:21–26

righteous
believers, justified in
God's sight, experi-
encing forgiveness

stranger
alien, of a different
nationality, race, cul-
ture, or social status

Needless to say, the boss was not pleased. "You wicked and lazy servant," he said (among other unpleasant things); then he took the $1,000 from him and gave it to the one who had $10,000.

The point is, Christ will be gone a <u>long time</u>, but he will return as promised. The interval is not to be spent dreaming of that future day or merely protecting the status quo. But the time is for serving the Lord, using what he has given you to advance his kingdom.

6. *The King's Disguise* (Matthew 25:31–46). When Jesus returns all the nations will stand before him as <u>judge</u>. Judge Jesus will <u>separate</u> the **righteous** from the unrighteous (25:32–33, 37, 41). As he does, a startling thing will take place in that cosmic court scene. At some point the Shepherd-Judge will reveal something neither the good guys nor the bad guys seemed to realize: While they were going about their daily lives, he was walking among them in disguise. At that moment the King will take off his mask: "I was hungry . . . I was thirsty . . . I was a **stranger** . . . I was naked . . . I was sick . . . I was in prison" (Matthew 25:35–36 NKJV).

A wave of astonishment will sweep the courtroom. The Shepherd–Judge will say to the righteous, "You fed me . . . you gave me a drink . . . you invited me in . . . you clothed me . . . you looked after me . . . you came to visit me [in prison]."

"Lord, when . . . ?" the righteous will reply, shaking their heads in amazement.

what others say

Ronald J. Sider

If Jesus' saying in Matthew 25:40 is awesome, its parallel is terrifying. "Truly I say to you, as you did it not to one of the least of these, you did it not to me" (verse 45). What does that mean in a world where millions die each year while rich Christians live in affluence? What does it mean to see the Lord of the universe lying by the roadside starving and walk by on the other side? We cannot know. We can only pledge, in fear and trembling, not to kill him again.[8]

The King will say, "Inasmuch as you did it to one of the least of these My brethren, you did it to Me" (Matthew 25:40 NKJV).

Chapter Wrap-Up

- Jesus's disciples were impressed by the magnificence of the temple in Jerusalem. His response was to tell them the time was coming when the temple would be destroyed. (Luke 21:5–7)

- In a lengthy prophetic teaching, he spoke of war, disaster, earthquakes, and other disturbances, and told them not to fear when they saw these things; they were signs that God's plan was unfolding as he promised. He also promised them persecution. (Matthew 24:4–14; Luke 21:8–18)

- He told them what to watch for and what to do when they saw the armies encircling Jerusalem poised for its destruction. (Luke 21:20–24)

- Jesus taught there would be a great time of worldwide distress, such as had never been experienced by mankind before. The Antichrist would be revealed. The heavens would be shaken. There would be national and international unrest. (Matthew 24:15–25; Luke 21:25–28)

- He promised to come like lightning, visible throughout the world. His angels would gather his followers to be with him. He would come when least expected. They must be ready at all times. (Matthew 24:26–42)

- He told six stories about being ready, emphasizing the unexpectedness of his return, the need for faithfulness, the need to be alert and watching, the need to invest what he has given us in his work, and the need to care for people he identifies as his "brethren"—the poor and powerless. (Matthew 24:42–25:46)

Study Questions

1. To what three questions from his disciples did Jesus's Mount of Olives teachings give the answers?

2. What were Christians told to do when they saw the armies surrounding Jerusalem?

3. List the six actions Jesus says will be used as a basis for judgment. In these six situations where do you feel best equipped to serve most naturally? In which of these six situations do you have the most trouble reaching out?

Chapter 30: Countdown to Glory

Let's Get Started

The final week of Jesus's earthly life moved closer to its climax. Few of the pilgrims gathered for the feast really knew this would be the most important Passover in Israel's history.

The Price of Treachery

MATTHEW 26:2 *You know that after two days is the Passover, and the Son of Man will be delivered up to be crucified.* (NKJV)

Two days before Passover, two groups were talking about the death of Christ. Jesus, spending the night with his men on the Mount of Olives, reminded them of what was ahead. Meanwhile, at the palace of the high priest inside the city, religious and civil leaders met to lay out a strategy to arrest and kill Jesus (Matthew 26:3–4).

The greatest challenge in their sordid business was to catch him alone, segregated from sympathetic festival crowds. If they seized him while he taught at the temple, the leaders risked setting off a riot (26:5), which would bring the Roman authorities down on their heads.

Judas made it easy.

gospel harmony

Matthew 26:1–5
Mark 14:1–2
Luke 22:1–2
John 11:47–53

The Mind of a Traitor

MATTHEW 26:14–16 *Then one of the twelve, called Judas Iscariot, went to the chief priests and said, "What are you willing to give me if I deliver Him to you?" And they counted out to him thirty pieces of silver. So from that time he sought opportunity to betray Him.* (NKJV)

What sort of confused thinking turned a man <u>chosen</u> to be Christ's ambassador into his betrayer for a mere **30 silver coins**? Not much information is given. Consider these factors:

go to

chosen
Luke 6:12–16

30 silver coins
Zechariah 6:12

30 silver coins
shekels, the price of a slave (Exodus 21:32)

loved money
Matthew 6:24;
Luke 16:13–15;
18:22–25

control by Satan
John 13:2;
Luke 22:3

fulfilled
Matthew 18:20;
Acts 2:4, 38–39,
42–47;
1 Corinthians
11:23–26

fervent desire
Greek: intense,
irregular, or violent
desire, passion

1. Judas was disillusioned with Christ's plans for the kingdom. He failed to see the kingdom of God as a spiritual community. Apparently he saw the kingdom as an uprising of the oppressed against the injustices of their oppressors. He missed the point that Jesus's primary mission was to rescue sinners. Judas had not signed on for that sort of kingdom.

2. Judas <u>loved money</u> more than he loved God (Matthew 26:14–15). He was a petty embezzler (John 12:6). His outwardly noble social concern was corrupted by a hypocritical, greedy heart.

3. Judas opened himself to <u>control by Satan</u> (Luke 22:3). Disappointment with Jesus's leadership coupled with his own greed made Judas vulnerable to the diabolical suggestion to sell his mentor out to his enemies.

The Last Meal

LUKE 22:15–16 *Then He said to them, "With **fervent desire** I have desired to eat this Passover with you before I suffer; for I say to you, I will no longer eat of it until it is <u>fulfilled</u> in the kingdom of God." (NKJV)*

After sunset on Thursday of Passover week, the thirteen friends gathered. Jesus began by sharing the intensity of his feelings.

J. B. Phillips translates the beginning of the above verse this way: "With all my heart I have longed to eat this Passover with you." Compassion was natural for him, even for his enemies. He wept openly and expressed anger more than once.

He loved these men. For three years they'd been through everything together. Now he was up against the greatest challenge of his life. "You are those who have continued with Me in My trials," he said (Luke 22:28 NKJV).

The Last Rivalry

LUKE 22:24 *Now there was also a dispute among them [the Twelve], as to which of them should be considered the greatest. (NKJV)*

At Mideastern festival meals, diners reclined on three-person couches (triclinia) around a square U-shaped table, their heads toward and feet away from the table. Traditionally, the host sat in the center of the closed side and guests were placed in the order of rank. The seats closest to the host were the most honored.

There's no evidence such <u>ranking</u> was observed at the Last Supper (see Luke 22:27), except in the minds of the disciples, who maintained a running argument about who was top banana! They brought their petty rivalry with them into the Upper Room. Like schoolboys they maneuvered for the best seats.

After three years of observing Jesus's model of leadership, had they caught nothing of his <u>servant style</u>? And how could they have been so woefully out of touch with his pain?

go to

ranking
Matthew 23:5–12;
Luke 14:7–11

servant style
Matthew 20:25–28

competition
Luke 22:24–30

removed
Passover is eaten
with shoes on
(Exodus 12:11)

Jesus the Slave

> JOHN 13:1b–5 *Having loved His own who were in the world, He loved them to the end. And supper being ended, the devil having already put it into the heart of Judas Iscariot, Simon's son, to betray Him, Jesus, knowing that the Father had given all things into His hands, and that He had come from God and was going to God, rose from supper and laid aside His garments, took a towel and girded Himself. After that, He poured water into a basin and began to wash the disciples' feet, and to wipe them with the towel with which He was girded. (NKJV)*

Pots of water were kept in every house for the purpose of washing guests' feet—a job usually assigned to the lowest slave. If both Jewish and Gentile servants were present, the Gentile did the foot washing; if no servant was there, women or children did it.

There were no slaves in the Upper Room. The disciples were too taken up with <u>competition</u> to volunteer to wash one another's feet.

So Jesus got up from the table and stripped off his robe. He tied a towel around his waist, filled a basin with water, got on his knees, **removed** each man's sandals, and poured water on their feet, gently washing away the road filth, and wiping them with the towel.

He would be their slave. In a few hours his slavery would climax on the cross!

go to

shall never
Mark 8:32–33

never
Greek: "not ever till
the end of time!"

what others say

Merril C. Tenney

The disciples' minds were preoccupied with dreams of eleva-
tion to office in the coming kingdom. They were jealous lest
one of their fellows should have the best place. Consequently,
no one of them was likely to abase himself by volunteering to
wash the feet of the others. They were ready to fight for a
throne, but not for a towel![1]

"To Be or Not to Be . . . Clean?"

JOHN 13:6–8a *Then He came to Simon Peter. And Peter said
to Him, "Lord, are You washing my feet?" Jesus answered and
said to him, "What I am doing you do not understand now, but
you will know after this." Peter said to Him, "You shall never
wash my feet!" (NKJV)*

Peter was stunned by Jesus's action: "You shall **never** wash my
feet!"

Jesus responded, "If I do not wash you, you have no part with
Me" (John 13:8 NKJV). In the simplest sense, he meant they couldn't
eat together unless Peter let him wash his feet.

Peter was sure he wanted to be friends with Jesus! He blurted out
his feelings: If washing made him Christ's partner, then wash "not
my feet only, but also my hands and my head!" (John 13:9 NKJV).

Jesus responded, "He who is bathed needs only to wash his feet,
but is completely clean" (13:10 NKJV). Banquet guests bathed before
coming to dinner. Upon arrival all they needed was foot washing.
Practically speaking, Peter didn't need his hands and head washed,
only his feet.

what others say

Revell Bible Dictionary

[Christ] was teaching two lessons through this [foot washing].
First, the washing of the disciples' feet symbolized the continual cleansing that would be available to them through his
death . . . Second, [it] provided an example for Christian leaders, who are to see themselves as servants to God's people
. . . Some Christian groups observe a ritual of foot washing,
taking literally Jesus' words, "I have set you an example that
you should do as I have done for you" (John 13:15). This prac-

tice, however, has never been widely adopted by the church. In fact, the only reference to foot washing in an **epistle** is an example of hospitality (1 Timothy 5:10).[2]

go to

early days
John 6:70–71

handpicked
Luke 6:13–16

became
Luke 6:16

inner circle
Matthew 10:1–10;
Luke 10:16–24

treasurer
John 12:4–6; 13:29

loyal
John 6:68–71; 11:16

The Last Appeal to a Lost Amigo

JOHN 13:21–27 *When Jesus had said these things, He was troubled in spirit, and testified and said, "Most assuredly, I say to you, one of you will betray Me." Then the disciples looked at one another, perplexed about whom He spoke. Now there was leaning on Jesus' bosom one of His disciples, **whom Jesus loved**. Simon Peter therefore motioned to him to ask who it was of whom He spoke.*

Then, leaning back on Jesus' breast, he said to Him, "Lord, who is it?" Jesus answered, "It is he to whom I shall give a piece of bread when I have dipped it." And having dipped the bread, He gave it to Judas Iscariot, the son of Simon. Now after the piece of bread, Satan entered him. (NKJV)

epistle
a letter, such as
Romans, 1 and 2
Corinthians,
1 Timothy, etc.

whom Jesus loved
John, writer of the
fourth Gospel

Separation between the traitor and the other disciples became increasingly apparent during the meal. Jesus had known the betrayer's identity and prophesied the betrayal since the <u>early days</u>. His treatment of the insider enemy was wonderful and heartbreaking.

- Jesus <u>handpicked</u> Judas to be his ambassador. There was no hint of treachery in the beginning—he was not chosen to be a traitor, he <u>became</u> one.

- Judas experienced the special privileges that went with being in Jesus's <u>inner circle</u>.

- Judas was given a place of honor and trust on the apostolic team, as <u>treasurer</u>.

- When others turned away from Jesus, Judas and the other eleven disciples remained <u>loyal</u>.

what others say

F. L. Godet

As a sign of communion, it was a last appeal to the conscience of Judas. If, in receiving it, his heart had been broken, he still could have received pardon.[3]

glorified
John 7:39; 12:16,
23, 28; 17:1, 5

spiritual family
Mark 3:31–35

Old Testament
Leviticus 19:18, 34

offering grace
Romans 15:7;
Galatians 6:1–2

sums up
Mark 10:28–31;
Romans 13:8–10

glorified
Christ's death and
resurrection; com-
pletion of the
Father's saving plan

little children
expression of affec-
tion rabbis used
with students

covenants
testaments, commit-
ments, promises
governing relation-
ship (with God)

Last Will and Testament

JOHN 13:31–33 *So, when [Judas] had gone out, Jesus said, "Now the Son of Man is **glorified**, and God is glorified in Him. If God is glorified in Him, God will also glorify Him in Himself, and glorify Him immediately. **Little children**, I shall be with you a little while longer. You will seek Me; and as I said to the Jews, 'Where I am going, you cannot come,' so now I say to you." (NKJV)*

Eleven faithful members of Jesus's spiritual family shared the last meal with him.

The double-crosser was gone.

The Last Commandment

JOHN 13:34–35 *A new commandment I give to you, that you love one another; as I have loved you, that you also love one another. By this all will know that you are My disciples, if you have love for one another. (NKJV)*

The command to love was not new; it was as old as the book of Leviticus. The word Jesus used for new doesn't mean "recent"; it means "superior, better in quality."

What makes this commandment superior?

- It establishes a family style of relationship among Christ's followers, identified throughout the New Testament by the phrase "one another" (John 13:34). Followers of Jesus are brothers and sisters in a way possible only to those who share his Spirit.

- It raises the standard for love (13:34). The Old Testament called for loving one's neighbor as oneself. Jesus calls us to love as he loves—putting others' welfare above our own, offering grace, laying our lives on the line for one another.

- It has a new impact (13:35). Nothing demonstrates the reality of Jesus Christ more clearly to the world than Christians visibly loving each other in word and action.

- It sums up the moral demands of the old and new **covenants** in a single principle.

does not tempt
James 1:13

Jesus's prayers
Hebrews 7:25;
1 John 2:1

equip
2 Corinthians 1:3–7;
Hebrews 2:18

what others say

John Powell

Going out to another in love means risk—the risks of self-disclosure, rejection, misunderstanding. It means grief, too, from the temporary separations, psychological or physical, to the final separation of death. Whoever insists on personal security and safety as the nonnegotiable conditions of life will not be willing to pay love's price or find love's enrichments. Whoever shuts himself or herself in the cocoon of self-protective defenses, keeping others always at a safe distance and holding on tightly to personal possessions and privacy, will find the price of love far too high and will remain forever a prisoner of fear.[4]

Damage Control

LUKE 22:31–34 *And the Lord said, "Simon, Simon! Indeed, Satan has asked for you, that he may sift you as wheat. But I have prayed for you, that your faith should not fail; and when you have returned to Me, strengthen your brethren." But he said to Him, "Lord, I am ready to go with You, both to prison and to death." Then He said, "I tell you, Peter, the rooster shall not crow this day before you will deny three times that you know Me." (NKJV)*

Peter was still hung up on Jesus's statement (John 13:33) that he was leaving. Jesus gave his well-intentioned friend four things to remember as the dust settled after the spiritual crash for which he was headed:

1. He must remember that the source of temptation is Satan (Luke 22:31). God <u>does not tempt</u> people to sin.

2. Because of <u>Jesus's prayers</u>, Peter's faith would survive (Luke 22:32).

3. Peter would bounce back after his spiritual lapse (Luke 22:32).

4. His failure would <u>equip</u> him to strengthen his fellow believers (Luke 22:32).

That night and in the days ahead, all the apostles would be at risk. And they would be without Jesus.

go to

remember
1 Corinthians
11:23–26

meal together
Acts 2:42, 46

gospel harmony

Matthew 26:26–29
Mark 14:22–25
Luke 22:15–20

"Remember Me"

LUKE 22:17–20 *Then He took the cup, and gave thanks, and said, "Take this and divide it among yourselves; for I say to you, I will not drink of the fruit of the vine until the kingdom of God comes." And He took bread, gave thanks and broke it, and gave it to them, saying, "This is My body which is given for you; do this in remembrance of Me." Likewise He also took the cup after supper, saying, "This cup is the new covenant in My blood, which is shed for you.* (NKJV)

As the Passover meal progressed Jesus used its most common elements—bread and wine—to introduce his friends to a new way to <u>remember</u> him. Christians call it "Holy Communion" or "the Lord's Supper."

Bread and wine were common fare at everyday meals. This memory meal was not introduced in church. It was designed for family and friends eating an ordinary <u>meal together</u> in someone's home.

It's appropriate for Christians to remember Jesus at every meal, not just special "communion services."

between you and God." . . . Because of what Jesus did for men, the way for men is open to all the loveliness of this new relationship with God.[6]

go to

eternal home
Hebrews 11:14–16;
12:22;
Revelation 21:9–22:5

Power Secrets

JOHN 14:1–6 *"Let not your heart be troubled; you believe in God, believe also in Me. In My Father's house are many mansions; if it were not so, I would have told you. I go to prepare a place for you. And if I go and prepare a place for you, I will come again and receive you to Myself; that where I am, there you may be also. And where I go you know, and the way you know." Thomas said to Him, "Lord, we do not know where You are going, and how can we know the way?" Jesus said to him, "I am the way, the truth, and the life. No one comes to the Father except through Me." (NKJV)*

There were at least three reasons for Jesus's disciples to shake in their boots that night:

1. Jesus, on whom they depended for everything, was leaving them (John 13:33).

2. Peter, the "Rock," strongman of faith (Matthew 16:18; John 6:68–69), would deny the Lord before sunup (John 13:38).

3. Deadly danger was around the corner, and they'd face it alone (Luke 22:36).

Reining in Galloping Fears

For these fears Jesus had one answer: "Believe in God; believe also in Me" (John 14:1 NKJV). Believing in Jesus when they saw him arrested, condemned, and crucified would not be a piece of cake! So Jesus gave them reasons to believe.

1. *You've got a home* (John 14:2–3). Peter asked, "Where are You going?" (13:36 NKJV). Jesus answered, "I'm going to get your room ready in my Father's house." God's "house" illustrates two "places" Christians call home: (1) heaven, God's <u>eternal home;</u>

go to

earthly home
1 Corinthians
3:16–17;
Ephesians 2:20–22;
1 Peter 2:5

access
Hebrews 10:20

truth
Colossians 2:3

life
John 14:19;
Galatians 2:20

only way
Acts 4:12

visible in Jesus
John 1:18;
John 5:17–23;
12:44–45

greater
not greater in
power, but in scope
and number, touch-
ing more people

and (2) the church, God's <u>earthly home</u>, the believer's spiritual family. Jesus's death and resurrection prepared the way to both places.

2. ***You know the way to God*** (14:4–6). Jesus is our <u>access</u> to fellowship with God, the <u>truth</u> about what God is like, and the giver of <u>life</u> from God. When we know Jesus, we've found the <u>only way</u> to God.

3. ***You've seen the Father*** (14:7–11). To know Jesus is to know the Father. Philip exclaimed, "Show us the Father" (14:8 NKJV). Jesus answered, "For three years you have been looking into the face of God—haven't you seen him, Philip?" (14:9, paraphrased). The invisible God is <u>visible in Jesus</u>! He and God are part of each other. Jesus speaks God's words and does God's miracles (14:10–11).

The Show Must Go On!

> JOHN 14:12–14 *Most assuredly, I say to you, he who believes in Me, the works that I do he will do also; and greater works than these he will do, because I go to My Father. And whatever you ask in My name, that I will do, that the Father may be glorified in the Son. If you ask anything in My name, I will do it.* (NKJV)

God's revelation of himself among us began in Jesus. It would continue in his followers. They would do the things he had done—even **greater** things! Jesus would do for them anything they asked. This would require fundamental changes in their relationship:

1. Jesus must return to his Father, at which time his Spirit would come to live in them (John 14:12, 16).

2. They must trust in Jesus even though he would not be physically present (14:12).

3. Their works must continue to be what Jesus would do (14:12).

4. Their requests must be **in Jesus's name** and must bring **glory** to the Father (14:13–14).

go to

I am
John 6:35; 8:12; 8:58; 9:5; 10:7, 9, 11; 14; 11:25; 14:6

what others say

John Charles Ryle

"Greater works" mean more conversions. There is no greater work possible than the conversion of a soul.[8]

in Jesus's name
consistent with his character, values, purposes

glory
praise, honor, revelation of his nature and redemptive plan

The New, Improved Relationship with Christ

JOHN 14:15–17 *If you love Me, keep My commandments. And I will pray the Father, and He will give you another Helper, that He may abide with you forever—the Spirit of truth, whom the world cannot receive, because it neither sees Him nor knows Him; but you know Him, for He dwells with you and will be in you. (NKJV)*

Jesus unveiled the exciting adventure into which the pain of the coming hours would be the gateway. When he was dead and buried, they might doubt it. But when he walked with them again in his resurrection body, these teachings would roar back to mind and set them on a course to share his glory. Following Jesus's instructions would lead to an intimacy with him beyond their wildest dreams!

Let's Get to Work!

JOHN 14:31–15:5 *Arise, let us go from here. <u>I am</u> the true vine, and My Father is the vinedresser. Every branch in Me that does not bear fruit He takes away; and every branch that bears fruit He prunes, that it may bear more fruit. You are already clean because of the word which I have spoken to you. Abide in Me, and I in you. As the branch cannot bear fruit of itself, unless it abides in the vine, neither can you, unless you abide in Me. I am the vine, you are the branches. He who abides in Me, and I in him, bears much fruit; for without Me you can do nothing. (NKJV)*

By now Jesus's men knew they were going to fail Jesus before morning (Matthew 26:31; Mark 14:27; John 13:38). His response to their fears was a model for all good leaders. Calling himself "the

go to

can do
Acts 1:8;
Philippians 4:13

fruit
John 4:35–36;
Romans 8:4–6;
Galatians 5:22–24;
Colossians 1:10–12;
James 3:17

prune
trimming that
ensures large, lus-
cious grapes rather
than tiny ones

true vine" and his disciples "the branches," he encouraged them by telling them the following six things:

1. *God would meet their failure by lifting them up.* John 15:2 should read, "Every branch that does not bear fruit, he raises up" (to keep it from trailing on the ground). Israeli farmers lift young vines out of the dirt and prop them up so sun and air can get to them.

2. *God would use their failures to **prune** and cleanse away spiritual hindrances to fruitfulness* (John 15:2). In fact, the process of cleansing had already been happening as they listened to his words (verse 3).

3. *If they'd hang on to him and let him hang on to them, they would be more fruitful than they'd ever been* (John 15:4–5). They'd learn a vital principle of Christian living: "Without Me [Christ] you <u>can do</u> nothing" (John 15:5 NKJV).

4. *What happened to Judas* (John 15:6) would not happen to them if they'd keep connected to Jesus (15:7).

5. *They would be fruitful branches.* God would be glorified in all the spiritual <u>fruit</u> they would bear (John 15:8–17).

6. *Jesus gave them promises to fall back on.* Promises of love, joy, friendship, and usefulness were piled like sandbags (John 15:8–17) to keep them from being washed away in the flood of failure and grief about to wash over them.

No Rose Garden

JOHN 15:18 *If the world hates you, you know that it hated Me before it hated you.* (NKJV)

Jesus promised he would be with us in the person of the Holy Spirit, empowering us, guiding us, enhancing our witness. He promised peace, joy, love, and usefulness to God.

He also told us to <u>expect to suffer</u> and be hated by the **world**, just as he was (and is), for no better reason than our association with him.

go to

expect to suffer
Mark 13:9–13;
Matthew 10:17–29;
Luke 12:2–9, 51–53

world
Ephesians 6:12;
Colossians 1:13–14;
2:20;
1 John 2:16; 5:19

all nations
Matthew 28:19–20

> what others say
>
> **Tertullian**
>
> The blood of Christians is seed. [It is] the bait that wins men to our school. We multiply whenever we are mown down by you . . . For who that beholds [martyrdom] is not stirred to inquire what lies indeed within it?[10]

world
human society as a system opposed to God

omnipresent
present everywhere at all times

Face-to-Face Versus Spirit-to-Spirit

JOHN 16:5–11 *But now I go away to Him who sent Me, and none of you asks Me, "Where are You going?" But because I have said these things to you, sorrow has filled your heart. Nevertheless I tell you the truth. It is to your advantage that I go away; for if I do not go away, the Helper will not come to you; but if I depart, I will send Him to you. And when He has come, He will convict the world of sin, and of righteousness, and of judgment: of sin, because they do not believe in Me; of righteousness, because I go to My Father and you see Me no more; of judgment, because the ruler of this world is judged.* (NKJV)

Jesus gave his followers reasons for his leaving and sending the Counselor:

1. *It is better for Jesus's followers not to be dependent on his visible, physical presence.* The physical Jesus was bound by human limitations that would have hindered the spread of the gospel to <u>all nations</u>; in human form it was impossible for him to live in and be with all his followers wherever they were at all times. Through his Holy Spirit Jesus is **omnipresent**.

go to

write his teachings
Hebrews 10:16;
1 John 2:20–21,
26–27

changing
2 Corinthians 3:18

atoned for
covered, paid for,
pardoned

convict
Greek legal term for
investigation or
cross examination

2. *The Holy Spirit could not come into the disciples until Jesus had finished his redeeming mission.* For people to be filled with God's Spirit, the estrangement between them and God must be healed. Sin must be **atoned for**. The price of forgiveness must be paid. Christ had to die and rise again.

3. *In Spirit, Jesus can get inside his people's heads and <u>write his teachings</u> on their hearts and minds, <u>changing</u> them from inside.*

The Holy Spirit prepares people's hearts for hearing the bad news about their sins and the good news about Jesus Christ. He can **convict** not just one person or a crowd, but the whole world (John 16:8–11). That is, he is able to expose hidden sin and unbelief, show where God's righteous standard has been violated, and convince people of impending judgment. When witnesses share their faith in Christ, they can be sure the Holy Spirit is already speaking to their listeners' hearts.

4. *Living in them, the Spirit teaches Christ's followers things they never understood while face-to-face with him* (John 16:12–15).

He gives disclosures about the future, insights into current situations, and enlightenment about his teachings, person, and relationship to God:

- The Holy Spirit does not draw attention to himself (John 16:13).
- The Holy Spirit reveals only what he hears from Christ (16:13).
- The Holy Spirit glorifies Jesus, making him the center of attention (16:14).
- The Holy Spirit concentrates on Jesus as the ultimate Revealer of God (16:15).

Chapter Wrap-Up

- Judas contracted with the chief priests to turn Jesus over to them for thirty pieces of silver. (Matthew 26:14–16)

- The night before he died, Jesus met the Twelve in an upper room to celebrate Passover and share many things with them. He washed their feet. He gave them his New Commandment: Love one another as I have loved you. (Matthew 26:17–35; John 13:1–38)

- Jesus told them he was going to his Father to prepare a place for them. Meanwhile, they would do the works he had done through the Holy Spirit living in them, empowering them, and revealing him to them. (John 14)

- He told them he was the vine and they the branches: they were destined to bear much fruit with the help of the Father's lifting and pruning. If they'd stay connected with him, they would have fruitful lives and ministries. (John 15:1–17)

- He warned them to expect the world to hate them as it hated him. The world would hate them because it does not know God. Many will think they are doing God a service by persecuting Christians. (John 15:18–16:4)

- He said it was good for him to leave, because the Holy Spirit could come. When the Spirit came he would convict the world of sin and teach Jesus's followers. (John 16:5–11)

Study Questions

1. When did Judas conspire with Jesus's enemies to sell him out? What was his price? What could a person buy with that amount?

2. What three factors may have contributed to Judas's becoming a traitor?

3. What "shocking" thing did Jesus do to begin the supper? How did Peter feel about it? How would you have felt? What reason did Jesus give Peter to let him do it?

4. What is the "new commandment"? Name three reasons it's "new."

5. What did Jesus mean when he called the Holy Spirit "another" Helper (John 14:16)?

6. In Jesus's picture of the vine and branches, what does the Father do if a branch does not bear fruit?

7. What is the main reason Jesus tells his disciples he must leave them? What role of the Holy Spirit have you come to appreciate most?

Part Six
THE PRICE OF REDEMPTION

Chapter 31: The Great Surrender

Chapter Highlights:
- The Insider Petitions
- The Great Surrender
- Night Trials
- Betrayer's Remorse
- Roman Justice

Let's Get Started

Around the Last Supper table in the <u>Upper Room</u>, Jesus told his friends they would very shortly be separated and experience a grief made more bitter because the world would be holding a victory dance around his crucified corpse. Then he left them with this bittersweet assurance: Eventually their weeping would give birth to joy so real they would forget the pain (John 16:16–28).

In a burst of "<u>insight</u>," the disciples were sure they understood everything. At last they were certain: Jesus was the Messiah (John 16:29–30)!

go to

Upper Room
John 13–16

insight
1 Corinthians 8:1–3

High Priestly
Hebrews 4:14–16;
7:22–28

priest
mediator, spiritual
bridge between
people and God

The Insider Petitions

JOHN 17:1–5 *Jesus spoke these words, lifted up His eyes to heaven, and said: "Father, the hour has come. Glorify Your Son, that Your Son also may glorify You, as You have given Him authority over all flesh, that He should give eternal life to as many as You have given Him. And this is eternal life, that they may know You, the only true God, and Jesus Christ whom You have sent. I have glorified You on the earth. I have finished the work which You have given Me to do. And now, O Father, glorify Me together with Yourself, with the glory which I had with You before the world was." (NKJV)*

How could these mere earthlings access the resources to deal with the responsibilities with which this night left them? Jesus mentioned the means of access several times that very evening. He taught them and made promises to them about prayer.

Sometimes John 17 is called Jesus's "<u>High Priestly</u> Prayer." (Sixteenth-century Lutheran theologian David Chytraeus called it that because it follows the pattern of the high **priest** on the Day of Atonement, or Yom Kippur.)

go to

on the cross
Luke 23:34

Prayer for the Magnificent Eleven

JOHN 17:9–12 *I pray for them. I do not pray for the world but for those whom You have given Me, for they are Yours. And all Mine are Yours, and Yours are Mine, and I am glorified in them. Now I am no longer in the world, but these are in the world, and I come to You. Holy Father, keep through Your name those whom You have given Me, that they may be one as We are. While I was with them in the world, I kept them in Your name. Those whom You gave Me I have kept; and none of them is lost except the son of perdition, that the Scripture might be fulfilled. (NKJV)*

Jesus did not pray for the world. He'd do that later, <u>on the cross</u>. Here he prayed for his friends, the insiders, his scouts, to blaze a trail for the kingdom of God deep into the wild, wicked, untamed territory of the world.

A Vision of the Future

JOHN 17:20–21 *I do not pray for these alone, but also for those who will believe in Me through their word; that they all may be one, as You, Father, are in Me, and I in You; that they also may be one in Us, that the world may believe that You sent Me. (NKJV)*

The night before he died, Jesus prayed for you and me—people who would believe in him as the result of the message of the apostles, in their preaching and writing of the New Testament.

what others say

William Barclay

If we really loved each other and really loved Christ, no church would exclude any man who was Christ's disciple. Only love implanted in men's hearts by God can tear down the barriers which they have erected between each other and between their churches.[1]

The Great Surrender

MARK 14:32–34 *Then they came to a place which was named Gethsemane; and He said to His disciples, "Sit here while I pray." And He took Peter, James, and John with Him, and He began to be troubled and deeply distressed. Then He said to them, "My soul is exceedingly sorrowful, even to death. Stay here and watch." (NKJV)*

The door opened and Jesus led his team down the outside stairs, through streets and along trails lit by the full Passover moon, out of the city, across the Brook Kedron, and up into the olive trees that gave Mount Olivet its name.

Among the groves was an old olive press surrounded by a garden, a place Jesus loved to go to spend the night or pray. Mark and Matthew identify the place as **Gethsemane** (see appendix B). John tells us it was a garden.

In this olive garden Jesus recommitted himself to carry through God's plan involving suffering and death for our sins. He confided in Peter, James, and John that he was on the verge of dying of grief! Luke uses the Greek word *agonia*, a word for intense emotion, violent inner struggle, emotional strain, "agony" (Luke 22:44 NKJV).

go to

punishment
Isaiah 53:4–6, 8, 10;
2 Corinthians 5:21;
1 Peter 2:24

cup
Job 21:20;
Psalm 60:3;
Isaiah 51:19, 22;
Ezekiel 23:32–34

Gethsemane
means "place of crushing" or "olive press"

Abba
"Daddy" in Aramaic, the language Jesus spoke

cup
expression for the experience of suffering or judgment

"Daddy, Must I?"

MARK 14:35–36 *He went a little farther, and fell on the ground, and prayed that if it were possible, the hour might pass from Him. And He said, "**Abba**, Father, all things are possible for You. Take this cup away from Me; nevertheless, not what I will, but what You will." (NKJV)*

At no time in Jesus's story is his humanity more visible and his commitment to the Father's will clearer. He had faced death before, while shaking his finger in its face. Now he confronted it with no less courage. The physical horror of crucifixion was not the major reason he dreaded the cross. He knew that as he took the punishment for our sin, his Father would turn away from him! That separation was the focus of his grief.

Three times, facedown on the ground, Jesus expressed his human wish that his Father might find some way for him to avoid the ordeal ahead. "If it is possible, let this **cup** pass from Me" (Matthew 26:39 NKJV). Three times Jesus affirmed his uninterrupted commitment to God's plan: "Nevertheless, not as I will, but as You will."

After each prayer Jesus came back to the disciples and found them asleep. The first time he woke Peter (Matthew 26:40–41) and reminded him to pray to keep from falling into temptation. The second time he left them sleeping (26:43). The third time he woke them up because the arresting force led by Judas had entered the garden (26:45–46).

---

what others say

Michael Card

Jesus cried out, "Abba." Never let anyone clothe that word in theological sophistication. It is not a sophisticated word! It is baby talk. Papa, Daddy, Abba—they are all the same thing: the first stutterings of an infant, not to be categorized in some systematic theological structure, but to be cried out from the heart of a child, a heart of faith . . . The agony of the cross, the crushing torment of it, was the separation Jesus experienced from the Father, the result of his obedience. That painful crushing began, appropriately enough, in the garden called Gethsemane [the place of crushing].[2]

Capture of the Desperado

MARK 14:44–46 *Now His betrayer had given them a signal, saying, "Whomever I kiss, He is the One; seize Him and lead Him away safely." As soon as he had come, immediately he went up to Him and said to Him, "Rabbi, Rabbi!" and kissed Him. Then they laid their hands on Him and took Him. (NKJV)*

Jesus could have been beyond the reach of the high priest's men. Instead he waited in a familiar rendezvous where the traitor could lead them to him.

When a disciple greeted a beloved rabbi, he put his hands on his mentor's shoulders and kissed him. That Judas chose this as the signal to identify Jesus deepens the sense of betrayal.

John records the same scene this way: "And Judas, who betrayed Him, also knew the **place**; for Jesus often met there with His disciples. Then Judas, having received a **detachment** of troops, and officers from the chief priests and Pharisees, came there with lanterns, torches, and weapons" (John 18:2–3 NKJV). As if expecting a fight, the arresting party came with weapons poised.

"Have you come out, as against a robber, with swords and clubs?" Jesus asked. "When I was with you daily in the temple, you did not try to seize Me. But this is your hour, and the power of darkness"

(Luke 22:52–53 NKJV). The dead of night was strangely appropriate for nabbing the young Messiah. After all, the real power behind the raid was the **dominion** of darkness!

Peter leaped to Jesus's defense. His blade flashed in the torchlight as it swung in a huge arc aimed at splitting the high priest's slave in two! Fortunately, it missed its mark and lopped off the man's right ear (John 18:10)! (Whew! Good thing Peter was better at casting a net than swinging a sword!) "Permit even this," Jesus said, and he touched the servant's ear and healed him (Luke 22:51 NKJV).

At that point, the disciples ran for their lives. Mark adds that a young man with "a linen cloth thrown around his naked body" was grabbed by the officers. Leaving his shirt, he "streaked" into the night. Mark is telling us he was there (Mark 14:51–52 NKJV).

go to

dominion
Colossians 1:13

Annas
John 18:24;
Acts 4:6

dominion
Satan's evil empire

Night Trials

> JOHN 18:12–13 *Then the detachment of troops and the captain and the officers of the Jews arrested Jesus and bound Him. And they led Him away to Annas first, for he was the father-in-law of Caiaphas who was high priest that year. (NKJV)*

At last it was time for the enemies of Jesus to do with him what they wished. It was the moment for the world's power structures—religious and secular—to take their turns on center stage, showing what they were capable of doing to preserve their positions of power and protect their sacred institutions and traditions.

By prearrangement Jesus was taken first to the palace of <u>Annas</u>, father-in-law of Caiaphas, the current high priest. Annas had once been high priest. Roman prefect Valerius Gratus fired him in AD 15, but Annas continued to be the power behind the throne. Many Jews considered this appropriate because the high priest was supposed to be appointed for life.

Trial of the Deposed "Patriarch"

> JOHN 18:19–21 *The high priest then asked Jesus about His disciples and His doctrine. Jesus answered him, "I spoke openly to the world. I always taught in synagogues and in the temple, where the Jews always meet, and in secret I have said nothing. Why do you ask Me? Ask those who have heard Me what I said to them. Indeed they know what I said." (NKJV)*

death
Deuteronomy
13:1–10

blasphemy
treat God with contempt by reducing him to mere human level

Annas interrogated Jesus. The bitter old Sadducee tried to get Jesus to incriminate himself as a false prophet, a crime punishable by death.

Jewish law prescribed the procedure for such inquiries. And this wasn't it! The accused was not to be questioned by the judge. Everything in a legitimate trial depended on the testimony of witnesses given under oath in open court. No witnesses were present. It was the middle of the night. Anyone who might have been called to testify in Jesus's favor was asleep.

Jesus was within his legal rights to object to Annas's illegal interrogation. But when he spoke, an officer doubled up his fist and hit Jesus in the face! "Is this any way to talk to the high priest?" the official demanded. Striking an uncondemned prisoner was also illegal! Jesus demanded witnesses be produced to testify he had said something wrong.

Trial of the Puppet Priest

> MARK 14:61–62 *But He kept silent and answered nothing. Again the high priest asked Him, saying to Him, "Are You the Christ, the Son of the Blessed?" Jesus said, "I am. And you will see the Son of Man sitting at the right hand of the Power, and coming with the clouds of heaven." (NKJV)*

Annas ended his interrogation. Jesus, bound like a dangerous outlaw, was taken across the courtyard to the adjoining palace of Caiaphas, the reigning high priest (see appendix B). In phase two of this kangaroo court scenario, Caiaphas's judgment was anything but impartial. He had already made up his mind that Jesus should "die for the people" (John 11:50 NKJV).

Joining Caiaphas were Sanhedrin members who "sought testimony against Jesus to put Him to death" (Mark 14:55 NKJV). Many witnesses perjured themselves. Their "testimony" was useless because they "did not agree" (verses 56–59). Jesus refused to answer their lies. But when Caiaphas asked him directly if he was the Christ, Jesus answered.

In a melodramatic gesture of outrage, Caiaphas tore his robe and shouted, "**Blasphemy**!" He called for a verdict (Mark 14:63–64). The unanimous judgment was "Guilty!" (Surprise! Surprise!) The sentence: Jesus of Nazareth is "worthy of death."

Since legal jurisprudence had nothing whatever to do with these hate-driven proceedings, what happened next was revolting but predictable. Powerful men, prominent leaders of Israel's religion and life, teachers, lawyers, and clergy, model citizens, and police, all drunk with the taste for Jesus's blood, became a mob of hooligans. They blindfolded, mocked, spit, slapped, and **beat** him, <u>striking</u> him in the face with their fists. Again! And again! And again! And those who did not participate stood with folded arms, approving.

go to

striking
Matthew 26:67–68;
Mark 14:65;
Luke 22:63–65

beat
with skin-flaying scourge (Luke 22:63); with fist or flat side of sword (22:64)

known
"familiar friend"; "kinsman"

Trial Beside the Enemies' Fire

> JOHN 18:15 *And Simon Peter followed Jesus, and so did another disciple. Now that disciple was known to the high priest, and went with Jesus into the courtyard of the high priest.* (NKJV)

Peter and another disciple, assumed to be John, had followed the arresting force to the high priest's palace. John was **known** to the gatekeeper, so when the officers, with Jesus in chains, entered the palace grounds, John was allowed to enter with them. When he found out where the interrogation was taking place, he returned to convince the gatekeeper to let Peter in. As Peter came through the gate, the keeper, a young woman, asked, "You are not also one of this Man's disciples, are you?" (John 18:17 NKJV). "I am not," he lied (18:17 NKJV). (That's once.)

The guardsmen and servants had built a fire in the courtyard to take the chill off the night. Peter joined them. A little time passed. Another person said to him, "You are not also one of His disciples, are you?" (John 18:25 NKJV). "I am not!" Peter lied (18:25 NKJV). (That's twice.)

An hour passed. A third person, a relative of Malchus, whose ear Peter had lopped off, identified Peter as one of Jesus's men: "Did I not see you in the garden with Him?" (John 18:26 NKJV). Mark's report adds: "You are a Galilean" (Mark 14:70 NKJV). Matthew 26:73 says Peter's accent gave him away.

That's Three!

> LUKE 22:60–62 *But Peter said, "Man, I do not know what you are saying!" Immediately, while he was still speaking, the rooster crowed. And the Lord turned and looked at Peter. Then*

three
Luke 22:34

wept bitterly
John 21:15–23

dissenters
Luke 23:50–51

Sanhedrin
highest Jewish
ruling council

tribunal
court of justice

Peter remembered the word of the Lord, how He had said to him, "Before the rooster crows, you will deny Me <u>three</u> times." So Peter went out and wept <u>bitterly</u>. (NKJV)

Matthew and Mark say that this third time, Peter backed his reply with a string of oaths. His denial was a crushing failure and showed, not only Peter but all of us, how weak humans are.

By failing to speak the truth and by doing nothing, Peter helped to crucify Christ as surely as the priests and the soldiers who drove the nails.[3]

Although Jesus was being moved across the courtyard to another trial, he knew what Peter had done. Jesus looked at him with sorrow and love. And take-charge, rush-ahead, self-confident Peter was reduced to a heap of sobbing flesh.

Jesus of Nazareth Versus the Sanhedrin

LUKE 22:63–65 *Now the men who held Jesus mocked Him and beat Him. And having blindfolded Him, they struck Him on the face and asked Him, saying, "Prophesy! Who is the one who struck You?" And many other things they blasphemously spoke against Him. (NKJV)*

The **Sanhedrin** (see Illustration #8) met at dawn. As the supreme court they had complete and final jurisdiction over religious and theological issues. They were bound by Jewish law to follow rules of procedure designed to give defendants the advantage. In the case of Jesus of Nazareth versus the Sanhedrin, however, most of the rules were broken.

Into this **tribunal**, Jesus was dragged, dripping with spittle, his face bruised from blows by many fists. "If You are the Christ, tell us" (Luke 22:67 NKJV). He replied, "If I tell you, you will by no means believe" (22:67 NKJV).

"Are You then the Son of God?" they demanded noisily (Luke 22:70 NKJV). "You rightly say that I am," he replied (22:70 NKJV). He spoke with the confidence with which he had emerged from Gethsemane. He knew his answer would bring a sentence of death.

The assembly rose to its feet, declared him guilty, and dragged him off to the Roman governor to demand the death penalty. If there were <u>dissenters</u> present, they were never given a chance to speak. No witnesses for the defense were called. No poll of individual members was conducted. A lynch-mob mentality prevailed.

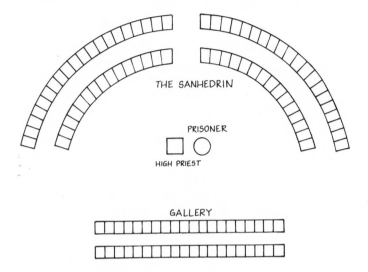

THE SANHEDRIN

PRISONER

HIGH PRIEST

GALLERY

Illustration #8
The Sanhedrin—The sketch shows the physical arrangement of the Jewish Sanhedrin with 71 members: elders, priests, teachers of the Law, Sadducees, and Pharisees.

Betrayer's Remorse

MATTHEW 27:3–4 *Then Judas, His betrayer, seeing that He had been condemned, was remorseful and brought back the thirty pieces of silver to the chief priests and elders, saying, "I have sinned by betraying innocent blood." And they said, "What is that to us? You see to it!" (NKJV)*

The tragic end of Judas Iscariot came when the Sanhedrin condemned Jesus. Putting together the facts reported by Matthew and Peter (Acts 1:18–19), it happened like this:

- Seized with remorse, Judas brought the thirty pieces of silver to the temple and tried to return them to the officials who hired him. They refused to take the money, so he threw it at them (Matthew 27:5). As the coins clattered across the temple pavement, he left.

- The next news of Judas came when his mangled body was found at the foot of a cliff owned by a local pottery maker. From the evidence it appeared Judas hanged himself from a tree at the edge of the precipice, the limb broke, and his body plunged onto the rocks below.

- The priests bought the land where he died for a pauper's burial ground using the returned silver. People called it Akel Dama, Field of Blood (Acts 1:19).

Praetorium
governor's palace,
Roman military
headquarters near
the temple

> **what others say**
>
> **Oswald Chambers**
>
> Never mistake remorse for repentance; remorse simply puts a man in hell while he is on earth, it carries no remedial quality with it at all, nothing that betters a man. An unawakened sinner has no remorse, but immediately a man recognizes his sin he experiences the pain of being gnawed by a sense of guilt, for which punishment would be a heaven of relief, but no punishment can touch it.[4]

Roman Justice

JOHN 18:28–32 *Then they led Jesus from Caiaphas to the **Praetorium**, and it was early morning. But they themselves did not go into the Praetorium, lest they should be defiled, but that they might eat the Passover.* (NKJV)

The delegation of religious leaders stopped outside the palace gate (see appendix B). They meticulously avoided entering the governor's palace, because entering a Gentile's house would defile them ceremonially, disqualifying them from eating the Passover meal that evening (John 18:28–29).

There were three reasons for doing this at the crack of dawn: (1) Roman officials began work before sunup; (2) Sanhedrin leaders wanted Jesus to be executed before the Passover; and (3) at daylight worshippers filled the temple and the potential for an uprising of support for Jesus increased.

> **what others say**
>
> **George R. Beasley-Murray**
>
> No more eloquent example than this can be found of the ability of religious people to be meticulous about external regulations of religion while being wholly at variance with God.[5]

Trial of the Ruthless Judge

JOHN 18:29–32 *Pilate then went out to them and said, "What accusation do you bring against this Man?" They answered and said to him, "If He were not an evildoer, we would not have delivered Him up to you." Then Pilate said to them, "You take Him and judge Him according to your law." Therefore the Jews said to him, "It is not lawful for us to put anyone to death," that the saying of Jesus might be fulfilled which He spoke, signifying by what death He would die. (NKJV)*

Pilate was expecting them (he would have ordered the detachment of <u>soldiers</u> to aid in Jesus's midnight arrest). He came out onto the platform overlooking the pavement in front of the palace.

He asked the question with which all Roman trials began: "What accusation do you bring against this Man?" (John 18:29 NKJV). Their answer (18:30) indicates they hoped Pilate would simply rubber-stamp their verdict and ratify the death sentence without further investigation.

After the initial retort, they brought charges against Jesus crafted to grab the Roman's attention (Luke 23:2):

1. He is the leader of a political insurrection.

2. He opposes payment of taxes.

3. He claims to be king in competition with Caesar.

Pilate responded, "You take Him and judge Him according to your law" (John 18:31 NKJV). But that wasn't their scheme. They wanted to transfer responsibility to the Romans for the popular young prophet's execution. And they wanted Jesus to die on a cross so they could tag him with the ancient **curse** of hanging.

Little did they know they were assuring the fulfillment of one of Jesus's own <u>prophecies</u>, that he would die on a Roman cross (John 18:32)!

"Who's on Trial Here?"

JOHN 18:33–34 *Then Pilate entered the Praetorium again, called Jesus, and said to Him, "Are You the King of the Jews?" Jesus answered him, "Are you speaking for yourself about this, or did others tell you this concerning Me?" (NKJV)*

Pilate went back inside the judgment hall to cross-examine the prisoner. He confronted him with the most serious charge first: "Are You the King of the Jews?" Jesus answered with a question of his own: whether this was Pilate's own idea, or whether he was parroting what others had said. The accused was cross-examining the judge!

soldiers
John 18:3, 12

curse of hanging
Deuteronomy 21:23;
Galatians 3:13

prophecies
Luke 18:32;
John 12:31–33

curse
"Cursed is anyone who is hung on a tree."

prophecy

go to

truth
John 1:14–18;
8:31–32; 14:6–11

untruth
John 8:44–45

untruth
darkness, hypocrisy,
dishonesty, false
promises

Incensed, Pilate said, "Am I a Jew?" (John 18:35 NKJV). (In other words, I have no personal interest in your peculiar Jewish notions. So how could I know?) "Your own nation and the chief priests have delivered You to me. What have You done?" (18:35 NKJV).

Jesus's response was to define what his kingdom was not. "My kingdom is not of this world" (John 18:36 NKJV).

"Truth? What's That?"

JOHN 18:37–38 *Pilate therefore said to Him, "Are You a king then?" Jesus answered, "You say rightly that I am a king. For this cause I was born, and for this cause I have come into the world, that I should bear witness to the truth. Everyone who is of the truth hears My voice." Pilate said to Him, "What is truth?" And when he had said this, he went out again to the Jews, and said to them, "I find no fault in Him at all." (NKJV)*

Having told him what his kingdom was not, Jesus proceeded to explain to the governor what his kingdom was: It was the kingdom of truth—the <u>truth</u> about God, his sovereignty, love, and redeeming purpose to rescue human beings from the kingdom of **untruth**.

"What is truth?" retorted the governor (John 18:38 NKJV). He did not wait for an answer. Cynical minds ridicule the idea there is absolute truth. Pontius Pilate had just been given his best chance to embrace the truth and the life truth opens up to the believing mind.

> **what others say**
>
> **Cal Thomas**
>
> True believers—including me—are beginning to sense that the kingdom of this world, which regularly demands compromise, cannot be reconciled to a kingdom not of this world that allows for no compromise. Consider John 18:36, when Jesus tells Pilate: "My kingdom is not of this world . . . my kingdom is from another place." His is not a realm that needs soldiers to establish or defend it . . . For Christians, the vision of worldly power is not a calling, but a distraction. It is a temptation Jesus rejected not because it was dangerous, but because it was trivial compared with his mission.[6]

Trial of the Petty Potentate

> LUKE 23:4–5 *So Pilate said to the chief priests and the crowd, "I find no fault in this Man." But they were the more fierce, saying, "He stirs up the people, teaching throughout all Judea, beginning from Galilee to this place." (NKJV)*

Pilate asked "if the Man were a Galilean" (Luke 23:6 NKJV). Galileans were under the jurisdiction of Herod Antipas (see appendix B), who happened to be in Jerusalem at the time. Roman law permitted Pilate to transfer jurisdiction to the home province of the accused. Relations between Pilate and Herod were strained. Herod would see this transfer as a compliment.

Herod was pleased, and the transfer led to friendship between the two political enemies (Luke 23:12).

Herod was a shallow man who tried to get Jesus to do something sensational. Jesus treated him as his insignificance deserved. He refused to answer any questions and was returned to Pilate (see appendix B), with his herd of accusers. Knowing he had a political hot potato on his hands, Herod didn't pronounce Jesus guilty or innocent.

Litany of Rejection

> LUKE 23:13–16 *Then Pilate, when he had called together the chief priests, the rulers, and the people, said to them, "You have brought this Man to me, as one who misleads the people. And indeed, having examined Him in your presence, I have found no fault in this Man concerning those things of which you accuse Him; no, neither did Herod, for I sent you back to him; and indeed nothing deserving of death has been done by Him. I will therefore chastise Him and release Him." (NKJV)*

Three times Pilate pronounced Jesus innocent (Luke 23:4, 14–15, 22). Five times he tried to let him go:

1. *He told the Jews to punish Jesus themselves* (John 19:6–7). They demanded he do it.

2. *He tried to get the Sanhedrin-led mob to accept Jesus's release as the governor's traditional Passover pardon* (Mark 15:6–11; John 18:39–40). As a gesture of goodwill, one prisoner was released each year at Passover. A man named Barabbas was in Roman custody awaiting execution as a violent revolutionary, assassin, rabble-rouser, and robber (Mark 15:7; Luke 23:18, 24; John 18:40). Pilate gave the mob a choice—should he release Barabbas the killer or Jesus the Christ? They chose Barabbas and screamed for Jesus's death.

what others say

Revell Bible Dictionary

The one who deserved execution was freed, and the innocent took his place. In this sense, the incident of Barabbas' release is a vivid image of redemption itself. Christ's death was, from the standpoint of human responsibility, a supreme injustice; nevertheless it proved to be the central element in the grand plan of God to release those who deserve punishment by taking on himself the stroke that justice decrees. In his death Jesus was not simply a substitute for Barabbas, but for all who receive him by faith.[7]

3. *Pilate tried to get Jesus's accusers to accept a compromise punishment: He flogged Jesus, intending to release him* (Luke 23:16, 21; John 19:1). When Pilate brought him out after the scourge had torn his skin to ribbons, they screamed again: "Crucify Him, crucify Him!" (Luke 23:21 NKJV).

4. *In disgust Pilate dared religious leaders to crucify Jesus themselves, repeating his not-guilty verdict.* They let the cat out of the bag, revealing their real beef against Jesus: "We have a law, and according to our law He ought to die, because He made Himself the Son of God" (John 19:7 NKJV). Like most Romans, Pilate was superstitious. Ingrained in the culture were stories of children of the gods visiting earth. If Jesus was one, it could mean bad luck for Pilate. His wife added fuel to the fires of superstition by sending him a message telling of a nightmare she'd had about the prisoner. "Have nothing to do with that just Man," she warned (Matthew 27:19 NKJV).

"Where are You from?" Pilate asked Jesus (John 19:9 NKJV). When Jesus did not answer his questions, Pilate demanded, "Are You not speaking to me? Do You not know that I have power to crucify You, and power to release You?" (19:10 NKJV). The power of which Pilate spoke was from the most powerful politician on earth, the Roman emperor. Jesus told Pilate he really had no power at all that wasn't granted by God (19:11).

5. *Pilate tried one last time to free Jesus* (John 19:12). So the Jews threw in a final zinger—the one accusation his instinct for survival could not ignore: "If you let this Man go, you are not Caesar's friend. Whoever makes himself a king speaks against Caesar" (John 19:12 NKJV).

on our children
Exodus 20:5–6

people
priests and people in the crowd, not whole city or nation

subterfuges
deceptive ploys

The Unwashable Stain

MATTHEW 27:24–25 *When Pilate saw that he could not prevail at all, but rather that a tumult was rising, he took water and washed his hands before the multitude, saying, "I am innocent of the blood of this just Person. You see to it." And all the **people** answered and said, "His blood be on us and <u>on our children</u>." (NKJV)*

With his political back against the wall, faced with the inferred threat to report him to the emperor, unable (unwilling) to silence the screaming demands for Jesus's crucifixion, and fearing the breakdown of order in the city, Pilate "delivered Jesus to their will" (Luke 23:25 NKJV) and set Barabbas free.

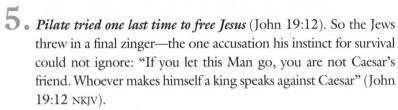

what others say

John R. W. Stott

It is easy to condemn Pilate and overlook our own equally devious behaviour. Anxious to avoid the pain of a wholehearted commitment to Christ, we too search for convenient **subterfuges**. We either leave the decision to somebody else, or opt for a half-hearted compromise, or seek to honour Jesus for the wrong reason (e.g. as teacher instead of Lord), or even make a public affirmation of loyalty while at the same time denying him in our hearts.[8]

Revell Bible Dictionary

One early Christian historian, Eusebius, reports that Pilate committed suicide in Gaul several years after Christ's death. Other Christian legends suggest that he and his wife became Christians. The **Coptic** Church honors Pilate on June 25th as a saint and maintains that he was ultimately converted and died as a martyr for his faith in Jesus.[9]

Chapter Wrap-Up

- Jesus's disciples were saddened by the news that he would be leaving. He assured them their grief would soon be turned to joy when he rose from the dead. At that point, a new, more wonderful way of relating to him and his Father would begin. (John 16:5–24)

- The final supper with his friends ended with Jesus praying his "High Priestly Prayer" for his restoration to glory, their protection against a hostile world, their unity, and for those who would believe on him through their witness. (John 17)

- In Gethsemane, Jesus struggled with the prospect of the separation from his Father that would occur when he bore God's judgment for sinners on the cross. He committed himself to do God's will. Judas led Jesus's enemies to the garden, and Jesus was arrested. (Luke 22:39–53)

- In the middle of the night Jesus was interrogated by the deposed high priest and the reigning high priest. Three times Peter denied knowing Jesus. At dawn the Sanhedrin pronounced Jesus guilty of blasphemy and condemned him to die. (John 18:12–27; Matthew 26:57–68)

- The religious leaders took Jesus to Pilate, demanding crucifixion on trumped-up charges. Pilate declared him not guilty and tried five times to release Jesus. Each time Jesus's enemies resisted. In an act of cowardice, Pilate gave in to their demands. (Luke 23:1–25; John 18:28–19:16)

Study Questions

1. In the opening sentences of Jesus's "High Priestly Prayer," he talks about eternal life. What is eternal life, according to what he says there?

2. Identify the three religious (Jewish) trials of Jesus and their locales.

3. What did Peter do after his third denial of Jesus and the rooster crowed?

4. What three charges did the Jewish religious leaders bring against Jesus when they took him to Pilate? What was the real charge—the one he was accused of by the Sanhedrin?

5. What was the "Passover Pardon"? How did Pilate use it to try to free Jesus? Who was the man freed instead of Jesus, and what kind of man was he?

6. What was the final thing Pilate did to claim that he was not responsible for Jesus's death? On a scale of 1 to 10 (1 is easiest, 10 is toughest), how difficult is it for you to accept responsibility for your own decisions and actions?

Chapter 32: The Ultimate Sacrifice

Chapter Highlights:
- **Man in Purple**
- **Street of Sorrow**
- **Father, Forgive Them**
- **The Day the Sun Refused to Shine**

Let's Get Started

The crucifixion of Jesus Christ in AD 30 was not just a Jewish problem or a Roman problem. It was not just a religious problem or a secular problem. Church and state were both to blame. The rejection and condemnation of Christ was and is a universal problem.

The Bible teaches that Jesus's death provided forgiveness for all sinners. And—hang on to your hat—all of us are sinners! Romans 3:10–12, 23 says, "There is none righteous, no, not one; there is none who understands; there is none who seeks after God . . . There is none who does good, no, not one . . . For all have sinned and fall short of the glory of God" (NKJV).

Jews
Luke 23:63–65

Rufus
Romans 16:13

Man in Purple

> **MARK 15:20** *And when they had mocked Him, they took the purple off Him, put His own clothes on Him, and led Him out to crucify Him.* (NKJV)

After the sentencing, Roman soldiers stripped Jesus and threw a purple robe over his bleeding shoulders. They twisted a crown of thorns and put it on his head, put a reed "scepter" in his right hand, and took turns kneeling before him in mock reverence, hailing him as "king of the Jews," spitting on him, and hitting him in the face. This was the second time in the hours before his crucifixion that Jesus was treated like this. The Romans carried the derision and abuse to even greater extremes than the <u>Jews</u>. In addition to their contempt for the man himself, they poured all their anti-Jewish hatred on this lone, defenseless prisoner.

Matthew 27:27–31
Mark 15:16–20
John 19:1–3

Street of Sorrow

> **MARK 15:21** *Then they compelled a certain man, Simon a Cyrenian, the father of Alexander and <u>Rufus</u>, as he was coming out of the country and passing by, to bear His cross.* (NKJV)

forced
Matthew 5:41

for themselves
Hosea 10:8;
Luke 21:20–24;
Revelation 6:15–17

in place of
Romans 5:6–8

cross
the crossbeam (simi-
lar to a railroad tie)

Cyrene
modern Tripoli

forced
Anyone could be
forced to serve the
Roman occupation
army.

nefarious
vicious, glaringly
wicked

Surrounded by four soldiers, one carrying a placard announcing his crime—his alleged claim to be "King of the Jews"—Jesus emerged from the judgment hall, carrying his **cross** (John 19:17). Hours of physical abuse had left him physically exhausted; his strength gave out, and he fell beneath the weight of the heavy beam. A traveler from **Cyrene** named Simon, just entering the city, was <u>forced</u> to carry Jesus's cross to the place of crucifixion.

Minority Opinion

LUKE 23:27–28 *And a great multitude of the people followed Him, and women who also mourned and lamented Him. But Jesus, turning to them, said, "Daughters of Jerusalem, do not weep for Me, but weep for yourselves and for your children."* (NKJV)

The crowd lining the road was not entirely hostile. A group of women filled the air with wails of grief. Jesus urged them not to grieve for him but <u>for themselves</u> and their children, because great suffering was ahead for them, too. He said, "For if they do these things in the green wood, what will be done in the dry?" (Luke 23:31 NKJV).

This was a Jewish proverb meaning, "If today God pours his wrath on his Son—an innocent 'green tree'—what will conditions be when he pours his wrath on the world that spurned his love and rejected his Son?"

Parade of the Doomed

LUKE 23:32 *There were also two others, criminals, led with Him to be put to death.* (NKJV)

Jesus was not the only one carrying a cross that day. Two criminals walked the death road with him.

Some wonder if a trio of felons had been originally scheduled to die this day—including the **nefarious** Barabbas. When Barabbas was released, Jesus merely replaced the pardoned bad guy on the execution calendar. Jesus had come to die <u>in place of</u> sinners.

Father, Forgive Them

not know
Luke 23:33–34;
Acts 3:17;
2 Corinthians
3:13–16

destroy the temple
Matthew 26:61;
Mark 14:57–58

nine o'clock
the third hour

asphyxiation
interruption of
breathing

LUKE 23:33–34 And when they had come to the place called Calvary, there they crucified Him, and the criminals, one on the right hand and the other on the left. Then Jesus said, "Father, forgive them, for they do not know what they do." And they divided His garments and cast lots. (NKJV)

New Testament authors give no space whatsoever to details about crucifixion itself. None mention the hammer or nails. None describe the pain or the precise cause of death. They simply say, as Luke does, "They crucified Him." The soldiers carried out their gruesome task as ordered by their commander, Pontius Pilate. They were professionals, and this was part of their job. Before they began driving the nails, they offered Jesus wine mixed with myrrh, a sedative to ease the pain (Mark 15:23). He refused it.

About **nine o'clock** in the morning, they drove the spikes through his wrists. Jesus kept praying out loud, "Father, forgive them, for they do <u>not know</u> what they do" (Luke 23:34 NKJV).

Crucified!

The *HarperCollins Atlas of the Bible* describes death by crucifixion: "Death would occur quickly if the body were allowed to hang without support. This would be through **asphyxiation**, as the weight of the unsupported body would lead to the shutting off of the breathing passage. To prolong the agony the victim was provided with support for the feet and, at times, a seat peg as well.

"A wooden pole was thrust into the ground, and the condemned man was then compelled to carry the top crosspiece which would then be fixed to the piece in the ground. When there were numerous victims, their arms would be simply roped to the crosspiece. In the case of the crucifixion of Jesus, our sources refer to only three being crucified at the same time. In that case, the victims were nailed both at the wrists—the nails passing between the radius and ulna—and at their feet."[1]

Opinion Poll at Golgotha

MATTHEW 27:39–43 And those who passed by blasphemed Him, wagging their heads and saying, "You who <u>destroy the temple</u>

deliver
Psalm 22:6–8

entire world
John 3:16

titulus
Latin: "title," here
a sign

and build it in three days, save Yourself! If You are the Son of God, come down from the cross." Likewise the chief priests also, mocking with the scribes and elders, said, "He saved others; Himself He cannot save. If He is the King of Israel, let Him now come down from the cross, and we will believe Him. He trusted in God; let Him <u>deliver</u> Him now if He will have Him; for He said, 'I am the Son of God.'" (NKJV)

To the crossbar above his head, the soldiers fastened Pilate's **titulus** naming Jesus's crime: "This is the King of the Jews." The sign was written in three languages (John 19:20)—Aramaic (language of the locals), Latin (language of the Romans), and Greek (the universal language).

People from all over the world would travel the nearby roads this feast day. Pilate, of course, had no idea he was symbolizing that Jesus's death was for the <u>entire world</u>.

When the chief priests protested the sign should be changed to read that Jesus claimed to be king of the Jews, Pilate responded tersely, "What I have written, I have written" (John 19:22 NKJV).

> **what others say**
>
> **Louis A. Barbieri Jr.**
>
> The irony of this scene was that Jesus could have done the things the crowd was shouting for him to do. He could have come down from the cross and physically saved himself. He did not lack the power to accomplish his deliverance. But it was not the Father's will to do that. It was necessary that the Son of God die for others.[2]

Sinners in Paradise

LUKE 23:39–43 *Then one of the criminals who were hanged blasphemed Him, saying, "If You are the Christ, save Yourself and us." But the other, answering, rebuked him, saying, "Do you not even fear God, seeing you are under the same condemnation? And we indeed justly, for we receive the due reward of our deeds; but this Man has done nothing wrong." Then he said to Jesus, "Lord, remember me when You come into Your kingdom." And Jesus said to him, "Assuredly, I say to you, today you will be with Me in Paradise." (NKJV)*

The two other men, presumably Barabbas's partners in crime, were crucified with Jesus—one on his right, the other on his left, with Jesus in the middle. Both watched him as he suffered the same calamity they were going through. Both were there to hear his prayer for his enemies' forgiveness.

At first both joined the sneering detractors, refusing to believe anything but what Jesus's enemies said about him, and refusing to accept responsibility for their own situation (Matthew 27:44). One continued to spew his bitterness until the very end. The other, however, began to see with different eyes.

Jesus interpreted his attitudes and words as expressions of faith and promised that he and the dying rebel would be together that very day in **paradise**.

paradise
place of the believing dead, also called "the bosom of Abraham"

"Take My Mother Home"

> JOHN 19:26–27 *When Jesus therefore saw His mother, and the disciple whom He loved standing by, He said to His mother, "Woman, behold your son!" Then He said to the disciple, "Behold your mother!" And from that hour that disciple took her to his own home.* (NKJV)

Relatives and friends of the crucified often came to be with them and were allowed to gather near the cross.[3]

A group of women stood near Jesus's cross, along with John, Jesus's dear friend and confidant, and others, including his enemies. In the group was his mother. What he said to her and John was no mere suggestion. He used the terminology of legal adoption proceedings.

what others say

E. Stauffer

A crucified man has the right to make testamentary dispositions, even from the cross. Jesus now makes use of this right, and with the official formula of the old Jewish family law he places his mother under the protection of the apostle John.[4]

The Day the Sun Refused to Shine

> LUKE 23:44–45a *Now it was about the sixth hour, and there was darkness over all the earth until the ninth hour. Then the sun was darkened.* (NKJV)

go to

Gethsemane
Luke 22:41–44

sixth hour
noon

ninth hour
three o'clock in the
afternoon

forsaken
expression of
emotional anguish
caused by
abandonment

About midday (the **sixth hour**), the land of Israel became shrouded in darkness for three hours. We do not know how dark it was or what caused it. It could not have been an eclipse of the sun, because an eclipse is impossible at full moon (by which the Passover date is determined).

New Testament writers don't connect the darkness with astronomical events but with the event taking place on Golgotha—the death of God's Son.

what others say

John R. W. Stott

Gradually, the crowd thinned out, their curiosity glutted. At last silence fell and darkness came—darkness perhaps because no eye should see . . . the anguish of soul which the sinless Saviour now endured.[5]

Cry of the Forsaken

MARK 15:34–35 *And at the **ninth hour** Jesus cried out with a loud voice, saying, "Eloi, Eloi, lama sabachthani?" which is translated, "My God, My God, why have You forsaken Me?" Some of those who stood by, when they heard that, said, "Look, He is calling for Elijah!"* (NKJV)

A cry pierced the air. In that day, before the constant hum of machinery that today so muffles sounds, such a cry would have been heard even in the heart of the city of Jerusalem. It came from the edge of the old quarry. The groans of the dying had often been heard from that place, but this was a cry of pain that went deeper than the physical suffering inflicted by nails and cross. It was in Aramaic, the language of the street.

"My God, My God, why have You **forsaken** Me?"

The pain the cry expressed was exactly what Jesus had struggled with in the garden of <u>Gethsemane</u>: the prospect of experiencing separation from his Father in heaven.

key point

what others say

Oswald Chambers

The cross is the crystallized point in history where eternity merges with time. The cry on the cross, "My God, My God,

> why have you forsaken me?" is not the desolation of an isolated individual: it is the revelation of the heart of God face to face with the sin of man, and going deeper down than man's sin can ever go in inconceivable heartbreak in order that every sinstained, hell-deserving sinner might be absolutely redeemed.[6]

go to

loud voice
Matthew 27:50;
Mark 15:37

into Your hands
Psalm 31:5

die
Hebrews 2:14–18

paschal lambs
Exodus 12:3–11;
1 Corinthians 5:7

breathed His last
literally, "breathed
out"

Pardon's Price Paid in Full

> JOHN 19:28 *After this, Jesus, knowing that all things were now accomplished, that the Scripture might be fulfilled, said, "I thirst!"* (NKJV)

Jesus needed strength for a final proclamation. "I thirst!" he said. Of the Gospel writers, only John heard it.

Someone dipped a sponge in wine vinegar and held it to his lips (John 19:29). Then, reaching deep inside for strength, Jesus cried out in a <u>loud voice</u>: "It is finished!" (John 19:30 NKJV).

In Good Hands

> LUKE 23:46 *And when Jesus had cried out with a loud voice, He said, "Father, '<u>into Your hands</u> I commit My spirit.'" Having said this, He **breathed His last**.* (NKJV)

The death of Jesus was no ordinary death, because Jesus was no ordinary man.

1. *Jesus's death was voluntary.* No one could take his life from him: "I lay [my life] down of Myself," he said (John 10:18 NKJV). He consciously yielded his spirit to God. John 19:30 describes it this way: "And bowing His head, He gave up His spirit" (NKJV). He literally sent away his spirit.

2. *Jesus's death was his destiny.* He'd left his Father's side thirty-three years earlier, to become mortal so it was possible for him to <u>die</u>, a substitute taking the death sentence for human sin.

3. *Jesus's death was the ultimate sacrifice.* As he died, <u>paschal lambs</u> were being sacrificed at the temple. Every bleeding lamb throughout the fifteen-hundred-year history of Passovers pointed to Jesus's sacrifice. He was the last—the Lamb of God taking away

once-and-for-al
Hebrews 9:26;
10:1–18;
Romans 3:25; 5:8–9

defile
Deuteronomy 21:23

Holy of Holies
the temple inner
sanctum, only the
high priest entered
once a year on the
Day of Atonement

special Sabbath
first day of the Feast
of Unleavened
Bread

the world's sin (John 1:29, 36), the <u>once-and-for-all</u> sacrifice to end all sacrifices. God brought a perfect Lamb to the altar and sacrificed him there.

4. *When Jesus died an earthquake generally shook things up* (Matthew 27:51)! Two amazing things accompanied the quake: (1) the heavy embroidered veil in the temple, symbolizing separation from God, tore in two from top to bottom as if Jesus's death had ripped open access to the **Holy of Holies** to let ordinary sinners barge into the presence of God for grace and mercy (Matthew 27:51; Luke 23:45; Hebrews 4:16); and (2) tombs, perhaps across the quarry from Golgotha, "were opened" (Matthew 27:52–53 NKJV). Deceased Jews, known for righteousness, were seen alive in the city.

Death Certificate

> JOHN 19:31–34 *Therefore, because it was the Preparation Day, that the bodies should not remain on the cross on the Sabbath (for that Sabbath was a high day), the Jews asked Pilate that their legs might be broken, and that they might be taken away. Then the soldiers came and broke the legs of the first and of the other who was crucified with Him. But when they came to Jesus and saw that He was already dead, they did not break His legs. But one of the soldiers pierced His side with a spear, and immediately blood and water came out. (NKJV)*

Jesus died about 3:00 p.m. Preparations for the Sabbath, which began at sundown, were under way. Because it was a **special Sabbath**, a feast day, Jewish leaders did not want dying bodies hanging around out on Skull Hill. Romans left the bodies of the crucified on the cross as a warning to others; Jews preferred to bury them so as not to <u>defile</u> the land.

Death by crucifixion could take several days. In cases where a speedier demise was to the advantage of the powers that be, legs of victims were broken. This made it impossible for them to push themselves up against the spikes in their feet. In the crucified position this movement was absolutely necessary in order to breathe. This brought a quick death by asphyxiation (a strange mercy).

Hard blows with a heavy mallet broke the legs of the other victims, but when they came to Jesus the soldiers discovered he was already dead. No need to break his legs. (God had instructed Moses that none of the Passover lamb's <u>bones</u> must ever be broken.) To be sure he was dead, one soldier drove his <u>spear</u> into Jesus's torso. A gush of blood and water confirmed his death. The spear pierced Jesus's chest, releasing blood from the heart and water from the **pericardial sac** around the heart.

bones
Exodus 12:46;
Numbers 9:12;
Psalm 34:20;
John 19:36

spear
Zechariah 12:10

pericardial sac
membranes enclosing the heart and large blood vessels

what others say

Max Lucado

The cross did what sacrificial lambs could not do. It erased our sins not for a year, but for eternity. The cross did what man cannot do. It granted us the right to talk with, love, and even live with God.[7]

Chapter Wrap-Up

- The Praetorium guards mocked and beat Jesus, calling him "King of the Jews." (John 19:2–3)

- Jesus was unable to carry his cross all the way to Calvary. Simon of Cyrene was forced to carry it for him. Along the way Jesus told some weeping women to weep for themselves because disaster was coming. (Luke 23:26–31)

- At a place called "the Skull" Jesus was crucified. As the nails were driven into his wrists and feet, he prayed, "Father, forgive them." His enemies milled around the cross insulting him. One of the thieves crucified with him believed in him. Jesus gave his mother into the care of his closest disciple, John. (Luke 23:32–43; John 19:25–27)

- At noon it became dark. Jesus cried out because he was forsaken by God as he bore the guilt and condemnation for the world's sins. At the end of six hours on the cross, he shouted, "It is finished!" and sent his spirit to God's control. His redeeming work was done. (Matthew 27:45–54; John 19:28–30)

Study Questions

1. For what three groups of people was Jesus praying when he said, "Father, forgive them for they do not know what they are doing"?

2. What did the sign read that Pilate put over Jesus's head? How did the Jewish leaders react to it? How did the repentant thief react to the idea it presented?

3. Identify three ways in which Christ's death was out of the ordinary.

4. When did the meaning of the death of Christ begin to make sense to you? How would you explain it to a friend who does not understand?

Part Seven
SONRISE

Chapter 33: He's Alive!

Let's Get Started

The young Messiah, Jesus of Nazareth, was dead. He died on the eve of Passover, Friday, April 7, AD 30, about 3:00 p.m.,[1] on a Roman cross on a hill overlooking an old stone quarry just north of Jerusalem—a place called the Skull.

Most biographies end with the person's death. Not this one. Jesus's followers intended to give him a decent burial, but they got the surprise of their lives. His enemies got the mother of all headaches. Sin's case against believing sinners was <u>thrown out</u> of court.

And the living church was born.

A Decent Burial

> **MARK 15:42–43** *Now when evening had come, because it was the Preparation Day, that is, the day before the Sabbath, Joseph of Arimathea, a prominent council member, who was himself waiting for the kingdom of God, coming and taking courage, went in to Pilate and asked for the body of Jesus. (NKJV)*

In an unexpected twist in the story, a member of the Sanhedrin, who dissented against the decision to condemn Jesus, appeared at Pilate's offices to ask that the body of Jesus be released to him.

The man's name was Joseph, from the town of Arimathea, a <u>rich man</u> (Matthew 27:57). He was joined by another dissenting council member, the Pharisee <u>Nicodemus</u> (John 19:39).

These two had apparently been absent when the Sanhedrin handed down its verdict on Jesus—perhaps they were purposely not informed of the early morning meeting. Nicodemus had given hints of pro-Jesus sympathies; Joseph is described as "a disciple of Jesus, but secretly, for <u>fear of the Jews</u>" (John 19:38 NKJV).

go to

thrown out
Romans 4:25; 5:1, 6–11

rich man
Isaiah 53:9

Nicodemus
John 3:1–2; 7:50–51

fear of the Jews
John 12:42–43

gospel harmony

Matthew 27:57–28:20
Mark 15:42–16:18
Luke 23:50–24:49
John 19:38–21:25

go to

caretaker
John 20:15

strips of linen
strips of cloth or a
single grave cloth

Sad Acts of Service

MARK 15:44–47 *Pilate marveled that He was already dead;
and summoning the centurion, he asked him if He had been
dead for some time. So when he found out from the centurion, he
granted the body to Joseph. Then he bought fine linen, took Him
down, and wrapped Him in the linen. And he laid Him in a
tomb which had been hewn out of the rock, and rolled a stone
against the door of the tomb. And Mary Magdalene and Mary
the mother of Joses observed where He was laid. (NKJV)*

When Jesus died, three hours of daylight remained before the
Sabbath when no work could be done. Preparing a coffin or even
moving a corpse's arm or leg was specifically forbidden on the seventh day. So Joseph, a strict Jew, had to act quickly.

When Pilate heard Jesus was dead after only six hours, he was surprised. Crucifixion victims often hung on the cross for days waiting
to die. Pilate quizzed the centurion in charge of the crucifixion, who
confirmed Jesus's death and released the body to Joseph.

Across the quarry from Skull Hill, Joseph had prepared a tomb for
his own burial (Matthew 27:60). It was cut into the soft limestone
of a craggy hillside and surrounded by a garden (John 19:41). Some
tombs of the wealthy were set in private, walled gardens, with care-
taker-guards to tend and watch them. This tomb had never been
used (John 19:41).

While Joseph secured release of the body, Nicodemus gathered
burial spices—probably a mixture of myrrh and aloes—to pack
around the body along with "**strips of linen** . . . as the custom of
the Jews is to bury" (John 19:40 NKJV). Egyptian burial was
designed to preserve the body from decay; Jewish burial was
designed to inhibit odors during decay.

> **what others say**
>
> **Byron R. McCane**
>
> The eyes of the deceased were closed, the corpse was
> washed with perfumes and ointments, its bodily orifices were
> stopped, and strips of cloth were wrapped tightly around the
> body—binding the jaw closed, fixing arms to the sides, and
> trying the feet together. Once prepared, the corpse was
> placed on a bier or in a coffin and carried out of town in a pro-
> cession to the family tomb.[2]

Decency and Disgrace

Customary Jewish burials took place immediately, in the family tomb. The burial was followed by a week of intense grieving, called *shiv'ah* ("seven"), then a month of less-intense mourning, called *shloshim* ("thirty"). The family continued to mourn for a year.

But Jesus died as a criminal. Different rules applied.

First, an executed criminal could not be buried in his family's tomb until a year after death. Many were buried in common graves, or even thrown on the city garbage dump to burn with the trash. Second, no public mourning was allowed for an executed criminal. While Joseph and Nicodemus honored Jesus by caring for his body, in actuality, his burial conformed to the prohibitions: He was never buried in his family tomb, nor were any of the rituals of mourning conducted for him. He was buried in disgrace like any condemned criminal.

The final task in the burial was to roll a large **stone** over the opening to the cave (Mark 15:46). As the sun was setting, the two Johnny-come-lately disciples completed their sad work and trudged home. Following Joseph and Nicodemus to the tomb and last to leave the burial site were Mary Magdalene and Mary the mother of **Joses** (Mark 15:47).

> MATTHEW 27:62–66 *On the **next day**, which followed the Day of Preparation, the chief priests and Pharisees gathered together to Pilate, saying, "Sir, we remember, while He was still alive, how that deceiver said, 'After three days I will rise.' Therefore command that the tomb be made secure until the third day, lest His disciples come by night and steal Him away, and say to the people, 'He has risen from the dead.' So the last deception will be worse than the first." Pilate said to them, "You have a guard; go your way, make it as secure as you know how." So they went and made the tomb secure, sealing the stone and setting the guard.* (NKJV)

stone
large, flat cartwheel-like stone; some weighing more than a ton still seen in Israel

Joses
brother of disciple James the Younger

next day
after sunset—on the Sabbath—probably shortly after Jesus's burial

what others say

Bill Bright
[Jesus's] little band of followers was now terror-stricken and scattered. His enemies were celebrating their victory.[3]

go to

angel
Mark 16:6–7;
Luke 24:5–7;
John 20:12

Bustin' Out!

> **MATTHEW 28:1–4** *Now after the Sabbath, as the first day of the week began to dawn, Mary Magdalene and the other Mary came to see the tomb. And behold, there was a great earthquake; for an **angel** of the Lord descended from heaven, and came and rolled back the stone from the door, and sat on it. His countenance was like lightning, and his clothing as white as snow. And the guards shook for fear of him, and became like dead men. (NKJV)*

At the crack of dawn Sunday, a group of women headed for Joseph's tomb with spices to offset the stench of the decaying body. Either Joseph and Nicodemus were unable to finish the job before Sabbath, or the women simply wanted to do something to honor Jesus's memory.

The number of women is uncertain. Several are named. All four historians mention Mary Magdalene (Matthew 28:1; Mark 16:1; Luke 24:10; John 20:1). Others who came were Mary the mother of James, called "the other Mary" (Matthew 28:1; Mark 16:1; Luke 24:10); Salome (Mark 16:1), Joanna (Luke 24:10); and unnamed "other women with them" (Luke 24:10 NKJV).

On the way, they wondered who was going to roll that humongous stone from the entrance of the tomb (Mark 16:3). Not to worry!

Before they got there, the grave guards suddenly got all shook up by a violent earthquake. While they were looking around for something to hang on to, a dazzling personage appeared from nowhere, and with a flick of his little finger rolled the boulder away from the cave opening and sat on it! The knees of battle-toughened legionnaires turned to Jell-O, and they keeled over from sheer terror.

By the time the women arrived, the guards had left for the city—there was nothing for them to guard!

---

what others say

George R. Beasley-Murray

The presence of angels is a witness that the powers of heaven have been at work here.[4]

"He's Gone!"

> **MARK 16:4–6** *But when [the women] looked up, they saw that the stone had been rolled away—for it was very large. And entering the tomb, they saw a young man clothed in a long white robe sitting on the right side; and they were alarmed. But he said to them, "Do not be alarmed. You seek Jesus of Nazareth, who was crucified. He is risen! He is not here. See the place where they laid Him." (NKJV)*

Matthew 28:1–8
Mark 16:1–8
Luke 24:1–12
John 20:1–10

Finding the grave open, they went in, expecting to find the body—but the corpse was gone! Luke says they were "greatly perplexed" (Luke 24:4 NKJV), wondering what was going on.

Suddenly a figure in bright garments stood beside them: an angel (Matthew 28:2)! Some of the women, telling this incident, said there were <u>two</u> angels, others said <u>one</u>. However many, the women were terrified.

"See the place were they laid Him," the angel said (Mark 16:6 NKJV). Examination of the open tomb by the women confirmed that the body of Jesus, so carefully placed there by Joseph and Nicodemus on Friday afternoon, was no longer there.

The women were so rattled by what they'd seen and heard—the deserted grave, the vision of angels, the announcement that Jesus had risen from the dead—they were speechless at first (Mark 16:8). But by the time they got to where the disciples were hiding out in Jerusalem, they found the story impossible to keep (Luke 24:9).

The Mystery of the Missing Corpse

> **LUKE 24:9, 11** *Then they returned from the tomb and told all these things to the eleven and to all the rest . . . And their words seemed to them like idle tales, and they did not believe them. (NKJV)*

The response of the apostles and other followers of Jesus was less than enthusiastic. The Greek term translated "idle tales" (Luke 24:11 NKJV) is a medical term for "the babbling of a fevered and insane mind."[5]

The apostles and others were sure that the women's grief had driven them off the deep end! Mary Magdalene proposed the theory that someone had moved the body without letting them know (John

two . . . one
Compare
Matthew 28:2;
Mark 16:5;
John 20:12;
Luke 25:23

go to

believed
John 5:44; 6:47;
19:35; 20:29

believed
in John, indicates
real faith

20:2). She'd seen the angels, but she was apparently having trouble believing her eyes! Peter and John decided to go see for themselves (Luke 24:12; John 20:3–10). Sure enough, the grave clothes, with the spices still in them, were there, along with the cloth that covered the corpse's face. But the grave clothes were empty. After seeing the empty tomb for himself, "the other disciple [John], who came to the tomb first, went in also; and he saw and **believed**" (John 20:8 NKJV). To John, empty grave clothes proved something wonderful had happened. Maybe Jesus had risen.

But "as yet they did not know the Scripture, that He must rise again from the dead" (John 20:9 NKJV). Peter and John returned from the grave scratching their heads. But they would soon be convinced beyond all doubt that what the angels said to the women was a fact: Jesus Christ, crucified, dead, and buried, had risen from the dead and was alive!

Hush Money

> MATTHEW 28:11–15 *Now while they were going, behold, some of the guard came into the city and reported to the chief priests all the things that had happened. When they had assembled with the elders and consulted together, they gave a large sum of money to the soldiers, saying, "Tell them, 'His disciples came at night and stole Him away while we slept.' And if this comes to the governor's ears, we will appease him and make you secure." So they took the money and did as they were instructed; and this saying is commonly reported among the Jews until this day. (NKJV)*

The sum of money offered the Roman guardsmen to spread this cock-and-bull story must have been significant considering the risk. A soldier who fell asleep on guard duty faced execution (Acts 12:19). If Pilate had to be paid off to protect the soldiers, it would be a royal pain in the priestly pocketbook!

gospel harmony

Matthew 28:9–20
Mark 16:9–18
Luke 24:1–12
John 20:1–10

what others say

Thomas Arnold

The evidence for our Lord's life and death and resurrection may be, and often has been, shown to be satisfactory; it is good according to the common rules for distinguishing good evidence from bad. Thousands and tens of thousands of persons have gone through it piece by piece, as carefully as every judge summing up on a most important case. I have myself done it many times over, not to persuade others but to satisfy myself. I have been used for many years to study the histories of other times, and to examine and weigh the evidence of those who have written about them, and I know of no one fact in the history of mankind which is proved by better and fuller evidence of every sort, to the understanding of a fair inquirer, than the great sign which God has given us that Christ died and rose again from the dead.[6]

not recognize
Luke 24:16, 31;
John 21:4

funereal
fit for a funeral

brethren
Jesus's unbelieving biological brothers or the disciples or both

The Magdalene Mourner

JOHN 20:14–16 *Now when she had said this, she turned around and saw Jesus standing there, and did not know that it was Jesus. Jesus said to her, "Woman, why are you weeping? Whom are you seeking?" She, supposing Him to be the gardener, said to Him, "Sir, if You have carried Him away, tell me where You have laid Him, and I will take Him away." Jesus said to her, "Mary!" She turned and said to Him, "Rabboni!" (which is to say, Teacher).* (NKJV)

Mary Magdalene was at the tomb again. She had shown Peter and John the way and then stayed when they left. She was crying.

Robbed of the chance to honor the body of her dead Master, she ignored the ban on public mourning for executed criminals and set up a **funereal** wail that could be heard inside the walls of Jerusalem.

Angels appeared again inside the tomb, asking why she was wailing. As she turned from the cave, someone was standing there. The gardener, she thought. She did <u>not recognize</u> Jesus.

"Mary!" he said (John 20:16 NKJV). The familiar voice, the special way he said her name, rang a bell. "Teacher!" she cried in Aramaic. As she realized it was Jesus, she threw herself down and hugged his feet in a spontaneous and appropriate expression of affection.

But he had a job for her to do. "Do not cling to Me, for I have not yet ascended to My Father; but go to My **brethren** and say to them, 'I am ascending to My Father and your Father, and to My God and your God'" (John 20:17 NKJV).

Mary Magdalene obeyed. She "came and told the disciples that she had seen the Lord, and that He had spoken these things to her" (John 20:18 NKJV). She was the first.

the eleven
the twelve apostles
minus Judas

Bewilderment and Joy

MATTHEW 28:9–10 *And as they went to tell His disciples, behold, Jesus met them, saying, "Rejoice!" So they came and held Him by the feet and worshiped Him. Then Jesus said to them, "Do not be afraid. Go and tell My brethren to go to Galilee, and there they will see Me."* (NKJV)

Finding the tomb empty and having seen and heard angels, the women who came to complete the embalming process were in a hurry to get back into the city to report the mysterious happenings to the disciples.

They were a giddy mix of wide-eyed bewilderment and joy. Their joy hit a crescendo when Jesus suddenly met them. They dropped their spices on the road, hugged his feet, and worshipped him right there in front of God and everybody!

Emmaus Encounter

On a seven-mile hike from Jerusalem to Emmaus (see Appendix A), a disciple named Cleopas and another, whose name isn't given, found themselves sharing the road with a knowledgeable stranger.

The stranger engaged them in conversation for two hours about the Old Testament's teaching concerning the necessity of Christ's death and resurrection. Their hearts were warmed as the stranger explained the Scriptures to them (Luke 24:32). But they recognized it was Jesus only after they got to Emmaus and were sharing a meal with him. As soon as they knew who he was, he vanished!

Even though it was after dark, the two hurried back to Jerusalem to share the news with **the eleven** and others huddling with them in the Upper Room.

gospel harmony

Mark 16:12–13
Luke 24:13–35

The Rock Sees the Risen Redeemer

LUKE 24:33–34 *So they rose up that very hour and returned to Jerusalem, and found the eleven and those who were with them gathered together, saying, "The Lord is risen indeed, and has appeared to Simon!"* (NKJV)

When the two from Emmaus arrived, they found a group of almost-believers, ready to listen to their tale. The risen Jesus had also appeared to **Peter** that day (see 1 Corinthians 15:5). They'd thought the women were hallucinating, but when Peter reported his encounter, they began to let a little hope trickle in.

Reveille for the Revived Redeemer's Routed Regiment

Unexpectedly, while Cleopas related the Emmaus incident to the jaundiced-eyed collection of apostles and disciples, Jesus himself stood in the midst of the gathering! Even then most of the people there couldn't believe it was really Jesus. He did four things to convince them:

- Jesus dragged their nagging doubts and fears out in the open and dealt with them (Mark 16:14; Luke 24:38).

- Jesus showed them his nail-scarred hands and feet and the wound in his side, to verify he was the crucified one (Luke 24:39–40; John 20:20).

- Jesus invited them to touch him, and ate a piece of broiled fish so they would understand that his resurrection was complete— he was not a disembodied spirit, but spirit and body (Luke 24:39, 41–43).

- Jesus reminded them of his predictions that he would rise from the dead, and that his rising fulfilled Old Testament prophecy (Luke 24:44).

John remembers the trickle of hope turning into a river of joy (John 20:20). Before he left them that night, Jesus gave his apostles and other disciples four extremely important things:

1. *He gave them his **Shalom**. "Peace to you!"* (John 20:21 NKJV). He had greeted them this way when he first appeared in the room (verse 19); now he repeated it. In his Last Supper talks Jesus promised them <u>peace</u> more real than the world could ever give. He assured them he would keep that promise as they went out to face the world in his name.

2. *He gave them authorization to continue Christ's ministry: "As the Father has sent Me, I also send you"* (John 20:21 NKJV). Christian disciples are sent to do Jesus's thing, not their own. The mission of Jesus's followers in the world is not a different mission

peace
John 14:27

Peter
"Simon" or
"Cephas"

shalom
wholeness; fulfill-
ment; inner har-
mony, peace with
others

Mark 16:14
Luke 24:33, 36–43
John 20:19–25

go to

body
1 Corinthians
12:12–27

work
Matthew 28:20;
Mark 15:15–16;
Luke 24:46–48;
John 14:12–14

breathed
Genesis 2:7;
Ezekiel 37:9–10

Holy Spirit
Luke 24:48–49;
John 7:37–39;
Acts 1:8

Pentecost
Jewish spring harvest festival, fifty days after Passover, when the Holy Spirit filled the disciples

retain
Greek: "hold, carry"

than his. It's in a different form—through men and women who share his resurrection life through the Holy Spirit, his corporate <u>body</u>—but it's his <u>work</u> they are being sent to do.

3. *"He <u>breathed</u> on them" and urged them to "receive the <u>Holy Spirit</u>" to enable them to carry on his ministry* (John 20:22 NKJV). The actual invasion of their lives by the Spirit was a few weeks away (**Pentecost**, see Acts 2), but in the context of being told their work was cut out for them, they needed assurance that they were not being sent out without the spiritual resources needed to do the job.

4. *Jesus gave the apostles and all Christians authority to deal with other people's sins.* "If you forgive the sins of any, they are forgiven them; if you **retain** the sins of any, they are retained" (John 20:23 NKJV). Jesus teaches that we are always to forgive (Matthew 18:21–22); the apostle Paul writes that when someone is "overtaken in any trespass," Christ's followers are to "bear" the burden of the sinning person in an effort to "restore" him or her (Galatians 6:1–2 NKJV). We have Jesus's assurance that God forgives sinners, and that he is bearing their sin as we are.

> ## what others say
>
> ### Dietrich Bonhoeffer
>
> As Christ bears our burdens, so ought we to bear the burdens of our fellowmen. The law of Christ, which it is our duty to fulfill, is the bearing of the cross (Galatians 6:2). My brother's burden which I must bear is not only his outward lot, his natural characteristics and gifts, but quite literally his sin. And the only way to bear that sin is by forgiving it in the power of the cross of Christ which I now share. Thus the call to follow Christ always means a call to share the work of forgiving men their sins.[7]

<u>Seeing Is Believing, But . . .</u>

JOHN 20:26–28 *And after eight days His disciples were again inside, and Thomas with them. Jesus came, the doors being shut, and stood in the midst, and said, "Peace to you!" Then He said to Thomas, "Reach your finger here, and look at My hands; and reach your hand here, and put it into My side. Do not be unbe-*

lieving, but believing." And Thomas answered and said to Him, "My Lord and my God!" (NKJV)

A week after the missed meeting, Jesus came again for a second visit with the disciples.

He offered his nail-scarred hands for Thomas to touch, and opened his shirt for Thomas to feel the wound in his side.

Thomas didn't need to touch Jesus. Overwhelmed at the sight of him, he blurted out his confession: "My Lord and my God!" Thomas did not simply mean he was convinced Jesus was alive. He understood the meaning of the Resurrection. The <u>Resurrection reveals</u> who Jesus is—Lord and God. For Thomas that was no abstract theological proposition. With the words "My Lord and my God," Thomas pledged his personal allegiance to Jesus as the Master he would serve and the God he would <u>honor</u>.

Believing Without Seeing

JOHN 20:29 *Jesus said to him, "Thomas, because you have seen Me, you have believed.* ***Blessed*** *are those who have not seen and yet have believed." (NKJV)*

John the writer reminds his readers that the faith of those who did not see Jesus alive after his resurrection is as solidly based as the faith of people like Thomas who did see. The written record of Jesus's life and works is in the New Testament. "These are written that you may believe that Jesus is the Christ, the Son of God, and that believing you may have life in His name" (John 20:31 NKJV). Believing even when you can't see is an act of faith, and God will bless you for it.

go to

Resurrection reveals
Romans 1:4

honor
John 1:1; 5:23;
14:7–11

blessed
happy, fortunate,
successful

what others say

George R. Beasley-Murray

They have not had the privilege of the disciples in seeing Jesus alive from the dead, nor of having their faith quickened in the extraordinary manner granted to Thomas. Theirs is a faith called forth by the word of the Gospel; but it is none the worse for that, for their trust in the Lord revealed through the Word is of special worth in his eyes.[8]

go to

breaking bread
John 6;
Luke 22:19; 24:30

Sea of Tiberias
Sea of Galilee

Nathanael
Bartholomew

James and John
sons of Zebedee;
John avoids giving
his name, as usual

apostasy
falling away from
the faith

Fishing with the Good Ol' Boys

The third time Jesus appeared to his friends after his resurrection happened like this: Passover and the Feast of Unleavened Bread were over. The disciples returned to Galilee, but stayed close to one another. Seven were together near the **Sea of Tiberias**—Peter, Thomas, **Nathanael**, **James, and John**, and two other guys.

One day Peter said, "I'm going fishing." "We'll go with you," chimed the others. So they went fishing while it was still dark (every good fisherman knows the fish are biting best before dawn).

Scholars have read all sorts of terrible things into this decision—everything from aimlessness, to quitting the ministry, to out-and-out **apostasy**! But, hey! Even if Jesus had been crucified and risen from the dead, a guy's gotta eat and feed his family. Or, maybe, out on the lake as the sun is coming up is just a good place to sort things out.

The fishing was lousy. As the sun cast light over the eastern hills, the boat was about one hundred yards out (John 21:8), and Jesus was standing on the shore (only they didn't realize it was Jesus). "Haven't caught anything, have you?" he called over the water.

"Nope," they answered.

He said, "Cast the net on the right side of the boat, and you will find some" (John 21:6 NKJV). Maybe the guy on the shore could see something they couldn't. They had nothing to lose. So they did what he said, and suddenly their net was full!

"It is the Lord!" John told Peter (John 21:7 NKJV). Peter jumped into the water and swam for shore. The others brought the boat in with the net full of fish. Breakfast was ready. Bread and broiled fish cooked on a little fire the Lord had kindled. They counted the fish they'd caught—153 big ones—what a great "fish story"!

And Jesus was in his old, familiar role, breaking bread and fish and sharing a meal with his friends (John 21:13). It doesn't get any better than this!

The Rehabilitation of Simon Peter

> **JOHN 21:15–16** *So when they had eaten breakfast, Jesus said to Simon Peter, "Simon, son of Jonah, do you love Me more than these?" He said to Him, "Yes, Lord; You know that I love You."*

He said to him, "Feed My lambs." He said to him again a second time, "Simon, son of Jonah, do you love Me?" He said to Him, "Yes, Lord; You know that I love You." He said to him, "Tend My sheep." (NKJV)

But Jesus wasn't out there for a fishing trip. In addition to reaffirming the reality of his resurrection for the seven (and us), this appearance had a highly personal purpose: to rehabilitate Peter after his dismal <u>spiritual failure</u>.

After breakfast, in the presence of the others, Jesus asked, "Simon, son of Jonah, do you love Me more than these [others do]?" (John 21:15 NKJV). Ouch! Just hours before denying Jesus to protect his own skin, Peter had brashly compared his loyalty with that of the other eleven. "Even if all are made to stumble because of You, I will never be made to stumble" (Matthew 26:33 NKJV).

Now the swagger was gone. No more comparing. No more bragging. No more overblown self-confidence. Peter answered simply, "Yes, Lord; You know that I love You" (John 21:15 NKJV).

Jesus asked the same question three times, not to "rub it in," but to give Peter a chance to wipe away the memory of his threefold denial by a threefold affirmation of his love. Understandably, the third time the question stung deep. All Peter could do was appeal to the Lord's knowledge of his heart: "Lord, You know all things; You know that I love You" (John 21:17 NKJV).

Jesus then reminded Peter of his call to **shepherd** Christ's sheep and prophesied that Peter would die when he was old, with **hands outstretched**, and his death would "glorify God" (John 21:18–19 NKJV).

Forty Amazing Days

Jesus showed up at many gatherings of his friends during the forty days between discovery of the empty tomb and his ascension. The disintegrating nucleus of the church was being irresistibly <u>drawn together</u> around his living presence. If you were a disciple, the best place to be was with other disciples—I mean, suppose you skipped church and Jesus showed up!

During those forty awesome days, Jesus did the following:

go to

spiritual failure
John 18:15–16, 25–26

shepherd
John 10:2–16; 1 Peter 5:2

drawn together
Matthew 18:19–20

shepherd
pastor, lead

hands outstretched
crucifixion

go to

laid aside
Philippians 2:5–11

ascension
act of rising upward
into heaven

1. *Jesus made more post-resurrection appearances:*

- The eleven saw Jesus on a mountain in Galilee (Matthew 28:16–20; Mark 16:15–18).

- More than five hundred saw Jesus at a single gathering (1 Corinthians 15:6).

- In Jerusalem, Jesus made a special post-resurrection visit to his biological half brother James (1 Corinthians 15:7), which turned his skeptical sibling's life around.

- Several times, in Jerusalem, Jesus met with his disciples and apostles (Luke 24:44–49; Acts 1:3–8).

- Many followed him outside Jerusalem to witness his **ascension** (Acts 1:9–12).

2. *Jesus did humanlike things:* What was Jesus's body like? A ghost? He emphatically answered, "No!" He said, "Behold My hands and My feet, that it is I Myself. Handle Me and see, for a spirit does not have flesh and bones as you see I have" (Luke 24:39 NKJV).

- They recognized his face and voice (Matthew 28:9; Luke 24:31; John 20:16, 19–20; 21:2).

- His body was recognizable by its identifying marks (Luke 24:39; John 20:27).

- They touched his body (Matthew 28:9; Luke 24:39; John 20:17, 27).

- He ate with them (Luke 24:30, 42–43; John 21:12–13).

3. *Jesus gave additional post-resurrection teachings:* The things he said were vital to the work he was leaving in their hands. Face-to-face with the resurrected Jesus, his disciples understood as never before.

Jesus made two important points about power. First, all the earthly and heavenly power and authority he had <u>laid aside</u> in order to take on humanity and mortality were now being given back to him after the successful completion of his redeeming mission. He said, "All authority has been given to Me in heaven and on earth" (Matthew 28:18 NKJV).

Second, spiritual power and authority would soon energize those who believed in Jesus, through the Holy Spirit, who would soon invade their lives. The Spirit's presence would give them power to confront evil spirits, speak new languages, risk danger, heal the sick, and boldly carry his message to the world. Jesus said, "And these signs will follow those who believe: In My name they will cast out demons; they will speak with new tongues; they will take up serpents; and if they drink anything deadly, it will by no means hurt them; they will lay hands on the sick, and they will recover" (Mark 16:17–18 NKJV).

Jesus also gave them the promise of his personal presence. Jesus said, "And lo, I am with you always, even to the end of the age" (Matthew 28:20 NKJV).

The Final Test

> 1 CORINTHIANS 15:14–19 *And if Christ is not risen, then our preaching is empty and your faith is also empty. Yes, and we are found false witnesses of God, because we have testified of God that He raised up Christ, whom He did not raise up—if in fact the dead do not rise. For if the dead do not rise, then Christ is not risen. And if Christ is not risen, your faith is futile; you are still in your sins! Then also those who have fallen asleep in Christ have perished. If in this life only we have hope in Christ, we are of all men the most pitiable. (NKJV)*

Paul wrote those words in about AD 56. In this same passage he says five hundred people at the same time saw Jesus after his resurrection, of whom "the greater part remain to the present" (1 Corinthians 15:6 NKJV). If any of his readers wished to do so at that time, there were eyewitnesses alive and kicking who could be interviewed about it!

The Christian faith rises or falls on the reality that Jesus Christ is alive. If Christ is not alive, the New Testament historians, Matthew, Mark, Luke, John, and all the apostles, upon whose testimony the Christian faith is based, are liars!

The resurrection of Jesus Christ is the test question on which the truth or falsehood of the Christian gospel turns. Either it is the greatest miracle that ever happened in the history of the world or the biggest lie ever told.

what others say

Philip Schaff

The miracle of the Resurrection and the existence of Christianity are so closely connected that they must stand or fall together. If Christ was raised from the dead, then all his miracles are sure, and our faith is not in vain. It is only his resurrection that made his death available for our **atonement**, **justification**, and **salvation**. Without the Resurrection, his death would be the grave of our hopes, we should be still **unredeemed** and under the power of our sins. A gospel of a dead savior would be a contradiction and a wretched delusion.[9]

Madeleine L'Engle

If it can be verified, we don't need faith. I don't need faith to know that if a poem has fourteen lines, a specific rhyme scheme, and is in iambic pentameter, it is a sonnet. I don't need faith to know that if I take flour and butter and milk and seasonings and heat them in a double boiler, the mix will thicken and become white sauce. Faith is for that which lies on the other side of reason. Faith is what makes life bearable, with all its tragedies and ambiguities and sudden, startling joys. Surely it wasn't reasonable of the Lord of the Universe to come and walk this earth with us and love us enough to die for us and then show us everlasting life? We will all grow old, and sooner or later we will die, like the old trees in the orchard. But we have been promised that this is not the end. We have been promised life.[10]

Chapter Wrap-Up

- A rich, secret disciple named Joseph of Arimathea and the Pharisee Nicodemus got permission from Pilate to bury Jesus's body. It was placed in Joseph's new tomb in a garden near the crucifixion site. A huge stone was rolled over the opening of the tomb. (Mark 15:42–47)

- The chief priests and Pharisees asked Pilate to seal the stone and post a guard of Roman soldiers to keep Jesus's disciples from stealing the body and claiming he'd risen from the dead. (Matthew 27:61–66)

- On Easter morning, the tomb was empty. An angel rolled the stone away. The terrified guards ran off to tell Jesus's enemies, who bribed them to lie about what they'd seen. Women disciples came to finish embalming Jesus's body and were met by angels who told them he had risen from the dead. (Luke 24:1–8)

- Examination of the empty tomb left the disciples puzzled. Mary Magdalene thought someone had stolen the body. Jesus appeared to her and sent her to his disciples with the news. (John 20:1–18)

- That day and the next forty days Jesus appeared to his friends one at a time, by twos, and in groups, in Jerusalem, on Emmaus Road, and in Galilee, and commissioned them to continue his work. More than five hundred people saw him alive after his resurrection. (Luke 24; 1 Corinthians 15:3–8)

Study Questions

1. Who were the secret disciples who came forward after Jesus's death to bury him? Who confirmed his death? Where did they bury his body?

2. In what two ways was the burial of a criminal different from the usual Jewish burial?

3. Who was the first person to whom Jesus appeared after his resurrection? How did she recognize him? When and how has Jesus spoken your name in a time of grief?

4. What did Thomas think he needed in order to believe Jesus had risen from the dead? When he saw Jesus, what did he discover he really believed about him? When you have doubts, what do you find helps you overcome them? (a) Bible study, (b) others' faith, (c) remembering past miracles, (d) historical evidence, and/or (e) a return to the basics.

Chapter 34: Liftoff!

Let's Get Started

One more event on God's calendar of redemption would cap the mission Christ had begun thirty-three years before in the womb of the Virgin Mary. Christians call this event "the **Ascension**." Christ's ascension made it possible for the Christian faith to become an inside job.

Up, Up, and Away!

LUKE 24:50–53 *And He led them out as far as Bethany, and He lifted up His hands and blessed them. Now it came to pass, while He blessed them, that He was parted from them and carried up into* **heaven**. *And they worshiped Him, and returned to Jerusalem with great joy, and were continually in the temple praising and blessing God. Amen. (NKJV)*

According to Luke's reports (Luke 24:50–51; Acts 1:9–12), forty days after he rose from the dead, Jesus led his followers to the east side of the Mount of Olives to a spot overlooking the village of Bethany, where they watched as he was lifted—up, up, up—until he vanished in a cloud.

To get the disciples' focus back down to earth (where the Christian action is), two angels ("men") suddenly appeared, standing with them on solid terra firma. The two terminated the sky-gazing party with the announcement that Jesus would one day <u>return</u> in the clouds, just as they'd seen him leave (Acts 1:11).

The ascension of Christ certifies the promise of his return. "This same Jesus, who was taken up from you into heaven, will so come in like manner as you saw Him go into heaven," said the angels to the men and women who saw Jesus bodily lifted up (Acts 1:11 NKJV).

return
Matthew 24:30

ascension
lifting up

heaven
the spiritual dimension; God's home

Mark 16:19–20
Luke 24:50–53
Acts 1:9–12

Linked with the Life of Jesus

MARK 16:19–20 *So then, after the Lord had spoken to them, He was received up into heaven, and sat down at the right hand of God. And they went out and preached everywhere, the Lord working with them and confirming the word through the accompanying signs. Amen.* (NKJV)

Jesus's resurrection and ascension made all the difference in the world for his early followers.

To them, Christianity was something more than a "religion" to be performed, traditions to be memorialized, creeds to be recited, or a moral code to follow with gritted teeth.

To the people who saw Jesus alive and those who believed on him through the testimony of those who saw him, the Christian life was a personal experience with Jesus Christ, which turned everyday life into an exciting adventure!

what others say

J. B. Phillips

We are apt to reduce the Christian religion to a code, or at best a rule of heart and life. To these men it is quite plainly the invasion of their lives by a new quality of life altogether. They do not hesitate to describe this as Christ "living in" them. Mere moral reformation will hardly explain the transformation and the exuberant vitality of these men's lives—even if we could prove a motive for such reformation, and certainly the world around offered little encouragement to the early Christians! We are practically driven to accept their own explanation, which is that their little human lives had, through Christ, been linked up with the very life of God.

Many Christians today talk about the "difficulties of our times" as though we should have to wait for better ones before the Christian religion can take root. It is heartening to remember that this faith took root and flourished amazingly in conditions that would have killed anything less vital in a matter of weeks. These early Christians were on fire with the conviction that they had become, through Christ, literally sons of God; they were pioneers of a new humanity, founders of a new Kingdom. They still speak to us across the centuries. Perhaps if we believed what they believed, we might achieve what they achieved.[1]

Chapter Wrap-Up

- After forty days, Jesus led his disciples to a hill outside Jerusalem, where he ascended back to his Father's right hand in heaven, with the promise to return, and to be with them wherever they went. (Acts 1:9–12)

- In his present ministry as our representative in the presence of God, Christ intercedes for us and is our defense attorney when we sin. (Romans 8:34; Hebrews 4:14–16; 6:20; 1 John 2:1)

- From his place at God's right hand, Christ sends his Holy Spirit to live in people who trust him and keeps his promise to be with us always. (Matthew 28:20; John 14:15–16; 15:26–16:16)

- The ascension of Christ carries with it the promise of his return, and his presence with us as we carry out his work in the world. (Acts 1:11)

Study Questions

1. What is meant by the statement that Jesus is now at the "right hand" of God?

2. Over whom does the ascended Christ have authority?

3. What are three things Jesus presently does as our representative in heaven?

4. How can Christ be with us always?

5. What future event did the angels who appeared at Christ's ascension promise?

Appendix A - Map of Palestine

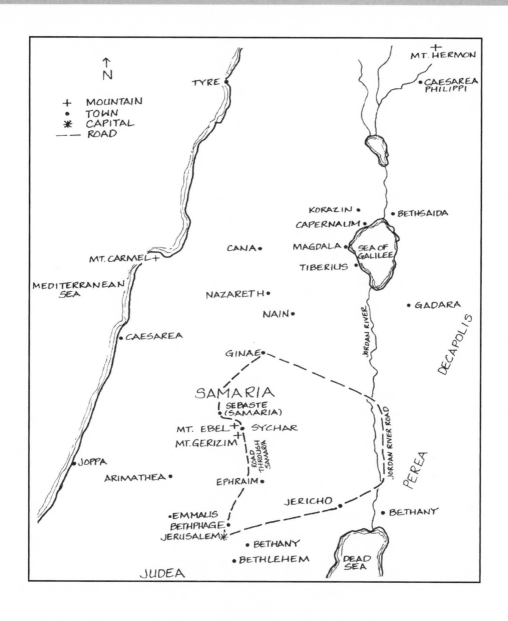

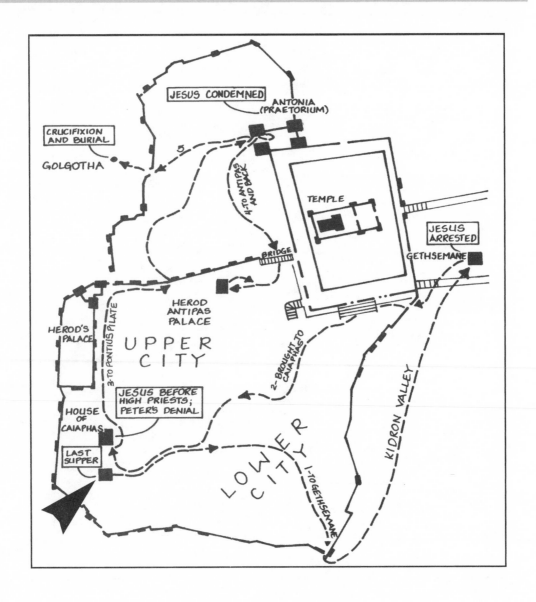

Appendix C - The Answers

Chapter 1: Breaking News

1. The Roman Empire was oppressing the Jews at the time of John's and Jesus's conceptions and births.

2. Old Testament promises concerning Christ's birth include those found in Genesis 49:10; Deuteronomy 18:18; 2 Samuel 17:12–16; Isaiah 7:14; Isaiah 9:6–7; Isaiah 61:1–4; and Ezekiel 37:21–28.

3. To keep Zacharias from expressing his doubts, his ability to speak was taken away. (Luke 1:20)

4. The three "revolutions" Christ accomplished are (1) spiritual, (2) social, and (3) economic. (Luke 1:46–55)

Chapter 2: Mary's Little Lamb

1. Joseph thought Mary was pregnant by another man and considered divorcing her-breaking off the betrothal-(Matthew 1:18-19). An angel in a dream convinced him Mary's baby had been conceived by the Holy Spirit (Matthew 1:20-21).

2. God moved Caesar Augustus to decree a census, requiring all Jewish men to return to their ancestral towns to be registered (Luke 2:1-30). This forced Joseph to go to Bethlehem. Knowing God arranged world events according to his plans in Jesus's day may make you feel more secure about God's control over today's current events.

3. Shepherds were likely to be outside with their flocks in February and March-thirty days prior to the Feast of Passover (though some might be there all winter). Their sheep were probably kept for sacrifices at the temple.

4. When a first son was born, three ceremonies were required: (1) circumcision, (2) redemption of the firstborn, and (3) for the mother: purification after childbirth. (Luke 2:21-24)

5. The Magi were scholars, scientists, astrologers, and priests in the countries from which they came. They were wise men who recognized who

Jesus was and worshipped him. From them we might learn to seek Christ, to bring him spiritual gifts, and to worship him.

Chapter 3: And God Said, "Today I Am a Man!"

1. (a) "Out of Egypt I called My Son," was a prophecy that Joseph, Mary, and Jesus would return to Israel after their escape into Egypt. (b) "He shall be called a Nazarene" expresses that Christ was despised like the little town where he grew up.

2. Jewish childhood religious education began with psalms sung and stories told while the child was still nursing.

3. *Bar mitzvah* means "son of the commandment." It was celebrated at age twelve (Luke 2:42). It signified the beginning of manhood.

4. Possible explanations of differences between Matthew's and Luke's genealogies: (1) Matthew gives Jesus's royal descent, establishing his right to David's throne; (2) Matthew gives Joseph's genealogy; Luke gives Mary's; (3) Jewish men were often known by more than one name; (4) a brother might marry his brother's widow and raise children in his brother's name; and (5) Luke shows Christ's identification with all mankind; Matthew shows Jesus is Joseph's legal son.

Chapter 4: Shout in the Desert

1. Old Testament prophecies foretold the work of Messiah's advance man (Malachi 3:1; 4:5–6; Isaiah 40:3–5). Israel looked for one like Elijah (Malachi 4:5–6; 2 Kings 1:2–8).

2. The essence of John the Baptist's message was repentance (Luke 3:3). Repentance is willingness to turn from sin and be changed in lifestyle and values.

3. Pharisees and Sadducees were told to share what they had with others (Matthew 3:8–10). Tax collectors were told to stop cheating the public and collect only what the law demanded (Luke

3:12–13). Soldiers were told to stop accusing people falsely and extorting money by threat of violence (Luke 3:14).

4. John insisted people who thought they were "God's special people" should approach God like pagans needing to learn from the ground up how to walk with the Lord.

5. Christ's baptism is greater than John's because (1) Christ baptizes with the Holy Spirit; (2) Christ baptizes with fire; and (3) Christ cleanses the useless chaff from a person's life. (Luke 3:16–17)

6. Many people feel affirmed as a child of Christ in a variety of ways from a deep feeling of peace to a new ability to refrain from former sins.

Chapter 5: First Blood

1. Jesus's tactics were these: (d) He quoted Scripture (Matthew 4:4, 7, 10), and (f) he ordered Satan to leave (Matthew 4:10).

2. The devil tempted Jesus to (1) turn stones to bread, which would appeal to Jesus because he was hungry; (2) jump off the temple pinnacle, which would appeal to Jesus as a quick way to prove he was God's Son; and (3) worship the devil, which appeared to be a less costly way to win the world than going to the cross. (Matthew 4:1–11)

3. (a) Turning stones to bread would divert God's gifts to a selfish purpose. (b) Jumping off the temple pinnacle would manipulate God to fit Jesus's purpose rather than God's and violate the trust relationship between them. (c) Giving the devil respect would compromise God's plan of salvation and roadblock the kingdom of righteousness.

4. Many believers say they struggle with selfish desires and wanting to seek shortcuts to spiritual growth. Jesus's experience may teach us to act for the good of others, to put up with difficulties, and to rest knowing God has our best in mind.

Chapter 6: Descent from Splendor

1. John's Gospel is different from Matthew's, Mark's, and Luke's Gospels because after fifty-plus years of walking with Jesus in the Spirit, John was the only one of the original Twelve left to write from the vantage point of a half century of experience with him.

2. A person becomes a child of God by receiving and believing in Christ. (John 1:12)

3. The Word (Christ) came into the world and lived among us. (John 1:9–10, 14)

Chapter 7: Choices at Jordan

1. Priests, Levites, and Pharisees were sent to investigate John's identity. (John 1:19, 24)

2. John claimed to be "the voice of one crying in the wilderness: 'Make straight the way of the LORD.'" He got his authority from God. (John 1:23 NKJV)

3. God gave John the sign of the Holy Spirit descending on Jesus like a dove. (John 1:32–34)

4. Peter and Nathanael were introduced to Jesus by a friend or relative. (John 1:41–42, 45)

5. Six titles for Jesus in John 1:29–51 are Lamb of God, Son of God, Rabbi, Messiah (Christ), King of Israel, and Son of Man. There is no one right answer to the second question. Many people today think of Jesus as Son of God or Son of Man because they emphasize either his divine qualities or his humanness.

Chapter 8: The Gush of New Wine

1. The temple market angered Jesus because the merchants were misusing religious rules to make unfair profits from worshippers, especially the poor. (John 2:16)

2. The merchants were misusing the following rules. (1) The temple tax rule: All money had to be exchanged for temple currency at very high exchange rates. (2) The rule of unblemished sacrificial lambs: temple inspectors tended to disapprove lambs purchased outside, and prices inside the temple were inflated. (3) The rule of alternate sacrifices for the poor: temple inspectors disapproved birds purchased outside, while high prices were charged inside.

3. Nicodemus believed Jesus was a teacher, from God, and that God was with him. (John 3:2)

4. Personal answers will vary. People have been attracted to Jesus through the Christlike qualities in one of their friends, by reading about Christ in Scripture, and hearing about Jesus in sermons.

Chapter 9: Operation Rescue

1. Those who trust in Christ are saved, but those who refuse to believe choose condemnation by their unwillingness to accept God's offer of salvation. (John 3:18)

2. When people followed Jesus, John knew he had succeeded in what God sent him to do-just as the bridegroom's friend succeeds when the bride and groom are married. (John 3:27–30)

3. Animosity between Samaritans and Jews developed because (1) Samaritans were a mixed race (2 Kings 17:24); (2) practiced a corrupt religion (2 Kings 17:25–41; John 4:20, 22); and (3) had

tried to stop the rebuilding of Jerusalem after the Exile (Nehemiah 4).

Chapter 10: The Rugged Hills of Home

1. Jesus is looking for people who believe in him because of his character and his word, with or without visible proof. (John 4:48; 20:29)

2. Herod's official demonstrated his faith by taking Jesus at his word. (John 4:50)

3. The five things the Lord anointed Jesus to do (Luke 4:18–19) are (1) preach the gospel to the poor, (2) heal the brokenhearted, (3) proclaim liberty to the captives and recovery of sight to the blind, (4) set at liberty those who are oppressed, (5) proclaim God's grace ("the acceptable year of the LORD"). Any one of these things may be what you need most.

4. The Nazarenes refused to believe because they knew Jesus's family and because he told them God loved Gentiles. (John 4:22, 25–27)

5. Jesus's authority over evil spirits tells us we should listen to whatever he says. (Luke 4:32, 36)

6. Jesus's authority may affect many areas of your life and include comfort or freedom from worry about enemies, evil, and illness.

Chapter 11: The Mighty Kingdom of the Weak

1. When success threatened to deter Jesus he got alone and prayed. (Luke 4:42)

2. The Jews believed (1) the universe is God's kingdom, (2) Christ came to govern as king, and (3) Christ will set up a political kingdom and rule the world from Jerusalem. They failed to understand the necessity for Christ to suffer and die as a sacrifice to atone for human sin (Isaiah 53).

3. When he saw Christ's power, Simon confessed he was a sinful man. (John 5:8)

4. Jesus restored the paralyzed man's ability to walk. (Luke 5:23–25)

Chapter 12: Religion Gone Rigid

1. The healed man defended himself by saying, "The man who healed me told me to do it" (John 5:11). Jesus defended his actions by saying, "God works on the Sabbath" (John 5:17).

2. The four witnesses who verify Christ's claims are (1) John the Baptist, (2) Christ's saving mission, (3) the Father's voice, (4) Old Testament Scripture.(John 5:35–39)

3. The scribes and Pharisees neglected God's desire for "mercy, not sacrifice" by condemning the disciples for plucking grain on the Sabbath. (Matthew 12:1–2)

4. By healing the withered hand Jesus demonstrated that "it is lawful to do good on the Sabbath" and that a person is more valuable than a sheep! (Matthew 12:12)

5. Examples of offering sacrifice while neglecting mercy could include giving a tithe to the church while being angry about doing so or denying yourself some comfort while failing to forgive someone who has hurt you.

Chapter 13: The Inner Circle

1. Jesus chose twelve disciples to be apostles (Luke 6:13). The names of the twelve chosen are Peter (Simon) and Andrew, fishermen and brothers; James and John, fishermen and brothers; Philip and Bartholomew (Nathanael), possibly brothers; Matthew (Levi the tax collector) and James, possibly brothers; Thomas; Simon the Zealot (the Canaanite), political radical; Thaddaeus (Judas son of James); and Judas Iscariot.

2. Jesus's Sermon on the Mount teachings were for his disciples (Matthew 5:1; Luke 6:17), people who are "born again" (John 3:3, 5).

3. Jesus fulfills the Law by giving his disciples a fuller understanding of sinful motives and attitudes as well as outward actions condemned by the Ten Commandments. (Matthew 5:17, 20)

4. We love our enemies by (1) doing good to them, (2) blessing them, and (3) praying for them.

5. Possible answers may include the need to forgive someone, to stop judging others, or to be honest about your faults.

Chapter 14: Revolution of Love

1. The centurion recognized Jesus's authority (1) is similar to earthly authority, (2) extends over people and created things (e.g., disease), and (3) transcends space and distance. (Luke 7:7–10)

2. God feels people's pain; his compassion moves him to help. (Luke 7:13–16)

3. If you are doing God's will by obeying Scripture in your daily life, those around you will probably view you as a close relative of Jesus.

Chapter 15: The Storyteller

1. A parable is a saying, story, or metaphor that communicates truth by comparison. "An earthly story with a heavenly meaning."

2. The seed is the word of God, Christ's kingdom teaching (Matthew 13:19). Rocky places are listeners with prejudices, stubbornness, or fear that keep the word from taking root in their lives.

3. Jesus's goal in teaching was to help his disciples become like their teacher.

4. When interpreting Jesus's parables: (1) note the context, (2) focus on the main point, and (3) consider the culture and customs of Jesus's time.

5. Depending on your circumstances, to get tuned in on Jesus's voice you might read Psalm 46 or 51, or Job 38:1–40:2.

Chapter 16: Storms over Galilee

1. When the storm hit the boat Jesus was asleep in the stern (Mark 4:38). Trials or losses can make us feel that God does not care about us, although we are wrong when we believe that.

2. The disciples asked, "Who can this be?" (Mark 4:41 NKJV). His ability to command the storm tells us Jesus is Lord—his word has authority over the elements.

3. The people of Gadara clamped the demon-possessed man in chains (Luke 8:29). We use drugs and confinement in hospitals to control the mentally ill, avoid them, and fear them.

4. The evil spirits were terrified, recognized who Jesus was, and begged him not to send them to the place of the dead (Mark 5:7; Luke 8:31). Jesus is more powerful than evil spirits, and they fear him (1 John 4:4).

5. The townspeople were afraid and asked Jesus to leave (Luke 8:37). They valued pigs and profits more than people and rejected any solution that was costly to them.

Chapter 17: Crusade for Galilee

1. Jesus saw that the crowds were harassed and helpless (Matthew 9:36). He felt compassion. He asked his disciples to pray for spiritual harvesters (9:38).

2. Jesus told his disciples to expect persecution when he sent them out.

3. Families may be united or divided when one member believes Jesus's claims. One believer could tell others in the family and bring them to Christ. Unbelieving family members may reject Jesus's claims, feel guilty or threatened, and cut off communication with the believer.

4. Herod thought John the Baptist had returned from the dead (Mark 6:16). He had beheaded John to please his illegitimate wife (Matthew 14:6–11).

Chapter 18: Good Bread

1. The only available food for feeding the five thousand was five barley loaves and two small fish. (John 6:9)

2. Jesus claims (1) he came down from heaven (verse 38); (2) he was sent by God (verses 38–39); (3) he does the Father's will, not his own (verse 38); (4) he safeguards those the Father gives him (verse 39); (5) he will raise the dead (verses 39–40); and (6) trust in him assures eternal life (verse 40).

3. To eat Jesus's flesh and drink his blood means to take him into our lives and maintain an intimate, daily, dependent, personal spiritual relationship with him.

Chapter 19: Religion Versus Reality

1. The Pharisees and lawyers nullified the authority of God's word (Mark 7:13). Jesus called them hypocrites (7:6).

2. Jesus demands that people deal with their dirty hearts (the sin inside). The Pharisees settled for "ceremonial" (external, religious, ritual) cleansing. (Mark 7:15–23)

3. The Pharisees, Sadducees, and Herodians.

4. Jesus used spit in three healing miracles: healing a speech impediment (Mark 7:33) and healing blind men on two different occasions (John 9:6; Mark 8:23).

Chapter 20: Road to Messiahship and Discipleship

1. God gave Peter his revelation about who Jesus is. The gates of Hades, place of the dead, will not stand against the church founded on the conviction that Jesus is the Christ, the Son of God. (Matthew 16:18)

2. Jesus called Peter "Satan" when Peter told him to stop talking about dying (Matthew 16:23). Peter was not seeing things from God's perspective but from man's viewpoint.

3. Moses and Elijah appeared with Jesus on the Mount of Transfiguration (Matthew 9:2–8). Reasons for this experience for the disciples may have included: (1) visual confirmation that Jesus was what they had confessed him to be (Matthew 16:16); (2) encouragement after Jesus's disclosure of the cost of discipleship (Matthew 16:24–27); (3) to teach that cross-bearing does not diminish Christ's majesty or ours; and (4) to affirm the supremacy of Christ over Old Testament Law and Prophets (Matthew 17:4–8). For Jesus, transfiguration was (1) reaffirmation of God's approval; (2) refocus on the purpose of his mission; and (3) encouragement for the ordeal ahead (Luke 9:31).

4. Jesus told Peter to forgive a person who wronged him seventy-seven times. Some translations say "seventy times seven" (Matthew 18:22 NKJV). We should never stop forgiving.

Chapter 21: Feast of Spirit and Light

1. Jesus explained, "I am not yet going up to this feast, for My time has not yet fully come" (John 7:8 NKJV). Jesus entered the feast exactly when God's timing called for him to be there.

2. God gave Jesus his teaching material and authority to teach (John 7:16). The person who chooses to do God's will and practices what Jesus says comes to know Jesus's teachings are from God (John 7:17).

3. Jesus promised that out of the heart of anyone who believes in him "will flow rivers of living water" (the Holy Spirit). (John 7:37–39)

4. Some people are relieved that Jesus accepts them as they are. They feel encouraged and desire to please God with right behavior.

Chapter 22: Bright Sonlight, Dark Shadows

1. What excited the returning seventy most was that demons obeyed them (Luke 10:17). Jesus suggested they should be most excited that their names were recorded in heaven (17:20). Personally, Jesus was thrilled they were discovering the secrets of his relationship with his Father (17:21–22).

2. Love God with your whole being and your neighbor as yourself (Luke 10:27). The Samaritan loved his neighbor by showing mercy to the robbery victim (10:37).

3. According to Luke 11:5–13, successful praying involves (1) the brashness of the person praying (11:5–8); and (2) the goodness of God (11:9–13).

Chapter 23: Seeing with New Eyes

1. This calls for evaluation of your personal handling of material possessions compared to Jesus's attitude and practice as revealed in Luke 12:13–34.

2. Jesus's investment strategy had three points: (1) Don't worry (Luke 12:22–28). (2) Seek God's kingdom (12:29–34). (3) Use resources to move the kingdom toward its goals—that is, help needy people (12:33).

3. To be ready for Christ's second coming: (1) be ready and working (Luke 12:35); (2) be faithful and filled with the Spirit (12:35); and (3) be watching—spiritually awake, alert, attentive, vigilant (12:37–38, 40).

4. The Pharisees cared more about their traditions than healing people. (John 9:14–16)

Chapter 24: Shepherd Lord

1. (a) The sheepfold is the kingdom of God. (b) The sheep are God's people. (c) The shepherd is Jesus. (d) The thief is the exploitive leader. (e) The gate is Jesus, our access to God. (f) The wolf is the enemy/the devil.

2. In addition to choosing the moment to lay down his life, Jesus said he could decide when to "take it again" (rise from the dead). (John 10:18)

3. God rejoices when lost people are found, accepts them, and celebrates their return (Luke 15:7, 10, 20–24). The reactions of the elder brother to the prodigal's return were anger, resentment, and refusal to join the party (Luke 15:25–30).

4. Depending on your experiences, you may identify with any of the three people.

Chapter 25: Your Money or Your Life

1. Lazarus had been dead four days (John 11:39).

2. Jesus told Martha, "Whoever lives and believes in Me shall never die" (John 11:26 NKJV). Even though a believer dies, his spirit lives on in heaven.

3. Martha believed: (1) God would give Jesus whatever he asked (John 11:22); (2) Jesus is the Messiah (Christ); (3) Jesus is the Son of God; and (4) Jesus is the Promised One—the one who "is to come into the world" (11:27 NKJV). Jesus promised if she believed, Martha would see "the glory of God" (11:40 NKJV).

Chapter 26: Final Journey to Jerusalem

1. In the parable of the widow and the judge, Jesus encouraged prayer for justice (Luke 18:1–8). In the parable of the Pharisee and the tax collector, Jesus encouraged prayer for forgiveness (Luke 18:9–14). Base your last answer on your real personal desires.

2. Marriage as God designed it is: (1) for a male and a female; (2) monogamous; (3) two becoming one flesh; and (4) permanent. (Matthew 19:4–6)

3. Jesus asked the man to sell all his possessions, give the money to the poor, and follow him (Luke 18:22). By giving away his wealth (1) he would demonstrate complete trust in Jesus, (2) renounce wealth as his idol, and (3) follow Jesus as an apostle.

4. Zacchaeus's story (Luke 19) reveals the following: Jesus knows where hungry hearts are (19:5); he takes the initiative to find sinners (19:5); he values lost people (19:5); he refuses to let man-made proprieties and public opinion get in the way of reaching the needy (19:7). Zacchaeus demonstrated his readiness to be saved: by acting on his desire to see Jesus; welcoming Jesus into his home; announcing his intent to live a new life; adopting a new attitude toward possessions; and

making restitution for wrongs done to others (19:4–8). Your final answer is based on personal experience.

Chapter 27: Parade

1. Jesus sought to correct the misconception that the kingdom would appear at once (Luke 19:11). The king represents Christ. The distant empire represents his heavenly Father. The enemies represent Christ's enemies. The servants are Christ's disciples. Your personal answer is based on consideration of your personal resources, including money, time, and abilities.

2. To Jesus, Mary's anointing was preparation for his burial. (John 12:7)

3. Jesus rode a donkey instead of a warhorse in the Triumphal Entry (1) to fulfill Zechariah's prophecy (John 12:14–15; Zechariah 9:9); and (2) to show he is the king of peace, not war (Zechariah 9:10; Luke 19:38).

4. They were afraid they'd be put out of the synagogue (John 12:42–43). For your final answer, consider the effect of people's approval or disapproval on your willingness to express your faith.

Chapter 28: Ambush

1. The brother who first said "no" and later changed his mind represents tax collectors and prostitutes. The brother who said "yes" but then never did the work represents religious leaders. To answer the second part of this question, think about your own track record on obedience to God.

2. The Pharisees joined with the Herodians, supporters of Herod (Matthew 22:15–16). Jesus showed them a Roman coin and said to give to Caesar what belongs to Caesar and to God what belongs to God (verse 21).

3. In the resurrection world, (1) marriage isn't necessary; (2) we will be like the angels; (3) it will be impossible for us to die; and (4) we will be recognized as God's children. (Matthew 22:30; Luke 20:36)

Chapter 29: Final-Hour Prophecies

1. The disciples asked: (1) When will the temple be destroyed? (2) What will be the sign of your coming? and (3) What will be the sign of the end of the age? (Matthew 24:3)

2. When you see armies surrounding Jerusalem, get out of town! (Luke 21:21)

3. Six actions upon which future judgment will be based are (1) feeding the hungry, (2) giving a drink to the thirsty, (3) showing hospitality to strangers, (4) clothing the naked, (5) caring for the sick, and (6) visiting prisoners (Matthew 25:35–36). The last two questions call for personal answers based on your abilities, interests, and limitations.

Chapter 30: Countdown to Glory

1. The conspiracy between Judas and Jesus's enemies was arranged two days before Passover. Judas betrayed Jesus for 30 pieces of silver. That was the going price for a slave. (Mark 14:1–2; Luke 22:3–6; Exodus 21:32)

2. Apparently Judas's decision to betray Jesus was based on (1) disillusionment with Jesus's idea of the kingdom (John 12:4–5); (2) greed (Matthew 26:14–15); and (3) that Satan had entered his heart (Luke 23:3–6).

3. Jesus washed the disciples' feet—the job of the lowest household slave (John 13:2–5). Peter refused to let Jesus wash his feet (13:6–8). You may have felt as Peter felt. Jesus and Peter could not have fellowship if Peter didn't let him wash his feet (13:8).

4. The new commandment is "Love one another as I have loved you" (John 13:33–35). It's new because it (1) establishes a new "family" relationship, (2) calls for a higher standard for love, (3) makes a new impact on the world, and (4) sums up Old and New Testament commandments into one (Romans 13:8).

5. Jesus meant the Holy Spirit would be to his disciples what he had been. (John 14:16)

6. John 15:2, in most translations, says he cuts off or takes away the fruitless branch, but a better translation is he "lifts it up" (to sun and air), giving it another chance.

7. Jesus had to leave so the Counselor (Holy Spirit) could come to the disciples (John 16:7). You may appreciate the Holy Spirit's presence, the power he gives for ministry, how he convicts you of sin, and how he teaches you (John 14–16).

Chapter 31: The Great Surrender

1. Eternal life is knowing the true God and Jesus Christ, whom he has sent. (John 17:3)

2. The three religious trials of Jesus were (1) before Annas at his house (John 18:13–15); (2) before Caiaphas at his house (Matthew 26:57–58; John 18:24); and (3) before the entire Sanhedrin at sunup (Matthew 27:1; Mark 14:53).

3. After his third denial the rooster crowed, and Peter wept bitterly. (Luke 22:60–62)

4. Before Pilate the leaders charged Jesus with (1) insurrection ("subverting the nation"); (2)

opposing payment of taxes to Rome; and (3) claiming to be a king in competition with Caesar (Luke 23:2). In reality, the Sanhedrin charged him with blasphemy for claiming to be God's Son (Mark 14:64; John 19:7).

5. The Passover Pardon was a goodwill gesture in which the governor pardoned one prisoner. Pilate tried to convince the crowd to let Jesus be the pardoned prisoner, offering them a choice between Jesus and Barabbas, an assassin and robber. Instead the crowd chose Barabbas. (John 18:39–40; Luke 23:25)

6. Pilate washed his hands and declared, "I am innocent of the blood of this just Person . . . You see to it" (Matthew 27:24 NKJV). Your personal answer should be based on evaluation of your ability to accept responsibility for your actions.

Chapter 32: The Ultimate Sacrifice

1. Jesus prayed for God to forgive (1) the soldiers (Luke 23:34); (2) Jewish leaders and people (Acts 3:17; 2 Corinthians 3:13–16); and (3) all unbelievers (2 Corinthians 4:4).

2. The sign read: "JESUS OF NAZARETH, THE KING OF THE JEWS" (John 19:19–20 NKJV). Jewish leaders asked Pilate to change it to say he claimed to be king of the Jews (John 19:21). The thief asked Jesus to remember him when he came into his kingdom, recognizing that Jesus was King of heaven. (Luke 23:42)

3. Christ's death was unusual because it was (1) voluntary, (2) his destiny, (3) a sacrifice, and (4) accompanied by an earthquake, tearing of the temple veil, and raising of some dead people. (John 10:18; Hebrews 2:14–18; John 1:29; Matthew 27:51)

4. Your answers will be based on your recollection. You might explain the Crucifixion by comparing Jesus to a perfect person who offers to take your sentence on himself, freeing you from death row in prison.

Chapter 33: He's Alive!

1. Joseph of Arimathea and Nicodemus buried Jesus (John 19:38–39). The Roman centurion confirmed his death (Mark 15:42–47). They buried Jesus's body in Joseph's new tomb.

2. The differences between burial of a criminal and others were (1) a criminal could not be buried in his family tomb for a year after death; and (2) no public mourning was allowed.

3. The first person who saw Jesus alive after his resurrection was Mary Magdalene (John 20:10–18). She recognized his voice and the way he said her name (20:16). Your personal answer will come from recalling personal experiences.

4. Thomas thought he needed to see and touch Jesus's wounds to believe he was alive (John 20:25). When he saw Jesus, Thomas confessed him as Lord and God (20:28). One or a combination of all these things may help you overcome doubt.

Chapter 34: Liftoff!

1. "At the right hand of God" means Christ occupies the highest position in the universe, and God is carrying on all his work through him.

2. Christ has power and authority over every other rule, authority, power, and dominion in the universe, and he is head of the church. (Ephesians 1:18–23)

3. As the Christian's representative in heaven, Jesus (1) intercedes for us (Hebrews 7:25), (2) is our advocate when we sin (1 John 2:1), and (3) is preparing a permanent place for us in God's heavenly home (John 14:1–3).

4. Christ is always with us in the person of his Holy Spirit, who lives in us. (John 14:15–16)

5. The angels at the Ascension promised that Christ would return. (Acts 1:11)

Appendix D - The Experts

Alford, Henry—Dean of Canterbury, England; author of *The New Testament for English Readers Bible* commentary.

Allen, Ronald B.—Professor of Bible Exposition at Dallas Theological Seminary.

Anderson, Neil T.—Chairman of the Practical Theology Department at the Talbot School of Theology of Biola University.

Arnold, Thomas—Headmaster of Rugby School from 1795 to 1842; professor of modern history at Oxford University; author of *History of Rome* (three volumes, 1838–1843) and *Oxford Lectures on Modern History* (1842).

Saint Augustine of Hippo—Fourth-century bishop of Hippo, North Africa; a major influence on Christianity; he made the grace of God the theme of Western Christian theology.

Barbieri, Louis A., Jr.—Professor of Bible at the Moody Bible Institute, Chicago; contributing author to *The Bible Knowledge Commentary*.

Barclay, William—New Testament scholar and writer; professor of Divinity and Biblical Criticism at the University of Glasgow; author of many books, including the multivolume *Daily Study Bible* commentary on all the New Testament books.

Barnes, Albert—Pastor, First Presbyterian Church in Philadelphia, for thirty-five years; his multivolume *Barnes' Notes* Bible commentary series has sold two million copies.

Barnhouse, Donald Grey—Founder of *Eternity* magazine and *The Bible Study Hour* radio program; pastor.

Beasley-Murray, George R.—Former principal at Spurgeon's College, London; professor of New Testament Interpretation at Southern Baptist Theological Seminary in Louisville, Kentucky; author of several Bible commentaries and other books.

Bede, Venerable—Seventh- and eighth-century Bible scholar and hymn writer.

Boice, James M.—Pastor of Tenth Presbyterian Church, Philadelphia; radio preacher on the *The Bible Study Hour*; author.

Bonhoeffer, Dietrich—German theologian, co-founder of the Confessing Church in Germany, martyred by the Nazis for resistance against Nazi persecution of Jews.

Brandt, Leslie F.—Lutheran minister, evangelist, and retreat leader; author.

Bright, Bill—Founder and president of Campus Crusade for Christ International.

Bruce, F. F.—Scotsman, preeminent evangelical scholar of the post–World War II era, president of both the Society for Old Testament Studies and the Society for New Testament Studies.

Calvin, John—Sixteenth-century leader in the Swiss Protestant Reformation; his *Institutes of the Christian Religion* form the basis for the theological system known as Calvinism.

Card, Michael—Contemporary Christian author, composer, performer, and recording artist who lives in Nashville, Tennessee.

Chambers, Oswald—Principal of Bible Training School, London; founder of two YMCA desert camps in Egypt during World War I where he ministered to British soldiers.

Chrysostom, Saint John—Fourth-century Bible expositor and preacher (his name means "golden-mouth"); exiled for attacks against church and civil government vices.

Clayton, Charles—Executive Director of World Vision in Great Britain.

Coleman, Robert E.—Professor of Evangelism at Trinity Evangelical Divinity School, Deerfield/Chicago.

Cosby, Gordon—Founder and pastor of Church of the Saviour, Washington, D.C.

Edersheim, Alfred—Scholar of Jewish history and society during Bible times.

Erwin, Gayle—Astronaut, editor of *Servant's Quarters* magazine.

Evans, Tony—Professor at Dallas Theological Seminary; inspirational author.

France, R. T.—Principal of Wycliffe Hall in the University of Oxford; lecturer in Biblical Studies at the University of Ife, Nigeria.

Graham, Billy—International crusade, radio, and TV evangelist; he has presented the gospel face-to-face to more people than any other man in history; author of many inspirational classics read by millions; founder of *Christianity Today* and *Decision* magazines.

Gutzke, Manford George—Author of two dozen books in the *Plain Talk Bible* commentary series.

Halley, Henry H.—Author of the well-known and widely used *Halley's Bible Handbook*, which has sold nearly two million copies.

Henry, Matthew—Seventeenth-century biblical expositor, expelled from the Church of England in 1662; Presbyterian pastor; authored multivolume Bible commentary still popular today.

Irving, Roy—Bible scholar; longtime editor of the *Scripture Press Adult Teaching Guide*.

Josephus—First-century Jewish historian.

Julian of Norwich—Fourteenth-century English mystic; author of *The Sixteen Revelations of Divine Love*, the first book published by a female author in English.

Keller, Phillip—A shepherd who writes about the Bible's Good Shepherd from his personal understanding of shepherds and sheep.

Killinger, John—Professor of preaching, worship, and literature at Vanderbilt Divinity School, Nashville; author of more than twenty books.

L'Engle, Madeleine—Prolific author; winner of the Newberry Award for her novel *A Wrinkle in Time*; poet; lecturer; Christian retreat leader.

Lewis, C. S.—Fellow of Magdalen College, Oxford University; author of books on theology and fantasy: including *The Chronicles of Narnia*.

Lindsey, Hal—Influential author of *The Late Great Planet Earth* as well as other books on biblical prophecy (thirty-five million of which are in print); TV personality.

Lucado, Max—Pastor of Oak Hill Church of Christ in San Antonio, Texas; poet, artist, apologist, prolific writer of inspirational books.

MacArthur, John F. Jr.—Pastor/teacher of Grace Community Church, Sun Valley, California; president of The Master's College and Seminary; speaker on the daily Grace to You radio broadcast.

Marshall, Peter—Chaplain of the U.S. Senate from 1947 to 1949; pastor of New York Avenue Presbyterian Church, Washington, D.C.; his life story is told in the popular film *A Man Called Peter*.

McCane, Byron R.—Professor of Religion at Converse College in Spartanburg, South Carolina.

McCartney, Dan—Associate professor of New Testament at Westminster Theological Seminary.

McFague, Sallie—Theologian, feminist, critic; author of books on metaphorical theology.

Miller, Stephen M.—Editorial adviser for *Christian History* magazine; freelance writer.

Morris, Leon—Anglican priest; principal of Ridley College in Melbourne, Australia; author of numerous books, including commentaries on Luke, John, 1 Corinthians, Thessalonians, and Revelation.

Mouw, Richard J.—President of Fuller Theological Seminary in Pasadena.

Nouwen, Henri J. M.—Taught at University of Notre Dame, Yale, and Harvard; from 1986 till his death in 1996 associated with L'Arche Community in France and Toronto.

Packer, J. I.—Theologian; professor at Regent College, Vancouver, British Columbia; former associate principal of Trinity College, Bristol, England.

Pascal, Blaise—Seventeenth-century French physicist; formulator of the mathematical theory of probability, a fundamental element of modern theoretical physics, member of the Roman Catholic reform movement known as Jansenism.

Peretti, Frank—Christian novelist and storyteller; author of *This Present Darkness*.

Peterson, Eugene H.—Professor of Spiritual Theology at Regent College in Vancouver, British Columbia; author of many books; contributing editor to *Leadership Journal*.

Phillips, J. B.—Pastor in London during World War II; Bible translator of *The New Testament in Modern English*; friend of C. S. Lewis.

Pollock, John—Cambridge-educated English clergyman; biographer of Billy Graham, Jesus Christ (*Master: A Life of Jesus*), and Paul (*Apostle: A Life of Paul*).

Powell, John—Jesuit; associate professor at Loyola University in the classics, English, psychology, and theology; popular lecturer, counselor, and retreat director.

Richards, Larry (Lawrence O.)—Theologian, Bible scholar, ecclesiologist; prolific author of more than 175 books, including Bible commentaries and reference works for pastors, church leaders, teachers, laymen, and youth.

Ryle, John Charles—Nineteenth-century bishop of Liverpool, England.

Schaff, Philip—Historian; author of a widely recognized eight-volume *History of the Christian Church*.

Sider, Ronald J.—Professor at Eastern Baptist Seminary; president of Evangelicals for Social Action.

Snyder, Howard A.—Formerly dean of Free Methodist Seminary in San Paulo, Brazil; Director of Light and Life Men International; author of books on church renewal.

Stafford, Tim—Editor of Campus Life Books; senior writer for *Christianity Today*.

Stott, John R. W.—Evangelist, preacher, Bible scholar, author; pastor of All Souls Church in London; active participant in Evangelical-Roman Catholic dialogue; director of London Institute for Contemporary Christianity.

Sweet, Leonard I.—Dean of the Theological School, vice president, and professor of Post-Modern Christianity at Drew University, Madison, New Jersey.

Swindoll, Charles—President of Dallas Theological Seminary; popular Bible expositor, radio preacher, author.

Tada, Joni Eareckson—Author of more than twenty books; founder and president of Joni and Friends, a ministry to the disabled.

Mother Teresa—Founder of the Missionaries of Charity in Calcutta, India and fifty-one other countries; Nobel Peace Prize winner in 1979.

Thomas, Cal—Syndicated newspaper columnist.

Thomas à Kempis—Fifteenth-century German mystic; copyist (copied the entire Bible four times); author of devotional writings, including *The Imitation of Christ*.

Tozer, A. W.—Editor of *The Alliance Witness*; pastor, conference speaker, author; described as "a twentieth-century prophet."

Unger, Merril F.—Biblical scholar and researcher; author of *Unger's Bible Dictionary*.

Wagner, C. Peter—Senior professor of church growth at Fuller Theological Seminary, Pasadena; church growth consultant.

Wesley, John—Founder of Methodism; traveled 250,000 miles on horseback, preached 42,000 sermons, authored 233 books of history, Bible commentary, and medicine; did more to change English society and religion than any other person of his time.

Willard, Dallas— Professor at the University of Southern California's School of Philosophy; visiting professor at the University of Colorado.

Endnotes

Chapter 1

1. Eugene H. Peterson, "This Profound Mystery" (an interview with Eugene H. Peterson), Cross Point (winter 1998), 2.

2. John F. MacArthur Jr., *God with Us* (Grand Rapids, MI: Zondervan, 1989), 46.

Chapter 2

1. Charles R. Swindoll, *Growing Strong in the Seasons of Life* (Portland, OR: Multnomah, 1983), 35.

2. Michael Card, *Immanuel: Reflections on the Life of Christ* (Nashville: Thomas Nelson, 1990), 63.

3. William Barclay, *The Gospel of Luke* (Philadelphia: Westminster, 1975), 22.

4. Matthew Henry, *Commentary on the Whole Bible*, one-volume ed. (Grand Rapids, MI: Zondervan, 1961), 1418.

5. Lawrence O. Richards, *The Victor Bible Background Commentary* (Wheaton, IL: Victor, 1985), 16.

6. MacArthur, *God with Us*, 114.

Chapter 3

1. Robert L. Thomas and Stanley N. Gundry, *A Harmony of the Gospels* (San Francisco, CA: HarperCollins, 1978), 32.

2. Robert E. Coleman, *The Mind of the Master* (Old Tappan, NJ: Revell, 1977), 21.

Chapter 4

1. Barclay, *Luke*, 32.

2. Stephen M. Miller, "Select Circle," *Christian History*, issue 59, p. 33.

3. John Killinger, *A Devotional Guide to Luke: The Gospel of Contagious Joy* (Waco, TX: Word, 1980), 27.

4. Clark Peddicord, *Jesus, The Powerful Servant* (San Bernardino, CA: Here's Life, 1984), 39.

5. Henry Alford, *The New Testament for English Readers* (Chicago: Moody, n.d.), 17.

Chapter 5

1. William Barclay, *The Gospel of Matthew*, vol. 1 (Philadelphia, PA: Westminster, 1975), 63.

2. Merilyn Hargis, "On the Road," *Christian History* 17, issue 59 (no. 3), 31.

3. Chrysostom, *The Gospel of St. Matthew*, Homily 13.1, quoted in Oden and Hall, *Ancient Christian Commentary on Scripture*, vol. 2: Mark (Downers Grove, IL: InterVarsity, 1998), 17.

4. Quoted in Donald Grey Barnhouse, *The Invisible War* (Grand Rapids, MI: Zondervan, 1965), 156.

5. Thomas à Kempis, *À Kempis*, 32.

6. *Adult Teaching Guide* (Wheaton, IL: Scripture Press, September-November 1994), 44.

7. Albert Barnes, *Barnes Notes: Matthew and Mark* (Grand Rapids, MI: Baker, 1979), 12.

8. Barclay, *Matthew*, 70.

Chapter 6

1. Raymond E. Brown, *The Gospel According to John* (New York: Anchor Bible, 1966), 1.

2. Card, *Immanuel*, 36.

3. Lawrence O. Richards, *The Victor Bible Background Commentary: New Testament* (Wheaton, IL: Victor, 1994), 212.

4. From the hymn "Holy, Holy, Holy," by Reginald Heber.

5. *Revell Bible Dictionary*, 995.

6. Coleman, *The Mind of the Master*, 22.

7. *The Amplified New Testament* (Grand Rapids, MI: Zondervan, 1958).

8. Billy Graham, *How to Be Born Again* (Waco, TX: Word, 1977), 183.

Chapter 7

1. Richards, *Background Commentary*, 219.
2. Morris, *John*, 140–41.
3. George R. Beasley-Murray, *Word Biblical Commentary* (Waco, TX: Word, 1987).

Chapter 8

1. Barclay, *John*, vol. 1, 95.
2. Leonard I. Sweet, *Quantum Spirituality* (Dayton, OH: Whaleprints, 1991, 1994), 85.
3. Halley, *Halley's Bible Handbook*, 434.
4. Billy Graham, *Just As I Am* (New York: Harper, 1997), 34.
5. Blaise Pascal, noted physicist, source unknown.
6. Oswald Chambers, *My Utmost for His Highest* (New York: Dodd Mead, 1946), 10.

Chapter 9

1. George Beasley-Murray, *Word Biblical Commentary*, vol. 36: John (Waco, TX: Word, 1987), 51.
2. Augustine, quoted in Barclay, *John*, vol. 1, 138.
3. Morris, *John*, 231.
4. Thomas and Gundry, *Harmony*, 44 (footnote).
5. Allen, *The Majesty of Man*, 111, 118.
6. Barclay, *John*, 150.
7. Packer, Knowing God, 109.

Chapter 10

1. Josephus, *Antiquities of the Jews*, quoted in Barclay, John, 41.
2. Barclay, *John*, 174–75.
3. Leslie F. Brandt, *Jesus/Now* (St. Louis: Concordia, 1978), 113.
4. Albert Barnes, *Notes on the New Testament* (Grand Rapids, MI: Baker, 1949), 81.
5. Neil T. Anderson, *The Bondage Breaker* (Eugene, OR: Harvest House, 1990), 25–26.

Chapter 11

1. Elizabeth O'Conner, *Call to Commitment*, quoted in World Vision, June-July 1990, 15.
2. Howard A. Snyder, *The Community of the King* (Downers Grove, IL: InterVarsity, 1977), 40–41.
3. Gordon Cosby, "New Servnt Leadership School," *Faith at Work*, January-February 1990, 8.
4. Joni Eareckson Tada, "The World's Weakest-516 Million Strong," *World Vision*, June-July 1990, 7–8.

Chapter 12

1. Quoted in Barclay, *John*, 182.
2. C. S. Lewis, *The Case for Christianity* (New York: Macmillan, 1965), 45.
3. John Charles Ryle, *Expository Thoughts on the Gospels: John*, 3 vols. (London, 1957), quoted in Morris, 334.
4. Barclay, *Luke*, 73.

Chapter 13

1. Barclay, *Mark*, 69.
2. F. R. Maltby, quoted in Barclay, *Luke*, 75.
3. Dietrich Bonhoeffer, *The Cost of Discipleship* (New York: Macmillan, 1963), 125.
4. Harry Emerson Fosdick, *The Man from Nazareth* (New York: Pocket Books, 1953; first published by Harper and Brothers, 1949), 126.
5. R. T. France, *Matthew, Evangelist and Teacher* (Grand Rapids, MI: Zondervan, 1989), 196–97.
6. Sweet, *Quantum Spirituality*, 89.
7. Chambers, *My Utmost for His Highest*, 180.
8. C. S. Lewis, *Mere Christianity*, bk. 4 (New York: Macmillan, 1952), 163.

Chapter 14

1. Barclay, *Mark*, 150.
2. Sweet, *Quantum Spirituality*, 90.

Chapter 15

1. J. R. Dummelow, *A Commentary on the Holy Bible* (New York: Macmillan, 1923), 1056.
2. A. W. Tozer, *The Pursuit of God* (Harrisburg, PA: Christian Publications, 1948), 83.
3. Frank Peretti, *Fiction Sampler* (Waco, TX: Word, 1998), inside front cover.
4. Willard, *The Divine Conspiracy*, 114.
5. Merril F. Unger, *Unger's Bible Dictionary* (Chicago: Moody, 1957), 824.
6. Halley, *Halley's Bible Handbook*, 348.

Chapter 16

1. Thomas and Gundry, *A Harmony*, 87.
2. Halley, *Halley's Bible Handbook*, 373.
3. Richards, *Background Commentary*, 480.
4. Edersheim, *Sketches of Jewish Social Life*, 282.

Chapter 17

1. Barclay, *Matthew*, 356.
2. Robert E. Coleman, *The Master Plan of Evangelism* (Grand Rapids, MI: Revell, 1964), 84.

3. Packer, *Knowing God*, 218.

4. Coleman, *Master Plan*, 87.

Chapter 18

1. John Pollock, *The Master* (Wheaton, IL: Victor, 1985), 93.

2. Augustine of Hippo, quoted in Morris, *John*, 339.

3. Coleman, *The Mind of the Master*, 91–92.

4. Oswald Chambers, *Still Higher for His Highest* (Grand Rapids, MI: Zondervan, 1970), 86.

5. Richards, *Background Commentary*, 234–35.

6. Card, *Immanuel*, 83.

Chapter 19

1. Dan McCartney and Charles Clayton, *Let the Reader Understand* (Wheaton, IL: Victor, 1994), 73.

2. Richards, *Background Commentary*, 124.

Chapter 20

1. Robert E. Coleman, *The Master Plan of Evangelism* (Old Tappan, NJ: Revell, 1963), 18.

2. Peter Marshall, quoted in *NRSV Classics Devotional Bible* (Grand Rapids, MI: Zondervan, 1996), 1171.

3. Gayle Erwin, "Forgiveness," *Servant Quarters* (Cathedral City, CA), September-November, 1994.

Chapter 21

1. Alfred Edersheim, *The Temple* (Grand Rapids, MI: Eerdmans, 1982), 279–80.

2. Ibid., 281.

3. Billy Graham, *The Holy Spirit: Activating God's Power in Your Life* (New York: Warner, 1978), 14.

4. Barclay, *John*, vol. 2, 6.

5. Oswald Chambers, *Run Today's Race* (Fort Washington, PA: Christian Literature Crusade, 1968), 35.

Chapter 22

1. Frank R. Klassen, *The Chronology of the Bible* (Nashville: Regal, 1975), 58.

2. Morris, *Luke*, 200.

3. John Wesley, *The Letters of the Reverend John Wesley*, ed. John Telford, vol. 6 (London: Epworth Press, 1931), 272.

4. Morris, *Luke*, 206.

5. Roy Irving, *Adult Teaching Guide* (Wheaton, IL: Scripture Press, September-November 1984).

Chapter 23

1. McCartney and Clayton, *Let the Reader Understand*, 271.

Chapter 24

1. Octavius Winslow, *No Condemnation in Christ Jesus* (1857), quoted in John Murray, *The Epistle to the Romans*, vol. 1 (n.p.: Marshall, Morgan and Scott, 1960–1965), 324.

2. Phillip Keller, *A Shepherd Looks at the Good Shepherd and His Sheep*, large print ed. (Grand Rapids, MI: Zondervan, 1978), 40.

3. Tim Stafford, *Knowing the Face of God*, 67.

4. Barclay, *Matthew*, vol. 1, 304.

5. Oswald Chambers, *Still Higher for His Highest* (Grand Rapids, MI: Zondervan, 1970), 87.

Chapter 25

1. Killinger, *A Devotional Guide to Luke*, 91.

2. Mother Teresa, *Words to Love By* (Notre Dame: Ave Maria Press, 1983), 31.

3. Charles Swindoll, *Growing Deep in the Christian Life* (Portland, OR: Multnomah, 1986), 319–20.

4. Leon Morris, *The Gospel According to John* (Grand Rapids, MI: Eerdmans, 1971), 542.

5. Henri J. M. Nouwen, *Seeds of Hope* (New York: Doubleday, 1989), 171.

Chapter 26

1. Stafford, *Knowing the Face of God*, 206.

2. Barclay, *Matthew*, vol. 2 (Philadelphia: Westminster, 1975), 216.

3. Richards, *Background Commentary*, 71.

4. Barclay, *Matthew*, vol. 2, 227.

5. Sider, *Rich Christians*, 174.

Chapter 27

1. Morris, *Luke*, 302.

2. Venerable Bede, *Homilies on the Gospel*, 2:37–38, quoted in Oden and Hall, *Ancient Christian Commentary on Scripture*, 199.

3. Josephus, *The Works of Flavius Josephus*, trans. William Whiston (Grand Rapids, MI: Associated Publishers and Authors, n.d.).

4. Michael Card, *Immanuel: Reflections on the Life of Christ* (Nashville: Thomas Nelson, 1990), 143–44.

5. Morris, *John*, 593.

Chapter 28

1. Barclay, *Matthew*, vol. 2, 285–86.

2. Sallie McFague, *Metaphorical Theology: Models of God in Religious Language* (Philadelphia: Fortress, 1982), 181.

3. Richard J. Mouw, *Political Evangelism* (Grand Rapids, MI: Eerdmans, 1973), 55.

4. Pierre Teilhard de Chardin, quoted in John Powell, *Unconditional Love* (Allen, TX: Argus Communications, 1978), 97.

5. Barclay, *Matthew*, vol. 2, 310.

6. John Chrysostom, quoted in *Ancient Christian Commentary: Mark*, 180.

Chapter 29

1. Josephus, *The Works of Flavius Josephus*, 555.

2. Chambers, *Still Higher for His Highest*, 66.

3. C. Peter Wagner, *On the Crest of the Wave* (Ventura, CA: Regal, 1983), back cover.

4. Josephus, quoted in Morris, *Luke*, 326.

5. Hal Lindsey, *The Late, Great Planet Earth* (Grand Rapids, MI: Zondervan, 1970), 171.

6. Richards, *Background Commentary*, 86.

7. Chambers, *Still Higher for His Highest*, 88.

8. Sider, *Rich Christians*, 69.

Chapter 30

1. Merril C. Tenney, quoted in *Adult Teaching Guide*, December 1995-February 1996, 46.

2. *Revell Bible Dictionary*, 394.

3. F. L. Godet, *Commentary on the Gospel of John* (Grand Rapids, MI: Kegel, 1978).

4. John Powell, S. J., *Unconditional Love* (Allen, TX: Argus Communications, 1978), 95–96.

5. Richards, *Bible Difficulties Solved*, 297.

6. Barclay, Matthew, vol. 2, 377–78.

7. F. F. Bruce, *The Gospel of John* (Basingstoke, England: Pickering and Inglis, 1983), 298–99.

8. John Charles Ryle, *Expository Thoughts on the Gospels, St. John* (London, 1957), quoted in Morris, *John*, 646.

9. James M. Boice, *The Gospel of John* (Grand Rapids, MI: Zondervan, 1979), 229.

10. Quoted in William H. C. Frend, "Evangelists to the Death," *Christian History* 17, no. 1 (issue 57): 31, 33.

Chapter 31

1. Barclay, *John*, 218.

2. Card, *Immanuel*, 153.

3. Girard, *Adult Teaching Guide*, December 1994-February 1995, 108.

4. Chambers, *Still Higher*, 133.

5. Beasley-Murray, *John*, 328.

6. Cal Thomas, "Not of This World," *Newsweek*, March 29, 1999, 60.

7. *Revell Bible Dictionary*, 130.

8. Stott, *The Cross of Christ*, 51.

9. *Revell Bible Dictionary*, 793.

Chapter 32

1. *Harper Collins Atlas of the Bible*, ed. James Pritchard (Phoenix: Borders/Harper-Collins, 1999), 167.

2. Louis A. Barbieri Jr., "Matthew," *The Bible Knowledge Commentary*, ed. Walvoord and Zuck, 89.

3. E. Stauffer, *Jesus and His Story*, trans. D. M. Barton (London: SCM, 1960), 111.

4. Ibid., 113.

5. Stott, *Cross of Christ*, 78.

6. Chambers, *Still Higher*, 50.

7. Max Lucado, *No Wonder They Call Him the Savior* (Portland, OR: Multnomah, 1986), 140.

Chapter 33

1. Ben Witherington III, "Primary Sources," *Christian History* 17, no. 3 (issue 59): 18.

2. Byron R. McCane, "The Scandal of the Grave," *Christian History* 17, no. 3 (issue 59): 41.

3. Bill Bright, Introduction to *Ten Basic Steps Toward Christian Maturity: The Uniqueness of Jesus* (San Bernardino: Campus Crusade, 1964), 31.

4. Beasley-Murray, *John*, 374.

5. Barclay, *Luke*, 305.

6. Thomas Arnold, quoted in Bright, *Ten Steps Toward Christian Maturity*, 33.

7. Dietrich Bonhoeffer, *The Cost of Discipleship* (New York: Simon and Schuster/ Touchstone, 1959), 90.

8. Beasley-Murray, *John*, 386.

9. Philip Schaff, *History of the Christian Church*, vol. 1 (n.p.: A.P. and A., n.d.), 81.

10. Madeleine L'Engle, *Walking on Water: Reflections on Faith and Art* (Wheaton, IL: Shaw, 1980), 22.

Chapter 34

1. J. B. Phillips, Foreword to *Letters to Young Churches*, quoted in Bright, *Ten Steps Toward Christian Maturity*, 31–32.

Index

definition, 151
bar mitzvah, 24, 28
Barnes, Albert, 88
Bartimaeus, 228
Bartholomew, 108, 109
basis of faith, 171, 226
Bathesda, Pool of, 63, 99, 105
Baudelaire, 40
beat
  definition, 291
Beatitudes, 110, 117
  definition, 110
Bede, Venerable, 236
Beelzebub
  definition, 188
beginning and end, 246
believed, 48, 56, 63, 84, 218, 320
  definition, 320
believers, 48, 110, 125, 180
beloved Son, 35, 40, 102, 122, 169
below the dignity
  definition, 205
Benedictus, 10
Bethany (town of), 55, 187, 212, 219, 234, 235, 333
  definition, 55
Bethlehem, 14, 15, 16, 17, 18, 21, 23
Bethphage, 237
Bethsaida, 58, 151, 161, 240
  definition, 58
betrayal, 271, 288
bima
  definition, 85
bitterness, 197, 307
blasphemous
  definition, 101
blasphemy, 95, 159, 243, 290
  definition, 95, 290
bleeding, 137, 138, 303, 309
  definition, 137
blessed, 4, 50, 110, 325, 333
  definition, 325
blessing, 3, 8, 18, 143, 333

Boice, James M., 278
Bonhoeffer, Dietrich, 324
born again, 51, 52, 67, 69, 110
  definition, 110
"born of God," 51
Brandt, Leslie F., 87
Bread of Life, 152
breathed His last, 309
  definition, 309
brethren, 25, 93, 265, 321
  definition, 321
Bright, Bill, 317
Brook Kedron, 287
Bruce, F. F., 276
Buddha, 47
burial, 216, 236, 315, 316, 317
burial cave, 216
  definition, 216
burnt offering, 17, 176, 250

C

Caesar, 247, 248
  definition, 247
Caiaphas, 31, 217, 289, 290
Cana, village of, 61, 62, 84, 109, 112
Cananite
  definition, 109
Capernaum, 64, 84, 88, 90, 119, 120, 170, 171
Capstone
  illustration #6, 246
captives, 4, 86, 135, 258
celebration, 6, 61, 180, 207, 233, 262
cemetery
  definition, 121
census, 13, 14
centurion, 120, 316
  definition, 120
Cephas, 58, 108, 323
ceremonial laws, 16, 89
  definition, 89
ceremonial washings, 62
chazzan
  definition, 85

chief priests, 142, 167, 177, 243, 288, 297
chief priests and the elders, 243, 293
  definition, 243
children of God, 51, 217, 249
children of the devil, 180
Christianese
  definition, 116
Christianity, 8, 250, 330
circumcised, 9, 120
circumcision, 16, 17
Clayton, Charles
  on Jewish tradition, 158
  on the obedient Christian, 195
cleansing, 33, 34, 68, 270, 278
coerce, 43
commitment, 144, 147, 156, 178
  to God, 287, 299
communion, 274
compassion, 104, 121, 141, 149, 160, 199, 206
  definition, 141, 199
condemnation, 72, 103, 137, 142, 303
confess, 89, 108, 111, 196, 213
congregation, 24, 104, 176
consecrated bread
  definition, 103
consequences, 15, 61, 184, 202, 218, 247
  eternal, 202
  serious, 247
consummate, 7
contradictory, 48
control by Satan, 268
conversion, 69, 277
converted, 120, 300
  definition, 120
convict, 279, 280, 281
  definition, 280
Coptic
  definition, 61, 300
Coptic gospel, 61

P

Packer, J. I.
  on acceptable worship, 78
  on the man of sorrows,
    143
pagan, 34, 48, 87
  definition, 48
pagan widow, 87
pair of doves, 65
Palestine, 192
papyrus scroll
  illustration #2, 86
paradise, 211, 306, 307
  definition, 307
parental authority, 25
Pacal, Blaise, 68
Paschal lambs, 65, 309
Passover, 24, 28, 65, 66,
    183, 268
Passover Lamb, 183, 311
Passover moon, 287
past sins, 68
patience, 194
patriarchs, 55, 76, 77, 289
  definition, 76
Peddicord, Clark, 36
Pentateuch
  definition, 103
Pentecost, 7, 324
  definition, 324
people
  definition, 299
Perea, 183, 189, 212
Peretti, Frank, 130
pericardial sac
  definition, 311
persecution, 257, 265
personal liberty, 3
personal sin, 72
person's eternal destiny, 211
perspective, 9, 51, 142, 174,
    195
  God's, 168
Peterson, Eugene H., 8
Pharisee
  definition, 18
Philip, 24, 31, 151
Philippi, 165

Phillips, J. B., 334
Philo of Alexandria, 48
phylacteries
  illustration #7, 252
place
  definition, 288
place of honor, 271
plan of God, 27, 39, 298
point of access, 59
political influence, 146
polygamy
  definition, 223
Pontius Pilate, 31, 296, 305
Pool of Siloam, 176, 195
poor and powerless, 265
poor people, 236, 252
Powell, John, 273
power
  of Christ, 98
  of Elijah, 56
  of God, 7, 89, 249
  over unclean spirits, 142,
    145
Praetorium, 294, 295, 311
  definition, 294
praise, 78, 125, 220, 236, 241
praise God, 237
prayer, 114, 187, 222, 240,
    286, 307
preaching, 31, 35, 73, 116,
    141, 147
presence and power of the
  Holy Spirit, 45
pride, 42, 84, 159, 170, 225,
    278
priest, 4, 25, 218, 220, 285,
    289, 290
  definition, 25, 285
priority, 57, 236
prison, 74, 264, 303
Promised Land, 259
promised messiah, 5, 9, 57,
    78, 200, 256
prophecies, 4, 31, 122, 241,
    255, 261, 265, 295
prophecy
  fulfillment of, 14, 122,
    261, 295
Prophet, the, 24, 56, 145,

    151
  definition, 151
prophetic, 4, 10, 18, 255
propitiation
  definition, 25
prune
  definition, 278
public ministry, 25, 64, 107,
    221
punishment, 134, 143, 287,
    298
purification, 17
put out of the synagogue
  definition, 196, 241

R

rabbi
  definition, 58, 251
rabbinical rule, 137
rage
  definition, 258
Rapture
  definition, 260
ravens
  definition, 192
reap, 114
rebellion, 136, 144, 202,
    247
rebuke, 206, 237
"receive Him," 51, 298
Redeemer, 27, 239, 322
redemption in Jerusalem
  definition, 18
redemption price
  definition, 17
rejection, 87, 94, 111, 167,
    168, 233
religious habits, 128
religious hypocrisy, 117
reluctant, 149
removed
  definition, 269
repent, 194, 198, 222
repented
  definition, 245
respect, 44, 46, 245, 248
resurrection
  definition, 214

retain, 324
revealed
  definition, 166
revelation, 276, 309
Revell Bible Dictionary
  on foot washing, 270
  on human responsibility, 298
  on the Coptic church, 300
reverence, 20, 78, 235, 241, 303
rich man, 191, 209, 210, 211, 226, 227
righteous, 4, 5, 206, 249, 264
righteousness, 111, 113, 115, 222, 279
  definition, 113
ritual, 33, 187, 270
robber
  definition, 200
"Rock," 108, 275
Roman Empire, 3, 48
Romans, 3, 120, 295, 310
Rome, 14, 74, 247
royal descent of Jesus, 26
Rule of Corban, 158
Ryle, John Charles
  on "greater works," 277
  on the truth of religion and idolatory, 102

S

Sabbath
  definition, 16, 84, 100
Sabbath police, 103
sack, 127
sacred scrolls, 85
Sadducees
  definition, 34, 248
Salome, 61, 108, 146, 318
Samaria, 74, 83, 219, 228
Samaritans, 75, 76, 77, 79, 80, 220
Samuel, 129
sanhedrin
  definition, 25, 183, 292
  illustration #8, 293

Satan, 39, 41, 44, 45, 46, 128, 168, 184, 268, 273
saved, 71, 115, 147, 202, 227
  definition, 202
Savior, 7, 9, 37, 79, 330
saviorhood, 9, 40, 42, 63, 165, 167
Schaff, Philip, 330
scholar, 26, 33, 69, 95, 131, 326
scribes, 104, 105, 113, 157, 167, 178, 203, 251, 306
Scripture, 8, 15, 43, 85, 120, 135, 176, 320
Sea of Galilee, 88, 135, 150, 326
  illustration #5, 150
Sea of Tiberias
  definition, 326
seclusion, 6, 8, 31
Second Coming, 193, 198, 25, 261
security, 195, 198, 273
self-confidence, 292, 327
self-denial, 168, 173
  definition, 168
self-indulgent, 42
selfish, 116, 200, 210
selfless, 58
sense, 20, 42, 94, 134, 155, 270
sensitivity, 143
sermon, 109, 116
Sermon on the Mount, 109, 110, 118, 187
sermon on the plain, 109
servants, 62, 205, 206, 234, 242, 261, 270
servant style, 269
service, 103, 193
seven days, 97
seven demons, 123
shadow, 237
shalom, 143, 323
  definition, 323
shame, 6
shameless adultery, 178
shekels, 17, 64, 171, 267

Shema, 49
shepherd
  definition, 327
Shiloh
  definition, 4
Sider, Ronald J., 227
siege works
  definition, 258
sign
  definition, 66, 234
significance, 165, 297
significant, 20, 28, 56, 77, 274
signs and wonders, 84
Simon Bar-Jonah, 166
Simon Peter, 58, 107, 155, 165, 270, 271, 291
sin offering
  definition, 17
sinful man
  definition, 94
sinners, 27, 36, 71, 96, 178, 203, 206, 227, 303, 304, 310
six days
  definition, 168
six days before
  definition, 234
Six Day War, 259
sixth hour
  definition, 308
Skull Hill, 310, 311, 315, 316
sleeps
  definition, 213
small fish
  definition, 151
Snyder, Howard A., 92
social outcasts, 96
soldiers
  definition, 34
Solomon
  definition, 115
Solomon's porch
  definition, 200
son of man, 27, 59, 111, 165, 260, 290
  definition, 26
son of the commandment
  definition, 24

songs, 128
source of life, 214
sovereign declaration, 113
sovereignty, 3, 4, 195, 296
Sower, the
   illustration #4, 129
special Sabbath
   definition, 310
speechless, 6, 119, 319
spikenard, 235, 236
spiritual bodies, 249
spiritual community, 268
spiritual conquest
   definition, 167
spiritual failure, 327
spiritual family, 272
spiritual gift, 42
spiritual helpers, 170
spiritual infidelity, 224
spiritual issues, 132, 203
spiritual lapse, 273
spiritual leader, 116, 200
spiritual life, 251
spiritual poverty
   definition, 57
spiritual pride, 55, 170, 278
spiritual rebirth, 67, 68
spiritual sustenance, 156, 157
spiritual transactions, 37, 67
spiritual truths, 59, 132
spiritual warfare, 167
Stauffer, E.
   on freedom to choose, 202
   on praise, 220
stayed
   definition, 213
Stoics, 48
stoning, 100
Stott, John R. W.
   on the last moments of
      Jesus's life, 308
   on whole-hearted commit-
      ment to Christ, 299
stranger
   definition, 264
strength, 9, 134, 145, 150,
      185, 273, 309
stress, 246
strips of linen

definition, 316
subterfuges
   definition, 299
suffering, 116, 168, 216, 287
Sunday
   definition, 237
superficial faith, 66
supernatural supper, 151
superstition, 298
surrounded
   definition, 201
swine's flesh
   definition, 75
sycamore
   definition, 228
Sychar (town of), 75, 83
symbolic
   definition, 239
synagogue
   definition, 84

T

tabernacle
   definition, 103, 169
Tada, Joni Eareckson, 93
talents
   definition, 263
Talmud
   definition, 137
tassels, 137, 139, 251
   definition, 251
tax collector
   definition, 34
taxes
   definition, 247
"Teacher," 58, 133, 138, 178
Teilhard de Chardin, Pierre,
      250
temple
   definition, 171
temple pinnacle
   definition, 43
temple tax
   definition, 171
temptation, 39, 40, 41, 43,
      45, 46, 152
tempter, 41, 42, 43, 44, 46
Ten Commandments, 100,

117, 158, 169, 226
Tenney, Merril C., 270
Teresa, Mother, 210
Tertullian, 279
testimony, 55, 95, 102, 290
Thaddaeus, 109
thanks, 96, 159, 274
thief
   definition, 200
theology, 71, 107, 110, 195
thirsty for peace, 78
thirty silver coins, 293
   definition, 267
thistles
   definition, 115
Thomas, Cal, 296
Thomas, Doubting, 109, 213
Thomas, Robert L.
   on a double miracle, 134
   on Jesus's life prior to his
      public ministry, 25
thornbrushes
   definition, 115
those days
   definition, 260
three years, 48, 91, 165,
      221, 269
Tiberius Caesar, 31
"times of the Gentiles," 258,
      259
timetable of God's will, 62
tithe
   definition, 222
tithing, 222
titulus
   definition, 306
Titus, 238, 258
tolmai, 108
total commitment, 144, 147
Tozer, A. W., 129
traditions
   definition, 55
trail,
   definition, 127
transfigured
   definition, 169
Tribulation, 259–61
   definition, 259
tribunal

definition, 292
trichinosis
    definition, 136
Trinity
    definition, 50
troubled, 6, 19, 184, 215,
    240
    definition, 215
truth
    definition, 52
Twelve, the, 127, 141, 151,
    153, 155, 156, 171, 173,
    243, 281
twin, 109, 213
two mites
    definition, 252

U

unbelievers, 48, 132
uncompromising, 123
unconditional surrender, 8
unforgiveness, 173
unheard of
    definition, 197
Unger, Merril F., 131
untruth
    definition, 296
upheavals, 260
Upper Room, 269, 285, 322

V

veil
    definition, 5
versions
    definition, 109
vineyard, 193, 194, 244, 245
virgin birth, 7, 8, 11
Virgin Mary, 11, 333
vision
    of the future, 286

W

wages, 64, 171, 235, 252
Wagner, C. Peter, 257
wailing women, 138, 213
    definition, 138
waiting

for Christ's return, 234, 262
for a miracle, 156
walk in the light, 72
water to wine, 42
wealth, 44, 191, 192, 205,
    227, 252
wedding, 61, 70, 123
wept, 215, 268, 292
    definition, 215
Wesley, John, 185
whom Jesus loved
    definition, 271
who sinned
    definition, 194
wickedness, 159, 189, 248
Willard, Dallas, 130
will of God, 8, 113, 116,
    125, 167
"will of man," 51
willpower, 46, 68
wineskins, 96, 97, 98
Winslow, Octavius, 200
wisdom
    divine, 48
    of God, 42
    God's, 39
"wise builder," 116
without visible proof, 43
witnesses, 102, 105, 143,
    280, 290
woes
    definition, 189
wonders
    definition, 84
"Word became flesh," 3, 49,
    52
Word, the, 42, 49, 128
world
    definition, 128, 279
world order
    definition, 39
worship
    definition, 78
worshipped
    definition, 197
worthy, 143, 236
    definition, 143
wrath, 72, 116, 239, 258, 304

Y

Yahweh, 13, 226
Year of Jubilee, 86
yeast, 43
Yom Kippur, 222
young ruler
    definition, 226
your God, 43, 44, 185, 250,
    321

Z

Zacchaeus, 227–29
Zacharias, 4–11, 31, 55
Zealots, 109, 172
    definition, 172
Zebedee, 88, 108, 109, 326
Zechariah, 237, 267, 311